The Criminal
Justice System
and Its
Psychology

The Criminal Justice System and Its Psychology

Alfred Cohn, Ph.D.
Hofstra University

and

Roy Udolf, J.D.; Ph.D.
Hofstra University

VNR VAN NOSTRAND REINHOLD COMPANY
NEW YORK   CINCINNATI   ATLANTA   DALLAS   SAN FRANCISCO
LONDON   TORONTO   MELBORNE

Van Nostrand Reinhold Company Regional Offices:
New York Cincinnati Atlanta Dallas San Francisco

Van Nostrand Reinhold Company International Offices:
London Toronto Melbourne

Library of Congress Catalog Card Number: 78-26097
ISBN: 0-442-28882-4

Manufactured in the United States of America

Published by Van Nostrand Reinhold Company
135 West 50th Street, New York, N.Y. 10020

Published simultaneously in Canada by Van Nostrand Reinhold Ltd.

15 14 13 12 11 10 9 8 7 6 5 4 3 2 1

Library of Congress Cataloging in Publication Data

Cohn, Alfred, 1936—
    The criminal justice system and its psychology.

    Bibliography: p. 313
    Includes index.
    1. Criminal justice, Administration of—United
States. 2. Criminal justice, Administration of—
Psychological aspects. I. Udolf, Roy, joint author.
II. Title.
HV8138.C595   345′.73′05   78-26097
ISBN 0-442-28882-4

To
Selig Lenefsky
Roy Udolf

To
F. S. C., J. C., M. P. C., M. M. C. and L. C.,
A. C.

Preface

While primarily intended as a text for our undergraduate course in the Psychology of the Criminal Justice System, this book has much broader objectives. The criminal justice system is a gigantic octopus stretching its tentacles in sundry directions without, it seems, a rational plan to guide its movements. Its very title is a misnomer. It is not a system, and it has little to do with justice as that term is ordinarily understood. The available evidence indicates that it is a costly failure. One indication is that it costs more today to incarcerate a felon for a year than it would cost to send him to a top-ranking private college for a similar period. The expense notwithstanding, the system probably *causes* more crime and recidivism than it prevents.

Lawyers, psychologists, social workers, and other professionals involved in the field all recognize the need for a revamping of this system, but few have the multidisciplinary background necessary to understand the problem in all of its ramifications. Lawyers, for example, understand the legal aspects of the system but know little of the psychology involved in changing human behavior. Most important, they are unaware of the limitations of the present state of psychology as an applied science. Psychologists, of course, are more knowledgeable in this area but, typically, have little conception of the limitations on the freedom of action of social scientists within the system which are imposed by such basic legal principles as due process of law or other constitutional requirements.

The purpose of this book is to present and integrate both legal and psychological principles involved in the criminal justice system. It is intended that the reader will be helped to view the problem broadly and to employ the skills of his or her own discipline more effectively when dealing with those problems that fall within his or her professional domain. More specifically, in order to accomplish this the book: (1) describes both legal and psychological principles involved in the criminal justice system; (2) introduces the basic language and concepts of each field; (3) indicates, by reference to current literature, ways in which behavioral scientists conceptualize various features of the system and some of the ways in which they study it; (4) assesses and describes some of the behavioral science techniques that are employed at various points in the system (e.g., the selection of police officers, the selection of jurors, and behavior modification in prisons); (5) attempts to provide the student and general reader with information that is interesting, even controversial. Our assumption is that knowing something of how the system works will make one wish to improve it.

It is not our purpose to provide an encyclopedic reference book for all matters touched on here. We will be pleased if our reader's interest is aroused to the point where he or she seeks information from more specialized sources about some of the issues considered.

All of us are, in some way, part of the criminal justice system, whether as victims, jurors, lawyers, court personnel, or concerned (i.e., tax-paying) citizens. The roles we play, our attitudes toward them and toward each other's roles and responsibilities, among many other variables, affect the way we function and, through us, the functioning of the system itself.

Our book[1] is addressed, in part, to the responsibilities that all of us share, for the functioning of our police, courts, and prisons, and for their effect on the people whose lives they touch.

ALFRED COHN
ROY UDOLF

[1]The order of authorship was determined by chance.

Acknowledgments

The authors wish to thank the following people for their help in the preparation of this book:

Lieutenant Felix Alfano, N.Y.C.P.D. Retired, reviewed the chapter on the police and Detective First Grade Erasmus Alfano, N.Y.C.P.D. Retired, reviewed all of the chapters dealing with the legal aspects of the criminal justice system. Both made many constructive criticisms concerning the content and the philosophy of the material presented.

Special thanks are also due to John D. Case Jr., Esquire, of the Nassau County District Attorney's Office for his painstaking line-by-line comments on the legal material presented herein, which resulted in the detection and correction of many errors and in the updating of portions of the text.

It should be emphasized that none of the foregoing consultants are responsible for any remaining errors, as their suggestions were not always followed (particularly in cases where being literally correct on comparatively minor points would have necessitated unduly involved explanations). It must also be emphasized that there were substantial philosophical differences between the authors, who tend to be "defense-minded," and these reviewers, who were "prosecution-minded." Thus, they are in no way responsible for any of the opinions expressed herein, and often differed quite sharply with them. We hope as a result of their help that the book is somewhat less one-sided and no longer conveys the erroneous impression that the authors regard either the police, the prosecutors, or any other subdivision of the criminal justice apparatus as principally responsible for its shortcomings and problems.

Dr. Paul Lipsitt reviewed the entire manuscript. We are grateful for the many valuable suggestions he made for its improvement.

Dean David C. Christman of Hofstra University's New College gave the authors warm encouragement and support.

Felicia Cohn helped in various ways, among them typing, editing, and offering constructive criticism.

Cheryl Steinberg, M.S.W., reviewed the material on Social Work.

Ms. Mary Joan DeMarco typed the manuscript for the legal portions of this book.

Contents

Preface   vii
Acknowledgments   ix
1. The American Legal System—Its History and Structure   1
2. The Purpose and Goals of the Criminal Law   12
3. Basic Principles of Substantive Criminal Law   21
4. Criminals   34
5. Victims and Bystanders   71
6. Police   94
7. Lawyers, Psychologists, Psychiatrists, and Social Workers 129
8. Overview of Criminal Procedures in a Typical State   139
9. Pre-Trial Procedures   150
10. Trial Procedures   173
11. Psychology and Jury Selection   203
12. Psychological Factors in Trials   220
13. Post-Conviction Procedures   265
14. Imprisonment   278

Epilogue   308

Bibliography   313

Name Index   325
Subject Index   329

The Criminal Justice System and Its Psychology

1
The American Legal System—Its History and Structure

This book is about the American system of criminal justice and its psychology. It is predicated on the assumption that no social scientist is likely either to work effectively within this system or to contribute significantly to its improvement without a basic understanding of what the system is all about and how it functions, both in theory and in practice. Hence roughly equal amounts of psychological and legal concepts will be presented herein. While the primary concern in this book is with principles of criminal law, the criminal law does not exist in a vacuum but within the context of a larger body of legal principles. It is the purpose of this chapter to give a bird's eye view of the American legal system and to show how the criminal law fits into this larger picture.

Before going any further the reader must understand what is meant by the term law or positive law, as the man-made body of legal principles that we are about to describe is often called, to distinguish it from natural law, which the reader may have studied in science courses.

Actually both types of laws are, in some way, identical. A law is simply a prediction. It is a statement of a probability that under a given set of conditions a particular result will occur.

Thus Coulomb's Law in physics predicts that if two bodies with a positive charge of 1 coulomb each are separated by a distance of 1 cm, they will repel each other with a force of 9×10^{18} dynes.

The Penal Law of the State of New York predicts that if the people establish beyond a reasonable doubt that a defendant willfully refused to help a police officer to capture a dangerous bank robber by calling for assistance when ordered to do so by the officer, the defendant will be convicted of a Class B misdemeanor.

These two laws are not different in kind but in degree. One is a law of the universe, the other merely arbitrary and man-made; but both are basically predictions. The probability is higher that Coulomb's Law will predict accurately than it is that the penal statute will predict accurately, but this is merely a difference in confidence levels. Had we chosen our example of natural law from psychology rather than the physical sciences, the legal prediction would suffer less by comparison, as psychology is still lacking a high level of predictive accuracy.

The understanding that positive law is in the nature of a prediction is of vital importance. Too often, as a result of our yearning for a better world, we are prone to take literally some of the poetic expressions that people use, and to think of the law as somehow related to the establishment of justice rather than being concerned with the prediction of the consequences of human behavior. One of the authors has vivid memories of an inscription on a county courthouse where, as a young man, he began to practice law. The inscription read, "Justice, God's idea; man's ideal." This inscription is both inspiring and, we suspect, true, but it really has little, if anything, to do with our legal system. By its very nature justice is both subjective and elusive. Two reasonable and intelligent people may differ sharply over what is justice in a given situation. If our legal system really depended on such an elusive concept, it would be unable to function. What the law is really concerned with is enabling people to predict the consequences of their behavior so that they can function reasonably in their everyday personal and professional lives. Imagine how chaotic life would be if it were impossible to predict the consequences of signing a lease, contracting a marriage, or driving through a red light.

A pair of basic legal concepts that are like the head and tail of a coin are the reciprocal notions of rights and duties. A right is a duty that is owed to you by another person, either to perform or to refrain from performing a certain act. If you have a right against a particular person, then there must be a corresponding duty that person owes to you. Some rights are said to be primary in that you acquire them against all other persons simply by virtue of being a human being. For example you have a right to be secure in your person against all other individuals, and they in turn have the duty to refrain from assaulting you. Other rights are secondary as they require some action on your part to attain them, and you do not enjoy them against all other persons but only against certain people. An example of a secondary right is one that arises out of a contract between you and another.

Violations of primary rights, i.e., rights not arising out of a contract, are called torts.

In legal theory, any time a right is violated, that right is destroyed, and in its place is created a new right called a "cause of action." This is a right to bring a lawsuit for redress. The basic idea behind a civil lawsuit is to remove a financial loss from the shoulders of the person who suffered it and put it on the shoulders of the person whose breech of a duty caused it. Thus the tort of negligence is committed by a defendant's breeching his duty to behave like a reasonable person and thereby protect the plaintiff from suffering financial loss. To be actionable in a lawsuit, whatever damage the plaintiff has suffered must be translatable into financial terms, as all the court can do is award the plaintiff a sum of money as compensation for the loss.

In order to understand the functioning of our court system, it is necessary to take a brief look at the early English legal system. The United States was a colony of Great Britain for over 150 years before the American Revolution, and when we declared our independence of Great Britain, we retained the basic system of English common law.

There was a time in Great Britain when the judicial system was composed of a vast array of local courts, each with its own rules and procedures. This chaotic state of affairs made it difficult for the crown to enforce its tax collection laws. There is nothing that governments are more sensitive to than any problem concerning the collection of tax revenues. In response to the problem, the King established a uniform set of King's Courts or common law courts, as they came to be known because they established a common law throughout England. These common law courts developed a principle of operation called the doctrine of *stare decisis*. This simply meant that any time a court rendered a decision in a case, that decision became a binding precedent on it and on any inferior court should the same situation arise again. *Stare decisis* (to stand decided) remains the basic principle in American law today, whether civil or criminal. This is the reason why court interpretations of statutes are so important. Once a decision has been made, it becomes binding on the court to decide the same way in all future cases. Hence the old legal saying that "Hard cases make bad law." Often a court will strain to find minor differences between two very similar cases to prevent a past precedent from working an injustice in the case at hand. *Stare decisis*, by its nature, is not designed to take account of the justice of each case. It is designed to provide uniformity and predictability in the law.

The common law courts, like all law courts today, could only give relief in the form of money damages. As these courts developed, their procedures became more rigid. In order to bring a case before the court, the plaintiff had to swear out a writ for the particular wrong suffered. As these writs became more formalized, it often occurred that there was no writ in existence for the particular wrong that the plaintiff had sustained. There was, therefore, no way for the plaintiff to get the case before the court and no remedy for the plaintiff at law. Since the King was generally assumed to be above the law, it was possible for him to grant relief in such a case; so he began to entertain petitions from litigants who had no adequate remedy at law. As these petitions became more numerous, he began to delegate them to his chancellor, who was usually a cleric and was generally regarded as the keeper of the King's conscience. From this practice there developed courts of chancery, now called courts of equity. Courts of equity will afford extraordinary relief in that they are not limited to declaring that the plaintiff is owed a sum of money by the defendant as are law courts, but may direct that the defendant perform or, more commonly, desist from performing some act. This type of relief is called an injunction; but because of the historical origins of courts of equity, it is only available to litigants who cannot be "made whole" by money damages alone, i.e., plaintiffs who have no adequate remedy at law.

Today there are at least three different types of civil actions: (1) actions in law to recover money damages only, (2) actions in equity for injunctive relief, and (3) special proceedings.

It is the trend today for formal distinctions in procedure between legal and equitable actions to be abolished. Jurisdictions like New York have only one form of civil action, but the substantive relief sought and requirements for attaining such relief are still very different. Thus to obtain injunctive relief the plaintiff must not only show that the defendant breeched a duty owed to the plaintiff and that the plaintiff was damaged, but must also show that money damages alone would not be adequate compensation for the loss.

Any civil action other than a suit in law or equity is classified as a special proceeding. Examples of special proceedings are *habeas corpus* proceedings designed for a judicial inquiry into the legality of a detention, applications for special writs such as a writ of *mandamus* to compel a public official to perform some purely ministerial and nondiscretionary duty, or a writ of prohibition to prevent a public official from exercising some power that he or she does not legally have. In the hands of a capable lawyer these special proceedings are the average citizen's most effective weapons against the abuse of power by public officials. However, they are not sufficiently relevant to the subject of this chapter to warrant discussion at any greater length here.

A criminal action differs from a civil action in the basic purpose of the proceeding. A criminal action is not designed to make the victim whole, either with money damages or injunctive relief. It is designed to punish the defendant.

A civil action involves a wrong against the plaintiff, who prosecutes the action in his or her own name and at his or her own expense. A criminal offense is regarded as an offense not against the victim but against all society. Hence it is prosecuted in the name of the state, by a public prosecutor at public expense.

The same physical act—for example, an assault—can be both a tort and a crime. Hence the victim may sue in his or her own name at law for money damages, while the people may prosecute the defendant for a crime in order to punish the behavior.

There are many similarities and some major differences between civil and criminal actions, but for the remainder of this book we will limit our discussion to criminal procedures.

Another basic legal concept that the reader must become familiar with in studying criminal law is the concept of jurisdiction. Jurisdiction is the power of a court to act in a given case. Unless founded on jurisdiction, every purported judicial action is a nullity without force or effect. There are several types of jurisdiction, and a court must have all of them to proceed.

First, there is subject matter jurisdiction. A court must have jurisdiction over the particular type of lawsuit before it. Some courts, like the New York State Supreme Court, are courts of unlimited trial jurisdiction in law and equity. They can try any case, civil or criminal. Most courts are courts of limited jurisdiction. Some are limited only to law cases and have no equity jurisdiction; others have only civil or criminal jurisdiction. Courts are commonly limited not just in the type of cases that they can hear but in the amount of money judgments that they can award or in the seriousness of the offenses that they can try. Thus a district court may have subject matter jurisdiction over traffic infractions or misdemeanors but no jurisdiction to try a felony. Usually trial and appellate jurisdiction are vested in different courts.

A second type of jurisdiction that a court needs in order to function is jurisdiction over the person of the defendant. In a civil case, jurisdiction over the person of the defendant is usually obtained by serving the defendant with a summons giving notice of the action against him or her and providing the defendant an opportunity to come in and defend him- or herself. Jurisdiction over the plaintiff is obtained by the plaintiff's action in initiating the lawsuit. In criminal cases jurisdiction over defendants is obtained either by arresting them or by summoning them to appear and be arraigned before the bar of the court.

Courts also need territorial jurisdiction over the locus of a crime. A felony committed wholly in New York cannot be prosecuted in a New Jersey court, even if the defendant is physically before the court, and the same act is also a crime in New Jersey.

The basic source of all American law, both civil and criminal (except in Louisiana, whose legal system was founded upon the Napoleonic code) is case law or the common law. Because of the doctrine of *stare decisis*, every time a court renders a decision in a case at the bar, a new increment is added to the body of existing legal principles. The common law is both ancient and pervasive. Justice Holmes referred to it as "The brooding omnipresence in the sky."[1] If there are no more modern precedents for a given case, the court can look back to the English common law. If there are no precedents at all for a given case, it is called a case of novel impression, and the court has more freedom in deciding how to handle the matter; but this situation is quite rare. It should be pointed out that not everything that a court may say in its decision becomes a binding precedent under the principle of *stare decisis*, but only those statements *necessary* to the decision. Other gratuitous statements may be persuasive in future cases, but they are not binding; hence they are called *dicta*. If they are really far removed from the controlling reasons for the decision, they are called *obiter dicta*.

In the case of *Erie v. Thomkins* the U.S. Supreme Court set down the principle that there is no federal common law.[2] The common law enforced by a federal district court is the common law of the state in which it sits. The reason for there being no federal common law is more important than the fact that there is none. It relates to the fundamental legal principle that the federal government is a government of limited powers. It has no power not expressly or implicitly granted to it by the U.S. Constitution. On the other hand, each state in the union is a sovereign and has all of the powers of a sovereign state unless such power is specifically or implicitly denied to it by the federal Constitution. Thus, in criminal cases, what we colloquially refer to as the constitutional rights of defendants are really restrictions on the powers of state governments that these governments would have enjoyed had the federal Constitution not expressly limited them.

The second major source of positive law is called statutory law. The term "statutory law" is somewhat misleading, as it includes both constitutional and statutory enactments. In the event of conflict between various statutory enactments, constitutional provisions take precedence over legislative enactments. The U.S. Constitution is the supreme law of the land, and it, and statutes enacted by Congress pursuant to it, take precedence over any state constitutional or statutory enactment. The U.S. Constitution is a very brief document designed to outline broadly the basic structure of government. State constitutions tend to be much longer and more detailed. What they have in common with the federal Constitution is that they are more difficult to amend than ordinary statutes because they were designed to produce long-term stability in basic legal principles.

The volume of statutory law, while extensive, is much less than the volume of case law. Statutory law may be declarative of the common law or in derogation of it. In the latter case there is a rule of construction which holds that statutes in derogation of the common law are strictly interpreted. This means that if a statute makes criminal an act that was not criminal at common law, the court will not extend the meaning of the statute to cover any act not clearly falling within the purview of the words used.

There is a third source of law so voluminous that it dwarfs the volume of the statutes enacted by legislatures. Indeed it is so pervasive that nobody really knows its full extent. This is the array of regulations enacted by administrative agencies. Contrary to what the reader may have learned in school about the legislative, judicial and executive branches of government, there are four, not three, branches of our government. The fourth branch is the administrative branch. There are countless administrative agencies set up by both the federal and state governments to administer particular branches of the law. The FCC, the IRS, the SEC, parole boards, and so forth, are just a few examples of administrative agencies. Because the legislature could not possibly consider all of the rules necessary (and unnecessary) to effectuate its legislative policy, it has delegated part of its legislative authority to these agencies, and they enact regulations having the force of law. The volume of tax regulations issued by the Internal Revenue Service is much thicker than the Internal Revenue Act itself.

In addition to exercising quasi-legislative functions, these agencies exercise quasi-judicial functions, such as a Motor Vehicle Bureau hearing to determine if a driver's license should be revoked.

Administrative agencies are the main reason for the government's being so expensive and out of control. No one really knows the full extent of the regulation of American citizens by these agencies; indeed, many lawyers who specialize throughout their professional lives in handling matters before individual agencies still do not know all about their operations. Many American presidents and governors have taken office with the firm resolve to bring these agencies under control and eliminate needless redundancies or harmful regulations; but, to date, none has been even slightly successful. Often one agency will be issuing regulations designed to produce one effect, while another will be issuing regulations to produce just the opposite effect. For example, one government agency requires health warning labels on cigarette packages, while another provides subsidies to tobacco growers.

Since the federal government is one of limited powers, and since Congress cannot delegate a power that it does not have, many of these regulations may be illegal and would be set aside under judicial review. The problem is that before a court can review an adverse decision of an administrative agency, the aggrieved party must exhaust all legal remedies within the agency. Thus if the agency has set up an extensive internal appeals system, finally getting into the courts can be both an expensive and a time-consuming operation. Administrative agencies are probably even more susceptible to lobbyists and special interest groups than are state and federal legislators who are elected from the population at large. Sometimes there are ludicrous examples of conflict of interest between the agencies and the people over whom they exercise quasi-judicial functions—for example, the Police Department of New York City issuing pistol permits or the local district attorney's office being designated the legal adviser to a grand jury. We will say more about the effects of administrative agencies on the criminal law later.

One thing that all students of the criminal justice system ought to do early in their careers is to get a copy of the U.S. Constitution and read it. It is interesting to contrast this simple document with the vast octopus of interlocking and overlapping administrative agencies that have developed from it. This is particularly so in view of the fact that the Constitution was drafted by men who were basically distrustful of the potentially oppressive powers of any form of government. By and large, the founding fathers had the view that any government is at best a necessary evil and that all of them tend to consolidate as much power as possible at the expense of the people. The experience of the past 200 years has tended to bear out this view. Hence, in order to persuade enough of the states to ratify this Constitution, it was agreed to amend it with a Bill of Rights to protect the citizens against the feared abuse of governmental power. This Bill of Rights and subsequent amendments, together with supporting judicial decisions holding that these basic rights were assertable against states as well as the federal government, provide the most important safeguards against oppressive methods of law enforcement that a defendant in a criminal action has. The subsequent history of American criminal jurisprudence is ample testimony to the necessity for these basic safeguards. Even today they are under attack by overzealous law enforcement agencies or politicians asserting the need for tougher law enforcement in the name of law and order. These sources claim that it is often too difficult to convict dangerous criminals. Indeed it is difficult; to make it so is the function of these protections. It is not possible for a society to protect the rights and civil liberties of its law-abiding citizens unless it is also willing to protect the same rights of other people who are not so socially acceptable. In view of the very serious consequences of a conviction for a criminal offense, it might be argued persuasively that it is not yet difficult enough to get a conviction.

Here we simply list a few of the basic protections that the U.S. Constitution affords all defendants in criminal proceedings, protections which take precedence over any federal or state law to the contrary. These rights will be dealt with in more detail later when appropriate. However, the reader must clearly understand that the real meaning and extent of these protections cannot be determined merely by reading the Constitution. These provisions actually mean what the courts have interpreted them to mean, and their range and limits of application are also subject to court interpretation.

Article 1, Section 9 states: "The . . . writ of habeas corpus shall not be suspended, unless when in cases of rebellion or invasion the public safety may require it." It also says that "No bill of attainder or ex post facto law shall be passed." A bill of attainder is a legislative enactment of guilt as opposed to a determination of guilt by a trial. An *ex post facto* law is one that either makes an act a crime which was not a crime at the time it was performed or increases the penalty for or reduces the requirements for a conviction of a crime after it was committed.

Amendment 1 provides: "Congress shall make no law . . . abridging the freedom of speech, or of the press; or of the people peaceably to assemble, and to petition the government for a redress of grievances."

Amendment 4 provides for "the right of the people to be secure in their persons, houses, papers, and effects against unreasonable searches and seizures. . . ."

It also requires search warrants to be issued only ". . . upon probable cause, supported by oath or affirmation and particularly describing the place to be searched and the persons or things to be seized."

Amendment 5 provides that no person can be held to answer for a capital or infamous crime (felony) unless indicted by a Grand Jury. Nor can any person be subjected to double jeopardy of "life or limb" for the same offense. An accused cannot be compelled to be a witness against himself in a criminal proceeding, nor can he "be deprived of life, liberty, or property without due process of law. . . ."

Amendment 6 provides a defendant in a criminal trial with the following very important rights:

1. ". . . a speedy and public trial . . ."
2. ". . . by an impartial jury . . ."
3. ". . . to be informed of the nature and cause of the accusation . . ."
4. ". . . to be confronted with the witnesses against him . . ." (i.e., the right to cross-examine them)
5. ". . . to have compulsory process for obtaining witnesses in his favor . . ."
6. ". . . to have the Assistance of Counsel for his defence."

Amendment 8 forbids the setting of excessive bail, the imposition of excessive fines, or the imposition of "cruel and unusual punishments."

Amendment 14, unlike the foregoing, was directed against the states instead of the federal government. It forbade any state to ". . . deprive any person of life, liberty, or property, without due process of law. . . ." This has been generally interpreted by the courts as imposing most of the limitations of the original Bill of Rights on the states as well as on the federal government.

DUE PROCESS OF LAW

It will be useful at this point to deal with the legal concept of "due process of law." The U.S. Supreme Court, instead of trying to define this idea formally, has chosen to define it by inclusion and exclusion, on a case-by-case basis, at least as far as its application to substantive law is concerned. It is basically concerned with notions of "fair play," however inadequate this concept may be. In the area of adjective or procedural law, due process requires at least that defendants be given notice that there are actions pending against them and be given a fair opportunity to come in and defend themselves. This is why the notion of due process necessarily includes some of the basic constitutional rights given in Amendment 6, which are designed to assure a fair trial. Due process, of course, also demands that a court have proper jurisdiction to proceed with a case. The fact that due process of law is not easily and precisely definable is one of its basic strengths. The simple fact of the matter is that any criminal trial is a contest between an individual citizen and the awesome power of the state. The concept of due process of law is one of the tools that the courts have at their disposal to protect the individual citizen from the ever-present threat of the abuse of this enormous power.

This brings us to the last basic characteristic of the American legal system. We have not only inherited the English common law system, but in a very real sense we have inherited the medieval custom of trial by combat. During the medieval period disputes could be settled by each litigant hiring a knight to fight for his cause in armed combat. The theory was that God would defend the right and give the victory to the knight representing the just claim. We still retain this basic method of trial by combat in American courtrooms, although, fortunately for the attorney on the losing side of the case, these battles are now fought with words rather than swords. Our legal system is based on the premise that the best way to arrive at the truth is to have two able advocates for the opposing positions fight it out before an impartial judge or jury. The idea that ours is an adversary system is fundamental to an understanding of the operation of our legal system. Attorneys and prosecutors are not impartial sifters of objective evidence but advocates of particular positions. It is their duty to present their side of the case in the most favorable light possible consistent with the facts and the rules of procedure. Indeed, the entire system is based on the supposition that they will do just that. A fair trial cannot be obtained unless both advocates are equally skilled, are equally dedicated, and have comparable amounts of time and financial resources available. A lawsuit, whether civil or criminal, is a fight between two opposing interests. There are rules that limit what the parties can do in this fight, but this doesn't change the essential nature of the proceedings. All of the rules of evidence and procedure that will be discussed later have one purpose: to make this fight even and fair enough so that the truth will emerge from it. The reader who understands this basic idea has gone a long way toward understanding the real nature of the criminal justice system.

In a criminal case one of the attorneys, namely the prosecutor, has an unusual double role. Besides being an advocate of a cause, like any trial lawyer, the prosecutor is also a public official with an ethical duty to see to it that justice is done in any case that he or she prosecutes and that innocent defendants are not convicted. For this reason a district attorney is ethically required to inform defense counsel of any evidence the former discovers that would tend to exculpate the defendant.[3] The defense attorney, having no such dual role, is neither required nor even permitted to inform the people of any inculpatory evidence that he discovers.

REFERENCES

1. Holmes, Oliver W., Jr. *The Common Law.* Boston: Little, Brown and Co., 1951.
2. *Erie v. Thomkins,* 1938, 304 U.S. 64, 58 S.Ct. 817, 82 L.Ed. 1188.
3. American Bar Assoc., *The Code of Professional Responsibility,* 1971.

2
The Purpose and Goals of the Criminal Law

An understanding of the complex and seemingly inconsistent criminal justice system must be predicated on a knowledge of the reasons for its existence, both theoretical and practical.

Nowhere can a better example of the Freudian defense mechanism of rationalization be found than in the reasons given in most law schools for the enactment of the criminal law. The most common justifications given for the establishment of a criminal code are the following:

1. To protect the public from unjustified risks to person and property, i.e., "to make the streets safe."
2. To provide a deterrent to potential offenders.
3. To deter others who might become offenders if not for seeing malefactors punished.
4. To provide public redress of grievances and thereby eliminate the possibility of private vendettas.
5. To reform and rehabilitate offenders and convert them into good citizens.
6. Because it is good for public morality to punish offenders.

The problem with these general goals, of course, is that while each purports to be a valid reason for having a criminal law, they are mutually inconsistent and, as a matter of simple fact, require very different and incompatible actions on the part of the state for their attainment. For example, it is psychologically impossible to punish an offender and reform him at the same time. Punishment, particularly when it is as far out of proportion to the offense as is commonly the case in American criminal proceedings, is much more likely to breed resentment and increase recidivism than it is to cure antisocial behavior. The weight of the evidence in psychological research on learning seems to indicate that punishment does not change behavior, it merely temporarily suppresses the behavior punished.[1] However, it would be simplistic in the extreme to try to extrapolate from the behavior of research animals to people. Rats are not capable of nurturing bitterness and hatred toward abstract con-

12

cepts, e.g., society, as people are. When training rats we have specific behaviors as goals. When rehabilitating people we have numerous classes of behaviors as goals. Rats, so far as we know, do not think about alternative courses of action; people do. Rats do not aspire to the satisfaction of more than biological needs; people do. Perhaps these are the reasons that the goal of rehabilitating offenders based upon techniques developed on rats has proven so elusive.

In practice the state must decide which of the foregoing goals it is most interested in attaining for a particular offense. Often these goals will be different for different offenses, and, equally often, the goals of the legislature in enacting a particular statute will differ from those of the prosecutors or judges enforcing it. Many crimes do not involve hazards to life or property, but are affronts to the dignity of the state or are enacted for regulatory convenience or to proclaim the legislature's views about morality. In view of this, it is quite conceivable that many people convicted of crimes are already good citizens and do not need any reformation.

On the other hand, if a state is attempting to enforce an oppressive and confiscatory tax system, it is very important for it to convict and punish comparatively minor cases of tax fraud as a deterrent to other potential violators, for the failure to do so would bring about the collapse of the whole system.

Any system as expensive as the criminal justice system ought to be evaluated to ascertain how well it is attaining its goals. Unfortunately, the multiplicity of the stated goals of this system makes it possible for advocates of any position to prove whatever they are interested in proving from the available data. Judged by the standard of reducing recidivism, the system is a colossal failure. If anything, there is good reason to suspect that it has had substantial negative results and actually increases recidivism. As to its success in deterring crime, this is a largely unanswerable question, since if a person does not commit a crime, there is no way of knowing whether it was the law or his conscience that prevented him (although the authors are inclined to guess that it was the latter). On the other hand, if the system is designed primarily to inflict punishment on offenders, then—at least with respect to that small minority of offenders who are actually apprehended, convicted, and sentenced—it must be admitted to be the most successful system ever designed. It often inflicts very substantial suffering on both offenders and their families, sometimes out of all proportion to the culpability of the offender, common sense, psychological knowledge, and even some very basic principles of human dignity and decency.

Historically and currently, the most universally agreed-on purpose of the criminal law is to vindicate public morality by punishing criminals. This is true in spite of all the talk about reformation of offenders by psychologists, social workers, jurists, and even some correctional personnel. It is not possible to understand the workings of this system without realizing just how fundamental the idea of culpability and punishment is to its design and operation. Courts are designed to resolve questions of guilt and innocence with great care for the protection of the innocent; however, once found guilty a defendant is no longer regarded as a human being with basic "inalienable rights," but has become an enemy of society, to be punished. The entire correctional system is primarily designed to administer punishment, not rehabilitation. Indeed the label of criminal attached to a convicted defendant makes it easier to stop considering the defendant as a person. A reader who is at all observant cannot help but be struck by the meticulous concern for all of the constitutional and basic human rights of a defendant during the course of legal procedures prior to conviction and the almost complete disregard of these same rights subsequent to conviction.

Whatever the major reasons for having a criminal law, the law itself must be effectuated in the form of specific criminal statutes. Some jurisdictions, like New York and the federal government, are statutory jurisdictions. Others are common law jurisdictions. In a statutory jurisdiction no act is considered a crime unless there is a specific statute making it such. Common law jurisdictions, on the other hand, enforce both statutory and common law crimes. Even in a statutory jurisdiction, however, the common law is still used to provide a basic body of definitions and interpretations that are used in conjunction with the criminal statutes.

A penal statute proscribes some act or omission and makes it a punishable offense. The main purpose of a criminal statute is to define a crime and its elements so that a prosecution can be based on it and the violator of the statute punished.

There are certain constitutional requirements that a valid criminal statute must meet. It must define the offense and the penalty in a clear and unambiguous way so as to give fair warning to potential offenders of the consequences of their actions. If a potential criminal of average intelligence could not read the statute and determine exactly what behavior it either prohibits or requires, then the statute will be held unconstitutional by the courts for being vague and uncertain. As one court put it, even though potential offenders are unlikely to read a statute before violating it, they have the right to be put on such constructive notice. An example of such an unconstitutionally vague criminal statute is New York's law against loitering, Section 240.35-6 of the Penal Law, which was held too vague to be enforceable.[2] This statute is worded as follows:

A person is guilty of loitering when he: . . . Loiters, remains or wanders in or about a place without apparent reason and under circumstances which justify suspicion that he may be engaged or about to engage in crime, and, upon inquiry by a peace officer, refuses to identify himself or fails to give a reasonably credible account of his conduct and purposes; or . . ."

Even if a statute is specific enough to be enforceable, there is a general rule of construction that criminal laws are interpreted by the courts strictly against the people. This means that any ambiguities of meaning of a criminal statute are interpreted in favor of the defendant (since the people drafted the statute and hence are accountable for it). Most states have a formal body or chapter of their laws called a penal law, which is limited to defining crimes. What many people do not realize is that crimes are defined throughout the general statutes as well as within the penal law. This results from the regrettable tendency of most state legislatures to try to regulate behavior by making non-conforming conduct a crime whether or not it has anything to do with anti-social behavior. (For example, in New York it is a misdemeanor to do business under an assumed name without filing a "certificate of doing business under an assumed name" with the county clerk's office.) As a result of this practice, there is probably no lawyer in any state who really knows just how many crimes are on the books in his own jurisdiction.

It is in the specific criminal statutes that the overall objectives of the legislature in creating a criminal law must ultimately be effectuated. Therefore, it behooves us to consider the types of behavior that are commonly proscribed in criminal statutes to understand their effects on the overall system.

Every state, in contemplation of law, is deemed to possess what is called "police power." This term has nothing to do with a police department. It is the concept that every state has the intrinsic power to protect the health, morals, and public welfare of its citizens. It is under this general power, as limited by the federal and state constitutions, that criminal statutes are enacted. Thus, the courts will require that to justify a criminal statute there must be some legitimate public interest served by such a statute. Unfortunately, they are extremely reluctant to place limits on this public interest; and short of an attempt to make an ordinary and innocuous activity, like private sunbathing, a crime, they are likely to find some public interest in the most oppressive types of legislation, such as the so-called Sunday Blue Laws. These laws were clearly originated for religious reasons, and many legal scholars see them as violations of the constitutional prohibition against laws "respecting an establishment of religion." Yet some courts have justified them with the specious argument that a community needs a day of repose. The courts are particularly prone to sustain statutes designed to protect public morality. After all, how many of us would like to take a public stand against morality?

Within these very loose constraints state legislatures have tended to create criminal statutes prohibiting the following types of behavior:

1. Behavior that most people would agree is clearly antisocial, e.g., aggressive acts against the person or property of another.
2. Purely regulatory types of crime, i.e., getting people to conform to the type of behavior required by a statute by making nonconformity a crime whether the behavior involved is antisocial or not (e.g., smoking in public places, violating zoning laws, failure to file an accident report, etc.).
3. Behavior violative of the legislature's pronouncements of moral standards, e.g., sex acts between consenting adults, drug usage, gambling, etc.

Very often, following some major coverage of a crime by the local newspapers, a deluge of ill-advised legislation is generated, either by public pressure on the legislature or by a desire on the part of the legislators to capitalize on the publicity available to them. New York's excessive drug law is a ludicrous example of this, as were the attempts to make hijacking an airplane a capital federal offense in spite of the obvious fact that existing homicide and kidnapping statutes were more than adequate to cover the situation.

The tendency of legislatures to overreact to crime news or political pressure for stricter law enforcement is frequently counterproductive. It results in making penalties so severe that judges, being by and large decent and reasonable people, refuse to enforce these excessive penalties and accept pleas to lesser offenses than they would be inclined to if they were given freedom to impose rational sentences for the more serious crimes charged.

Actually newspaper stories on crimes have very little relationship to the extent of the crime problem—they are designed to sell newspapers. Reports of a crime wave are often a good sign that nothing really horrible is happening in the world that week; to fill out its columns the paper reports local crimes that would normally not be newsworthy.

While it is hard to disagree with the need of society for some form of protection against aggressive or antisocial offenses, there are some very serious problems created by offenses designed to produce social conformity or to legislate morality.

With respect to criminal statutes drawn to force compliance with purely regulatory enactments, the situation is made even more difficult by the fact that state legislatures have delegated an enormous amount of legislative authority to purely administrative agencies, such as motor vehicle bureaus, tax departments, consumer protection agencies, and so on. These departments not only enforce and administer statutes but issue regulations often many times more voluminous than the statutes of the state. To make the situation even worse, the people preparing these regulations are often not lawyers, and the regulations frequently have an effect very different from the one intended. Sometimes they create a greater harm than the situation that they were designed to correct.

The same problem of laymen drafting laws applies to state legislatures. It is not deemed a good idea in a democracy to limit service in a legislature to a special class of people, such as lawyers. Thus, in many respects our legislative process is analogous to having laymen perform delicate surgery. The best compromise to date has been to have legislators guided by attorneys on their staffs and among their colleagues and by recommendations made by the appropriate committees of bar associations. However, even lawyers are not always trained in law school on the proper drafting of legislation.

The real problem results from the fact that we seek to have "a government of laws not men." This means that we seek to treat everyone alike in the courts (which is just the opposite of what true justice would require, for by its nature it would mean treating people as individuals). The idea behind having a government of laws was to protect citizens from the abuse of power in the hands of individual office holders and what Shakespeare so aptly called the "insolence of office." But to the extent that it protects us from these harms, it must also insulate us from human compassion and good judgment. If we are to have a government of laws then laws have to be enforced as they are written, not necessarily as their drafters may have intended. Thus, there are standardized rules of construction for determining what a statute means if it is ambiguous. These rules may or may not coincide with the citizens' notions of common sense; usually they do not. Average citizens who have learned to handle their day-to-day living decisions on the basis of ordinary common sense and good judgment may suddenly find themselves in violation of many such obscure statutes. For example, common sense may tell a motorist involved in an accident with a parked car that he has complied with the statute requiring him to exchange names and addresses with the car's owner by leaving a note on the windshield. Technically, however, he has not complied and is, in fact, a violator. For the most part these statutes are enforced sporadically and thus do not have a major impact on the daily affairs of citizens; but there is something fundamentally wrong with a criminal law that, if strictly enforced, could label as criminals the vast majority of the law-abiding and productive citizens of a community.

There is a tendency on the part of legislatures to believe that all human problems can be cured by passing a law. In fact, few if any such problems are so summarily curable. The logical conclusion of this type of thinking would be to wipe out cancer by making it a crime to develop a malignancy. Unfortunately for this tactic, the courts have decided that it is unconstitutional to make being sick a crime (at least with respect to being alcoholic; there are still many sex and drug crimes on the books that require a mentally ill defendant to commit them).

The third category of criminal statutes, dealing with the legislation of morality, includes what are usually called "victimless crimes." Recently, in defending this type of statute, a politician observed that he didn't think that there was any such thing as a victimless crime because, after all, isn't a prostitute herself a real victim? We will not attempt to make any judgments as to whether an adult woman voluntarily engaging in sexual activities in exchange for what are often large quantities of tax-free money is properly considered as a victim. If she is, one might ask what sense it makes to punish the victim of a crime. However, we are inclined to agree that there is a victim in these crimes. The real victim is society. Not only is a great deal of tax money required to apprehend and convict these offenders, but if half of a city police department is tied up in chasing prostitutes and bookmakers, then, of necessity, there cannot be enough patrolmen available to handle the more important function of keeping the streets safe from muggers.

The most basic problem in legislating morality is determining whose ideas of morality we are going to enforce. Nowhere is this basic disagreement over moral issues more evident than in the controversy over abortion. There are those who feel that the right to have an abortion on demand follows from a woman's rights over her own body; others consider it a form of murder. How can we legislate on this subject without violating both the spirit and letter of the constitutional principle of the separation of Church and state? Even if you consider an abortion immoral, not making it a crime does not require a person to have one. Not legislating at least does not impose one person's moral or religious beliefs on another.

Another interesting example of legislating public morality can be seen in the anti-gambling laws of most jurisdictions. Bookmaking is illegal in New York. The idea behind this presumably is to prevent children from going hungry while their parents gamble away their earnings. However, when the state discovered it could make good money by running a lottery, it saw no moral difficulty in taking out ads on television to encourage these same family breadwinners to gamble. In fact, even the churches sought permission to conduct their own gambling operations, although some legislators expressed concern that organized crime might take over these operations. The simple fact is that by outlawing gambling and prostitution we did not eliminate them. The reason for this is that the actual morality and wishes of the public are not in consonance with public pronouncements on these issues. All that could be accomplished by this type of legislation was to give a monopoly to professional criminals while assuring a loss of tax revenue to the state.

Another way in which this type of legislation hurts the public interest is in the corrupting influence it tends to have on law enforcement personnel and politicians. Because of the vast amounts of money to be made in these illegal enterprises and because they require the cooperation of public officials to be able to flourish, they pose a very serious threat to the integrity of the entire criminal justice system and to public confidence in it. When prohibition was finally repealed, the only people mourning it, besides a handful of fanatics, were bootleggers and corrupt public officials. The widespread violation of unpopular and unenforceable laws inevitably leads to a general contempt and disregard for all laws, which is one of the major problems confronting this country.

Another problem with trying to enforce laws that are unenforceable because they are out of touch with real public morality, is that police departments trying to do the impossible may get the idea that the ends justify the means and resort to illegal actions of their own in an attempt to get convictions. These actions may range from illegal arrests and harassment of suspected prostitutes, to entrapment or the actual manufacturing or planting of evidence. In fact, in the name of society the police may be guilty of much more serious antisocial behavior than the alleged offender. This is a situation that no society can allow if it is to survive.

With respect to the issue of sex crimes between consenting adults, the history of adultery in New York is both interesting and instructive. Originally adultery was a felony. Juries, however, tended to take the view that it was a private matter concerning only the people involved and not society at large. Hence, they refused to convict for this crime. District attorneys, concerned with their record of convictions, stopped prosecuting. The legislature, therefore, reduced the crime to a misdemeanor. Juries still refused to convict. When adultery was the major ground for divorce in New York, there were thousands of divorces granted annually but no prosecutions for adultery.

By the 1960s, New York had a whole variety of victimless sex crimes that, by their very nature, were basically unenforceable even if anyone was inclined to enforce them. For example, enforcement of the statute against sodomy (which applied to married couples) would have required the posting of policemen in the bedrooms of citizens. These statutes were sporadically and abusively enforced, however. For example, the sodomy statute permitted someone who posed for a pornographic picture to be convicted of a felony although the manufacture of pornography was only a misdemeanor.

While most legislators realized that this type of case did not belong on an already congested court calendar, none had the political courage (or stupidity) to advocate the repeal of any of these offenses. However, a valiant attempt was made to clear the statute books of this type of sex crime by the simple expedient of completely rewriting the state's 90-year-old Penal Law and leaving out any sex crimes between consenting adults.

The results of this rewriting were not completely successful. Consensual sodomy was restored in a diluted and reduced form. It is now a Class B misdemeanor aimed primarily at homosexuals, but it is also applicable to unmarried heterosexual couples. Adultery, of course, was reinstated as a Class B misdemeanor in spite of the recommendation of the law revision commission to delete it. Prostitution was ostensibly reduced from a misdemeanor to a violation. Actually, it was never really a crime at all prior to the new penal law. What was criminal was not prostitution but soliciting for prostitution. This distinction was ignored in the past as a result of the policy of law enforcement agencies and the practicalities of judicial interpretation. This is a good example of the courts interpreting a statute to mean something totally different from what the legislature had enacted.

Often the courts will interpret a statute to mean something directly opposite to what it expressly says. For example, the U.S. Supreme Court has held that the mandatory language of the U.S. Constitution which says that when a person charged with a felony in one state flees to another, the governor of the state in which he is found *shall* on demand render him up to the state seeking him, is not really mandatory at all but permissive, and the aforesaid governor *may* render him to the demanding state.[3]

The problem of ill-advised or politically inspired criminal legislation is a very serious one in effective law enforcement. It has been said that the greatest problem that the legal profession has and the one over which it has the least control is the annual deluge of stupid legislation. The old legal maxim that "No man's life or property is safe while the legislature is in session" is still true.

We have included this chapter on the goals of the criminal justice system and the criminal statutes before considering the basic principles of substantive criminal law because no system can ever be any better than the goals set for it, and we feel it is necessary for the reader to be aware not just of the stated goals of the criminal justice system but also of the practical considerations involved in criminal legislation.

REFERENCES

1. Hall, John F. *The Psychology of Learning*. Philadelphia: J. B. Lippincott Co., 1966.
2. *People v. Bambino*, 1972, 69 Misc. 2d 387, 329 N.Y.S. 2d 922.
3. *Kentucky v. Dennison*, 1861, 24 How. 66, 16 L.Ed. 717.

3
Basic Principles of Substantive Criminal Law

Human beings seem to have a universal desire to classify and pigeonhole things. This is probably because classification provides some order in what would otherwise be a confusing array of isolated incidents, facts, and observations. Sometimes, as in the case of medical diagnosis, classification may be useful, as when it relates directly to treatment and prognosis. At other times, as in the case of psychological diagnosis, it may be worse than useless. It may be unrelated to treatment and prognosis, be quite artificial, and give the classifier the illusion of knowing something about a psychological condition because of having given it a name. In the case of the criminal law there are many ways of classifying offenses, and some methods of classification have more practical consequences than others.

The most important criterion for the classification of offenses is by their seriousness as measured by the length of authorized sentences. Since it is desirable to be specific, even though there are 51 different jurisdictions comprising the United States, we will, unless otherwise noted, use the law of New York as illustrative of the general principles of the criminal law. While the details of the criminal law will vary from state to state, the general principles will remain basically the same.

An offense is some act or omission proscribed by law and punishable by fine, imprisonment, forfeiture of office, death, or some other penalty. Offenses in New York are classified into:

Traffic infractions
Violations
Misdemeanors
Felonies

A traffic infraction is an offense defined as such in the Vehicle and Traffic Law. A violation is a minor offense for which a sentence of imprisonment in excess of 15 days cannot be imposed.

Traffic infractions and violations are not crimes. They have been expressly defined so as to avoid giving a criminal record to a citizen guilty of these relatively minor offenses.

Misdemeanors and felonies are crimes. A misdemeanor is an offense other than a traffic infraction for which a sentence in excess of 15 days but not in excess of one year may be imposed. A felony is a crime for which a sentence in excess of one year may be imposed. It should be noted that it is not the sentence actually imposed but the sentence that could legally be imposed which determines the classification of the offense.

When New York rewrote its Penal Law in 1967, it subclassified felonies into letter grades ranging from A for the most serious to E for the least. Class A felonies were later subdivided into A I, A II, and A III felonies. Misdemeanors were also subclassified, into A, B, and an unclassified grade to take into account misdemeanors created outside of the Penal Law in the general statutes. All misdemeanors defined in the Penal Law are specifically labeled A or B. A Class B misdemeanor carries a maximum term of three months. All violations created in the Penal Law are labeled as such. Any offense created outside of the Penal Law that has a maximum sentence of 15 days or less, however labeled, is deemed to be a violation. All other offenses, regardless of the length of the prescribed sentence, are also violations if they were not crimes at the time of the enactment of the new Penal Law. Felonies created outside of the Penal Law that are not expressly labeled are deemed to be Class E felonies regardless of the sentence authorized. Hence, an appellate court sustained a four-year term for a second conviction of drunken driving even though the statute creating this offense specified a two-year maximum term.[1] In this case, the criminal law superceded the Vehicle and Traffic Law and authorized a four-year maximum term for a Class E felony. We will discuss the specific maximum and minimum terms of imprisonment authorized for the various grades of felonies in Chapter 13.

Since both misdemeanors and felonies are subclassified into letter grades based on seriousness, the reader may be wondering why the primary division of crimes into misdemeanors and felonies has been retained. There are many practical differences between prosecutions for misdemeanors and those for felonies. For one thing, sentences for misdemeanors are required to be definite sentences and are served in local or county jails, while sentences for felonies are indeterminate in that a minimum term and a maximum term are set. Felony sentences are served in state prisons, which are often far removed from the defendant's community and family. A felony conviction carries with it the loss of certain civil rights which are not lost in a misdemeanor conviction. Since felonies are more serious crimes, trial jurisdiction over these offenses is usually vested in higher courts than those having trial jurisdiction over misdemeanors.

A second way of classifying offenses is in terms of the victim. Crimes may be primarily offenses against people (e.g., homicide, assault, rape, robbery, etc.), offenses against property (e.g., larceny, arson, forgery, etc.), offenses against the dignity of the state (e.g., tax evasion, bribery, etc.), or offenses against "public morality" (e.g., gambling, prostitution, drug offenses, etc.). It is in the last category that most of the "victimless crimes" occur. Some offenses will, of course, fall into more than one of the above categories. For example, robbery is a larceny (a crime against property) aggravated by the use of force or intimidation (a crime against a person). In a sense all crimes are affronts to the dignity of the state, and many challenge public morals. Hence, the foregoing classification scheme is really of little practical value except that the courts and legislatures tend to view offenses whose major thrust is against people as more serious than those primarily against property. This is why offenses classified higher up on this list tend to carry longer sentences than those further down.

A third important way of classifying offenses is into the dichotomy of *malum in se* v. *malum prohibitum* crimes. These are also referred to as offenses of mental culpability and offenses of strict liability, respectively. A *malum in se* crime is one that is "bad in its very nature," i.e., an act, such as murder or rape, that anyone in a civilized society would recognize as wrong without having to consult a statute. A *malum prohibitum* offense is one that is bad merely because it is prohibited by some penal statute but which is not intrinsically wrong or immoral. An example of such an offense would be the refusal to aid a police officer in apprehending a criminal when ordered to do so if no personal risk was involved. The New York Penal Law specifies that unless a clear legislative intent to create a crime of strict liability is evident in the language of the statute, the crime should be interpreted as one of mental culpability. The reason for the importance of this distinction is that if a crime is *malum in se*, there are at least two necessary elements for its commission: there must be (1) a voluntary act or omission accompanied by (2) a culpable mental state. This culpable mental state or criminal intent is what lawyers refer to as the *mens rea* or "guilty mind."

The specific elements that constitute a given crime are defined in the statute creating the crime and are referred to as the *corpus delecti* of the crime, literally "the body of the crime." A *mens rea* or a criminal state of mind is required as part of the *corpus delecti* of all crimes of mental culpability, and the creating statute will describe exactly what this state of mind must be. Terms frequently used in describing this mental state are: "intentionally," "knowingly," "recklessly," and with "criminal negligence."

In the cases of strict liability the mental state of the defendant is not part of the *corpus delecti* of the crime and is irrelevant. All the people need prove is that the defendant committed the act or omission in question, without regard to the defendant's state of mind at the time. Even in *malum prohibitum* offenses, however, the criminal act or omission has to be performed voluntarily, i.e., the only mental state required is that the criminal act itself be intended and not the result of accident, duress, or lack of capacity to form intent.

The common mental states required for criminal responsibility are defined with reasonable precision in the Penal Law, but these definitions often cause considerable difficulty when one tries to apply them to the facts in a particular case.

"Intentionally" means that a person has the conscious objective of performing a certain conduct or effecting a certain result.

"Knowingly" means that a person is aware of the nature of his or her conduct and of the existence of certain specified facts and circumstances.

"Recklessly" means that a person is aware of and consciously disregards a substantial and unjustifiable risk that a certain circumstance exists or that a certain result will occur.

"Criminally negligent" means that a person fails to perceive a substantial and unjustifiable risk that a certain circumstance exists or a result will occur.

The difference between reckless and criminally negligent conduct is that in the latter the risk is not perceived, while in the former it is perceived and disregarded. In either case, however, the failure to perceive or to be influenced by the circumstances in question must constitute a gross departure from the standard of care that a reasonable person would exercise in the situation. To prove criminal negligence one must demonstrate a much more extreme and cavalier type of behavior than is necessary to prove a case of civil negligence. The difficulty for the courts is in determining what the line of demarcation is between ordinary or civil negligence and a "gross deviation" from the behavior of a reasonable person.

As a practical matter, the problem in prosecutions for crimes of mental culpability is to establish the existence of the required mental state on the part of the defendant at the time of the commission of the crime. Notwithstanding Justice Cardozo's famous statement that "The state of a man's mind is just as much a question of fact as the state of his digestion," the fact remains that a person's subjective experience is not subject to inspection by anyone but that person. To get around this difficulty lawyers have a presumption that should appeal to behavioristically oriented psychologists: a person is deemed to intend the natural consequences of his or her actions. If a defendant has a fight with another person and points a loaded gun at him and pulls the trigger, the court will not be swayed by his arguing that he really didn't intend to hurt the other party. The natural consequence of pointing a loaded gun at a person and pulling the trigger is to inflict grievous physical harm or death. This is a perfectly reasonable rule and it makes it possible for the courts to function on a pragmatic basis. The problem arises when the defendant suffers from some "defect of reason" or mental disease.

While it may make sense to assume that a normal person intends the natural consequences of his or her actions, few mental health professionals would agree that such an assumption has any reasonable application to a catatonic or other severely deranged individual. Since this presumption breaks down with regard to the mentally ill, special rules were needed to deal with the criminal liabilities of these individuals. These will be discussed in Chapter 10. Some of these rules, notably the M'Naghten Rule, have been severely criticized by some mental health professionals on the grounds that they do not seem to make much sense psychologically. They excuse some mentally ill defendants but not others. Some rules even excuse one defendant but not another suffering from the same mental condition. At this point we merely wish to point out that such criticism, while perhaps justified from a psychological point of view, really reflects an ignorance of the legal purpose of the rule. A mentally ill defendant is not excused from criminal liability under these rules as an act of grace on the part of the state simply because he is mentally incapacitated. The real reason he is excused is that he has not committed the crime in question because he lacks the capacity to form the mental state required by the statute. In other words, he simply did not commit an element of the *corpus delecti* of the crime and is, therefore, innocent.

The defendant's mental condition at the time of the commission of the offense must be sharply distinguished from his mental condition at the time of trial or at the time of execution of the sentence because here the tests differ from those used to determine criminal responsibility.

The test of mental capacity to stand trial is that the defendant must have sufficient capacity to cooperate effectively with counsel. If a defendant lacks this capacity, a trial cannot be held until he recovers it. The reason for this requirement is that there is a constitutional right to be represented by counsel, and this right, to be vindicated, requires an effective, not just a *pro forma*, legal representation. Such effective representation cannot be obtained if the defendant cannot cooperate with counsel. While this rule was designed to protect the rights of people accused of a crime, it has often worked against them. Because they were mentally incapable of assisting in their defense, people have been incarcerated in mental hospitals under criminal commitments for periods far in excess of the sentence that they could have received for the offense charged.

One such defendant, after being held for years in a mental hospital, moved to be declared competent and granted a trial. His motion was opposed by the people, whose psychiatrist admitted under cross-examination that he really did not know what mental capacity the defendant needed to cooperate with counsel in defending the particular charge involved. His main reason for thinking the defendant incompetent was that the defendant asserted his constitutional rights and was "uncooperative" with the people's psychiatrist. The defendant's motion for a trial was denied.

In New York it is no longer possible to send a defendant to a mental hospital under a criminal commitment prior to conviction of a crime. However, it is still possible to be imprisoned for life in a mental hospital for a relatively minor offense under a civil commitment without any trial, particularly if the defendant cannot afford good-quality legal representation.

If a defendant becomes mentally incompetent after a trial, a sentence cannot be executed as the defendant is deprived of the opportunity to say something in mitigation. However, the law has been reformed so that time served in a mental hospital under a criminal commitment is counted against sentence time. The former situation of a patient recovering after 10 years in a mental hospital and then having to serve the sentence *ab initio* has been eliminated. This really was not much of a reform, as very few, if any, long-term patients in mental hospitals either recover or get any meaningful treatment. If a patient confined in a mental hospital under a criminal commitment has completed two-thirds of the sentence, the commitment must then be changed to a civil one, which may or may not have any practical benefits for the patient.

While it is neither practical nor desirable to deal with specific criminal offenses in this book, there are certain basic and general types of crimes that require discussion. These occur constantly in connection with a wide variety of other specific criminal behaviors and are conventionally charged along with these other crimes. These general crimes are: attempt, conspiracy, criminal solicitation, and criminal facilitation.

The crime of attempt is committed when a person with the intent to commit a crime engages in conduct tending to but falling short of its commission. If the crime is, in fact, consummated, the attempt merges into the crime of which it is a necessary element, and the defendant cannot be convicted separately for it. If, however, the crime has fallen short of being committed, the defendant may be convicted for the attempt. Thus, a prosecutor who has failed to prove a case for the principal crime may get a conviction for the attempt to commit it. An example of this type of prosecution could be seen in prosecutions for forcible rape where the prosecution was unable to get a conviction because it lacked the corroborative evidence formerly required. The defendant might still be convicted for attempted rape or some other related crime, such as assault which was necessarily involved in the rape but which required no corroboration. Prior to the new criminal code, the maximum sentence for an attempt to commit a crime was half of the maximum sentence for the completed crime. Today (with some exceptions) an attempt to commit a crime is a crime one degree lower than the completed offense, e.g., an attempt to commit a Class C felony is a Class D felony.

A conviction for the crime of attempt always requires the performance of some overt act in furtherance of the criminal intent. A scheme that has not gone beyond the planning stage can never amount to an attempt, as "the law does not punish evil thoughts." In addition to the requirement of an overt act, the crime must come "dangerously close" to completion. For example, in a crime against a person, the defendant must at least come within the presence of the prospective victim.

A conspiracy is an agreement between two or more persons to commit a crime. As in the case of an attempt, there must be some overt act committed by one of the co-conspirators in furtherance of the criminal plan for the crime of conspiracy to be consummated. The crime of conspiracy is a separate and distinct crime from the subject matter of the conspiracy, and the defendant may be convicted of both. No person can be convicted of a conspiracy or any other crime on the uncorroborated testimony of an accomplice. The corroboration required must independently link the defendant to the crime. The common law distinction between accessories to a crime before and after the fact has been abolished, and all co-conspirators are principals to the crime. Each is fully responsible for the actions of the other in the furtherance of the conspiracy. Also, it is no defense for a conspirator that a co-conspirator cannot be convicted of the crime because of some personal defense like the lack of mental capacity or infancy (i.e., the defendant is under the age of 16). Not only can one conspirator be found guilty while another is acquitted, but they each may be found guilty of different degrees of the crime as the circumstances indicate. The majority of crimes in the Penal Law are subdivided into degrees based on seriousness, and the four basic offenses that we are now discussing are no exceptions. Thus, Conspiracy in the fourth degree (a Class B misdemeanor) is an agreement to commit any crime, while Conspiracy in the third degree (a Class A misdemeanor) is an agreement to commit a felony. Conspiracy in the second degree (a Class E felony) is an agreement to commit a Class B or C felony, and Conspiracy in the first degree (a Class B felony) is an agreement to commit a Class A felony.

From the foregoing, it can be seen that the commission of a higher degree of conspiracy necessarily involves the commission of a Conspiracy in the fourth degree; hence, the defendant can only be convicted of the highest degree of Conspiracy that fits the facts in his or her case, and the fourth degree necessarily merges therein. This means that the defendant cannot be convicted of both the higher and the lower degree of the crime for the same act. If the people attempt to prove conspiracy in the second degree, the defendant may be convicted of that or any lesser degree of the crime that the evidence may support.

Criminal solicitation is a new crime as far as New York is concerned. It is committed when a person solicits, requests, commands, importunes or otherwise attempts to cause another to commit a crime. Like conspiracy, it occurs in many degrees and the defendant may not avail himself or herself of personal defenses available to the other party. For example, if a defendant solicits an infant of 12 to commit a murder, he cannot claim that since a 12 year old is legally unable to commit a murder that he cannot be convicted of soliciting a person to commit a murder. The reader may be wondering why the crime of solicitation is necessary since if A solicits B to commit a crime and B does so, they are both equally guilty of the crime solicited as well as the additional crime of conspiracy. However, if B refuses to agree to commit the crime solicited, then there has been no conspiracy and A would be guilty only of criminal solicitation.

Criminal facilitation, which is also a new concept in New York, further extends the range of inchoate criminal culpability to the situation in which a person knowingly provides another, who he believes is about to commit a felony, with the means and opportunity to do so. He must, in fact, have aided such person in the commission of the crime.

A less common non-specific type of crime is called compounding a crime. People often misuse this term to mean making a crime worse, but it really means accepting money or other consideration in exchange for not prosecuting for a criminal offense. The rewritten Penal Law makes it possible for a complainant to accept reparations from a defendant and agree not to prosecute him without being guilty of compounding a crime, provided that the consideration received is limited to a fair compensation for his actual losses.

Besides mentally disturbed people, there are other classes of defendants to whom the law gives special treatment. These include juvenile delinquents, youthful offenders and wayward minors. In these cases, the special treatment is in recognition of the limited life experience and maturity of these individuals and is motivated by a desire to protect these immature defendants from the consequences of their presumed lack of judgment.

There is a conclusive presumption that a person under the age of 16 is incapable of committing any crime except that children between 13 and 16 years of age may be criminally responsible for certain specifically listed offenses. A conclusive presumption is not rebuttable and is, in fact, a substantive rule of law. If such persons commit actions that would constitute crimes if committed by an adult, they are merely guilty of juvenile delinquency. A conviction as a juvenile delinquent is not a conviction of a crime. In addition to the possible reduction in length of sentence (sometimes the permissible sentence may be lengthened), the defendant is spared a criminal record. Also, these cases are tried in Family Court rather than in a criminal court, so that the record is sealed, protecting the defendant from the publicity attendant upon a public criminal trial. Under the former law the presumption was that no person under 15 years of age could commit any crime, and persons from 15 to 16 could commit only crimes punishable by death or life imprisonment. It was decided by the legislature that if an immature person needed protection from his own conduct in ordinary crimes he needed it even more, not less, in capital or very serious crimes. The exception concerning capital punishment or life imprisonment crimes was therefore dropped. Recently, due to all of the newspaper publicity concerning violent street crime by juveniles, there was much pressure to lower the age of criminal responsibility, and at the time of this book's going to press the legislature enacted a change in the law creating a category of offender called a "juvenile offender". This new law created criminal liability for children as young as 13 charged with second degree murder and for children 14 and 15 charged with second degree murder or one of a series of listed serious felonies. These juvenile offenders are to be tried in criminal courts like adults but are subject to lesser indeterminate sentences. Also the court has some discretion to remove the matter to the Family Court and treat the child as a juvenile delinquent. It can do so on its own motion if the child is not charged with second degree murder or an armed felony and it must do so under such circumstances on the people's request. If the charge is murder in the second degree or an armed felony the court must find extenuating circumstances or other listed factors to treat the child as a juvenile delinquent.

While the use of juvenile delinquent treatment for young offenders was intended to protect their interests, it must be pointed out that more often than not it has worked against them. For one thing, the courts have tended to take the position that, since the offense charged was not a criminal one, juveniles could be denied rights that the constitution mandates in criminal proceedings. In addition many states have enacted wayward minor statutes or statutes concerning persons in need of supervision (PINS). A child who is chronically disobedient or runs away from home repeatedly can find himself adjudicated as a PINS (on the complaint of a parent anxious to get rid of him) and confined in an institution for an act which, if committed by an adult, would not be an offense. Such youngsters are known as "status offenders". The courts are finally beginning to realize that the road to hell is indeed paved with good intentions and that even children have constitutional rights. The trend is now toward incorporating the safeguards of criminal procedures into juvenile proceedings.

People who are accused of crimes committed after they have reached the age of 16, but before the age of 19, may, at the option of the court, receive special treatment as youthful offenders. To be eligible for such treatment, the defendant must not be charged with a Class A I felony, a Class A II felony, or an armed felony, and must not have been previously convicted and sentenced for a felony or given youthful offender treatment. He must also not have been previously given juvenile delinquent treatment for an act for which he was criminaly responsible. Under the old practice the defendant had to agree to an investigation by the court and if, following this investigation, the court decided to treat him as a youthful offender, the proceedings were sealed and the case was tried by the court without a jury. Today the defendant is no longer deprived of his right to a jury trial nor can he be forced to be tried before a judge who may well have been prejudiced as a result of reading the pretrial investigation. The decision to treat the defendant as a youthful offender is now made at the time of sentence after conviction in a regular criminal trial with all of the defendant's rights preserved. If youthful offender treatment may be granted, the record is sealed, and the jury, at the onset of the trial, is instructed to keep its deliberations and the case confidential. The conviction in the criminal trial is wiped out by the according of youthful offender treatment, and the defendant is spared a criminal record. In cases of serious felonies, youthful offender treatment limits the maximum sentence to four years; but in misdemeanors, the price of preventing a criminal record may be a maximum sentence of up to four years rather than the one year authorized for the original crime.

By not adjudicating a person as a youthful offender until after the conviction for a crime, the former practice of keeping youthful offenders incarcerated under high bail until trial to give them a taste of what prison is like has been eliminated. This practice came to be known as "the Treatment" in the criminal courts. Despite its total disregard of the possibility that the defendant might be innocent, many defense attorneys were reluctant to protest too strongly against this high-handed abuse of judicial power, on the theory that the incarceration would be a powerful argument at the time of sentencing that the defendant had indeed "learned his lesson," and that any further commitment would serve no useful purpose.

In presenting the foregoing principles of criminal liability, we have shown that what would otherwise be criminal behavior may be rendered noncriminal because of certain defenses. The lack of mental capacity to form the required criminal intent is one such defense. The age of the defendant is another. At this point in our discussion, it might be pertinent to consider the effect on criminal liability of a "mistake" on the part of the defendant. Mistakes can be of two types: mistakes of law and mistakes of fact. In general a mistake of law is no defense in a criminal prosecution unless such mistake is based on a statute or other enactment, a judicial decision, an administrative order or grant of permission, or an interpretation of a statute by a public official responsible for administering or enforcing the law. The fact that a defendant did not believe that the act in question was illegal is no defense. This is so even if the defendant sought legal advice and was told by an attorney that his or her actions were legal. It is not a matter of the defendant's good faith. It is simply that the courts cannot help it if a defendant has had bad legal advice. Sometimes this principle is stated erroneously as "Everyone is deemed to know the law." This is, of course, not true. At times even lawyers are unsure of what the law is until a court of last resort rules on a specific issue. What it really means is that ignorance of the law is no excuse. While this may seem like a harsh rule, and at times it is, it would be manifestly impossible to enforce a criminal code if a defendant were required to be personally rather than constructively apprised of its provisions prior to being held accountable under it.

Mistakes of fact on the other hand may be a defense if they negate the required criminal intent, or if, had the facts been as the defendant believed them to be, they would have constituted the defense of justification to be discussed below.

Intoxication is not a defense *per se*, and indeed it may even be part of the *corpus delecti* of some crimes such as drunken driving; but the defendant may offer evidence of it if it tends to negate the required mental state for the commission of the crime charged.

The defenses of infancy and mental disease both involve a lack of criminal responsibility. They are called "ordinary defenses." Once they are raised by the defendant, the people have the burden of disproving them at the trial beyond a reasonable doubt.

There are other defenses that involve a lack of culpability as opposed to a lack of capacity to commit a crime. These are the defenses of justification, duress, entrapment, and renunciation. Justification is an ordinary defense, but the remaining three defenses are called affirmative defenses. The concept of an affirmative defense is new in New York criminal law and relates to the question of who has the burden of proof with respect to these defenses.

Prior to the new Penal Law the people had the burden of proof on every contested issue in a criminal case. Furthermore, they had to sustain this burden beyond a reasonable doubt. This is considerably more than the requirement in a civil case that the party with the burden of proof must sustain it with a preponderance of the evidence. A defendant raising a defense had merely to go forward with some evidence establishing the defense. Thereafter, the burden was on the people to disprove it beyond a reasonable doubt. This is still the rule with respect to ordinary defenses. However, in an affirmative defense, the legislature felt that the defendant would be in a better position than the people to establish the facts relating to such a defense, and, for these defenses the defendant was given the burden of proof. However, his burden is limited to proving the defense by a preponderance of the evidence, as in a civil case. The U.S. Supreme Court has held that once a defendant has established an affirmative defense by a preponderance of the evidence, the people have the burden of disproving it beyond a reasonable doubt.[2] This decision probably resulted from the reluctance of the court to admit that the concept of an affirmative defense really places the burden of proof of any element of a prosecution on the defendant because of the constitutional issues raised by such a departure from traditional criminal procedure. A rule of construction requires courts to interpret a statute in such a manner that it would be constitutional if such construction is reasonably possible.

The ordinary defense of justification is that the otherwise criminal behavior is either required or justified by law (e.g., the use of force in arresting a resisting felon) or is an emergency measure necessary to avoid some imminent public or private injury (e.g., the use of force to defend oneself or another from an illegal attack). With respect to the use of force the statutes are quite detailed as to what persons are authorized to use it, under what circumstances, and to what degree. There is also a distinction made between ordinary and deadly force, and the permissible use of the latter is, naturally, more restricted.

The trend is to restrict the use of force as much as is practical. Under common law a person had a right to kill to prevent an illegal arrest. Today, it is illegal to use any degree of force in resisting an illegal arrest, and the defendant must rely on his legal remedies. As one court put it, "The sanctity of human liberty must give way to the sanctity of human life." Formerly, a police officer could kill to prevent the escape of a felon. Now the officer may use deadly physical force only in certain very serious felonies involving the use, attempted use, or threatened imminent use of physical force against a person; or in case of kidnapping, arson, burglary, or escape in the first degree; or if the felony was committed by a person armed with a deadly weapon; or if necessary for the officer to defend himself or another person against the imminent use of deadly physical force.

The affirmative defense of duress involves the claim that the defendant was forced to commit the offense by the use or threatened imminent use of unlawful physical force against him or some third person, and the force was of such a nature that a person of reasonable firmness would have been unable to resist it. Mere blackmail or threat to expose the defendant's previous illegal or immoral conduct doesn't amount to duress. Physical force or the threat of it must be involved.

The affirmative defense of entrapment asserts that the defendant engaged in the proscribed conduct because he was induced to do so by a public servant or a person acting in cooperation with such public servant. The public servant involved must have induced the defendant to commit the act; merely giving a defendant who is inclined to commit a crime the opportunity to do so, does not constitute entrapment. The reason for this defense is that it is contrary to public policy to have police officers going around inducing people to commit crimes so that they may arrest them.

The affirmative defense of renunciation is a restatement of the old legal principle of *locus penitentiae* (a place of repentence). It involves the defendant's having a change of heart and completely and voluntarily renouncing his criminal purpose prior to the commission of a crime. To establish this defense the defendant must show that: (1) he withdrew from participation prior to the commission of the crime, and (2) he made a substantial effort to prevent the crime's commission.

The latter requirement is new and is more than just the requirement of the old law that he communicated his withdrawal to his co-conspirators so that they no longer relied on him. Renunciation of criminal purpose is not voluntary and complete if it is motivated by: (1) a belief that circumstances exist which make commission of the crime more difficult or detection and apprehension more likely, or (2) a decision to postpone the criminal act or to transfer the effort to another victim.

While this chapter was intended to give the non-legally trained reader some idea of the technical legal principles involved in the substantive criminal law (as opposed to the procedural or adjective criminal law, to be discussed in Chapters 8 to 10 inclusive), it cannot be expected to convey a feeling for the diversity of behavior that is subsumed under the label "criminal" in any given jurisdiction. This insight can only be obtained if the reader will take the trouble to read through the penal law of his or her own jurisdiction. Such a reading will usually require only a few hours for a rapid perusal, but will readily convince the reader of how ridiculous it is for some authors to talk glibly about "criminal types" or make recommendations for the reform of criminals as though they were a homogeneous group. What society calls "criminal behavior" is actually the most diverse assortment of conduct that anyone could conceive. About all that these activities have in common is that they have the potential for causing the perpetrators some very expensive, traumatic, and destructive contacts with the judicial process. It is this diversity in criminal behavior that makes necessary the next chapter, dealing with some types of offenders who find their way into the criminal courts.

REFERENCES

1. *People v. Bouton*, 40 A.D. 2d 383.
2. *Mullaney v. Wilber*, 421 U.S. 684.

4
Criminals

While we do not really know what makes one person a criminal and another a paragon of virtue, many theories exist, and considerable data support and contradict virtually all of the theories.

In this chapter we will consider such issues as: Who are "criminals"? What are some of the biological, psychological, sociological, and economic explanations for criminal behavior?

Generally, certain types of crimes receive much more attention than others. Murderers, rapists (especially of young girls and old women), armed robbers who are very brazen or flamboyant, never lack for press coverage. Embezzlers, forgers, conspirators in fraud, shoplifters, and petty thieves tend to be of less concern to the media, to the public, and to the professional criminologist. Female criminals are generally ignored in the press unless their crime is in some way "unwomanly," e.g., murdering a spouse or a child. This chapter will include discussion of female criminals, shoplifters, and petty criminals, as well as murderers and others.

A first point to make about criminals is that they are people, human beings, men and women with thoughts, feelings, needs, and values, much like other men and women. It is so easy to stereotype offenders as vicious, as brutal, as animals. It makes us that much safer from our own antisocial impulses and fantasies; we, after all, are not vicious, brutal animals and could never do the terrible things that these monsters did. That is why they must be punished, locked up, ostracized, and why we feel no guilt at the severity of the punishments we mete out. This is not to deny for a moment that many criminals *do* do terrible things to other people; it denies only the comfortable rationalization that only subhumans are capable of such evil.

A second point is that most crimes are not solved; in fact, many are not even reported. This may mean that there are far more criminals among us than we think, but that some unknown proportion of them are successful enough to remain at large. It may mean, too, that the information we do have about the psychology of criminal behavior is derived from the behavior of those who are least competent or who have some unconscious need to be apprehended. Another possibility is that most crimes are the work of a relatively small number of offenders. If so, while we do not know who committed each and every crime, we may have a pretty good idea of who most of the criminals are.

34

HISTORICAL THEORIES OF CRIMINAL BEHAVIOR

We will leave to others the task of tracing the earliest theories concerning criminal behavior and merely cite several of the more recent forerunners of contemporary theories.* Fink[1] discusses a number of them: phrenology, the doctrine of moral insanity, anatomical and "physiological" theories, and theories of heredity and "feeblemindedness." He concludes that criminal behavior is caused by biological, environmental, and psychological factors.

Phrenology. Like most of the other ideas discussed by Fink, phrenology originated in Europe. It was, initially, a serious attempt to link philosophical notions of the nature of human intellect, sensibility, and behavior with empirical data. In essence, phrenologists promulgated the views that:

1. Human beings have desirable and undesirable faculties (destructiveness, acquisitiveness, secretiveness, are a few associated with criminality).
2. The development of a faculty is directly related to the amount of brain tissue devoted to the faculty.
3. These faculties are localized in particular areas of the brain.
4. The shape of the skull accurately reflects the development of the underlying brain area, and, therefore, one's character can be assessed by measurement of the regions of the skull.

A famous phrenologist, Fowler, wrote that destructiveness could be located "beneath the temporal bone, and, when large, extends from three to six eighths of an inch above the top of the ear. When it is very large, it thickens the middle of the base of the head."[2] How were the locations of these faculties assigned? Individuals were identified who appeared to have certain dominant traits. Their skulls were carefully examined to determine which regions were especially prominent or undersized, and the inference was made that the prominence was responsible for the presence, or the deficiency for the absence, of the trait. According to this theory one was not doomed to act upon the faculties with which one was endowed most generously. Other faculties, alone or in combination, could enable one to control behaviors if one wished. That is, free will could still be exercised.

Phrenology did not endure as an explanatory system, at least as far as science is concerned. It was possible for the believer to demonstrate anything he wished, since if the behavior could not be attributed to one region of the skull, it could be attributed to others. This theory which could explain everything, could, therefore, predict nothing; and so it fell by the wayside of science.

*See Bibliography for references not cited at end of this chapter.

Moral Insanity. This disorder was described as a separation of feelings from intellect in which the latter was left intact and the former were in various ways perverted. Fink traces the history of the doctrine of moral insanity from its origins in the writings of Pinel (who discussed *manie sans delire* in the eighteenth century) to its formal naming in 1835 and its demise in the writings of Healy in 1915.[3]

Without using the term moral insanity, Benjamin Rush described a "diseased state of the will in which the understanding was unimpaired."[4] Rush listed nine characteristics of this condition, among them the following: The acts which this state produced were unprovoked and seemed to be the products of irresistible impulses; they were often directed at friends or relatives and seemed cruel and deliberate; the perpetrator did not rob the victim and rarely attempted to escape; he might mutilate himself or attempt suicide; sometimes the offender suffered delusions of a religious nature. Rush also pointed out that, for some of these persons, a despicable crime which would lead inexorably to execution was a means of indirectly committing suicide. Opponents of capital punishment have, in more recent years, argued that capital punishment is more an incentive than a deterrent to murder; Rush might have agreed.

While destruction of life is the act most often linked to moral insanity, other criminal behaviors were also attributed to it, particularly, it seems, acts committed by otherwise "respectable" men and women. Compulsive stealing or shoplifting and fire-setting were among them. (The well-known nineteenth century terms for these behaviors are, in fact, suggestive of disease: kleptomania and pyromania.)

That a moral deficiency was involved was suggested by the absence of grief or remorse on the part of the offender. His behavior had no apparent motive, save perhaps an unspoken or delusional one; and, unlike the murderer whose crime is clearly motivated, the morally insane would neither confess nor deny and would have committed no other crime at the time of his impulsive act.

This doctrine did not survive the nineteenth century unscathed, however. Among other reasons for the controversy may have been the insanity plea of Charles Guiteau, the assassin of President Garfield, who went to the gallows reciting a poem he had written about his execution. One attack on the doctrine put it this way:

> Under this . . . gospel petty larceny is a crime, while murder or arson are diseases—and the more perfect in lying, stealing, cheating or murdering a man becomes, the more indubitably is he irresponsible.[5]

The argument of the opponents of the doctrine of moral insanity seems to have centered on the assumption that the human brain cannot be divided into separable compartments and that, therefore, insanity involves both intellect and emotions. Phrenology notwithstanding, moral insanity, in this view, is an impossibility. Recent research on differences between the two cerebral hemispheres and the capabilities that each governs will probably not resurrect this doctrine, but it does suggest that there may have been more to it than met the eye. The view that parts of the mind can be healthy and other parts diseased is similar to more modern legal references to paranoids as sane men with insane delusions. We deal with this matter elsewhere in this book. There are also diagnostic labels for behavior subsumed under the archaic term moral insanity, e.g., psychopathy and character disorders, as well as paranoia.

Anthropometry: Anatomy is Destiny. At various periods certain ideas or themes seem to dominate and direct the intellectual life of a nation, a culture, a civilization. This phenomenon is referred to as the Zeitgeist or "the spirit of the times." One such idea, whose impact cannot be overstated, was that of evolution. The view that organisms change, develop, become better suited to survival over the eons, affected every aspect of life and thought in western civilization. Criminology was no exception.

Darwin's contribution to the theory of evolution was not the idea that more complex forms of life evolved from simpler ones; others had said that before him (and there is compelling evidence for this view from such diverse fields as embryology, comparative anatomy, paleontology, and hematology). His contribution was the description of the mechanisms of evolutionary change and his postulation of the following points:

1. Random changes in the germ plasm appear spontaneously and make minor alterations in the structure of individuals.
2. Any change that can occur eventually will.
3. Organisms live in constant competition for limited supplies of food, mates, and so on.
4. Most random changes impede the organism's competitive efforts and make it less likely to survive to mating age. Hence these changes die out with the individual mutant.
5. Rarely, a mutation enhances the individual's competitive position and makes it more likely that it will survive to reproduce and transmit this characteristic to its progeny.
6. Changes in species evolve slowly by an accumulation of these more beneficial mutations.

This postulate contradicted previous views (e.g., Lamarck's idea that acquired characteristics could be passed on to the next generation). Modern psychologists tend to view behavior not as accidental or spontaneous in the Darwinian sense but as the predictable product of two types of factors and their interaction. This is summarized in Lewin's famous equation: $B = f(P, E)$. That is, behavior is a function of the momentary structure and state of the person (P) and of his psychological environment (E).[6]

One bio-evolutionary view of the etiology of criminal behavior is that it may be reflected in physical measurements of the body (not just of the head, as the phrenologists had taught).

Cesare Lombroso, an Italian anthropometrist, was the pioneer advocate of the view that persons who engage in criminal behavior are, in some manner, less evolved or less developed than law-abiding persons. His major research technique was the detailed measurement of the bodies (or remains) of persons who had committed crimes of various types. He generally found what he called anthropological anomalies, e.g., malformations of skull, brain, face, limbs, or of secondary sex characteristics. These anomalies, particularly the more extreme or complex, were generally accompanied by psychological anomalies of a relatively morbid sort. In studies of female offenders, for example, Lombroso and his associates compared cranial capacities of the skulls of prostitutes, infanticides, thieves, "lunatics," and normal women and found that the averages varied (though he used no tests of statistical significance) according to the nature of the crime. They reported that poisoners had the highest cranial capacities and accomplices in rape the lowest.

Among the anomalies reported were asymmetrical crania, receding foreheads, flat heads, moles, hairiness, and prehensile feet. Such anomalies were interpreted as throwbacks to an earlier stage of human development. Lombroso used the term *atavism* to describe them. In his book on female offenders Lombroso writes of the relative rarity of such "retrogressive characteristics" in women and their more frequent appearance among prostitutes than among "occasional" criminals who are *not* different in physiognomy from people in general. Only the "profoundly depraved" woman bears the physiognomic "brand of criminality." Since the "criminal type" is a reversion to a more primitive body form, and since more primitive people were less differentiated along sexual lines, it follows that male and female criminals are less distinguishable in respect to stature, cranium, and so forth, than noncriminals of the two sexes. Or so Lombroso reasoned.

An interesting observation among the many he made is that tattooing is extremely common among male criminals and nearly nonexistent among female offenders. With characteristic attention to detail he lists the frequencies of different types of tattoos, their locations, the age at which they were acquired. Like Münsterberg and many others of his generation, Lombroso looks at woman and sees deficiencies. Discussing tattooing he writes:

Here we have another effect of the smaller ability and fancy, the lower degree of differentiation in the female intellect; for even the female criminal is monotonous and uniform compared with her male companion, just as woman is in general inferior to man.[7]

In fairness to Lombroso, it should be pointed out that he does describe the exploits of the infamous Belle Starr with some enthusiasm.

Atavism, then, is one form of bio-evolutionary explanation for criminality. Related to it is a concept of a psychologist, G. Stanley Hall, who described delinquency as a form of arrested development. Not a throwback to an earlier ancestor, the delinquent is one who has not yet "grown up." This view has its contemporary counterpart in the observation that most violent crime is committed by persons under 30 and that these offenders seem to "burn out" by the time they reach that milestone.

Erik Erikson, too, remarks on the relationship between delinquent behavior and maturation. He suggests that the delinquent is engaging in his behavior as a form of psychosocial moratorium, a taking "time out," a temporary postponing of the responsibilities of adult life which serves to keep one's options open. As maturity brings a greater sense of identity, suggests Erikson, the young person is no longer compelled to engage in antisocial acts or to take on a "negative identity" characterized by behaviors he knows are "bad."[8]

Cerebral Degeneration.   Atavism and arrested development were two approaches to understanding the abnormal nature of criminal behavior. Another approach is that which views criminality as "degeneracy." Influenced by theories of heredity, disease, and neurology and by observations of the brains of decapitated evildoers, a number of writers in the decades around 1900 expressed the view that criminal behavior is not a throwback to what was *de rigueur* in earlier times, but is a consequence or a correlate of deterioration of brain tissue either by disease or through inheritance. Degenerate behavior is the product of a degenerated brain. While it is no doubt true that certain tumors or lesions can produce unanticipated and uncontrollable violence, it is equally true that consistent differences have not been found between the brains of criminals and those of noncriminals (and no one has systematically studied the brains of embezzlers or forgers).

In addition to structural notions which proposed that criminals are "built" differently, there were a number of functional notions, as well, which proposed that criminals' bodies operate differently. Fink describes several studies of heart functioning, sensitivity to pain, blushing, susceptibility to fatigue, and so on, among criminals and delinquents. Unfortunately, they, like the various early schools discussed, offer little of value beyond their historical antecedence to contemporary views. As Fink points out, there were any number of methodological and conceptual shortcomings in these studies. Those that were conducted on incarcerated men and women did not take into account the effects of prison itself on their functioning. There were no control groups of unincarcerated criminals who had committed similar acts. There were rarely control groups of noncriminals matched with criminals on pertinent variables. In most of these studies statistical tests were not employed, either because the study antedated the development of these techniques or because the researcher was unfamiliar with them. Accordingly, generalizations were made without due regard for the effects of chance or extraneous factors. Implicit in this comment is the point that alternative explanations were overlooked or denied without being given due consideration. Where correlations were (or appeared to be) found, they were often interpreted as showing a causal relationship in spite of the fact that correlation does not logically lead to an inference concerning causation. The possibility of other variables affecting both of the correlates was rarely considered.

Despite these after-the-fact criticisms, however, most of these approaches won some measure of support.

Heredity.   There was another movement in the quest for explanations of criminal behavior. It, too, had to do with heredity and with one of its presumed manifestations, "feeblemindedness."

By the 1880s, reports Fink, penologists at the Eastern State Penitentiary of Pennsylvania had changed the attributions they made to account for inmates' crimes from such phrenological ones as jealousy, combativeness, destructiveness, and acquisitiveness to much more explicitly hereditary causes such as "inherent depravity." While they were not oblivious to external factors, they viewed the great majority of offenders as innately criminal. That many were repeatedly imprisoned raised certain questions of justice. If an offender lacks the ability to restrain his criminal tendencies and, in consequence, is repeatedly incarcerated with no deterrent effect, what *ought* to be done with him? Crime was viewed by several writers as a disease akin to insanity and transmitted, like other sins of fathers, unto the third and fourth generations. Whether the inherited criminality worked through cerebral instability, insensitivity to sensory impressions (an issue that recurs in the 1970s—cf, *infra*), or other factors was not understood, although there was considerable speculation about it.

Some believed that physiological, psychological, and intellectual traits were directly inherited, just as are skin color and physique; others viewed the legacy as more subtle, as a *tendency* toward criminality rather than "the very germs of theft and murder . . . stirring in the blood of (one's) progenitor ages back."[9]

In short, there was considerable advocacy of the view that criminality is inherited. But the diversity of mechanisms and specific inheritances that were assumed was great. Some wrote that persons inherited specific criminal activities; others, that they inherited tendencies towards certain kinds of acts. Some wrote that inherited crime will take place regardless of environmental circumstances; others, that "good" upbringing may reduce the likelihood of crime. Their views were based on their experience as prison physicians, on the works of authorities in many countries, and on medical practice, but not on research as we know it. Not until 1914 was there an attempt to conduct systematic studies of offenders. These ultimately distinguished between the inheritance of criminal traits *per se* and the inheritance of other characteristics which appeared to make certain persons more likely to engage in antisocial behavior. Healy studied 1,000 juveniles in Chicago in discounting the notion of what Lombroso had called the "born criminal," but Fink sees his emphasis on the criminal rather than on the crime as in the Lombroso tradition.

One hundred years ago Dugdale published a remarkably influential book, *The Jukes*, about the 709 descendants of a "degenerate" couple who, collectively, cost New York State millions in prison and relief monies. His book was cited for years as support for the view that antisocial behavior is inherited. Dugdale, in fact, did note the relevance of environment in the lives of the hapless Jukes family. His successors did so even more vigorously. One of these was H. H. Goddard, who wrote a work about another family, the Kallikaks, in order to demonstrate the inheritance of "feeblemindedness."

"Feeblemindedness." Mental disease and mental defect were distinguished for the first time in 1838 by Esquirol in France and Ray in the United States. The criminal responsibility of those whom we would today call profoundly retarded was, like that of the "morally insane" (whose intellects were normal), a matter of debate by legal and medical writers. For scores of years, estimates of intellectual ability had been based upon the guesses of authorities and, later, upon some tests of memory or association. Sir Francis Galton tried to measure intellectual ability by means of tests of sensory acuity, on the theory that all learning is based on information concerning the outside world coming into the nervous system through the sense organs. If this is so, it follows that persons with highly developed sensory apparatus should be in a position to learn more readily and so are more "intelligent."

In 1904, Alfred Binet was given the task of developing an objective means of discriminating between children of normal and those of subnormal intelligence. He used tests of memory, word comprehension, recognition of objects, and the like. While Binet and his associate, Simon, were still working to perfect their test in France, Goddard employed a translation of their attempt to identify "feebleminded" children. Before very long there were numerous studies of the intellects of prison inmates and juvenile offenders. Goddard viewed "feeblemindedness" as closely related to criminal behavior, and argued that because intellectual subnormality is inherited, we are misled into thinking that criminal behavior *per se* is inherited. He also asserted that the person who is intellectually incapable of distinguishing right from wrong and who is mistreated and misunderstood must almost inevitably turn to crime if he is to survive. Many researchers accumulated data to support this position. Fink points out that it represents a replacement of Lombroso's physical anomalies position with a position based upon mental anomalies. Similarly, "moral insanity" ultimately gave way to "moral imbecility." Interestingly, though, Healy found not a single case of moral imbecility among his 1,000 subjects.

We will comment only briefly on the use of intelligence tests for the purposes described here. The very high rates of "feeblemindedness" found in some of the studies to which we have alluded cannot be taken at face value without consideration of some factors that may have rendered these tests invalid. One wonders: how motivated the prisoners were to do "well"; to what extent the testers' preconceptions affected their scoring of responses; whether any attempt was made to establish rapport with the subjects; how comfortable subjects were in the testing situation; how able they were to concentrate on the task; how willing they were to make responses that might possibly be wrong; whether the language of the test was the language of the respondent; and, how familiar the latter was with the culture represented by the test items. In short, the findings of these early researchers leave ample room for doubt. Unfortunately, those of some more recent scholars are not totally convincing either. We turn now to some of them.

MODERN THEORIES OF CRIMINAL BEHAVIOR

Learning.   An interesting and provocative book appeared late in 1977 concerning *Biosocial Bases of Criminal Behavior*. Based upon records of the Danish National Police Register, among others, it presents a series of carefully controlled studies of biological correlates of criminal activity. The variables investigated are far more subtle than those studied by Lombroso, and the interpretations and generalizations far more cautious. *In toto* the book is an attempt to examine how biological and social forces interact in the production of criminal behavior. In essence, the conclusion is that genetic and physiological factors are linked importantly to crime but that the connection depends for its effects on such social variables as social class, family, and economic deprivation. To discern effects of social forces clearly, says Mednick, one first must control (statistically) the effects of genetic and physiological variables, and vice versa.[10] We will consider one of the studies in that volume and Mednick's intriguing theory which his data support.

He begins with the assumption that law-abiding behavior must be learned and that certain abilities and conditions are required for this learning. He does not claim that antisocial behavior is perfectly correlated with deficiencies in environmental conditions or in individual abilities, only that they each may have partial responsibility for it.

Like many of his predecessors, Mednick found that a small number of offenders are responsible for a majority of all reported crimes. Of nearly 31,500 men born in Copenhagen between 1944 and 1947, slightly more than 4,100 had some record of criminal behavior. Of these, the great majority had very few contacts with the police; in fact, 1% of the 31,500 (about 315) were responsible for more than half of all the reported offenses charged to this group.[11] His theory and research are addressed to the issue of what produces this small group of multiple offenders. Are these the men whose physiology interferes with the learning of lawful behavior? Do they tend to be the victims of social deprivation as well? Why do others, equally deprived socially, manage to learn lawful behavior?

Mednick does not neglect the fact that many crimes go unsolved and many criminals undetected. He does comfort himself with the thought that of those whose crimes remain "hidden," i.e., those who have never come to police attention, most are less serious and less habitual offenders. By working with respondents who have police records whether or not they have been incarcerated, he does avoid the bias of many studies which involve only incarcerated felons. However, merely having a police record makes it more likely that a person will be re-arrested any time a crime is committed having an M.O. (*modus operandi*) similar to that of the previous offense.

Small infants and children tend to be self-concerned, acquisitive, angry in response to frustration, incapable of empathy. Most learn to control anger, to feel empathy, to recognize the property rights of others. How do they learn this?

Modern psychologists recognize at least two types of learning: classical and instrumental conditioning.

Classical conditioning is also referred to as stimulus substitution, respondent, or Pavlovian conditioning and is based on the famous studies in which Pavlov trained dogs to salivate at the sound of a bell. Initially, the bell lacked the power to elicit salivation. That is, it was neutral with respect to salivating behavior. By sounding the bell as he placed meat powder in the dog's mouth, the meat powder having always had the ability to cause salivating, Pavlov caused the dog to salivate at the sound of the bell alone. Only a few such pairings were necessary to bring about this "conditioned response."

Pavlov had noticed this effect while engaged in research on digestion. The last 40 years of his life were devoted to studying the phenomenon and the various conditions that affect it.

Since there was no physiological reason for the bell to produce salivation, Pavlov called the phenomenon "psychic salivation" and worked out the paradigm and terminology of Figure 4-1 for this conditioning, or learning, process.

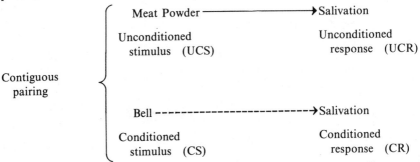

Fig. 4-1. The classical conditioning paradigm.

Research indicates that these responses which are brought under the control of a conditioned stimulus by the technique of classical conditioning generally involve the operation of the autonomic (or vegetative) nervous system (ANS).

A second major type of learning paradigm is based on the work of such investigators as Thorndike and, more recently, Skinner. It is known as instrumental, operant, or trial-and-error learning.

This method is described by the following paradigm:

$$S \longrightarrow R \longrightarrow S \text{ Reinforcement}$$

In other words, when a response is made in the presence of a stimulus and this response is followed immediately by a reinforcement or reward, the response becomes more likely to occur in the presence of this stimulus thereafter.

Instrumental conditioning (despite some bio-feedback studies to the contrary) basically utilizes responses of the muscular-skeletal system or the voluntary nervous system.

Both classical and instrumental conditioning are forms of learning and are similar in that previously neutral stimuli gain the ability to elicit responses.

Since human emotions (e.g., fear or anger) involve responses of the ANS, they are learned by classical conditioning. How we react to our emotions, e.g., sulking or attacking when angry, involves the voluntary nervous system and is learned instrumentally. That is, we are likely to take actions that, in the past, have been rewarded.

A special subtype of instrumental conditioning is called punishment training. Whenever an undesirable response is followed by a punishment instead of by a reward, the effect is to suppress the response. For example, Jeffrey takes a toy from Matthew who tells Mommy who hits Jeffrey. After one or a few such instances, Jeffrey learns to associate the unacceptable behavior with punishment. In fact, he may begin to feel fearful at the very thought of transgressing. Such fear is the product of classical conditioning, an emotional response that may inhibit the proscribed behavior even in the absence of a real external mother who inflicts punishment. In effect, the child has developed an internalized parent, which Freudians call a superego. In the mature person this becomes a basis for conscience. By not performing the proscribed behavior when tempted, the child experiences a reduction of the internal response of fear. The reduction of fear itself serves to reinforce the child's inhibition of his aborted offense and increases the likelihood that inhibition of this sort will occur again whenever the temptation recurs. Thus do all of the libidinal, acquisitive, aggressive urges of infancy give way to social control.

For Mednick's theory, the critical factor is the rapid dissipation of fear, which reinforces the inhibition. Researchers have consistently demonstrated that prompt reinforcement has the greatest effect on the learning of new responses. But fear reduction cannot be bestowed like a piece of candy; it takes place *within* the organism, it is not given *to* it. How does fear reduction occur? The queasy feeling one gets when one is frightened, the racing heart, the cold sweat, the tremor, are the results of the activity of a portion of the autonomic nervous system known as the sympathetic nervous system. The other division of the autonomic nervous system is called the parasympathetic. It is primarily involved in vegetative processes like digestion that go on when the person is relaxed and free of stress.

The sympathetic division of the ANS has been called the fight or flight system and is concerned with the mobilization of the body's resources for short-term emergency situations. The parasympathetic division, on the other hand, serves to build up resources between emergencies so that they are available to the synmpathetic system when needed.

It appears that the sympathetic nervous system reacts differently in different people. In some, it is prompt and efficient; in others, it appears sluggish. How do we know this? We know it by means of several physiological responses that can be measured directly. Among them are blood pressure, heart rate, respiration rate, resistance to a weak electric current on the surface of the skin. Lie detection, incidentally, involves such measures as these.

Lie Detection. Typically, a lie detector or polygraph involves the recording of several of the foregoing measures of ANS activity simultaneously. The rationale is that the act of lying causes emotional responses which are detected as changes in ANS activity.

Most often a subject is instructed to lie during the initial calibration of the machine so that his physiological reactions to lying can be determined. For example, he may be instructed to deny his name when it is spoken to him.

The actual testing consists of several key questions interspersed among innocuous "filler" items. Responses following key questions are compared with responses made when the subject was known to be lying in order to determine the accuracy of the answers.

There are differences of opinion concerning the accuracy of the polygraph when used in lie detection. The federal government and many private employers seem to be enamored of its use. The State of New York, on the other hand, tends to agree with the authors that this device is unreliable, so much so that polygraph results are not admissible into evidence in New York.

While a polygraph is a fine tool for research in which ANS activity is a dependent variable, the additional step of offering its results as evidence of truthfulness leads to a variety of difficulties. For example, a pathological liar who is unaware that he is lying is unlikely to show physiological indications of lying. Nor is a psychopath, a person who lacks any appreciable superego or conscience, likely to be detected on the basis of these data.

Now back to Mednick. A child whose ANS permits rapid recovery from fear will be promptly and effectively reinforced when he inhibits an antisocial act for which he had previously been punished. So he will learn quickly and well. On the other hand, one whose ANS reestablishes balance slowly, will be less adequately reinforced and should learn to inhibit his impulses less well. All of this leads to the prediction that, all else being equal (e.g., social status, economic condition, and so forth), "those who commit asocial acts would be characterized by slow autonomic recovery."[12] Moreover, the slower the recovery, the more such acts would be expected. Where slow recovery coexists with deficient sympathetic arousal (hyporeactiveness) so that the person experiences relatively little fear and what he does experience is reduced very slowly, we would expect to have a candidate for criminal or other antisocial behavior, par excellence.

The measure selected by Mednick (and by many others whom he cites) has to do with electrodermal recovery (EDRec)—the rate at which the skin's resistance to electrical current returns to its normal level following emotional stimulation.

Six different studies conducted in Denmark, Sweden, England, and Canada support the hypothesis that one of the variables that facilitates the learning of law-abiding behavior involves the prompt reduction of autonomic arousal. Persons with criminal records seem to show slower EDRec than those free of criminal histories; and the more serious the record, the slower the EDRec. Further, criminals "reared in a noncriminal milieu have slow EDRec,"[13] and children whose early lives and parentage suggest a criminal life but who resist criminality show fast EDRec.

Many writers of environmentalist bent attribute criminal behavior to bad companions, poverty, shady role models, and broken families. Others note that criminals also develop in privileged, intact families where the youngster's associates are in all ways admirable. How can this be?

To see whether criminality had something to do with EDRec as well as intelligence and criminal parentage, Mednick and his associates collected data from and about all men born in a particular Copenhagen hospital during 1936, 1937, and the first nine months of 1938. Of the 1,944 men in this population, 1,158 could be traced whose fathers had committed either a serious offense or no offense at all. (Those whose fathers had minor records were not included.) A serious offense was defined as one that had resulted in a jail sentence. Of these fathers, 92 offenders and 513 nonoffenders, some of each group had sons who were criminals and sons who were not. In short, four groups were studied: criminal sons of criminals ($n = 26$), criminal sons of noncriminals ($n = 20$), noncriminal sons of criminals ($n = 24$), and noncriminal sons of noncriminals ($n = 24$ randomly chosen from among 477 in this category).

These subjects were given intelligence tests, exposed to a sudden loud tone (to produce ANS arousal), and given several other tests as well. Results were as follows:

First of all, there was a high degree of association between the seriousness of the father's offense(s) and the seriousness of the son's. Of 372 fathers with serious records, 20% had sons with similar behavior; of 786 fathers with clean records, fewer than 11% had seriously criminal sons. By the same token, of 190 sons with serious records, 40% had fathers with serious records; of 839 sons with clean records, only 21.5% had seriously criminal fathers. Obviously, these data could be interpreted in several ways. Perhaps criminal fathers indoctrinate their sons into criminal lives; perhaps they pass on some criminogenic genes (e.g., for ANS functioning); perhaps the sons' behaviors reflect these factors acting in combination with other social factors to determine the youngsters' fate.

Second, consistent with some previous research, criminal sons had lower IQ scores than noncriminal sons. Noncriminal sons of criminals had especially high IQ scores (mean IQ = 113), suggesting to Mednick and his associates that intelligence may offer "protection" from a criminal career.[14] On the other hand, criminal sons of noncriminals were not unusually low in IQ (mean = 105).

Tentative analysis of the physiological data indicates that criminal sons of noncriminals showed low levels of ANS response following exposure to the very loud tone and slow recovery. (This was especially true among those diagnosed as psychopaths.) On the other hand, the noncriminal sons of criminals showed very fast EDRec. Mednick et al. were surprised at the high level of autonomic response of the criminal sons of criminal fathers. It may be, they suggest, that these young men acquired their criminal propensities from their fathers' examples.

Genetics.   Given that ANS responses are related to learning to inhibit criminal or antisocial behavior, it is possible that a genetic mechanism may someday be established by which a parent passes to the next generation particular patterns of ANS activity. These, in combination with various social conditions, may make it difficult for the youth to learn to avoid punishment or to inhibit asocial behavior. That a tendency to certain psychoses may be inherited has been demonstrated by studies of identical and fraternal twins.[15] If one of a pair of twins is schizophrenic, for instance, the odds are far greater that the other twin will have the disorder if the two are monozygotic (identical) than if they are dizygotic (fraternal). Since identical twins have identical heredity and fraternal twins are no more alike genetically than ordinary siblings, and since co-twins are equally likely to be reared similarly whether they are fraternal or identical, the foregoing data suggest that there is a genetic factor in the etiology of schizophrenia.

Christiansen reviewed a number of studies of criminality among twins to test the value of this approach for understanding criminality. Examination of data from countries as diverse as Japan, Finland, and the United States led him to the view that no conclusive statement can be made concerning the dominance of genetic over environmental influences on the emergence of criminality. While most of the studies (not all) indicate greater similarity regarding criminal behavior between identical than between same-sex fraternal twins, he points out several pertinent cautions. For one thing, most of the studies employed relatively small and probably unrepresentative samples of the population of twins that existed. Second, the determination of zygosity (whether the twins were fraternal or identical) was subject to error of an indeterminate magnitude. It may be, for example, that some fraternal twins were misclassified as identical. Third, the conclusion that the twins had similar histories vis-à-vis crime was based, in several instances, on vague or undependable criteria. Sometimes, this judgment was made with full knowledge of the zygosity of the twins in question, making possible a biasing error in favor of the expected finding. Underlying these studies and basic to any conclusion as to the importance of genes in producing criminal behavior is the assumption that the environments within which the two types of twins are reared do not differ systematically. If, as may be the case, identical twins, who do look more alike, are treated more similarly than fraternal twins, who resemble each other less, these studies would lose whatever importance they might have had, as far as clarifying the impact of genetics is concerned.

Christiansen reports that greater similarity in the environments of identical twins is generally assumed. If this is true, the greater similarity between the criminality of identical twins could stem from the greater similarity of their genetic inheritance or from the greater similarity of their environments before, during, or after their birth, or a combination of these factors.

In his "preliminary" study, Christiansen investigated nearly 3,600 pairs of twins (of the 13,500 pairs) born in Denmark between 1870 and 1920. Of these, at least one twin in each of 799 of the pairs had some criminal record. There was somewhat greater similarity among identical than among fraternal pairs; but, more interestingly, the degree of similarity varied according to several other variables. For example, females are more likely to be criminals if their co-twins are than males are. Twins of older generations are more likely to be criminals (if their co-twins are) than twins of younger generations. Rural-born twins are more likely to be criminals (if their co-twins are) than urban-born twins. Twins whose fathers are of a higher social class are more likely to emulate their co-twins' criminal careers than twins of lower-class fathers, and so on. In other words, under some circumstances the supposed genetic effects are altered by conditions more than under other circumstances. In any event, to regard criminal behavior as inherited in the same manner as hair or skin color is patently unjustifiable.

On the other hand, the foregoing data suggest that one's genetic makeup may affect how one reacts to specific environmental conditions. Thus, what may be inherited is not criminal behavior *per se*, but a propensity to develop such behavior under the proper environmental conditions. This is probably similar to the situation with schizophrenia, in which the disorder itself is not inherited (if it were the concordance rate in identical twins would be 1.00 as opposed to about .8 as typically reported), but a predisposition to develop it probably is.

The greater degree of similarity in criminal behavior between co-twins who are female, older, of upper class fathers, and rural can all be subsumed under the proposition that where deviance is more strongly resisted by the community (as it is in each of these instances), the deviant becomes a deviant because of unusual conditions that are not prerequisites of crimes for others. In other words, for a rural woman to become a criminal requires that she overcome restraints of both sex and community, restraints that are far stronger than for, say, an urban man. Therefore, if, in fact, she does deviate, her doing so suggests the existence of some factor that reduces the impact of group pressure. This factor may be either hereditary or environmental or, most likely, both.

The role of genes in criminal behavior is a complex matter. The search has gone on for decades and may be expected to continue. Two problems must be cited concerning the foregoing type of research, however. First, if a behavior is determined by both environmental and hereditary factors, it is not sensible to ask which factor is the dominant one. The behavior is determined 100% by both. Such a question is like asking whether the multiplier or the multiplicand is more important in determining the product of 5×4.

Second, behaviors that are considered criminal are classed as such arbitrarily. Since such a diversity of actions is proscribed by the criminal law, the results of any research into the causes of "crime" are probably valid only with respect to the particular type and subtype of criminal behavior studied. In other words, there may be little commonality in the etiology of burglaries, rapes, and murders. There may, in fact, be gross differences in the causal factors of different sub-groups of crimes, e.g., of felony or premeditated murders.

Chromosomes.   Every once in a while a discovery is made that captures the popular (and media) imagination, causing a widespread belief that a breakthrough has been made in the understanding of some medical or psychological mystery. Such an event is the recent suggestion that men whose chromosomal makeup includes an extra Y chromosome are likely to be criminals and, particularly, to be violent criminals.

The reader will recall that females have two complete sex chromosomes, one from each parent, called X chromosomes. Males, on the other hand, have one complete X chromosome from their mothers and an incomplete X, or "Y," chromosome from their fathers. While studies of newborns have indicated the rate of XYY boys born during various periods (Stock cites estimates of 1 in 300; Witkin et al. cite estimates of from 1/1000 to 1/3000), the prevalence among adults is hard to pin down, and it is unwise to infer incidence or prevalence in one population from incidence or prevalence in another.

Stock reviews a number of the early research efforts, some on aggressive fish, another on inmates of a Scottish prison–mental hospital. He mentions a 21-year-old Australian who was acquitted of murder by reason of insanity because "every cell in his body was abnormal," i.e., had two Y chromosomes.

The XYY syndrome, discovered in the early 1960s, was thought to include unusual height, low intelligence, acne, antisocial behavior, and perhaps "unusual sexual tastes." Stock does cite some evidence to the contrary, however.

More evidence to the contrary emerged in a recent study by Witkin et al. These authors begin their report with a discussion of the limitations of earlier studies on the subject. First, earlier studies may have employed biased samples—very tall men and/or institutionalized men whose ranks were assumed to include XYY types. That is, the samples were not random samples of all XYY men. Second, several reports were based on one or a very few cases. Third, few studies employed normal (XY) men as controls; those that did often were marred by the investigator's knowledge of the individuals' chromosomal makeup. Fourth, studies tended to focus on one or another aspect of the subject's life without considering the interaction of psychological, social, *and* bodily aspects.

Studies conducted since Stock's article have led to conflicting data concerning the relationship between XYY and aggressiveness, as one might expect given the above problems. Witkin and his associates attempted a study that would correct as many shortcomings of their predecessors as possible. Their ultimate goal was to determine whether society should be wary of XYY men simply because they are XYY types.

Specifically, they sought to identify all XYY men in a large population without undue biasing due to institutionalization or height, to compare them with XY controls in aggressiveness, intelligence, and height, and, if XYYs were more inclined to criminality, to try to determine *why* they were.

All males born in Copenhagen in 1944 through 1947 inclusive comprised their basic population. By age 26 all Danish men must undergo a military physical examination during which their heights are recorded. The tallest 15% of these men became the targets of special interest, since any XYYs would be likely to be among them. Many of these men could not be found because they had emigrated, died, moved at an early age, and so forth. Of the tallest 16%, 4,558 were to be sought out for chromosomal testing. The shortest among them was 184 cm (6 feet, .4 inch). The forthcoming study was widely publicized to encourage cooperation when the men were finally approached, and 90.8% of them (4,139) agreed to take part (after as many as 14 persuasive visits by the research team).

What sorts of data were obtained? Blood samples and smears from the inside of the cheeks yielded chromosome types. Military records had previously yielded data on height. Criminal convictions were noted from the very thorough records of the Danish National Police Register. Intelligence was estimated in a rough way from an army test and from the number of years of schooling each man had completed. (In Denmark, exams are given after 9, 10, and 13 years of schooling; for purposes of this study, the more exams passed, the higher the assumed intelligence.) Socioeconomic status was estimated according to the father's occupation at the time of the subject's birth.

What was found? Of the 4,139 men, 12 were found to have XYY chromosomal makeup, a rate of 2.9/1000. Five of these men (41.7%) had police records, significantly more than the XYs (9.3%). Since the syndrome was supposed to include a high level of aggressiveness, the nature of the offenses was examined. Only one of the 12 XYYs (8.4%) had been convicted of a violent crime, a proportion not significantly greater than the 1.8% figure for the 4,096 XYs. The five XYY offenders had committed 149 crimes among them. Nearly 140 were committed by just two of them, however. Of these 149 crimes only one involved violence ("a mild form of violence," at that) against another person. Further, of the five XYY offenders, three had not committed an offense in five years and a fourth, who alone had committed 90 offenses, was mentally retarded. All five of these men, in fact, were well below average in intelligence as measured by the army test, and none of the twelve XYYs had reached the 13th year examination. As a group their intelligence was significantly lower than that of the XY controls. In both XY and XYY groups, men who had committed crimes had significantly lower intelligence scores than their counterparts who had clean records. Witkin et al. view this finding as support for their hypothesis that intellectual impairment may lead to the commission of crimes and, equally important, to a greater likelihood of arrest than is the case for criminals of normal intelligence. In other words, whether low intelligence may lead one to crime or simply to incompetent crime is still at issue.

Concerning height, the XYYs were taller than the XYs; but, unexpectedly, among the XYYs the noncriminals were taller than the criminals.

As for socioeconomic status (SES), XYYs did not differ from XYs; but SES for criminals was lower than for noncriminals.

A more sophisticated analysis was employed, which matched XYYs with XYs on several variables to determine whether one could predict criminal behavior from knowledge of these combined measures and whether criminality was predictably higher among XYYs than among the XYs with whom they were matched. The XYYs did have a higher crime rate (5/12) than would have been predicted had they been XYs of the same height, intelligence, and SES (2.06/12); but the study did not support the hypothesis that XYYs would be unusually prone to violent crime.

Sociological Approaches.   A number of attempts to understand the causes and nature of crime focus upon the nature of society rather than on the biological nature of the criminal. Since far more crime occurs in urban than in rural settings, many of these studies have been concerned with crime in cities.

Cities consist of large numbers of neighborhoods. Some are residential, some industrial, some mercantile, some recreational, and so on. In addition, many cities are subdivided into ethnic and socioeconomic enclaves. Different neighborhoods offer different opportunities to the criminally inclined. The embezzler needs a business from which to embezzle; the burglar needs homes or other settings in which his intended loot may be found. Boggs cites evidence that offenders do not generally live where they "work." Most urban crime occurs in central business districts; most offenders dwell in lower class residential neighborhoods. These generalizations may be misleading, however, depending on how the crime rate is computed and on the particular sorts of crimes studied.

Data on homicide-assault and residential burglary suggest that offenders and their victims are very often neighbors. The victim's habits or the residence's layout are known to the offender from his own experience as a dweller in the area. Business robberies, auto theft, grand larceny, and so forth, are likely to occur in high status areas that are adjacent to low status ones. Forcible rape seems to occur less predictably; that is, it is not associated with particular areas as the other crimes are.

Public housing has been singled out for attention by some writers as a setting that, under certain circumstances, seems almost to invite criminal activity. Indeed, Suttles views "deviant behavior as an unanticipated consequence of public housing."[16] He suggests several factors which, if they do not promote crime, at least do not inhibit it. For one thing, in large public housing projects (and, one might add, in many large *private* housing projects, too) families feel anonymous. They may live for years in a particular apartment and know very few, if any, of the other residents in their building. In public housing, in particular, families are compelled to keep any major gains in employment or income secret lest they be forced to leave the project before they are ready to move voluntarily to more desirable quarters. Suttles suggests that one consequence is that many families feel superior to, or estranged from, their neighbors who cannot be allowed to know of their success. One consequence of this is that relationships which do develop among residents tend to be superficial, distant, and random. In communities where people have more positive characteristics in common, e.g., they are all young families attending graduate school, patterns of relationships are not random. They tend, in fact, to be related to proximity. That is, the nearer two families live to each other the more likely it is that they will have a friendly relationship.[17]

Further, in the public housing projects, residents' feelings of helplessness, of poverty, of powerlessness are exacerbated. They have no middle class neighbors; they are unlikely to have friends with political connections, or a family doctor, or very much influence in determining how the local schools function. The landlord could not be more faceless or absent. The merchants with whom they deal do not live among them. Living among hundreds of people at best requires one to "tune out" a great many stimuli.[18] When one feels overwhelmed not only by numbers but by lack of control over his own fate as well, the tendency to avoid contact with others is probably heightened. Residents of public housing feel vulnerable not only to the city authorities, who often seem arbitrary, capricious, or indifferent; they also feel threatened by one another, and by the unknown visitors and intruders who frequent the area. Suttles submits that in the traditional slum community people do know one another, visit, establish meaningful relationships with neighbors. Dwellers in public housing, on the other hand, are very reluctant to have visitors in their apartments. They do not want others to know too much about them, their possessions, or their employment. So they use their apartment as a place to sleep, and seek social contact elsewhere.

Suttles' essay complements the controversial work of Newman on "defensible space." Newman cites the detailed records that the New York City Housing Authority maintains on the tenants of its 169 projects—their ages, incomes, years in residence, previous backgrounds, and family problems. The Authority's police maintain crime records that pinpoint the site of any crime committed in or around the projects. Since these many projects differ in countless ways from one another, it was possible for Newman to compare projects that are large and small, low-rise and high-rise, elevator and walk-up, on spacious or sparse acreage, etc. Relatively constant is the economic and social status of the residents.

Among many other things, Newman found that high-rise developments are "catastrophic," particularly for the poor, for the broken family, for immigrants from other lands or rural areas. Where children are involved, the dangers to them and to the physical plant of the project are great indeed. High-rise middle class buildings that have superintendents, elevator operators, and doormen are manageable. High-rise public housing that lacks all of these amenities (or necessities) are dangerous even where crime is not a key factor.

But crime is a key factor in many projects, and Newman discovered several relationships between the nature of the buildings and the rate of criminal activity. For example, in high-rise buildings vandalism, robbery, and arrests of drug-addicted loiterers were seven and a half times more frequent than in *neighboring* two-story row houses inhabited by families of similar characteristics. The fact that high-rise buildings house so many people that intruders are all but impossible to recognize increases the vulnerability of their tenants. Newman urges that public housing be limited to three-story walk-ups, 50 units per acre, with very few families per lobby or entry. In this way those who "belong" there will be known to one another, and a sense of "ownership" of the lobby and surrounding grounds will increase the attentiveness of the residents to what takes place there.

It has been assumed by many writers that the density of population is an important correlate of crime. Social psychologists have been among those who believe that if an area becomes very crowded social constraints on deviant behavior break down. More recently the complexity of the relationship has begun to be recognized. Freedman et al. report that with income levels controlled there is little relationship between density (number of people/square mile) and crime. Such relationship as appears, they find, is due to the fact that income seems to be negatively correlated with density; i.e., poor people live together in larger numbers than wealthier people do and are more likely to be the victims of crime. Newman, also, finds crime unrelated to density *per se*, but significantly correlated with building type and height. High-rise, elevator, double-loaded corridor buildings (apartments on both sides of the corridor) generally have high crime rates. Unfortunately, this sort of building is typically employed when the project is to have more than 80 dwelling units per acre. This is not the place to restate Newman's many suggestions for making living space defensible. Our point is that buildings in which many people live increase the probability that residents will be crime victims purely as a result of their design and setting. The proper design of housing could minimize this risk. Some of Newman's suggestions, as well as others concerned with the use of the premises by the community, surveillance over entries, and restricted access, are key parts of current experimental programs known as Crime Prevention Through Environmental Design (CPTED).[19]

One of the great controversies in American society is that between those who attribute crime to willful, freely chosen, evil and those who believe that people do not choose to be evil but are driven to evil acts by circumstances over which they have no control. These positions lead to divergent solutions for crime (punishment or rehabilitation v. social change). One's position on this issue may be related to one's political and economic attitudes.

One writer whose essay attributes crime to social causes rather than personal ones is Lewis, who selects two kinds of behavior for examination: the "hustle" (e.g., numbers-running) and the activities of organized juvenile gangs. He concludes that "deviants" who engage in such behavior are actually strongly committed to conventional norms (achievement, demonstration of personal skill, dependability, integrity). The offenders commit these criminal acts *not* because they have deviant values, but because the circumstances in which they live impede efforts to enter legitimate fields of endeavor. Lewis argues that we must deal with the problem by recognizing some of these activities as legitimate rather than deviant or by making available opportunities for the pursuit of legitimate goals. "It is not the criminal who must change," says Lewis, "but the situation which turns his conventionality (conventional motives) toward illegal expression."

Other Psychological Approaches. A common view is that people who commit crimes are "sick," that "normal" people do not do "abnormal" things. The cost of the support of a drug habit is cited as an indication of the need for rehabilitation (or free access to drugs). One does not punish the sick, one "cures" them. In the chapter on prisons some of the more grievous results of this position will be made clear.

Yochelson and Samenow describe their "reluctant coversion" from this view in their recent volume *The Criminal Personality*. Working at St. Elizabeth's Hospital in Washington, D.C. as researchers, the authors started out interested in the causes of criminal behavior. For more than 15 years they had access to large numbers of individuals who were hospitalized after being acquitted of crimes by reason of insanity, or who were in St. Elizabeth's for psychiatric evaluation related to criminal prosecution. Other subjects were parolees, probationers, and offenders who had never been arrested but had heard of their work from other research subjects and had volunteered to participate in the research.

The men with whom they worked varied in socioeconomic status, religion, the stability of their families, and age (15–55). All were of average intelligence. Some were drug abusers; some were not. More were black than were white.

At first, the authors tried to understand what motivated these men. They began with a modified psychoanalytic approach, naively trusting in the wish of their patient-subjects to "get well." Only later did they come to realize that these men wanted to get *out*, not well. The responses of the subjects to the therapeutic attention were varied. Some preferred to think of themselves as "sick" because it seemed to them to justify their criminal acts. Where the authors had anticipated that the attainment of insight into their psychological processes would free the men of the compulsion to commit crimes, they found that it merely produced more insightful offenders who now could explain why they were engaging in their continuing criminal activity. Some quickly learned to say what their therapists hoped to hear, and, for some time, the investigators were taken in by this type of response.

One group of men seen as a therapy group became a mutually cooperating criminal gang when they were not in therapy.

Most of the men reported having had hard-working, caring parents, a point that the authors learned to their surprise early in the study. It was not until later, though, that they began to question another assumption with which they had begun their work. They gradually became less confident that the prisoners' criminality resulted from economic or emotional deprivation. For one thing, many subjects had brothers who had not turned to crime and yet had presumably experienced similar hardships. More important, however, was the emergence of patterns discernible in the lives of many of these men regardless of their socioeconomic status, race, or educational level. In general, these were men who had rejected school and jobs (although they perceived themselves as having been rejected by them). They blamed "bad companions" for misleading them into criminal activity. At length, Yochelson and Samenow came to disbelieve the self-justifying stories they had heard so often.

In most of the men, antisocial activity began very early in life, in some before they had even started school. Each admitted to the researchers responsibility for large numbers of crimes for which they had never been apprehended. Virtually all had been thieves, had committed assault and various sexual violations. Yet virtually all regarded themselves as "good" men, never as "criminals." They may have recognized that their actions were illegal or were disapproved by others, but they regarded their criminal acts as "right" for themselves at the time.

Most appeared to have a kind of "shutoff" mechanism that enabled them to suppress fear of capture or qualms of conscience. Such a mechanism made it possible for them to shift abruptly from sentimentality to brutality and back again.

Their investigations led the authors to develop a new view of the criminal personality. These men who felt battered by fate and at the mercy of forces outside themselves seemed, to Yochelson and Samenow, to be very much *in control of their actions*. Most of their criminal activity seemed deliberately and rationally planned; they were not impulsive acts or crimes of passion.

These men tended to be ridden by numerous and intense fears, e.g., fears of darkness, heights, water, enclosed spaces, bodily injury, and being seen as "weak." In addition, they viewed themselves as worthless, a trait they seemed loath to reveal to one another. Lying was virtually a conditioned response among them, as was their suspiciousness. The seeming inconsistency between these self-perceived traits and their perceptions of themselves as "good" is not unusual. Many people harbor self-contradictory beliefs, which Rokeach accounts for in terms of "logic-tight" compartments in the mind.

From a focus on causation, the authors turned to an investigation of the thought processes of their population. Once they stopped thinking of "criminal behavior" as the product of illness, they began to make what they considered to be substantial gains in grasping its nature. They began to focus on the fact that criminals make choices and have personal responsibility for their actions. Instead of accepting what subjects said, they began to confront them with their responsibility for their own actions, i.e., that they were, in fact, the exploiters, not the exploited.

Yochelson and Samenow came to believe that what was needed was not therapy but conversion: a total cessation of criminal activities and thinking and the adoption of a new noncriminal way of living. To facilitate this conversion they hit upon what they called "phenomenologic reporting." The men were taught to be aware of their own thought processes and self-perceptions and to report them during their therapeutic meetings with the researchers.

In short, the investigators gave up the quest for motives; they gave up persuasion and exhortation and tried to educate the criminals to understand themselves and to know something about how the rest of the world thought and behaved. Talk was not sufficient to bring about change. Change itself was necessary to bring about the "conversion." This, it should be noted, is very consistent with findings of researchers in the realm of cognitive dissonance who have demonstrated that attitudes and beliefs change to be consistent with changes in behavior. Other data from an earlier time suggest that attitude change is most easily and lastingly effected when it takes place in the context of a group, particularly when there is an explicit commitment to the new behavior.

Yochelson and Samenow kept in touch with many of their subjects over the years, and, of those they treated, they found that "one dozen" had shown change to impeccably upright behavior. They do not indicate the number who did not succeed. This and numerous other omissions make it difficult to evaluate this provocative work.

This work has been roundly criticized on methodological grounds by social scientists and on philosophical grounds by persons committed to the view that our social system and institutions bear primary responsibility for crime and recidivism. It has been welcomed, on the other hand, by some corrections officials, who feel that their problems are, at last, beginning to be understood.[20] However one reacts to it, it seems clear that this study requires confirmation with some well-designed research procedures before its conclusions can be accepted with confidence.

WHO ARE THE CRIMINALS?

Whether or not a particular act is treated as a crime is not totally determined by what the law says. Police officers, for example, may elect whether to deal with a situation as a crime or not. When police stand by as youths riot, the rioting is not treated as a crime; when they take action, it is. When they "move in" with inordinate force as in Chicago during the Democratic Convention of 1968, and higher authorities take no remedial action, the behavior of the police is not dealt with as "criminal." Whether or not police officers perceive an event as a crime may depend upon the way that they define their own responsibility. It may be affected by the location of the event or the appearance of the offender, among other extraneous factors.

Just as the characterization of an act as criminal or not is sometimes uncertain, so, too, are the numerous causes to which crime has been attributed.

We have discussed biological, sociological, and psychological approaches to understanding crime. A conclusion of Yochelson and Samenow is that quests for causes are fruitless and pointless. Be that as it may, one thing *is* clear: there is no single cause of crime. Neither broken homes, nor neuroses, nor XYY chromosomes distinguish between those who become criminals and those who do not. Even where there is some degree of association between such factors and crime, it is far from perfect.

Therefore, crime must have many causes and combinations of causes. For one thing, it takes many forms—from embezzlement to adultery to felony murder. These behaviors are linked only by virtue of the fact that at some time they have been declared to be illegal. Such diverse activities must have diverse causes although the student or scientist who seeks a "scientific" understanding of the nature of crime must necessarily look for generalizations.

Most scientific generalizations are in the context of a theory about the phenomenon in question. A single theoretical explanation of all criminal behavior would have to include a number of propositions, of which some, at least, would be capable of empirical test. In addition, they would be related to each other on logical grounds and would specify the conditions under which criminal behavior occurs. Finally, they would distinguish between those who engage in criminal behavior and those who do not. Such a theory will not soon be developed, however; and given the diversity of behaviors that are classed as criminal, such a comprehensive theory may never be realized.

One way in which criminologists have tried to cope with the variety and complexity of criminal behavior in lieu of such a theory is to identify particular types of crime or of criminals that permit at least *some* degree of generalization. They have studied "naive" and "systematic" forgers, professional thieves, white collar criminals, murderers, vandals, car thieves, and delinquents, among others. Few writers, though, have tried to relate different criminal behaviors to one another. Hood and Sparks provide a helpful discussion of some of these attempts to link crimes or criminals according to consistent principles of classification or typologies.

Typologies. There are several reasons for attempts to develop typologies:

1. They organize the field, simplify it, make it more amenable to study.
2. They help to pull together data gathered over the last 150 years, make it more usable, and alert us to gaps in our knowledge.
3. They help us to distinguish between types of crimes and criminals, to note differences as well as similarities.
4. They prevent us from assuming that there is such a "thing" as criminal behavior, *per se*.

It has been argued that a typology is, in fact, prerequisite to a general theory although it would seem that in order to develop a typology one must have at least some rudimentary theory to begin with, some notion of which characteristics are important and which are not.

When we consider types of crimes or criminals, we divide the general sets "crime" or "criminal" into subsets. Most classifications of crimes have employed such variables as the target of the act, its nature, and its seriousness. Most classifications of criminals have employed a few simple, broad variables (e.g., age, sex, social class, race, criminal record).

One major distinction which is often made is that between social and individual criminals. The former are part of a culture that approves and rewards the criminal act, provides collaborators, and accords status as a function of the daring or success of the crime. The individual criminal works for personal reasons with no prestige or recognition from other criminals. This latter group might include the person who murders in a fit of passion, the insane "criminal," or most professional criminals.

Another distinction relates to the frequency with which the criminal act is performed. The habitual offender or career criminal is very different from the one-time or casual offender.

A third basis for classification concerns the offender's motives: proving his toughness, excitement, displacement of anger onto the victim, and so on.

One can approach the construction of typologies in two general ways. In an empirical approach we observe the characteristics of each case and group those that seem similar in some important way. We establish mutually exclusive and, as far as possible, exhaustive categories. We may have some general idea of which traits to look for in categorizing based on some inchoate theory, but no one theory completely determines the categories employed. The ultimate basis for classification is usually some easily observable criterion, e.g., age, current offense, and so forth.

The second approach to the construction of topologies is theoretical. Instead of starting with observable data, one starts with a theory, whether about the nature of human behavior in general or, for example, the behavior of rapists in particular. One selects the bases for classification according to the specifications of the theory from which one is working. For instance, basing her work on Freudian theory, Friedlander[21] classified delinquents as follows:

1. Antisocial character
   caused by:
   a. environmental stress
   b. emotional stress
   c. neurotic conflict

2. Organic
   disturbance

3. Functional
   psychotic
   ego-disturbance

For each of these categories she provided descriptive criteria.

Empirical and theoretical classification schemes have different advantages and disadvantages. Science proceeds by an alternation of the methods of inductive and deductive reasoning. Inductive reasoning involves going from the specific to the general, as in the generation of hypotheses to account for a series of specific experimental findings. For example, if three criminals are all found to have lower than average IQ scores, the hypothesis might be generated that stupidity is associated with criminality.

Deductive reasoning, on the other hand, involves going from the general to the specific. It is employed after certain general assumptions have been made or after certain hypotheses have been formulated. Specific testable propositions are derived from general hypotheses or assumptions that can either be confirmed or disconfirmed by observations. These observations, which give us our data, either support the hypothesis or demonstrate that it needs to be modified. For instance, starting with the hypothesis that there is a relationship between low IQ and criminal behavior, one would predict a high crime rate for a low-IQ population. If this, or any, hypothesis is confirmed enough times, it becomes elevated to the status of scientific law.

In this way empirical classification schemes are useful in the early stages of research as a guide to hypothesis development, while theoretical classification schemes are more useful later in generating research to evaluate these hypotheses.

Of the typologies that presently exist, most are primarily empirical in origin although they are related to one or another general theory, whether sociological or psychological.

Whether empirical or theoretical, typologies are not without drawbacks. Many of these were discussed by Allport.[22]

Theoretical typologies depend on the author's preconceptions and are likely to be only as fruitful as the author is insightful. Empirical typologies are based upon data rather than preconceptions, but are still limited by the investigator's ability to interpret the data fruitfully. More important, any classifying takes into account only part of the individual, not his wholeness or his uniqueness. Further, typologies cause us to stress the differences between people and to disregard the many ways in which people of different "types" are, in fact, similar. Finally, within a given category some people are more accurately classified or more fully described by the criteria for classification than others are.

As far as criminology is concerned, a critical issue is the purpose for which the typology is developed. One that helps us to understand the origins or etiology of crime may have no relevance for helping us understand how to treat (or punish) the criminal. A typology that distinguishes among offenders with different treatment needs may not help us to understand the criminal behavior or its origins. A typology of criminals would be useful that included:

1. The total range of offenses among its types.
2. Mutually exclusive categories.
3. Types that are readily identified in accordance with clearly stated operational definitions.

This last requirement is a problem particularly for theoretical typologies, since the "types" in question may have a number of characteristics in common which obscure those that distinguish them.

If the typology is to be used in prescribing treatment, there should be as many types as there are modes of treatment. If its purpose is to explore etiology, the number of types would depend on the number of varieties of behavior that the theory is intended to incorporate.

An example of an attempt to classify offenders by their criminal behavior is that of Roebuck, who randomly selected 400 offenders in Virginia and identified among them 13 different patterns of behavior. Of the 13, eight were "single patterns." That is, the offender typically committed one kind of crime or predominantly one type of crime. Three other patterns involved either two crimes or three that were characteristic of the offender's activities. Other offenders were classed as showing a mixed pattern ("jack-of-all-trades") or no pattern because of too few arrests.

Offenders in different categories differed in more than just the patterns of their criminal careers. Armed robbers, for example, tended to be relatively young and to have belonged to juvenile gangs.

Thirty-seven percent of all the offenders Roebuck studied were classified as single-pattern types. Among these the most frequent were narcotics offenders (12.5%) and robbers (8%). Gamblers, car thieves, burglars, and other criminals were rare among single-pattern offenders. While 25% of the offenders studied were double-pattern types, the only two combinations found were larceny and burglary (16%) and drunkenness and assault (10%). Of the 400, more were "jack-of-all-trades" than any particular single-, double-, or triple-pattern offenders (17.8%).[23]

An important problem with approaches such as this is that classification must necessarily be based on one's criminal record rather than on one's actual criminal activity. The two can be quite different.

Gibbons takes the position that many criminals do behave in relatively predictable ways, adhering to patterns of conduct or "role careers" that are related to the offenders' backgrounds and personalities.

His approach is largely empirical but it is guided by some theoretical considerations. He attempts to compromise between very broad ways of classifying (e.g., whether the crime is against property or against persons) and very specific ways. The 15 adult criminal types he does distinguish are described in terms of what he calls "role careers," which include the nature of the offense, the interactional setting in which it occurred, the offender's self-image (as criminal or not), and his attitudes about life, family, work, and so forth.

Among the 15 types are embezzlers, psychopathic assaultists, one-time losers, and so on. His type 10 (personal offender–one-time loser) has usually committed a murder, manslaughter, or serious assault against someone he knew well (spouse, child, friend). He does not regard himself as a criminal and, feeling remorseful and contrite, will often call the police to report his crime. He usually has pro-social attitudes, had lived a conventional married and working life before the offense, and plans to return to it. Gibbons' type 2, by way of contrast, is the professional "heavy" criminal. This person usually gets his start with a delinquent gang, becomes more and more involved with older professionals from whom he learns basic skills, and, in middle age, retires from crime into a noncriminal occupation. He usually is of urban, lower class background, was either neglected as a child or was cared for by criminal parents or siblings, and was involved with the police as a juvenile but not so much as an adult. By that time he had become far more skilled in criminality. His crimes are usually well planned, involving much skill and little violence. Burglary, armed robbery, or other crimes against property are carried out by a team each member of which is a specialist (in safe-cracking, etc.). He is generally scornful of the police, except for especially competent officers, although he is not especially hostile toward them. He despises normal work and defines himself as a criminal, taking satisfaction in what he does and the skill and nerve it requires. He sets himself well above amateur criminals.

It is probably clear that any explanations of the origins of the acts of these two types will be quite different from one another. For this and similar reasons, typologies like this can be useful points of departure in the quest for origins of crime; it should be obvious that they are not the end of the quest.

Female Criminals.   In the wake of the women's liberation movement, there is growing interest in female offenders and the growing numbers of them. Adler describes the "rise of the female crook" since the early 1960s. Her general thesis is that as women achieve equality in other spheres of life, in access to job opportunities, higher education, and self-expression, so will women increasingly resemble men in the frequency and nature of criminal acts. Burglary, larceny, robbery, embezzlement are being perpetrated by more women than ever before (by more men, too, for that matter). Arrests among women are rising four times faster than arrests among men (only twice as fast among those under 18 because offenses by youths are rising six times faster than arrests of men in general). Table 4-1 summarizes data concerning

TABLE 4-1. Arrest trends by sex, 1960–1975.[a]

OFFENSE CHARGED	TOTAL		PERCENT CHANGE	UNDER 18		PERCENT CHANGE
	1960	1975		1960	1975	
	MALES					
Murder and nonnegligent manslaughter	3,936	9,376	+138.2	331	1,012	+205.7
Robbery	28,627	89,985	+214.3	7,034	32,448	+361.3
Motor vehicle theft	52,376	71,021	+35.6	31,936	38,174	+19.5
"Violent" crime[b]	84,912	217,797	+156.5	14,277	53,925	+277.7
Property crime[c]	336,311	708,207	+110.6	170,665	348,186	+104.0
Stolen property	8,916	54,845	+515.1	2,469	17,832	+622.2
Driving under influence	144,700	381,994	+164.0	1,166	6,879	+490.0
	FEMALES					
Murder and nonnegligent manslaughter	830	1,707	+105.7	28	105	+275.0
Robbery	1,439	6,915	+380.5	355	2,651	+646.8
Motor vehicle theft	1,978	5,206	+163.2	1,268	3,047	+140.3
"Violent" crime[b]	10,139	25,937	+155.8	1,065	6,427	+503.5
Property crime[c]	38,526	205,209	+432.7	16,524	85,994	+420.4
Stolen property	837	6,924	+727.2	189	1,747	+824.3
Driving under influence	9,026	34,725	+284.7	63	596	+846.0

[a]Adapted from Table 31 of C. M. Kelley, *Uniform Crime Reports of the United States 1975*, Washington, D.C.: U.S. Department of Justice, Federal Bureau of Investigation, 1976. Based on comparable reports from 2,090 cities representing 82,195,000 population and 636 counties representing 14,234,000 population.

[b]Violent crimes are offenses of murder, forcible rape, robbery, and aggravated assault.

[c]Property crimes are offenses of burglary, larceny-theft, and motor vehicle theft.

the relative increase in the criminal behavior of men and women in those categories in which increases have been most marked.

Simon takes a position much like Adler's on the subject of women in crime. She, too, sees a connection between the women's movement and crime among women. For one thing, women have greater access to temptation now than they used to have. A woman could not embezzle from a firm that would not hire her. On the other hand, she anticipates that crimes of violence which may be attributed, in part, to frustration, should diminish among women as they win greater access to well-paying jobs and independence. As shown in Table 4-1, that trend has not yet developed clearly although the rates of increase in violent and property crimes are, *in toto*, consistent with that prediction.

Simon briefly reviews the position that the increase in arrests among women is due to a drop in police willingness to overlook many offenses by women. This position holds that the increase in arrests is due to an increase in equality of treatment rather than to an increase in offenses by women. While Simon acknowledges that law enforcers are, in general, treating women less chivalrously and more equally than may once have been the case, she points out that the different rates of change in numbers of arrests for different crimes are incompatible with this alternative explanation of the data.

Of one thing, at least, we can probably be sure. Just as women are entering legal and police professions and others formerly closed to them, so, too, are they entering into active participation in criminal activities in greater numbers. In property crimes, particularly, they have come a long way toward closing the gap between rates for male and female offenders.

Dangerousness.   Another distinction that should be mentioned in this chapter, although it is considered further in Chapter 14, is the dangerousness of the offender. It has been estimated that from 85 to 90% of all incarcerated offenders pose no threat to the personal safety of members of the public. The other 10 to 15% may have to be kept apart from the rest of society. The trick is to identify who is and who is not dangerous. There is some evidence that identification can be made with some success. But how much failure is too much?

Only recently has there begun to be research on rates of recidivism of dangerous behavior. Yet psychiatrists and psychologists are constantly asked to predict dangerousness, in some civil commitment proceedings before the subject has done *any* harm to anyone.

Murderers.   This leads us to a closely related matter, however. While we lack data on this point we would predict that most people equate murderers with "dangerous offenders." Are murderers likely to repeat their crimes? In a study in a prison hospital in England of 293 murderers who were released in a given period of time, only one repeated his act. Of 7,000 released from the same facility over the course of 50 years, only two were subsequently convicted of murder.[24] Who are these murderers, and who are their victims?

Lunde has been an interested student of these questions. He reports that the murder rate is twice what it was 20 years ago, and that during 1975 one person in 10,000 could be expected to die violently. Actually, 18,642 persons were murder victims in 1975, a 22% increase since 1970.[25] Of these victims, 42% were between the ages of 20 and 35, 76% were males, 51% were white, 47% were black, and fewer than 1% were "native Americans." Lunde attributes the increased murder rate to economic problems, and points out that very few of the killers were professional criminals. In fact, one murderer in four is closely related to his or her victim. One in eight is the spouse of the victim, who is as likely to be the husband as the wife. According to Lunde's data, one victim in five is a woman killed by her husband or lover. If that remains true, it appears that very few women are killed by anyone else, since only 23.9% of victims in 1975 were women. One third of all victims are related to their slayers.

Lunde offers descriptions of certain patterns that emerged from his studies of murder. Only his major categories will be mentioned.

Many men who kill do so impulsively. They reach a point of rage or extreme frustration and strike out unthinkingly at their spouses, teen-aged sons, or lovers. Young people who kill younger siblings often appear to be displacing aggression from their parents to the sibling substitute.

About one-third of victims are killed by friends or acquaintances in the course of fights, arguments, or other confrontations. Generally both parties involved are men. Where the victim is a casual acquaintance, the killer is often a young man who regularly carries a weapon and is accustomed to responding physically to challenges or insults, real or imagined.

Another 30% die as victims of felony murder. Most murderers use guns; half of them handguns, while another 15% use rifles or shotguns. About one-fifth use knives or ice picks (particularly women), blacks more than whites. Lunde cites Wolfgang's well-known study of homicide in Philadelphia in which it was found that of 588 killings between 1948 and 1952, about two-thirds occurred on weekends, half late Saturday night or early Sunday morning.

There are regional differences, too, in the rate of murder, the type of weapon used, and the circumstances in which the killing occurs.

Firearms tend to be the weapon of choice (70%) in the South and in the North Central States. Knives, clubs, and "personal weapons," (fists, feet, and so forth) are as popular as guns in the Northeast and West. In 1975, at least, killings of relatives were more frequent in the South than elsewhere, and felony murders were less frequent there than elsewhere.

While murder is a more common crime in cities than in rural or suburban areas, neighborhoods within cities also vary in murder rate. Lunde cites a study which showed that two-thirds of Cleveland's murders occur in only 7% of its neighborhoods.

Murderers are tending to be younger nowadays although women who kill are older than their male counterparts. Blacks are far more likely to be the victim of murder than whites (males ten times, females five times more likely). Blacks commit homicides at a rate four times greater than whites but, in absolute terms, more whites are murderers.

Murder is usually an intraracial crime, as often as 90% of the time. Where it is not, blacks are more often the victims of whites than vice versa.

A point that should not be overlooked is that many victims of murder precipitate their own demise. Wolfgang defines victim-precipitated murders as those in which the victim is the first to display or to use a weapon or to strike a blow. Twenty-six percent of the cases he studied fell into this category! Lunde cites a Chicago study in which the figure was 38%.

Alcohol appears to be a frequent contributor to quarrels that lead to murder, a point which supports the view that since most murders occur without concern for, or even a thought about, possible penalties, the death penalty is not an effective deterrent. While Lunde consistently uses the term "murder," the context seems to indicate that he is also talking about other types of homicide such as manslaughter under the general rubric "murder." Capital punishment is probably overkill if imposed for deterrent purposes, since the number of murderers who repeat their crime if given the opportunity is very small.

Some murderers kill en masse.[26] Most mass murderers are psychotic; nearly all are white males. Some seem to experience very great hostility that they control as totally as they can until they reach a bursting point. Berkowitz has conducted a number of studies of aggression, not murder, to be sure, but of a subject's willingness to hurt or punish another person. He found that this willingness increases in the presence of cues which have been associated by learning with aggressive behavior. For example, in the presence of a gun, subjects were more willing to administer electric shock than in the absence of a gun. This was so despite the fact that the gun was ostensibly unrelated to what was taking place. Judge Edwards, a former Detroit police commissioner, draws a controversial conclusion from similar but unrelated data. He argues that possession of a handgun increases the likelihood of one's being a murder victim, and, in arguing for gun control, points to data of the sort we have discussed.[27] Lunde, too, expresses concern about the 50 million guns Americans own, and notes the impact of such factors as the large number of

men with military training, permissiveness of parents, the decline of organized religion, and feelings of being controlled by forces outside the self. On
the other hand, opponents of gun control argue that such laws may encourage
violent crime against a disarmed and helpless victim.

Shoplifting.   The same factors cited by Lunde as causes of homicide may
also be behind the rise in another type of crime that is far more common and,
in economic terms, far more costly than murder. It is a crime we rarely read
about. The offenders are more likely to be women and girls than men and
boys. Among all crimes only chain store and bank robberies have shown a
greater rate of increase since 1970, and only bank robbery shows a comparable rate of increase in the period 1973–1975. The offense in question is shoplifting, and, according to one study reported *before* the skyrocketing increase,
"one shopper in ten is a shoplifter."[28] In the preceding ten years store thefts
had increased by 150%, second only to purse-snatching. In the period 1970–
1975 purse-snatching *declined* by 5%, while shoplifting increased by 73%.[29]
Hellman describes young women with well-paying jobs who shoplift on their
lunch hour. They appear to do it for "kicks." Others steal to support drug
habits. That some stores routinely prosecute all shoplifters has not deterred
people from attempting it. It might even raise the "kick" value. Many of us
enjoy risky adventures. Hellman seems to feel that shoplifting is another indication of the corruption of values in American society.

Commercial Dishonesty.   Another form of this corruption is the behavior of what Horn calls "the arrogant crook." He describes a study by
Vaughan and Carlo of a case of repair fraud or, more accurately, 157 cases
of repair fraud perpetrated by the same appliance repairman in a community
in Ohio. The repairman in question frequently changed the name of his business. He employed small-print contracts that he presented to customers as a
bill, a receipt, or a work contract. The small print included an agreement not
to contact the Better Business Bureau, not to stop payment on checks, and
not to sue him. His respectable-looking ads and his customers' ignorance and
gullibility brought him a great deal of business. The victims' reluctance to
undertake legal proceedings or to pursue them once having initiated them
enabled him to prosper.

Consumer fraud is often very difficult to distinguish from incompetence;
this makes the customer reluctant to prosecute and the court reluctant to convict. A control group of neighbors of this man's victims was studied; members
of the control group had made no complaints to any agency. Investigation
revealed only that equal percentages of complainants and noncomplainants
had been victimized by consumer fraud and/or by street crimes. Even the

complainants, incidentally, had not reported all instances of consumer fraud that they had experienced.

We will consider the reasons why victims do and do not report crimes in the next chapter. Suffice it to say that nonreporting is a major element in the success of many criminal ventures.

When most people think of criminals, we would guess, they think of the kinds of crime they see on television or in the movies: the armed robbers or professional killers who are chased and caught by one or another hero of the electronics age. Criminals are much more varied than most people think. We have tried to show that they are human begins, that no stereotype is adequate to describe the perpetrators of even one type of crime, and that no present theory is sufficient to enable us to understand why they do what they do.

NOTES AND REFERENCES

1. Fink, A. E. *Causes of Crime: Biological Theories in the United States 1800–1915.* Philadelphia: University of Pennsylvania Press, 1938.
2. Fowler, O. S. *Fowler's Practical Phrenology (Etc.).* New York: Nafis and Cornish, 1845, pp. 85–86.
3. Fink, *Causes of Crime*, Chapter 3.
4. B. Rush letter to J. Priestley. Paraphrased in Fink, *Causes of Crime*, p. 49.
5. Ordronaux, J. Moral Insanity. *American Journal of Insanity.* 1873, 29, p. 321. Quoted in Fink, *Causes of Crime*, p. 67.
6. Lewin, K. *A Dynamic Theory of Personality.* New York: McGraw-Hill, 1935, p. 79.
7. Lombroso, C. and Ferrero, W. *The Female Offender.* New York: Appleton, 1915, p. 122. And see Introduction by W. D. Morrison.
8. Erikson, E. Ego identity and the psychosocial moratorium. In *New Perspectives for Research on Juvenile Delinquency.* pp. 1–23. Washington, D.C.: U.S. Department of Health, Education and Welfare, Children's Bureau, 1956. See also Erikson, E. H. *Identity: Youth and Crisis.* New York: W. W. Norton, 1968.
9. Drähms, A. *The Criminal: His Personnel and Environment.* New York: Macmillan, 1900, p. 142. Quoted in Fink, *Causes of Crime*, p. 169.
10. Mednick, S. A. and Christiansen, K. O. (Eds.). *Biosocial Bases of Criminal Behavior.* New York: Gardner Press, Inc., 1977, p. x.
11. Mednick, S. A. A biosocial theory of the learning of law-abiding behavior. Chapter 1 in Mednick and Christiansen (Eds.) *Biosocial Bases of Criminal Behavior.*
12. Ibid., p. 4.
13. Ibid., p. 5.
14. Ibid., p. 21.
15. Meehl, P. E. Schizotaxia, schizotypy, schizophrenia. *American Psychologist* 1962, 17, 827–838.
16. Suttles, G. Deviant behavior as an unanticipated consequence of public housing. In D. Glaser (Ed.) *Crime in the City.* New York: Harper and Row, 1970.

17. Festinger, L., Schachter, S., and Back, K. W. *Social Pressures in Informal Groups: A Study of Human Factors in Housing.* New York: Harper and Row, 1950. Also, Whyte, W. H., Jr. *The Organization Man.* New York: Simon and Schuster, 1956.
18. Milgram, S. The experience of living in cities. *Science* March 13, 1970, 167, 1461–1468.
19. Kohn, I. R., Locasso, R. M., Bell, L. S., Minor, W. W., and Dubnikov, A. Crime prevention through environmental design: Theory and framework. Paper presented at symposium on Crime Prevention through Environmental Design. 85th annual convention of American Psychological Association, San Francisco, 1977.
20. Serrill, M. S. The criminal personality in perspective. (In) A cold new look at the criminal mind. *Psychology Today* February, 1978, 11(9), 86ff.
21. Friedlander, K. *The Psycho-analytical Approach to Juvenile Delinquency.* London: Routledge, 1947. Cited in R. Hood and R. Sparks *Key Issues in Criminology.* New York: McGraw-Hill World University Library, 1970.
22. Allport, G. W. *Pattern and Growth in Personality.* New York: Holt, Rinehart & Winston, 1961.
23. Roebuck, J. *Criminal Typology.* Springfield, Ill.: Charles C. Thomas, 1965. Cited in R. Hood and R. Sparks *Key Issues in Criminology.* New York: McGraw-Hill World University Library, 1970.
24. Cited in H. J. Steadman and J. J. Cocozza. We can't predict who is dangerous. *Psychology Today* January, 1975, 8(8), p. 33.
25. Kelley, C. M. *Uniform Crime Reports of the United States 1975.* Washington, D.C.: U.S. Department of Justice, Federal Bureau of Investigation, 1976. Chart 6, p. 17.
26. Campbell, C. Portrait of a mass killer. *Psychology Today* May, 1976, 9(12), 110ff.
27. Edwards, G. Commentary: Murder and gun control. *Wayne Law Review* 1972, 18(4), 1335–1342.
28. Hellman, P. One shopper in ten is a shoplifter. *The New York Times Magazine* March 15, 1970, pp. 34ff.
29. Kelley. *Uniform Crime Reports.* Chart 14, p. 33.

5
Victims and Bystanders

A number of writers have recently reminded us that crimes usually have victims. Of all the persons involved in the criminal justice system, the victim is the one who has most often been overlooked. The situation is slowly being rectified. A variety of studies employing diverse methods are yielding information about such issues as: who the victims are; what encourages or discourages the reporting of crimes; what causes bystanders to offer or withhold help; and, what restitution opportunities exist in the various states to compensate the victim for injuries, lost property, and lost time due to court appearances. These issues will be discussed in the present chapter.

WHO THE VICTIMS ARE

Data concerning the characteristics of crime victims were not systematically gathered at all before 1965 when their usefulness in combatting crime was recognized by the President's Commission on Law Enforcement and the Administration of Justice. Since then there has been a growing number of such surveys, some of which will be reviewed in this chapter.

Victimization Surveys. The first survey we will consider is the Impact Cities Victim Survey.[1] The Census Bureau selected representative samples consisting of 10,000 to 12,000 households and businesses in each of eight cities (Atlanta, Baltimore, Cleveland, Dallas, Denver, Newark, Portland, and St. Louis). Everyone in the selected households 14 years old or older was interviewed, and information was gathered concerning 12- and 13-year-olds, as well. The interviews (about 21,000 in each city) focused on victimizations experienced in the 12 months preceding the period of the interview (July to October, 1972). Householders were asked whether there had been an attempted or successful break-in or whether anything had been stolen. Individual respondents were asked whether they had been robbed, beaten, or threatened, and so forth, as well as the time and place of the incident, the extent of injury or loss, and whether the incident had been reported to the police. Owners, or other knowledgeable spokesmen, were asked, in the commercial part of each survey, whether the place of business had been broken into, or a break-in attempted, whether there had been a hold-up, and so on.

These data were further subdivided by the National Criminal Justice Information and Statistics Service into three major categories: personal, household, and commercial victimizations. Secondary categories were based upon: whether the crime was completed or only attempted, whether a weapon was used, whether there was personal injury, whether there was a financial loss, and, if so, how great a loss. The levels of victimization varied from city to city, but the types of incidents and their circumstances were similar enough to make presentation of general findings feasible.

Personal Victimization. The events included in this category are crimes that threatened or caused personal injury (excluding murder), or threatened or caused loss of property. It is worth noting that a given incident might have more than one victim, so that there are generally more victimizations than incidents. Further, an individual may be victimized more than once. (In fact, the suggestion has been made that certain people appear to be singled out, by virtue of their frailty, isolation, or reputation for wealth, to be repeatedly victimized.)

Rate of personal victimization was determined by dividing the number of victimizations by the total number of persons in the category under discussion. Rates are stated in terms of the number of cases per thousand. The overall rate, across the eight cities, was about 60/1000 or one in sixteen. (The readers are invited to ask themselves whether or not they have experienced victimization firsthand during the past year. Both authors, who live and work in a low-crime suburban area, have been victimized within the year, and our sad guess is that many of our readers have been, too.)

Several points can be made based on the data of these surveys. For one thing, rates in the eight cities varied from a high of 73/1000 (Denver) to a low of 47/1000 (Dallas). Second, the greater one's income, the less likely he was to be victimized. The very poor suffered victimization most of all. Third, nonwhites were victims of robbery and larceny at higher rates than whites, while whites suffered a higher rate of assaults.

The late teen years are the most dangerous time as far as victimization is concerned, particularly where the offense is assault. For persons over 35 victimization is related increasingly to property and less to personal injury. That is, older people are much less likely to be assaulted than younger people are, but are only slightly less likely to be victims of theft.

Table 5-1 combines data by race, sex, and age. It shows that the 16–19 age group is consistently the most victimized except for nonwhite women, who are most often victimized between ages 20 and 24. Race and sex relate less and less to rate of victimization as age increases, and sex differences in rate are greater than race differences.

Persons married or widowed are less than half as likely to be victims as those who never married or were separated or divorced. Hindelang infers that

Table 5-1. Estimated Rates of Personal Victimization by Age, Race, and Sex.*

SEX OF VICTIM	RACE OF VICTIM	VICTIM'S AGE						
		12–15	16–19	20–24	25–34	35–49	50–64	65 OR OLDER
Females	White	81[a]	93	70	48	30	29	28
	Black/Other	41	61	63	57	48	47	32
Males	White	145	177	119	74	51	40	28
	Black/Other	78	120	98	72	62	54	35

*Adapted from Table 2.3 in Hindelang, M. J., *An Analysis of Victimization Survey Results from the Eight Impact Cities: Summary Report,* Albany, N.Y.: Criminal Justice Research Center, 1974. Washington, D.C.: U.S. Government Printing Office, 1976.
[a] Entries indicate rate per 1000.

the high frequency of victimization among young, unattached males is related to differences in "life style" which expose these persons to circumstances that facilitate victimization. The film and novel *Looking for Mr. Goodbar* can serve to illustrate this inference although the protagonist was a female. A curious pattern shown in Table 5-1 may be inconsistent with this notion, however. It appears that whites are more likely to be victimized than nonwhites younger than 25, while nonwhites are more vulnerable than whites over 25. One wonders whether this too, relates to differences in "life style," or whether it has to do with the protection that life's circumstances confer. Clearly, we need to know more.

A more recent study of an extreme form of personal victimization— murder—yields some noteworthy data. The New York City Police Department recently issued the results of an analysis of 1,622 murders committed in New York in 1976. The rate, .205/1000, places New York eighth among the ten largest cities in the United States. Among 124 victims over 60 years of age, almost half were slain during robberies. Of the 1,622 murders, 654 occurred during or resulted from altercations, and 290 more occurred during or resulted from robberies. For present purposes, though, the most interesting finding is that 867 of the victims (53.5%) had criminal records! Thirty-five had been arrested for murder! Of the murder victims who had been arrested, 104 had been arrested in connection with drugs, 95 for robbery, and 90 for assault. In discussing criminals we considered victim-precipitated murder. It does not seem unlikely, in view of these data, that many of these victims precipitated their own murders.[2]

Relationship between Victim and Offender. Generally, where the offense was theft, the victim and the offender were unacquainted. (See Chapter 4 for very different data concerning the crime of murder.) Almost 95% of thefts were committed by strangers. Where the crime was assaultive violence without theft, only about two-thirds of the crimes were the work of strangers.

When race and sex are included in the equation, the situation becomes a bit less clear. Assault without theft against white males involved strangers about 75% of the time. If the victim was a white female or a nonwhite male, the assault was committed by a stranger just over 67% of the time. Of nonwhite females who were assaulted, just over half were the victims of strangers.

Assaults without theft tended to be committed by persons about the same age as their victims. Where theft was involved, younger people were more likely to victimize older people, but older offenders were unlikely to victimize younger people. Offenses by more than one perpetrator were generally the work of persons perceived by the victims to be younger than 21 years of age.

Considering all instances of personal victimization, nonwhites were the victims of persons perceived to be nonwhites 94% of the time. Whites were victimized by offenders perceived to be white 63% of the time.

Hindelang notes that white offenders worked alone 65% of the time, while nonwhite offenders worked alone 49% of the time. Offenders who worked in pairs or larger groups were likely to be perceived as younger than 21 and as nonwhite. In presenting these data, Hindelang rightly notes that identification of the age or race of offenders is of dubious value. As will be shown in our discussion of eyewitness behavior, during time of stress one's ability to note and remember pertinent facts may be reduced. One's expectations or assumptions about who would be likely to commit such a crime can affect the way in which one perceives the perpetrator or recalls the perpetrator's characteristics. Moreover, the Census Bureau lists Hispanics as whites in its figures, but victims may not know this and may perceive or describe a Hispanic offender as nonwhite. Such a tendency would spuriously inflate the number of offenders listed as "black/others". As a matter of fact, it makes no sense to refer to all Hispanics as either white or nonwhite, as their "ethnic group" includes people of all racial backgrounds.

Attempts at Self-Protection.   Respondents were asked whether they had tried to protect themselves or their property during the offense, and, if so, how. In about 51% of the 208,720 cases some such action was taken. It was more likely to be the case where assault was involved than where the offense involved no assault. Specifically, protective measures occurred in 54% of cases of assaultive violence with theft, in 63% of cases of violence without theft, in 42% of cases of robbery without injury, and in 22% of cases of larceny.

Since larceny "relies more on stealth than on force,"[3] the relative lack of self-protection is not unexpected. Similarly, since robbery generally involves a lethal weapon, the relatively low figure is not surprising.

Where it did occur, self-protection involved hitting, kicking, or scratching the offender 34% of the time; it also involved fleeing the scene (27% of the time), yelling (14%), "reasoning" with the criminal (12%), and maintaining a grip on the property (5%). About 19% of the victims used more than one of these measures.

Which method was employed depended on the nature of the offense. Assaultive violence with theft led to striking the offender in 61% of those cases in which *any* protective action was taken. Few victims of personal larceny sought to protect themselves in this fashion (13%); they preferred to yell (36%). Only 10% of victims of assault without theft chose the latter tactic.

Age was closely related to the likelihood that a victim would attempt self-protection. Younger victims were more likely to attempt it than older ones. Older victims who did attempt it were more likely to yell and hold on to their property than younger victims, who were more likely to hit or flee.

Male and female victims were equally likely to attempt to protect themselves, but they went about it differently. Males were more likely to hit, kick, or scratch, females to yell. White victims were more likely than nonwhites to attempt to thwart the crime (56% v. 42%). Whites and nonwhites did not differ in the self-protective measures employed.

Injury and Hospitalization. Where the crime was assault and theft, 40% of victims required some medical treatment, most of them in an emergency room (65%). Where the assault involved no theft, only 11% required any medical attention, 60% of them also in an emergency room. There was almost no difference between these two groups in the duration of hospitalization. Eight percent of all the injured in both groups required hospital stays of eight days or longer.

Fewer than 10% of business robberies led to injury, and only 2% to hospitalization.

Characteristics of the Crimes. Among the issues about which the victimization surveys collected data were such characteristics of the crimes as the time and place at which they occurred, whether or not weapons were employed, and the number of victims and offenders involved.

Most personal victimizations involving assault occurred at night. Larceny was more often committed during the day. Most of these offenses occurred outdoors in public places, with nonresidential buildings and public transport being next in the order of frequency. Where the offender was known to the victim, the scene of the offense was more likely to be the victim's home than outside. Where they were strangers, the reverse was true. Weapons were used in 38% of the cases of personal victimizations, particularly in cases of robbery without injury; 52% of these crimes involved a weapon. Forty-four percent of cases of assaultive violence without theft and 42% of cases of assaultive violence with theft involved use of a weapon.

Victims of personal offenses were alone in 90% of the instances. Only 2% of the cases involved three or more victims in a single incident. On the other hand, offenses were often committed by more than one criminal. Only assaultive violence without theft tended to be a loner's crime. Sixty-five percent of these encounters involved a lone perpetrator. Thefts, whether or not coupled with violence, involved more than one offender between 60 and 65% of the time.

REPORTING OF CRIMES

Near the end of the chapter on criminals, an appliance repairman is discussed who arrogantly bilked customers, harassed them, ignored court orders, and so on. One of the reasons he was able to continue in this manner more or less indefinitely is that many of his victims declined to complain to the authorities. Some were intimidated by his threats of legal action. Others wanted to avoid trouble or could not be bothered. Some regarded it as a personal matter; some felt that their case would be hard to prove. And some could not say why they failed to report the offense. The most common reason for failing to report him, however, was the feeling that it would do no good. Whatever the reasons, the result was that the repairman was free to continue exploiting his customers.

Survey Findings.   The issue of reporting of crimes is an important one in the psychology of the victim, and it will be considered in detail below. For the moment, let us return to the Impact Cities Victim Surveys and learn what they have to teach us about the nonreporting of victimization.

To begin with, fewer than half of the personal and household victimizations were reported to the police. More than three-fourths of the business victimizations were reported. Of the personal incidents the type most likely to be reported involved assaultive violence with theft (65% reported); the least likely were assaultive violence without theft (42%) and larceny without injury (42%). Among household victimizations vehicle theft was the most likely to be reported (77%) and larceny the least (30%). In these two broad categories there were no major differences in the patterns of the eight cities. Business victimization differed from them, however, in two ways. Almost all robberies were reported (90%), and most of the burglaries (76%). One city showed a startlingly different pattern from the other seven. Of the victims of robbery in Newark, one-fourth declined to report the crime, a figure twice the rate of any other city.

Several variables were related to reporting rates. One was the amount lost. Only 20% of household larcenies under $50 were reported, but 60% of those amounting to $250 or more were reported. Similarly, in business robberies, 82% were reported when the loss was less than $50, while 98% were reported when the loss was from $50 to $249. Of more costly robberies, 99% were reported. For burglaries, the comparable figures were 61%, 81%, and 95%.

A second related variable concerned whether the crime was completed or merely attempted. As one might have guessed, completed offenses were considerably more likely to be reported. Of robberies without injury, for example, only one-third of the attempts were reported, while 60% of the completed crimes were. Even when completed, larceny was considerably less likely to be reported than assaultive violence.

Among household crimes, attempts were unlikely to be reported, but completed burglaries and vehicle thefts (not other larcenies) were much more likely to be reported.

A third pertinent variable was the use of a weapon. In cases of robbery with injury to the victim, the crime was more likely to be reported when a weapon was used (70%) than when it was not (59%). Robberies without injuries showed a similar pattern. Where the assault did not involve theft, the difference was greater (51% v. 34%).

The pattern holds up in business robberies, too. Ninety-five percent of instances involving weapons were reported, as compared with 78% of robberies in which no weapon was displayed.

Fourth and last among the variables related to crime reporting is the age of the victim. This was the only victim characteristic which bore any relation to the probability of reporting the crime. Young victims reported only one-third of the incidents; elderly victims reported more than half of them.

Reasons for Failure to Report.   The most common reasons given for not reporting an incident to the police were: nothing could be done, there was no proof, or the offense was not important enough. These reasons were given in 65% of the unreported personal victimizations, in 81% of the unreported household victimizations, and in 78% of the unreported business victimizations. Other reasons given much less frequently were: the police would not be receptive to such a complaint, it was too inconvenient to report the incident, it was a personal matter, or there was fear of reprisal.

Failure to report crime may be an important factor in the ability of the offender, particularly the petty offender, to engage repeatedly in his or her "employment." Since many criminals commit numerous crimes, a failure by the victim to report an incident helps to sustain a criminal career. Accordingly, the failure to report crimes is an important concern of the criminal justice system.

Before examining this phenomenon in greater depth, however, we wish to note the existence of a study comparing the data cited with similar data collected in the same eight cities three years later (1974–1975).[4]

The more recent data show no consistent trend. Of the eight cities, five (Baltimore, Cleveland, Dallas, Portland, and St. Louis) show overall increases in crime rates, one (Denver) no significant change, and two (Atlanta and Newark) a mixed picture of unchanged and lower rates.

Hindelang and Gottfredson provide some information about crime reporting drawn from the foregoing and other surveys. Whether or not a crime is reported depends upon its nature. Therefore, comparison of reporting rates by different types of victims must be based upon the same type of offense. For personal robbery, older victims are more likely to report the incident regardless of race. Two-thirds of victims 35 or older reported the robberies. Among victims 12–19 years old, 32% of whites and 42% of blacks reported the crime. In general, both groups are more likely to report the crime as their income levels go up.

One would expect a prior relationship with the offender to have some effect on crime reporting, but this was found only in cases of "larceny with contact"; unfamiliar offenders were more likely to be reported than familiar ones. As stated above, the characteristics of the crime were more closely associated with reporting or not reporting it than were characteristics of the victim.

The other side of the failure-to-report coin is the reporting of a crime. Just as one may wonder why someone declines to do so, so may one inquire as to what causes a victim to report a crime. Smith and Maness addressed this issue in connection with burglary.

Every reported residential burglary in Columbia, South Carolina that occurred in January and in June of 1974 was studied. There were 184 such burglaries. The researchers considered the meaning that the victims assigned to the burglary and to the act of reporting it on the assumption that people act toward things and events according to the meaning that these things and events have for them. The meanings derive from social interaction concerning the matters at issue. Social interaction shapes the meanings and provides a context in terms of which events are interpreted. The meaning, or "social reality," derives from what social psychologists call "social comparison processes," a matter discussed elsewhere in this chapter. Given this orientation, it becomes necessary to understand how events and actions acquire their meaning and what the meanings are. More specifically, what led the victim to report the burglary? Was it to seek help in understanding what had happened? Was it a result of the urgings of other parties? What did the victim hope to accomplish by reporting it?

Of the 184 victims, 88 were available and willing to discuss the matter with an interviewer by telephone. Most people probably would guess that a major motive for calling the police was to pave the way for recovery of losses by means of an insurance claim. (This may be the reason for the higher rate of reporting of crimes against businesses, which are more likely to be insured than individuals are.) Unless there is something to be gained, this reasoning goes, no one would bother to involve him- or herself in making a complaint and so undergo the inconveniences that follow. The data do not support this assumption.

Most respondents indicated that they had reported the crime because it was the proper step to take, a civic responsibility, or because they were urged to do so by other parties. The next most frequent reason was that reporting the crime would facilitate the capture of the perpetrator. Self-interest did enter the picture insofar as some said they did so for personal protection, to recover what had been stolen, or to recover losses through insurance; but insurance was the least mentioned of the three. It was mentioned by only 17% of all respondents and was listed as the major reason by only 10%. In fact, more than one-third claimed to have no insurance coverage at all. Of those who were insured, half had had no property taken, or what was taken was uninsured or was worth too little to exceed the deductible limit. One cannot help being mindful, however, of the possibility that some respondents were seeking the interviewer's approval in making these reponses.

The respondents, who were a subgroup of all who had reported burglaries (the 48% willing to be interviewed), were more likely than the general population to be homeowners and were somewhat better educated. With respect to race, sex, and age they were comparable with the general population.

Those who called the police were no more hopeful than nonreporters interviewed in other studies that it would do any good. But they did feel a responsibility to report the crime or wished to alert the police to be more watchful in their neighborhood. In this study there was, of course, no information on victims who had not reported the crime.

Smith and Maness suggest that the act of reporting may help the victims put the upsetting affair behind them. The victimization surveys described above suggested that crime reporting is related to certain characteristics or aspects of the crime. This study focused on only one type of crime and therefore dealt with another issue, the relationship of victim characteristics to crime reporting. It found that the decision to report it is a function of the significance of the crime, and of reporting it, to the victim.

The results might well be different if crimes of another sort were involved. Forcible rape, for example, appears to be a crime that many victims are reluctant to report. Some are afraid that the offender will return and do them further harm. Others are afraid of what they expect will be unsympathetic police officers. Others do not wish to relive the trauma as would be required if they chose to make a statement to the police, let alone face cross-examination in court. Then, too, victims of rape are often assumed by others to have somehow brought the crime upon themselves. Consistent with the "just world hypothesis" (see Chapter 12) we tend to believe that terrible things do not happen to nice people. Therefore, if this traumatic incident is reported, it must mean that the victim either deserved it or is lying.

Victims may be no less subject to this distorting view of the world than jurors or the uninvolved. To the extent that they do have these feelings they may be too embarrassed or guilt-ridden to wish to report the crime.[5]

Hindelang and Gottfredson suggest that the public may be growing increasingly aware of the low and declining rate of apprehension for crimes. In the years from 1960 to 1973 the rate of "clearance" for crimes of all sorts dropped: for burglary from 30% to less than 20%, for robbery from 40% to less than 25%, for forcible rape from 70% to 50%. Perhaps more crimes are being reported than in earlier years, and the proportion cleared has declined simply because the total number of offenses is greater. In any case it seems that large numbers of victims have little hope that the offender will be apprehended.

To the extent that this is so, the situation can be expected to continue deteriorating. Most criminal occurrences are brought to the attention of the police by the victim or by bystanders. In one study in Chicago, only 5% of criminal incidents were discovered by police officers. If every crime were reported, it might overload the already strained system. Maybe many instances not presently reported would not be pursued either by the police or the district attorney, because the cases are weak or questionable ones. The fact remains, though, that most of the time it is the victim who initiates the process of investigation, arrest, and trial.

It would be interesting to know whether or not a victim's readiness to report a crime is a function of the circumstances in which the crime occurs. Ethical constraints prevent researchers from conducting experiments capable of answering this question. Therefore, permissible experimental work has been limited to tests of the willingness of bystanders or witnesses to report staged offenses.

Experimental Data. Bickman and his associates have been among the more active researchers in this area. In a series of papers they varied the conditions under which shoplifting apparently occurred and measured the effects of these conditions on the reporting of the "crime." In one instance, a shopper behaved (by prearrangement) either rudely, neutrally, or positively toward the person behind her in the check-out line. Shortly thereafter, she "lifted" either two glasses (low cost) or two rolls of film (high cost) while the clerk's attention was elsewhere but the subject was watching her. She then paid for her groceries, left the store, and stood, plainly visible, outside the store window.

Thirty-two subjects said they had seen nothing amiss and three declined to be interviewed at all. Of 128 subjects who admitted to an interviewer that they had seen the theft, 50 had intervened. Of the 160 interviewed subjects, the proportions of interventions were unrelated to the cost of the loot or to the earlier behavior of the thief. Since attitude toward the thief was successfully manipulated, as shown by interview data, it appears to be of little importance, at least in this specific situation. Those who did report the young woman also indicated a stronger feeling that shoplifting should be punished than did those who failed to report her.[6]

A second study by Bickman, conducted in a department store, manipulated attitudes towards a sales clerk by having her bump into a second confederate in the subject's presence and behave rudely or apologetically. A third confederate conspicuously stole some merchandise, which she stashed in her pocketbook. Subjects were given up to 90 seconds to report what they had witnessed before an interviewer intervened. Once again there was no relationship between the subject's attitude towards the sales clerk and the reporting of the theft. Forty percent did intervene in some way (compared with 31% in the previous study), but neither the form nor the probability of their intervention was related to their attitudes towards the sales clerk.

Another study reported in the same paper showed that reporting can be increased, at least under very special circumstances. Undergraduate women were led to believe that they were viewing a live TV broadcast from a supermarket. Ostensibly, they were to record shoppers' reactions at the check-out line. In reality, what they saw was a videotape on which a shoplifting incident was staged. In preparing them for the experiment, the experimenter "offhandedly" suggested to half of the subjects that if they happened to see any shoplifting, they should report it to the store manager, with whom they believed they would soon be talking. He gave no such cue to the remaining subjects. When subjects "called the store" to ask that the camera be turned on, they were treated either courteously or brusquely by the "manager's secretary." Subjects who had been "cued" were significantly more likely to report the shoplifting than subjects who had not been "cued." Attitudes induced by the secretary's rudeness or politeness had minimal effects. Further, cued subjects who reported the theft did so more quickly than noncued subjects who reported it.[7]

The last of Bickman's papers to be discussed here is concerned with situational cues.[8] It describes two field studies of the impact of instructional signs on how to report a theft. In the second study, the effect of a third party's defining the theft as a shoplifting is examined as well.

In the first, Bickman and Green devised a series of signs, all of which said, "See a shoplifting? Tell the manager," and bore one of three last lines: "We need your help," "Don't be a guilty bystander," and "Shoplifting costs you money." These last were designed to appeal, respectively, to altruistic, guilty, and selfish motives. This study demonstrated that the signs increased the likelihood of subjects' agreeing that customers should help in curbing shoplifting. However, only 6% of the subjects intervened when a confederate slipped something from a shelf into a tote bag. The signs, then, had no effect on the reporting of shoplifting. It is interesting to note that the reporting rate was considerably lower in this study in which the theft was committed from supermarket shelves, than in the previous and subsequent studies in which the theft occurred at the check-out counter. Bickman and Green suggest that this may have been because the sign was not salient at the time the theft was witnessed.

These researchers cite a cognitive model of intervention in emergencies (that of Latané and Darley),[9] which distinguishes among five stages in the process of deciding whether or not to intervene. They apply this model to the shoplifting situation. The stages are: (1) noticing the occurrence, (2) interpreting it as an emergency, (3) taking responsibility, (4) deciding what to do, (5) doing it. This model and the low salience of the signs suggested some modifications in the next study.

First, the location of the signs was changed. Signs were placed on the magazine rack at the beginning of the check-out counter and on the back of the cash register. It was assumed that they would be inescapably salient, since the crime was to take place at the check-out counter. Also, the Latané-Darley cognitive model underscores the importance of defining the event as an emergency (in this case as a shoplifting), which was the second modification in the present study. This was accomplished by having a confederate say to the subject: "Say, look at her. She's shoplifting. She put that into her purse." Having said this the confederate suddenly disappeared to find her fictitious little brother. Meanwhile, the shoplifter paid for her purchases and left the store, remaining within view outside the store's window. This was an experimental design in which the independent variables were the presence or absence of signs and the definition of the event as a shoplifting (or not).

Interpreting what took place as a shoplifting had a significant effect of the intervention behavior of the subjects. Sixty-six percent of them intervened when in the interpretation condition; 44% did so when no interpretation was made. The sign (which did not include the motivating lines described in the previous study) had no effect at all. Of those who did intervene, most were female, "older," married, had gone beyond high school in their education, and had been reared in a rural or small-town setting. Inasmuch as the shoplifter was a college student, one wonders how shoplifters of different appearance (e.g., older, impoverished, wealthy, minority, sloppy, and so on) would have been reacted to.

Bickman and Green interpret the outcome in terms of the greater potency of interpersonal communication as compared to nonpersonal communication. The conclusion is questionable, at best, since the two types of communications conveyed different contents. One would expect, too, that characteristics of the communicator would have a bearing on the impact of her message. Not all interpersonal communications are likely to be equally effective. In fact, it has been demonstrated that the effectiveness of a communicator depends both on his or her characteristics and the context within which the communication is occurring. A very credible communicator may have little influence in persuading a person to do something which that person does not wish to do. A less credible but more powerful communicator who can reward or punish the other person may be expected to have less difficulty.[10]

Whether or not characteristics of the shoplifter interact in some way with characteristics of the victim or of the witness in determining reporting behavior is an interesting matter. Do people inform more readily on people like themselves, on people very different from themselves, on people whose appearance is intimidating, etc.?

Gelfand and her co-workers conducted a field experiment to assess some of these issues.[11] As in other shoplifting studies, the victim was an impersonal business (drug-variety store), not a mom-and-pop operation in which bystanders might take a more personal interest. Variables were the socio-. economic character of the community (upper income suburban v. lower income urban) and the appearance of the 21-year-old coed shoplifter (hippie v. conventional). In addition, the age and sex of bystanders were recorded. Items measured were the rate at which the shoplifting was noted and whether or not it was reported. Data were recorded on videotape for later analysis. Only 28% of those who had been exposed to the event even noticed it (despite various steps taken to attract their attention). In general the thievery was noticed more by wealthier, younger persons observing the hippie thief. Of those who observed the theft, only 28% reported it. (Security personnel had led the researchers to expect a substantially smaller rate than this.) Two of the three high socioeconomic status (SES) middle-aged male observers of the conventionally dressed thief reported her. More generally, and maybe more convincingly, males were twice as likely to report the theft as females; middle-aged people were more likely to report it than younger or older people; higher-SES-area shoppers were slightly more likely to report it than lower-SES-area shoppers. Persons raised in communities of fewer than 100,000 were more likely to report it than those from more populous places. The appearance of the shoplifter was unrelated to her being reported although it was related to her being seen shoplifting.

These studies all dealt with the reporting of a crime by a bystander who had lost nothing in the crime and had had no firsthand interaction with the criminal (except for the first study discussed in this section). Greenberg[12] describes an experimental procedure in which a subject was victimized and chose whether or not to say something about it.

Greenberg presents a model of crime reporting reminiscent of Latané and Darley's and of some other well-established theories in the realm of social psychology. Whether or not a crime is reported, he suggests, is contingent upon whether or not one decides that a crime has been committed and whether the costs–benefits ratio is higher for reporting the event or for not reporting it. The costs–benefits ratio is the proportion of effort, expense, or other loss, to compensation or other gain occasioned by a behavior. The decision as to whether or not a crime has been committed is, in turn, related to the victim's noticing something amiss (e.g., something is missing from her purse), attributing the loss to the actions of another rather than to her own carelessness, interpreting the other's presumed actions as intentional rather than as accidental or "an honest mistake," and interpreting the intent as a harmful one rather than a practical joke. One might go further and speculate that more trusting people will be more reluctant to define a given act as an intentional crime, particularly where the victim sees the apparent perpetrator as very similar to him- or herself.

The costs–benefits ratio will be determined according to the victim's embarrassment, intimidation, anger, and so forth, as well as the value of the stolen articles, the apparent motives or needs of the criminal, the certainty of the latter's guilt, and so on. Such variables as these were implemented in an experiment conducted by Greenberg's student, C. Wilson.

Subjects were told that they would compete with a peer (actually a confederate of the experimenter) in a test of clerical skills. They were each given $5 and told that their performance could increase or reduce the amount taken home, depending upon which of the two performed faster. The experimenter left each subject and "peer" alone and thereafter communicated with them by intercom. While the two worked, the confederate surreptitiously removed some of the subject's completed work from the "outbox," a task made easier by the physical arrangement of the room and by the concentration required for the task. Given a chance to check their work before submitting it to the experimenter, subjects became aware of the mischief. Observers could see (through a one-way mirror) behaviors that indicated first surprise, then searching and confusion, and finally contemplation and suspicion. Following instructions to turn in their work and the experimenter's announcement that the confederate had outperformed the subject so that the latter had to forfeit the $5 (a step which appeared to convince many subjects that they had been cheated), subjects were directed to the office of the Project Director, where they were to secure credit slips for their participation. The dependent variable was whether or not the subject's suspicions were reported and with what degree of certainty. Variations on this pattern included the use of confederates who "witnessed" the theft or who were themselves victimized, and who advised the subject either to report or to ignore it. Only when they advised against reporting the theft were co-victims more persuasive than bystander witnesses. The co-victim who urged reporting was less persuasive than the witness who did so (not very surprisingly, since reporting a "crime" is a serious matter and another victim is not as certain to be correct in his or her suspicions as an eyewitness is assumed to be). Greenberg interprets the data in terms of the attribution that the lone victim had somehow been singled out and was *personally* victimized, while the presence of another victim made the crime less personal and therefore less offensive.

In any event, 52% of the victims reported the "crime," a considerably higher proportion than was suggested by the survey data considered earlier. Greenberg suggests that the immediate presence of the authority may have encouraged reporting; a genuine victim would not have so prompt an opportunity.

It is worth pointing out that the process of defining an ambiguous situation as a crime or in any other fashion is facilitated by the opportunity to exchange views with others like oneself. In general, when we are in unfamiliar circumstances we look to others around us for clues as to how we ought to feel or respond. If everyone else is calm or indifferent, we will probably respond similarly; if others are agitated or frightened, we will be, too. Two theories in the field of social psychology are pertinent here: social comparison theory and the theory of emotional contagion.

Festinger's social comparison theory[13] assumes that we wish to have accurate opinions. We like to feel that we are responding correctly to ambiguous situations, cognitively, emotionally, and behaviorally. It would make little sense to compare ourselves with people who are obviously very different from us on some relevant dimension (intelligence, mental health, and so on). Accordingly, we seek out persons who seem to be pretty much like ourselves and compare our response with theirs. Students who compare answers after a test in order to see whether it was as easy (or difficult) as they had thought are engaging in this process. The others' responses give us a "social reality" where there is no objectively verifiable physical reality. And our responses are likely to be similar to the responses of the similar others with whom we compare ourselves. Other considerations enter in, too. The greater the chance or the more severe the consequences of being wrong, the more dependent we will be on the opinions of others unless, as in the co-victim situation, the "available other" has no better information than we have and action is not *required*.

Emotional contagion can be subsumed under social comparison processes.[14] It is said to occur when a situation that somehow upsets one person acquires the power, due to the first person's emotional response, to upset other people in a similar fashion. Their responses are triggered not by the event or situation *per se* but by the combination of the event and another's strong reaction to it. Panic may build upon one person's fear; mob violence upon one person's anger. If one bystander becomes angry (or foolhardy) enough to intervene in a crime, it is likely that others will follow that person's lead.

The present authors share the view that there are ethical constraints on experimental studies of victim behavior. One cannot victimize an unwitting subject without running the risk of causing stress, anxiety, or other emotional states which cannot be warned of in advance. Similarly, role-playing the part of a victim can yield data that are of questionable validity, at best. Accordingly, it seems likely that most experimental research will focus on the bystander rather than the victim. Since the bystander has some measure of choice of how to respond and whether to "get involved," the bystander has more control over any stress reactions than the victim would have, and the stress or conflict that the bystander does experience is likely to be less intense than the victim's.

Bickman summarizes several pertinent studies and points to the ways in which bystander intervention benefits victim, police, and society. Whether the intervention is direct (coming to the aid of the victim) or indirect (summoning help), one or more benefits accrue. The victim may be directly assisted or "rescued" by the intervention of the police called by the witness. The police can be materially assisted in the detection and prevention of crime by alert citizens. The nature of crime patterns can be better understood as more crimes are reported, and this understanding can assist law enforcement agencies in allocating their limited resources more effectively. Bickman also suggests that the degree of citizen intervention can provide an index of public support for various laws, and that mutual concern among citizens as reflected in their willingness to assist one another provides researchers with an index of social cohesiveness.[15] For some of these reasons the National Institute of Law Enforcement and Criminal Justice of the Department of Justice initiated a number of projects to encourage citizens to report crimes that they witness or even actions that are "suspicious."

Citizen Crime Reporting Projects. One program of this sort was sponsored by the New York City Police Department. Volunteers were sought to become "blockwatchers." They were instructed in what to look for, how to describe what was seen, and how to go about reporting the event. They were each given an identification number designed to facilitate responses to their calls; but the responding officers were not informed of the callers' identity, thus affording the blockwatchers some measure of anonymity. These people were taught to distinguish between emergencies requiring immediate response and non-emergency matters (street lights out, derelict autos, open hydrants, and so on). Blockwatchers were also given a list of city agencies responsible for non-police matters and their phone numbers, in order to reduce the number of inappropriate calls to the neighborhood station house.

Bickman and his associates conducted an evaluative study of the effectiveness of citizen crime reporting projects.[16] These projects did not originate with the murder of Kitty Genovese but appear to have gotten their impetus in many communities from that and similar crimes. Genovese was a young woman slain in the doorway of her apartment house by an assailant who attacked her on two occasions separated by nearly one half hour while more than three dozen of her neighbors watched and did nothing to aid her either directly or indirectly. Several other such incidents were widely publicized in the 1960s, but it was the Genovese killing and an article about it in *The New York Times* that had two effects pertinent to this volume. The first effect was the growth of a body of research literature on helping behavior and altruism. Latané and Darley were among the pioneers in this still burgeoning area;[17] but since their work has not been directly related to criminal matters, it will not be discussed here. Suffice it to say that such research as theirs caused social psychologists to consider for the first time why people do good things for each other.

The second effect was an effort to encourage citizen involvement in coping with crime. This required changes in the social environment and in the relationships among people. Of more than 300 Citizen Crime Reporting Projects, Bickman and his colleagues investigated 78. They describe two general types of projects. First, are those designed to encourage reporting of criminal or suspicious activity. Three different approaches are mentioned:

1. Whistlestop projects make whistles available to citizens who are instructed not to attempt a personal intervention in a crime but simply to blow the whistle, which will alert a resident to call the police (and perhaps frighten away the offender). Over 100,000 whistles have been bought by Chicagoans.

2. Radio Watch projects employ the two-way radios of cabs, CBers, and ham operators, encouraging them to alert the police to criminal situations.

3. A number of the projects involve the use of special telephone numbers. Some are permanent; some are temporary. Some offer rewards; others do not.

These are the special numbers publicized by the media to attract phone calls from witnesses on other than the standard police emergency line. A permanent "Crime Stop" line in San Antonio receives an average of 28,000 calls each year.

The second general type of project is educational. There are also three subtypes of educational projects:

1. Presentations to community or school groups by police officers or others offer instruction in what constitutes suspicious activity and what to do about it.
2. Membership projects involve a measure of public commitment by the citizen. He or she must sign up with the organization, and receives a membership card and even code numbers to use in making reports.
3. Home Presentation projects involve presentation of information (and sometimes membership cards, and so forth) to neighborhood groups. These may take the form of a single meeting, or they may involve a community organization for purposes of maintaining participation by residents in the block or community.

Each of these approaches can be linked to one of the numerous reasons why citizens do not report crimes. They lower the costs of reporting by making the process easier, providing anonymity, and minimizing the risk of embarrassment. They increase the rewards for reporting by restoring some sense of control over one's own fate to those who had felt powerless, and by increasing mutual concern among neighbors and the sense of belonging that goes with it. They reduce apathy and the (usually mistaken) assumption that someone else will take responsibility. They increase alertness so that fewer untoward events go unnoticed. They increase citizens' confidence in deciding to take action and in doing so. No longer is the station house a mysterious, intimidating unknown to these participants, as it is to many citizens who are reluctant to draw police attention to themselves for any reason at all.

At least these programs do some of these things in theory. Whether they do so in fact is another matter, not easily demonstrated. Such data as exist are correlational in nature, and even where increased reporting has occurred, it cannot be attributed with certainty to these programs. Of the programs studied, half reported more calls, and one-third reported more informative calls; but the Bickman team expresses reservations about the adequacy of these data. Control groups are lacking; dispatchers do not routinely rate the quality of each call. Where other populations are compared with these, the data show no increase in calls as a consequence of these programs.

Bickman considers six measurement problems that, individually and collectively, cast doubt upon the data and assumptions of these projects.

1. Propensity to report is hard to assess because it requires the citizen's presence at the time and place of suspicious activity, and that does not occur very often.
2. The degree of commitment to the program and the stability of the commitment are hard to measure.
3. The citizens who do participate may be the very ones who would have reported suspicious occurrences without a special project to encourage them.
4. Crime statistics cannot be used to assess these projects because reporting rates vary from crime to crime and from one area to another.
5. If more reporting and/or alertness reduces crime, there will be fewer calls so that it will seem that the program has had a negative effect.
6. The programs are designed to alter witness behavior but most reporting data are based upon victims' reports.

These problems notwithstanding, Bickman et al. offer some tentative predictions and conclusions. First, vehicular Radio Watch projects may be expected to increase watchfulness, the number of reports, and their quality. This is based on the readily available means of reporting and the mobility, which makes witnessing more likely than it is for stationary citizens. Whistlestop projects are generally not capable of assessment, since they merely encourage use of a whistle, not greater surveillance or more helpful reporting. Bickman et al. have little faith in special telephone number projects because they involve no contact with individual citizens, no commitment by them, and no training in reporting or in surveillance. Of group and membership projects, the most promising appear to be those involving neighbors working together to improve the safety of the community. Newman also indicates a belief that such mutual concern is a factor in reducing crime.

Programs of this sort affect more than the quantity and quality of crime reports, however. They may improve police–community relations, although that is not at all certain. They may affect fear of crime, but it is hard to predict in which direction. People may feel more safe and secure knowing that their fellow citizens are watching over them, but, at the same time, they may become more sensitized to, and so more fearful of, suspicious behaviors. One might have predicted that these efforts would tax the capacities of police agencies to process all the calls. This does not appear to be a real risk. Whether or not they increase community cohesiveness is not yet demonstrated. Tendencies of citizens to define more behaviors as criminal, to be unrealistically suspicious, or to take the law into their own hands are potential risks of these projects; but Bickman et al. do not view them as important risks. Some citizens' groups have formed their own neighborhood patrols in high crime areas. They have the highest potential for the realization of vigilante-like or illegal behavior. The organization of Auxiliary Police units in certain communities makes it possible to minimize these dangers by permitting professional police officers to exercise more effective control over the type of person who might otherwise join some independent neighborhood patrol force.

BYSTANDERS WHO HELP

Huston and his associates consider the advisability of encouraging bystander intervention and the characteristics of the "angry samaritans" who do intervene. Their findings are pertinent to the issues under discussion.

In most European countries bystanders are required by law to intervene when they see someone is in danger. In 1975, there were 24 people convicted in France for failing to do so. In the United States, only Vermont has such a requirement and has had it only for ten years (since the Genovese case). There are two conflicting pressures, aside from the rewards–costs ratios. We are taught that we are responsible for our fellow human beings and that helping others is a laudable act. We are also taught not to get involved and that minding our own business is a virtue. In 14 states, the first being California, these pressures are brought into some degree of congruence by "Good Samaritan" laws which authorize compensation for persons injured in the act of assisting a victim of a crime or in capturing an offender. Like so much of the research we have recounted, this innovation was stimulated by the Genovese murder. It permits compensation of up to $5000 for the injured samaritan.

By early 1976, 70 men and one woman had been compensated in California. Huston et al. investigated the characteristics of 41 of these individuals.

They did not differ from crime victims in age, place of residence, and so on. Ninety percent came from one of the four largest California cities; 51% were younger than 35, and only 7% were older than 54. While men are twice as likely as women to be crime victims, they are even more likely to intervene. Perhaps this has some relationship to motives of machismo or chivalry, or to the greater physical strength of men. Perhaps it relates to the disproportionate number of male criminals.

Interviews with 40 of these individuals suggest little resemblance to the Samaritan of Luke 10:29–37. These people appear to be risk-takers who are not merely famliar, but are comfortable with violence. They tend to be far more concerned with capturing the offender than with aiding the victim, and, in fact, are unsympathetic to the victim. They tend to derogate others who intervene with them. Many stated that the victim had in some way brought about his own victimization. They tend to be persons who are quick to anger, and their interventions are motivated more by that anger than by compassion or humane feelings. Upon intervening they gave little thought to any risk, and none had anticipated any form of compensation. Yet several said that they would not intervene again (remember, these were injured persons). This is a startling admission, since they could have kept this socially undesirable response to themselves.

Huston and Geis conclude that, on balance, the compensation law has been a worthy innovation. They do recognize that there are pros and cons concerning the encouragement of intervention. Among the pros are the likelihood that a victim will be spared injury or loss, that an offender will be apprehended, that an ethical society is based upon mutual concern among its members. Among the cons are the possibility that the intervener may, by his actions, increase the danger to the victim as well as to himself and that vigilantism may become more common. All of these things considered, however, Huston and Geis favor the law and even suggest that consideration be given to the arguments for and against making intervention mandatory. They also recommend that consideration be given to rewarding or recognizing all interveners, not simply those who suffer injury.

The present authors are strongly opposed to any legal requirement that an ordinary citizen with no special training or weapon be required to intervene in an ongoing crime. Such intervention is more likely to result in additional injuries than in the reduction of crime.

The law in New York requiring a citizen to aid a police officer when ordered to do so had to be modified to limit this duty to situations in which the aid would involve no personal risk to the citizen. This change was made to take account of the citizen's lack of police training.

COMPENSATION TO VICTIMS

As recently as 20 years ago a major text in psychology and law appeared with the total space allotted to victims being 11 *lines*.[18] It may be Kitty Genovese's legacy that this is no longer the case. But studies of victims are still relatively few. Often victim data are a byproduct of studies designed to investigate other issues.[19]

Victims are the initiators of the great majority of criminal proceedings. If justice is to be served, their participation is essential. But as many as half do not wish to pursue the matter, whether as complainants or as witnesses. Even if they report the crime and a suspect is arrested, they may decline to testify or to cooperate in other ways with the prosecution. A study of 4,188 cases of murder, rape, robbery, burglary, and assaults by strangers revealed that 47%

did not get beyond the initial screening because victims or witnesses refused to cooperate. The victim-witness may be afraid to testify because of fear that the defendant will be acquitted or fear of retaliation by the defendant's friends. The pre-trial delay may be so great that the victim no longer trusts his or her memory and is vulnerable to cross-examination. The time required of the witness for court proceedings may also discourage cooperation.

One way to encourage victim cooperation with the prosecution would be to provide that the victim be compensated either by the state or by the offender for any damages or loss occasioned by the offense. The victim has always had the right to sue the perpetrator of a crime for such losses, and some district attorneys' offices have the policy of informing the victim of this right. However, the right is more theoretical than real if the perpetrator lacks financial resources.

In discussing alternatives to incarceration, we will consider restitution by the offender. Compensation of victims by the state is provided for in 24 states, and 16 have such legislation pending.

Of the 24 extant programs, only Virginia's bars compensation for lost earnings. No state compensates for lost property, but all 24 compensate for medical expenses. Five of these states limit compensation to state residents, and 23 have filing deadlines which require that a claim be made within a limited period of time following the crime. All 24 compensate for burial expenses, 10 grant pensions, and 15 grant lump sum payments (9 offer either). The state of Nevada has a program only for compensation of "good samaritans," not of victims. Georgia compensates only persons who have helped police officers or helped to prevent a crime.

These programs can be costly. New York, one of two states that sets no limit on overall benefits (Washington is the other), spent $3.1 million in 1975. California, which limits payments to $23,000 at present, has paid out over $7 million.[20]

Victims, it seems, are no longer forgotten, at least in some states.

REFERENCES

1. Hindelang, M. J. *An analysis of Victimization Survey Results from the Eight Impact Cities: Summary Report*. Washington, D.C.: Law Enforcement Assistance Administration, U.S. Department of Justice, 1974; Albany, N.Y.: Criminal Justice Research Center, 1976.
2. Buder, L. Half of 1976 murder victims had police records. *The New York Times* August 28, 1977, Sect. 1, p. 1.
3. Hindelang, *Victimization Survey Results*, p. 51.
4. *Criminal Victimization Surveys in Eight American Cities: A comparison of 1971/72 and 1974/75 findings*. Washington, D.C.: Department of Justice, National Crime Survey Report, 1976.

5. Jones, C. and Aronson, E. Attribution of fault to a rape victim as a function of respectability of the victim. *Journal of Personality and Social Psychology* 1973, 26, 415–419.

6. Bickman, L. and Green, S. K. Is revenge sweet? The effect of attitude toward a thief on crime reporting. *Criminal Justice and Behavior* 1975, 2(2), 101–112.

7. Bickman, L. Attitude toward an authority and the reporting of a crime. *Sociometry* 1976, 39(1), 76–82.

8. Bickman, L. and Green, S. K. Situational cues and crime reporting: Do signs make a difference? *Journal of Applied Social Psychology* 1977, 7(1), 1–18.

9. Latané, B. and Darley, J. *The Unresponsive Bystander: Why Doesn't He Help?* New York: Appleton-Century-Crofts, 1970.

10. Kelman, H. C. Processes of opinion change. *Public Opinion Quarterly* 1961, 25, 57–78.

11. Gelfand, D. M., Hartmann, D. P., Walder, P., and Page, B. Who reports shoplifters? A field-experimental study. *Journal of Personality and Social Psychology* 1973, 25(2), 276–285.

12. Greenberg, M. S. An experimental approach to victim crime reporting. Paper presented at 84th Annual Convention, American Psychological Association, Washington, D.C., 1976.

13. Festinger, L. A theory of social comparison processes. *Human Relations* 1954, 7, 117–140.

14. For example, see Kerckhoff, A. C. and Back, K. W. *The June Bug: A Study of Hysterical Contagion.* New York: Appleton-Century-Crofts, 1968.

15. Bickman, L. Bystander intervention in a crime. Chapter 11 in E. C. Viano (Ed.) *Victims and Society.* Washington, D.C.: Visage Press, Inc., 1976.

16. Bickman, L., Lavrakas, P. J., Green, S. K., North-Walker, N., Edwards, J., Borkowski, S., Shane-DuBow, S., and Wuert, J. *National Evaluation Program Phase I Summary Report— Citizen Crime Reporting Projects.* Chicago: Applied Social Psychology Program, Loyola University of Chicago (undated).

17. Latané, B. and Darley, J. Situational determinants of bystander intervention in emergencies. In J. Macaulay and L. Berkowitz (Eds.) *Altruism and Helping Behavior.* New York: Academic Press, 1970.

18. Toch, H. (Ed.). *Legal and Criminal Psychology.* New York: Holt, Rinehart and Winston, 1961.

19. McDonald, W. F. Criminal justice and the victim: An introduction. Chapter 1 in W. F. McDonald (Ed.) *Criminal Justice and the Victim.* Beverly Hills: Sage Publications, Inc., 1976.

20. Rule, A. At last—Help for innocent victims of crime. *Good Housekeeping* July, 1977, 185(1), 84–93.

6
Police

This chapter will deal with a number of aspects of police work: those who do it, the processes by which they are selected, the training they receive, and their relationships with the civilians whose lives and property they protect.

CANDIDATE RECRUITMENT AND SELECTION

Probably many civilians, if they have considered the matter at all, think of those men and women who are attracted to police work as brave, lovers of adventure, and athletic. Like most stereotypes, this one may be true of some police candidates, but certainly not of all.

Niederhoffer, discussing the New York City Police Department in the 1960s, makes the point that prospective police officers are drawn to the job because it is *secure*. They can usually count on steady employment for at least 20 years, a sizable pension, and an opportunity for a second career commencing while they are relatively young. In fact, the pension has the effect of forcing the most experienced police officers to retire at an early age lest they, in effect, be working for half pay. The strength of their expectations of security may account, in part, for the great anger of young officers who unexpectedly found themselves laid off by New York City in 1975.

For various reasons, historical, economic, and cultural, interest in police work appears to be related to ethnicity. Lefkowitz reports data showing that motives for choosing police work differ between black and white officers and between Irish-American and other groups.

For many, police work amounts to a family tradition. A sizable proportion of new recruits are the sons, nephews, and brothers and, increasingly, the wives, daughters, nieces, and sisters of police officers. The strange hours that most police officers must work may discourage applicants who have not been accustomed to them by close contact with police relatives.

Police work often represents a sizable step up the socioeconomic ladder. There are a number of recruits from working or lower middle class backgrounds, to whom the pay, status, and benefits of police work are very attractive. The dangers are less likely to be taken seriously until the officers are out on the street, by which time their training and public commitment to police work probably compel them to minimize the perceived risk.

Many young officers are veterans whose applications were given preferential treatment because of their military service. In times of high unemployment, as in the 1930s and early 1970s, many persons seek appointment to police training who, at other times, would probably not do so. In 1973, the New York City Police Department had 6,000 anticipated openings for patrolman. Approximately 117,400 persons registered for and 51,655 actually took the test to qualify as police trainees. At the present time more and more police agencies are requiring applicants to complete from 6 to 30 or more college credits. The rationale is that professional status is important in winning public support for the police. Since professions require post-secondary education, college programs for police officers are proliferating, and college requirements for applicants are becoming increasingly common. Data pertinent to this development are discussed below.

Since the late 1960s, in the wake of the civil rights movement, women and minorities have applied for appointments in greater numbers. In this context, it is appropriate to consider who get the jobs and how the selections are made.

Selection Procedures.   Most large police departments have more or less elaborate selection procedures. Psychological testing, intelligence testing, investigation of applicants' backgrounds and private lives, and tests of physical fitness are commonplace. Are the tests of any value? Possibly so, but it would be very difficult to prove that they are.

In order to understand the process we have to consider the nature of personnel selection procedures in general and then apply them to police selection in particular.

Suppose you are the psychologically sophisticated personnel manager of a major business. Your task is to select, from among numerous candidates, those persons who can be expected to do the best job for your organization. How should you proceed?

The first thing you should do is think about the nature of the job in question and prepare a formal job description. What skills, talents, or aptitudes does it require? Must the candidate be attractive and well-groomed? Is an ability to deal with abstract concepts important? Does the job require physical stamina? Does it require the ability to get along with people of all types?

If you have done your job properly, you will be able to answer each of these questions positively *or negatively*, and you will be able to have a clear idea of the kind of person you want and to devise a limited number of procedures with which to screen candidates. You will probably wish to construct a test on which the candidate performs tasks similar to those the job requires. For example, to hire a secretary one might dictate a letter and ask the candidate to type it in a form suitable for mailing. The candidate's product could be evaluated in terms of spelling, neatness, speed, and so on.

Psychological Tests.   A psychological test is a sample of behavior taken under standard conditions to: (1) assess some personal characteristic of the testee and express it in numerical terms (e.g., an intelligence test or a classroom examination); (2) be used as a shortcut method of forcing a testee to respond in a contrived situation that permits conclusions to be drawn about the testee which would otherwise require prolonged observation (e.g., a personality test); (3) permit prediction of future behavior based on test performance (e.g., job selection or college admissions tests).

A good psychological test must have all of the following characteristics:

1. Reliability
2. Validity
3. Sensitivity
4. Ease of administration and scoring

Reliability refers to the repeatability of measurement. An unreliable test is analogous to an elastic tape measure, which will give a different reading each time the same object is measured. A test that is unreliable is, in fact, measuring nothing and is as useless as an elastic tape measure.

Validity refers to the test's ability to measure what it purports to measure. A test that is unreliable cannot be valid (if it does not measure anything, it surely cannot measure what it purports to measure), but a test can be reliable without being valid. For example, a highly accurate bathroom scale is, by definition, quite reliable, but if offered as an instrument for measuring intelligence, would be manifestly invalid.

Reliability of a psychological test or instrument may be demonstrated by administering the test to the same group of subjects on two different occasions. Each subject will then have two scores, and correlations may be calculated between the first and second administrations to determine whether the results are consistent. This method of establishing reliability is called *stability*. It can be used only if the attribute being measured is stable over the time interval between the two test sessions.

If the attribute being measured is relatively unstable, such as an attitude concerning a new rock group, reliability may be demonstrated by the method of *equivalence*. Here two equivalent forms of the same test are administered at the same time. If their two scores correlate, they must necessarily be measuring the same thing. They are, therefore, measuring *some* thing. In short, they are reliable.

There are several mutually independent types of validity:

1. Face validity
2. Content validity
3. Predictive validity
4. Concurrent validity
5. Construct validity

A test is said to have face validity if it appears "on its face" to measure what it purports to measure. For example, a test of marital happiness based on the number of subjects that a couple fights about might be thought to have face validity. This would be so if one's theory was that the more subjects the two fight over, the more fights they have, and, the more fights they have, the less happy the marriage. But it may be that there is a real need for these emotional exchanges in both parties. In fact, their ability to express hostile feelings freely to one another may be the basis for a very strong relationship. Face validity, then, is no validity at all. However, the presence or absence of face validity can affect the layman's acceptance or rejection of a psychological instrument.

Content validity relates to the definition of a psychological test as a *sample* of behavior. The tester is not really interested in the specific responses made to the test items *per se*, but in what these responses reflect about a larger population: all the possible items that might have been included if time permitted. Content validity is established by an expert's saying that the test is a representative sample of the larger population of items that could have been used. This may seem very similar to face validity, since the expert appears to be saying that the test "looks good." The difference is in the key word "expert." Being an expert implies that there is something to be expert about. That is, there are objective standards by which it can be determined how good a sample a test is. Content validity is the most common method of validating classroom examinations.

Predictive validity involves demonstrating that a test effectively predicts some future behavior or criterion. This is demonstrated by giving the test to all persons who are later to be evaluated on this criterion, waiting until they have achieved a score on the criterion or job performance rating, and then correlating the two sets of scores. If the correlation is high, the test may then be used to predict future criterion scores of other testees.

Concurrent validity is demonstrated in an identical manner except that the criterion score is available at the same time as the test score. For example, one might wish to compare a brief and inexpensive diagnostic test with a more costly and extensive schedule of diagnostic interviews. If both procedures yield the same diagnosis, the test is said to have concurrent validity.

All of the foregoing methods of validating tests are independent of one another. An instrument may have a great deal of one type of validity and none at all of another.

Construct validity must be resorted to in those situations in which there is no other way to validate a test. For example, there may be no expert around to declare it a representative sample of some larger universe of items, there is nothing it predicts, and there is no other instrument measuring the same attribute with which to correlate it.

In such a case, one must create a hypothetical construct, a mini-theory which specifies the variables that ought to be related to the one in question. One proceeds to determine the extent to which these variables are related to one's test of the hypothetical construct. For example, it might be expected that a new test of "Ethical Standards" would correlate with church attendance. If so, more frequent attenders would have higher scores on the Ethical Standards test than less frequent attenders. If the data verified this and similar predictions, there would be some evidence of construct validity.

Construct validity is the least preferred method of validation because we can establish it least firmly.

To the extent that an employment test encompasses all of the skills necessary to a job, it may be said to have content validity. To the extent that it accurately predicts how well the candidate would perform if hired immediately, the test has concurrent validity. If the test predicts not how well the candidate would perform now, but how well he or she would perform in the future, after training or "breaking in," the test has predictive validity.

If one's private definition of a good secretary includes brewing great coffee and being an effective public relations agent, typing and stenographic skills may be less important, and a test based only on these skills will have little validity of any type. Steno and typing skills may be necessary but not sufficient for ultimate success.

Selection of Police Officers. Selecting effective police officers is a very difficult task for several reasons. For one thing, there is no widespread agreement as to the criterion for being a "good cop." For some, it is being an incorruptible person who keeps the streets free of crime. For others, it is being someone the people in the neighborhood can relate to, an officer willing to pass the time of day, who overlooks the familiar double-parker's bad habit, and stops for a cup of coffee in the luncheonette. Some view the "good cop" as the one who can react quickly in crisis and who makes the most arrests. Others think of the "good cop" as one who helps people in trouble but issues few summonses. Until there is some degree of consensus about what the characteristics of a "good cop" are, it is not possible to develop a valid procedure for selecting one. Such a criterion is unlikely. What would be desired in one type of situation or beat would be undesirable in another. It may be that flexibility and adaptability are the important dimensions.

Since there is no single criterion for a police officer's job performance, it is not possible to design an effective selection test which meets the requirements described above. One well-established criterion in selecting police officers is the need to exclude from the force those who are likely to bring disgrace upon the department. In fact, the proportion of officers who get into difficulty is very small. This may reflect well on the selection procedures used; it may simply indicate the reluctance of police officers to investigate one another. Even if there were additional well-established criteria, it would be a foolish administrator who would advocate hiring all who took a selection test regardless of their scores (particularly for a job involving the carrying of weapons and the exercise of substantial authority); yet that is precisely what one would have to do at the outset to evaluate a selection test properly.

In short, a genuinely validated screening procedure is not likely to be employed for police officers.

In effect, the goal is not the selection of the best candidates for police work, but rather the exclusion of those who appear most likely to do poorly. The selection task is made more difficult by the fact that since relatively few officers get into trouble, they are unlikely to be identifiable in advance for statistical reasons. Further, since those with questionable test scores are not given a chance to show what they can do, there is no way to know whether the requirements are too strict. The cut-off points may exclude many competent people, as well as a few who would be poor risks.

Another reason that it is difficult for outsiders to evaluate the efficacy of screening methods is the secrecy with which most police agencies surround themselves. Police departments are extremely reluctant to permit "outsiders" access to personnel records because they include information about people working "under cover" whose identities must be kept confidential. Also, some of the information gathered about applicants is of a very personal nature. Lastly, the police department is a partisan in an adversary system of justice, and its records may have strategic value in legal proceedings. Thus, those forms that are made available to researchers are frequently so vague as to be useless.

A 1972 review of literature on police selection by Kent and Eisenberg was concerned, in part, with predictive validity as described above. Four types of predictors and four types of criteria were distinguished by these authors.

The types of predictors used were:

1. Psychological tests of various types, including measures of intelligence, aptitudes, interests, and personality.

2. Biographical data concerning ethnicity, education, work history, and so on.
3. Situational tests in which the applicant is confronted with a task similar to one likely to be encountered on the job.
4. Standard civil service examinations of the paper-and-pencil variety.

Criteria of job performance included:

1. Grades in the Police Academy.
2. Premature retirement or dismissal.
3. Performance ratings by supervisors.
4. Objective measures, including number of arrests made, commendations, complaints, promotions, and the like.

Their review of a substantial number of studies left Kent and Eisenberg generally dissatisfied with the quality of the research and with the reasonableness of conclusions drawn by the authors whose work they cited. They concluded that some of these predictors have *potential* value for selection, but more and better research is necessary if their validity is to be confirmed. The only clear-cut evidence that the screening procedures studied predict anything is that recruits who score well on intelligence and some aptitude tests do better at the Academy than those who score poorly. Since a good deal of the Academy training is "academic," that is not very surprising. If the more intelligent don't do well, who will? Such tests are generally designed to measure "intelligence" in an academic sense.

Kent and Eisenberg did single out one study as especially laudable, that by M. Baehr and her associates, who sought to develop or validate predictors of performance of members of the Chicago Police Department. They used several innovative tests of motivation, intellect, aptitude, and behavior, as well as a number of standard techniques.

Consistent with our description of what one must do to select an employee, these writers undertook an in-depth analysis of the nature of police work. They concluded that there are 20 behavioral or psychological requirements for effective police work. These include, for example: the ability to endure monotony; to make prompt, effective decisions; and to endure verbal abuse.

As criteria they used data routinely maintained by the Chicago Police Department: absenteeism, number of arrests during 1966, the ratio of complaints to sustained complaints, citations, and so forth. The criteria were selected because the authors had confidence that the Chicago Police Department records on these points were accurate, meaningful, and available.

The major criterion was evaluated by a technique known as *paired-comparison* ratings. In this technique, which greatly increases the likelihood that data will be reliable, each of a group of patrolmen was compared with every other officer in the group by a supervisor who knew all of them well. For every pair of patrolmen (A and B, A and C, B and C, etc.) the sergeant or lieutenant was asked which man "is the better performer on the street—which is the better patrolman in terms of performance in the field?"[1] The alert reader will have noted how ambiguous the word "better" is and will wonder whether all raters interpreted this term similarly. Apparently they did. The ratings were reliable and did correlate with several predictors.

This praiseworthy study notwithstanding, recruitment and selection of police officers continues to be problematic. In a speech to the American Psychological Association, Crosby related some of the problems to the philosophies and traditions of police personnel management. Many departments, he noted, follow a military model of organization. Like the military, these departments require not only a rigorous program of training, but also very explicit standards of deportment and appearance, often extending to off-duty hours. Whether or not by design, they encourage strong feelings of in-group loyalty, of pride in the uniform, of being different from the "civilian" population. Each officer has specific, well-defined responsibilities and is led to expect that, in the course of a 20-year career, there will be few changes in the way things are done.

Crosby asserted that these expectations are unrealistic. In reality, there is change in the characteristics of the citizenry, the community, and public mores. A police officer's job involves numerous ambiguities and discretionary judgments. Also, police officers return daily to their families and neighborhoods and to the demands of civilian life.

A second issue is the seeking by police agencies of what Crosby calls the "supercop," a real-life equivalent of the TV hero, with whom, lamentably, our readers are probably all too familiar.

These two factors are among those responsible for the rather rigid procedures commonly used in police selection. Instead of there being freedom to select individuals with particular skills that could be utilized in most good-sized departments, applicants are sought who, in theory, can do everything fairly well, rather than some things especially well. Applicants are sought who will adhere unquestioningly to paramilitary standards of appearance and attitude, rather than bring individuality and creativity to the police task.

All departments do not seek applicants with identical virtues, however. A 1973 news story[2] indicated that recruitment standards varied even within a relatively small geographic area around New York City. One county required applicants to have two years of college; others required only a high school diploma. Height, age, and weight standards also varied, partly in relation to the ethnic group in the community. For instance, where there are numerous Hispanics, the minimum height is lower than where there are few.

Among communities that differ in location and size there are even wider differences in the standards applied in the selection of police officers. Major studies of these standards have been conducted in few places, generally the larger cities. Funds and personnel are required to conduct such studies, and small towns and rural communities are unlikely to have enough of either.

Wall and Culloo list standards of several states for selecting law enforcement personnel. U.S. citizenship was required (as of 1973) in only 28 states and Washington, D.C. The minimum age was 21 in 19 states, 20 in four states, 18 in four others. Philadelphia and Houston began appointing teen-age police officers in 1970 and 1966, respectively,[3] a controversial move, particularly at a time when major departments had begun moving toward professionalization. The upper age limit for recruits ranged from 29 in New York (except for veterans, who were given an additional year for each year of military service), to 60 in Iowa.

Twenty-six states require that applicants have no criminal record. Some cities are seeking young recruits before they have acquired a record of antisocial behavior, especially a factor where the youths live in high crime areas.

Half the states require a physical examination. Among those that do, standards vary. For example, Alabama and Kansas accept applicants as short as 5'2"; New Hampshire sets a minimum of 5'8". In New York, minimum height requirements have been lowered, but an applicant may not be taller than 6'5". In Alabama, maximum height may be 6'10".

Wall and Culloo point out some less common requirements. Indiana requires a minimum I.Q. of 90. South Carolina requires a credit check. Several states require psychological testing, although few tests are in general use among them.

A large community with a sizable police department might be expected to employ a procedure of this sort: Applicants first take a Civil Service examination which measures their general level of information, skills, or aptitudes. Passing that, they are subjected to an intensive investigation of their backgrounds. Any of a number of findings could jeopardize their appointment: arrests, marital difficulties, indebtedness, a poor driving record, "immoral" habits, "poor character," and so on. The applicant who survives the investigation may be required to take a battery of psychological tests. One of those most often used is the Minnesota Multiphasic Personality Inventory (MMPI), an extensive paper-and-pencil test that purports to reveal tendencies toward pathologies of various kinds. The MMPI yields a set of scores called a profile. The various scores that comprise the profile are compared with *norms* (average scores of large numbers of people—in this case, people with a given pathological diagnosis). If any scores are unusually high, indicating possible peculiarities, (e.g., excessive suspiciousness or aggressiveness), the applicant may be interviewed by a psychologist or psychiatrist, who may employ additional tests in assessing the risk involved in appointing the applicant.

The applicant who is permitted to undergo training is, of course, on probation not only while in training but for six months or more after training has been completed. Any transgression during this period is likely to cause dismissal from the department. Police officers, in general, are very vulnerable in this respect. Rightly or wrongly, many feel that they are under almost constant surveillance by "shoo-flies," undercover police officers who are waiting to catch them in the most trivial error. Some years ago, a study was conducted in New York City of the readiness of officers to return, intact, "lost" wallets containing various amounts of money. Not everyone returned them. The Patrolman's Benevolent Association leadership, greatly angered by this study, conducted a similar one with civilian subjects and demonstrated that civilians were less trustworthy than the police.

Recruitment and Selection of Minorities.   Efforts to recruit minority officers in order to improve police–community relations and services have brought with them a great deal of controversy about traditional and new selection procedures. One traditional technique has been the paper-and-pencil test. Tests of this sort have many advantages: they can be administered efficiently, to many people at once; they can be scored objectively, often by computer; they have been validated, albeit for purposes which may be totally different from that for which they are used in police selection.

There is some evidence, however, that tests of this sort discriminate against minority groups.[4] If it had been shown that these tests predict police performance, those concerned about discrimination would be hard-pressed to justify discarding these selection procedures. As has been shown, though, there is no hard evidence that most paper-and-pencil tests do relate to performance on *this* job. Therefore, the charge of discrimination is a more difficult one to dismiss than it would otherwise be. If the test does not distinguish police officers who will be effective from those who will be ineffective, and if it is related more to ethnicity than to police performance, why should it be continued in use? One reason is that the tests are a tradition in police selection, and traditions are very hard to overcome. Another is that we have nothing very compelling with which to replace them. A third is that many police officers and civilians maintain that dispensing with these tests would lead to a "lowering of standards" among new recruits, this despite the fact that the relationship between test performance and job performance (presumably the pertinent criterion) is very weak.

Following a review of some of these issues, Eisenberg and Reinke propose an alternative procedure to be used when a truly "culture-free" test is developed. They propose that there are some characteristics of police candidates which are legitimately pertinent to performance as a police officer. These include:

1. Height and weight, vision, and age, as well as minimum levels of education, and U.S. citizenship.
2. Some aspects of personal background, including psychological and family adjustment as assessed by psychological tests, personal interviews, and lie detector tests.
3. Successful completion of a probationary period.

Since some of these requirements may themselves discriminate against members of minorities, they must be weighed with respect to their pertinence to job performance.

Margolis, in a report for the United States Commission on Civil Rights, evaluated the efforts of five cities to increase minority recruitment. He studied in particular the police departments of Detroit, Miami, Washington, Denver, and Waterloo, and the State Police of Michigan, California, and Connecticut. His findings indicated a number of ways in which recruitment and selection standards interfered with attempts to encourage minority applicants:

1. Minimum height requirements, especially those of state police agencies, may place Hispanics and Orientals at a disadvantage.

2. Educational requirements have a similar effect on minority applicants, particularly where what is required is not a high school diploma but from 6 to 30 college credits. This more stringent requirement is spreading because the complex demands of police work, particularly in urban communities, are said to require better trained and educated officers. There is no compelling evidence, however, that better educated police perform their jobs better, and there is some evidence that the better educated officers resign prematurely to seek other jobs.

3. The long and complex application form is a barrier. Fear of failure and a sense of being unwanted may inhibit some persons from returning it; others appear to view it as a means of justifying their rejection.

4. Most formidable among the hurdles is the written test. In some communities as many as 90% of black applicants have failed it. Such tests are often abbreviated intelligence tests of the sort used to predict academic success. The assumption is made that such tests measure the subject's native ability and that to do poorly is to be insufficiently intelligent for police work. It is widely documented, though, that many of these tests discriminate in favor of the better educated, the middle class, and against those whose schooling has been substandard or whose home life has not been preoccupied with book

learning. Margolis quotes one expert who suggested that a better indicator of success as a police officer would be what the applicant has accomplished in his own life and milieu, not his ability to report the meaning of R.S.V.P., as is required on one such test. It is worth reiterating that none of these tests has been shown to be correlated with the officer's on-the-job performance, although some have accurately predicted success in the Police Academy.

5. Background investigations appear to arouse suspicion among some minority applicants as to the police department's true attitude toward recruiting them. If the interviewer is prejudiced and/or the applicant's circumstances are not consistent with the majority's standards, the applicant may be at a disadvantage.

Some screening procedures may have validity. Margolis believes that personality and lie detector tests can be used to reveal antisocial attitudes and tendencies (including extreme racism). He evidently has much more confidence in lie detection than the present authors have. Medical examinations also may have validity, although they, too, have the potential for discriminating against minority applicants. For example, some respiratory disorders that are more common among urban dwellers may prevent appointment to a department, and Margolis suggests that there may be an anti-urban bias in some of these procedures.

Assuming that an applicant clears all of the foregoing hurdles, and knows how to drive and (in some communities) to swim, the applicant may be admitted to the Police Academy, where another hurdle is waiting, a hurdle that generally gives more difficulty to minorities than to other recruits. This will be commented on below.

The New York Times has described the efforts of a number of cities from coast to coast to recruit black applicants by employing black recruiters, shorter forms, and special recruitment vehicles driven into predominantly black neighborhoods.[5] But, Margolis pointed out that, in 1971 at least, most black and Hispanic applicants *were* ultimately rejected. Perhaps this makes their reluctance to apply more comprehensible. The *Times* reported that among these cities there were poor results in nearly every case. The exception was Washington, D.C., whose campaign was especially imaginative and persistent.

Despite all of these difficulties there are growing numbers of blacks and other minorities being employed as police officers in many areas. The Washington effort yielded 1,000 more black officers, raising the percentage in the department from 24.4 in 1968 to 35.9 in 1970. (At the time 75% of Washington's population was black.) Several books and articles have appeared concerning the black police officer,[6] who is often subjected to pressures from the public and from fellow officers that are not directed at whites. Female officers, another growing minority among police, are discussed below.

POLICE TRAINING

What is taught in the Academy? In a 1969 investigation entitled *Police Training and Performance Study*, a detailed description was given of the curriculum of the New York City Police Academy. The curriculum has been altered since, but the general content remains unchanged.

In 1968 there was a 26-hour introduction to the police career. Topics discussed were the police mission, organizational structure and functions, and ethical and other standards. Seventy-two hours were devoted to police procedures and techniques. What does the officer do in the event of an accident or illness? What procedures govern the tasks of patrol, traffic duty, summonses, and arrests? How does the officer proceed in investigating complaints or in securing prisoners? Aspects of government and law were covered for 66 hours. Included were discussions of the relationships among various branches of city government, the structure and functions of the courts, criminal law, municipal law, and the care and handling of evidence. The role of the police in human and race relations was discussed for 65 hours. Almost a fourth of this time was concerned with causes of crime and delinquency. Among other issues considered were human relations, the Constitution and due process, the history of the Negro in America, and Puerto Rican culture and customs.

Field trips and practice in driving skills consumed 83 hours. The total academic program (in 1968) consisted of 312 hours. Firearms training consumed 56 hours, during which the recruit fired 340 rounds at distances from 7 to 25 yards. Training in self-defense, first-aid, riot control, and so forth, took an additional 192 hours. This study proposes a longer program of training, the inclusion of some civilian instructors, and more on-the-job experience.

Since the time of the study, recruits have been required to attend college courses for one day per week for a semester. They have been assigned to field training officers, i.e., experienced officers who are entrusted with the responsibility of developing good habits of patrol among the young officers assigned to them. In a number of major police departments, approaches such as transactional analysis and sensitivity training are part of the curriculum.

The point made by Margolis that training should be made more relevant to the job is echoed by McEvoy, who points out that studies of the patrolman's activities show that from 75 to 90% of his time is spent on noncriminal matters.

The Minority Trainee.   The minority trainee is likely to be unique among the trainees, and, in fact, there may be no minority-group faculty on the Academy staff. He may be required to conform to standards of grooming that are uncommon in his own group, such as a very short haircut, no facial hair or sideburns. The discipline is strict. He may feel awkward about discussing personal problems with anyone and may get little or no encouragement or feedback. To the extent that grades on written exams are critical in the Academy, the minority trainee may be at a disadvantage if he did not develop studying or test-taking skills in school. Margolis argues that the curriculum ought to stress human relations skills rather than articulateness or physical training. Badalamente et al. also urge that police receive training for their social role. Nowadays police are called upon to perform social work functions more often than law enforcement functions and, in many departments, this part of the job is virtually ignored during training.

JOB DESCRIPTION OF A POLICE OFFICER

Whenever one moves from one niche in life to another, whether from single to married, from high school to employment or to college, from convicted felon to prison inmate, one has to learn "the ropes." One learns from more experienced others which behaviors are expected, which are unacceptable, what the range of acceptable behaviors is (norms). In short, one becomes part of a new culture, or, if a small child, learns the values and norms of one's own culture. This process is called *socialization*, and, as we have tried to show, it continues in one form or another throughout life.

One of the authors had an opportunity to teach large numbers of police trainees and probationary patrolmen (and patrolwomen) in a college of criminal justice. Because some graduated from the Police Academy while still attending his course in Social Psychology, it was possible to suggest as a term paper topic a diary of the transition from trainee to officer. The author of the following account worked for a major metropolitan police department. He was assigned for his first tour to a precinct with a moderately high crime rate.

Today was my first day in the ___ precinct and I was anxious to find out what police work is really like. But just as in the Academy, we spent eight hours in class learning about the problems of the community we would work in and about the various groups that lived there. Puerto Ricans are the majority in the area; others are Greeks, Blacks and Irish. We were briefed about prostitution, robbery, homosexual beatings as well as such customs as sitting on the steps in the summer drinking beer. I was disappointed at not meeting the people but . . . it's certainly an improvement over the old way of sending guys right out onto the street with no information about what's going on. I'll probably get pretty anxious before my next tour 'cause I've got the next two days off.

(Three days later) Well, today finally arrived. I was assigned to patrol ___ Street with an experienced officer. Now I was worried about how I'd do and about looking like an idiot to all the people on the street.

We'd been patrolling about 15 minutes when we got a complaint about an armed robbery about a block from where we were. We got there and found an old lady very upset by the robbery. My partner has been on the job a long time and he took charge while I listened to try to find out how to act, how to be compassionate and understanding of what she'd gone through. She was relieved to see us and tried hard to describe the people and the property that was stolen. My partner asked the questions. I kept quiet and filled out the complaint report. We turned in the report and went back on patrol. Seeing us walking in the cold a lot of people greeted us with smiles. They seemed glad to see us. I became less afraid of how I'd do my job. By just being there I was helping people. They were relieved to see us standing there in uniform at night. I had never thought of how just seeing us makes shoppers feel less tense and afraid of getting mugged.

I didn't accomplish much my first night but my presence on ___ Street was enough for the people who live there and so the first night seemed worthwhile to me.

(Two days later) Today I was assigned to a radio car and was told that since it was Saturday it would probably be a busy night. I knew that anyhow since there would probably be a lot of drinking and partying going on. It started slow. We stopped for coffee. I went into the shop and got two light coffees. When I tried to pay for them by reaching over the counter with a dollar in my hand the guy refused to take it. I really felt like a fool. The people were looking at me and the proprietor was getting annoyed. Finally, I told him I needed the change for cigarettes. When he gave it to me, I left fifty cents on the counter and walked out.

It was the first time I realized how hard it would be to please the people. They get offended when you don't accept their gratitude. They see nothing wrong in your accepting coffee and they're offended if you don't. I discussed it with my partner and he said I'd done the right thing and that sometimes things aren't as easy as I'd been taught in the Academy. Paper and people are different things. I knew he was showing the effects of 14 years on the street in this precinct; he knows a lot more about dealing with the people than I do with all my book learning.

Well, as the night went on we got a couple of motorists for moving violations. I observed what kind of tact to use—being courteous and keeping your cool while being called every so-and-so in the book. Then we got a call for my first dispute. We arrived at a rundown apartment building and were walking through a really smelly hallway when we heard the sound of crashing and several people screaming. We knocked and identified ourselves. The noise inside lessened. We were let in and observed two males and three females, apparently intoxicated, arguing over who kicked in the door of one of the girls' apartment on the floor above. While we were trying to find out the facts, a back-up arrived. It was very confusing to me with all the different stories that were being told: one male was chasing the girl with a butcher knife and she wanted him locked up and the other girl wanted the third girl to pay for the door that was kicked in. When we got them separated my partner's skill came through. We found out that two of the girls were lesbians and one of them locked the door on the other and she kicked it in and that the male downstairs threw a butcher knife at the lesbian to keep her away from his girl friend. After twenty minutes of arguing and trying to keep them apart no one would press charges. We told them if we got called again we would take them all in. That seemed to quiet them and they went to their separate apartments.

Even after the incident I was still confused about the whole thing. I hadn't handled myself very well. I'd kept almost completely quiet except when separating the parties (sometimes physically). My partner told me not to worry about it; he said it takes experience. There were a couple of other, minor, incidents but I'd rather be busy and on the go anytime.

(The next afternoon, the 4–12 tour) I'm still assigned to a radio car. Tonight was to be a slow night. Most people were getting ready to go to work Monday morning. But it turned out to be a good summons night for me because of the activity at ___ (an entertainment center). I learned how to fill out a parking summons and served five of them. The rest of the time we cruised our sector with very little activity. My partner told me Sunday night is usually a quiet tour so most of the time we talked and found out a lot about each other.

(The next day) Today was my first aided case. It was a sight to see. A wino had fallen down the stairs and hit his head on a radiator. The top of his head was split open and the blood was just gushing down his head. We called for an ambulance and put a towel on his head and told him he was going to the hospital. He insisted he wanted to go to bed, that he was tired and didn't want to go to the hospital. My feelings were colder than they should have been. I'd seen men wounded in Viet Nam and rushed around frantically trying to help them but I didn't do it in this case. I felt sorry for him but in a sense I didn't because of his attitude. He didn't care if he lived or died. Finally the ambulance came and they removed the towel from his head. This time I really saw how bad the gash was and my stomach turned when they told me to carry him down the stairs. I grabbed him and told him not to move his head but it was like talking to a wall. After I'd placed him in the ambulance I was covered with his blood on my hands and uniform. After this the rest of the tour and especially lunch hour was ruined and left me wondering if I was cut out for these kinds of jobs.

(Three days later) The same thing started out today. We were cruising when a bystander pointed out to us a man lying flat on the sidewalk. My partner told me to see what was wrong. In my mind, I expected this to be another wino. While I was bending over him, the incident from the other day came to mind and later I realized how prejudiced I was about someone who was sick thinking he was on a trip or drunk. When I grabbed the man he opened his eyes and was startled at the sight of the blue uniform. In an unclear voice he said that he was an epileptic and had just had an attack. We helped him stand up and asked him if he wanted an ambulance or to be taken to the hospital. He asked us to take him home, instead. When we got him into the car we learned that four patrolmen had mistaken him for an OD or a drunk and had stood him against a wall and left him there with instructions to "Get lost." We arrived at his house and asked him if everything was all right. He said he had medicine at home and thanked us. He was still in a daze but was talking a lot more clearly now.

Thinking back over the incident I felt that if he had been a wino I'd have treated him a lot more harshly than I would have before the aided case earlier in the week.

Before I knew he had had an attack I grabbed him . . . rudely and asked . . . arrogantly what the matter was. When I learned the nature of the problem I became gentle and understanding just as I should have been whether he was a wino or a drunk or anyone else for that matter.

This account of a police officer's first week on the job in a busy precinct paves the way for a discussion of several issues pertinent to the socialization of a police officer and to the actual requirements of the job.

J. G. Rubin discussed the similarity between establishing one's identity as an adult and establishing one's identity as a police officer. A number of the points he made echo the reactions of the young patrolman just quoted.

Rubin saw the identity *qua* police officer as shaped by six functions that officers are called upon to perform: maintaining order, fighting crime, providing community service, and performing paramilitary, quasi-judicial, and possibly establishment-protective activities. He suggested that conflicts arising from the first three functions are the most serious for the young officer. Providing the kinds of community services that our student offered the "wino" and the epileptic is different from what many police officers feel is their major responsibility, catching criminals. This is so despite the fact that study after study has shown community service and maintenance of public order (e.g., at parades, strikes, demonstrations, and so forth) occupy the great majority of the working hours of the officer. Unlike our student, who, in his first week at least, felt welcomed and appreciated by the public, many officers feel otherwise. Rubin described the hostility that greeted the officers he rode with in the black community of Miami. George Kirkham, a criminologist-policeman, describes a similar feeling in Jacksonville–Duval County, Florida.

Rubin noted that service calls leave the officer with a lack of closure. That is, he does not know the ultimate outcome of his intervention in a dispute or of his aid to an injured citizen. Hence, he has no feeling of accomplishment such as accompanies the arrest, booking, and jailing of a lawbreaker. This frustration is compounded when the same family or individual repeatedly comes to the officer's attention with no apparent resolution of the problem. Even when an arrest is made, many policemen find that the offender is back on the street (on bail or released on his own recognizance) before they have completed the paper work required with each arrest.

In most communities, police officers spend the bulk of their tours patrolling either on foot or in a car. Rubin reported data which suggest that at least 3.6 hours of every eight-hour tour are devoted to cruising around and around the same area. He found that contact with citizens averaged 3.6 hours per shift.[7] In describing the personality of police recruits, Rubin indicated that most are not introspective, i.e., they look to the world around them for stimulation.

Recently, the term "sensation-seeking" has been applied to persons who have a high need for novelty and change in the stimuli around them. This trait, in combination with a tendency to restlessness and a dislike of routine, means that patrolling is itself a source of boredom and tension. Our student expressed this view when he wrote, "I'd rather be busy and on the go anytime." In many communities not much happens on a typical weekday evening. Patrolling gets tedious.

One mode of coping with boredom is "cooping," the practice of sleeping in an out-of-the-way spot for a few hours during the tour. Most experienced commanders have a pretty good idea of where the favorite coops are located, and some assign other officers to keep track of those patrolling with special attention to the coops. The situation is much worse when the patrolman is riding alone and has no partner with whom to pass the time in conversation. Rubin reported that some officers will initiate contact with civilians during the quiet hours. On occasion sexual liaisons have been reported.

Another characteristic of police officers is what Rubin called a healthy suspiciousness. On night patrol, particularly in a community where the officer feels vulnerable and afraid, this valuable trait may give way to paranoid-like fears and prejudices. It may even develop into an inability to discriminate between the law-abiding and the trouble-making citizens.

Our student was concerned, as most young police officers are, with providing service and protection to the community. In the evaluation and advancement of police officers, these services do not always receive adequate recognition. No one gets a medal because he helped a heart attack victim or because no crimes were committed on his beat in two months. Prestige and advancement come from the "good collar" (i.e., an arrest which will be sustained in court), or a newsworthy arrest. As a consequence, crime fighting quickly becomes the focus of the officer's attention.

These forces—boredom, dislike of routine, suspiciousness, restlessness, rewards for some but not for other police functions, and so on—may serve to estrange the officer from the public. The "tough cop" image begins to take priority over that of the "public servant."

Rubin offered some recommendations for clarifying the roles of the police officer in order to reduce the variety of expectations the officer must meet and to provide both civilian and officer with a more clear-cut concept of what police work entails. He suggested that there be two distinct functions: crime prevention and crime fighting. The former would be attempted by enhancing community service efforts. This approach encourages good relations with the citizens and increases the likelihood of their cooperation in maintaining surveillance in the neighborhood and in supporting police efforts to keep the peace.

In this context, Rubin discussed the neighborhood police team—a group of officers who become familiar with and known to the community to which they are permanently assigned. Their tasks are to keep the peace, prevent crime, control traffic, and, in general, provide community services. Ideally, the rewards to the team members would be for preventing crime, a criterion that may be evaluated by using the crime statistics of previous years as a baseline.

The present authors disagree with the view that traffic control is a desirable police function. The problem is that the only contact of the average middle class citizen with the police or court system occurs when he or she receives a citation for a traffic violation. This is not a desirable type of contact if it is desired to enhance the esteem with which the public regards the police department, particularly if the individual officer is less than courteous. If the attitude of the public toward the police is to be improved, it might be a good idea to assign traffic violations to an independent agency such as the New York City meter maids who issue parking violations. In general, though, the concept of a neighborhood police team is a promising one.

One such team has recently been described as having had beneficial effects on the tensions in a crime-ridden section of Brooklyn.[8] Officers there visit residents in their homes and stores. Each of the 110 officers assigned to the area was asked to become acquainted with residents and merchants on one or two of the 130 blocks in the precinct. Officers began to help organize block associations and to attend their meetings. Those who saw this as inconsistent with their image of police work reportedly have been won over. Violent crimes are fewer. Help to officers in difficulty is commonplace where, a few years ago, it would have been very rare. Police and civilians have begun to know one another as individuals and not as an occupying army and a hostile citizenry. Stereotypes on both sides have been broken down, and both police and civilians feel safer knowing that they know each other and can freely turn to one another for assistance.

The neighborhood police team represents an application of social psychological principles from several sources. It has long been thought that one way to reduce intergroup prejudice is to bring about contact between the prejudiced person and his target so that the two parties meet as equals.[9] It has also long been known that a way to reduce hostility between groups is to provide the two groups in conflict with a superordinate goal, one in which the efforts of both are needed if either is to achieve its goal.[10] To the extent that either side employs labels in categorizing the other ("Pig," "Nigger," "Hippie") no need is felt to know the other. The label says it all. If A knows that B is a _____, A has no other interest in B and will react to B strictly as a _____. In the same way opponents in war employ labels for the foe—"Huns," "Gooks," and so forth. It is much easier to direct violence at someone who is a _____ than at someone who is a living, breathing person, perhaps a parent, perhaps a poet.

More recent research has shown that to gain cooperation in major things, it helps to start by gaining cooperation in minor things.[11] The police officer or civilian who feels free to ask the other for a match or the right time will more likely feel free to ask the other's help in an emergency.

Further, if policeman and civilian perceive themselves as friends under ordinary circumstances, they will be much less likely to interact violently in times of crisis.[12]

This line of argument is consistent with the call by Reiss for recognition of the interdependence of police and citizenry in the effective execution of police functions. Each must be able to trust the other.

Family Crisis Intervention.   In addition to the general responsibility for crime prevention, individual officers might specialize in any of several areas. One that has recently received considerable attention is family crisis intervention.

Just as many more homicides involve friends or relatives than strangers, most injuries to police officers occur when they are called upon to take action in family disputes or other disturbances between parties in close social relationships. Growing numbers of police departments have begun to take action to train officers for effective intervention. Some, who have been on the job for several years, may resist such training because they do not want to be "social workers." New training programs have been implemented, however, which are consistent with changes in the perception of police functions.

The best-known program of training was designed by M. Bard. Eighteen of 42 experienced officers who volunteered for this program in New York were selected to undergo training. Each had shown aptitude for family crisis intervention. Their training included over 160 hours in four successive weeks at City College in New York. The goals of the training were to provide a background in the behavioral sciences that was pertinent to the job and gradually to bring about some attitude change and insight concerning the nature of family conflict intervention. The on-campus training included lectures on family patterns and problems within different ethnic groups, role-playing of intervention techniques, field trips to facilities to which referrals might be made, and human relations or sensitivity training.

A student of the authors had been among the 18 selected, and he gave the following description of the sort of learning that he had experienced. Prior to this training his custom in dealing with family disputes had been to threaten his way into the apartment, shout down the quarreling family members, ask whether A wanted B arrested, tell them to keep quiet, and leave. He learned in the training to think of himself not as a disciplinarian but as a helper, to respect the fact that he was in someone else's home, to try to listen to the conflicting sides and lower the level of tension, and to make suggestions designed to encourage the parties to seek help for themselves. One technique that he found helpful in lowering the tension was to ask the man of the house for permission to smoke. While his intervention might otherwise have been a threat to the latter's manhood (which might then be asserted violently), this simple act reestablished the man's status in the situation, signaled respect for the family and their home, and shifted attention away from the matter at issue to the new person present, who could then more easily be perceived as a nonthreatening helper.

For two years after the training had been completed a single radio car answered all family crisis calls in the experimental precinct. The car, which patrolled in the usual fashion when not required in a crisis, was staffed around-the-clock by members of the Unit. Psychological consultants were available to the officers, and group training sessions continued for a time. Both of these measures helped to strengthen the new attitudes and behaviors as well as to provide clarification of abstract concepts and mutual support. (The consultants benefited at least as much as the officers from the sessions; they had had stereotypes of their own that they learned to overcome.)

The training program was evaluated by means of comparison with an adjacent precinct. In general, there were more interventions by police and more homicides in the experimental precinct than in the neighboring one. But, in the 962 families visited by the Family Crisis Intervention Unit (FCIU), there was no homicide although family homicides increased in general during the same period. There were fewer family assaults in the experimental precinct, and no FCIU officer suffered any injury.

The reader will recall Rubin's suggestion that, in the interests of reducing role identity confusion, police functions be divided into crime prevention and crime fighting. He advocated that the latter group of officers not be assigned to a particular community but be mobile, ready to respond to reports of crime anywhere in the area. Large urban departments have found it desirable to have specially trained units for particular types of crime: burglary squads and anti-mugging details are examples. The New York City Tactical Patrol Force was designed to serve a purpose akin to that envisioned by Rubin.

One type of unit is particularly pertinent to the relationship between psychology and the criminal justice system—the hostage unit.

Hostage Units. Shortly after the killing of eleven Israeli athletes and four of their captors in Munich in 1972, a training program was begun by the

New York City Police Department for coping with hostage situations in ways that would minimize loss of life. Police officer and psychologist Harvey Schlossberg applied psychological theories to the hostage situation and developed a program that has been copied or adapted in many departments throughout the nation.[13]

The major strategy is to attempt to make contact with the perpetrators without threatening them, to wait them out while maintaining control and/or surveillance over their movements. Sometimes friends or relatives are brought in to try to persuade them to surrender. Sometimes they are given an opportunity to make a public statement (if the hostage-taking is a symbolic act). Generally, attempts are made to minimize unauthorized access to the media lest, as in the case of the Hanafi Muslims in Washington, D.C., a reporter should inadvertently undercut the attempts by police to win the perpetrators' confidence. The success of this strategy is evidenced by the lack of fatalities in cases where it has been used and by the rapidity with which it has been imitated in other places (e.g., in the South Moluccan seizure of a train and school in the Netherlands in May of 1977).

The reason for this strategy is that hostage-takers are viewed as persons temporarily deranged by desperation. Patient discussion with them is intended to lower their anxiety or fear to a point where they will once again be willing to "listen to reason." Simultaneously, an attempt is made to avoid encouraging their threats or their violent actions by making it clear that these acts will not have the effects that they desire.

Giving political (rather than profit-seeking) hostage-takers the opportunity to make public statements through the media may, as mentioned, reduce the likelihood of violence or loss of life in a particular instance. But it will do so at the cost of encouraging future kidnappings.

The major reason for many political kidnappings is to secure this type of publicity, and, if public authorities make it freely available, they are effectively assuring the success of the criminal venture. If all press coverage of such incidents could be prohibited, such politically inspired crimes would probably cease. This situation is impossible, of course, in a free society, but one can hope that the press will develop an increasing sense of responsibility in these matters.

FEMALE POLICE OFFICERS

According to data gathered by Cramer in the 1960s, about 53% of the countries of the world employed female police officers in some capacity. Most often, it appears, they are assigned to responsibilities similar to those of male officers. In a substantial proportion of the countries surveyed, however, they are restricted to clerical or other non-patrol functions. With the growth of feminist concerns throughout the world, there are pressures to expand the roles of women in police work.

According to Sherman, women comprise only about 2 or 3% of the police officers in this country even though there have been female officers since 1911 (in Los Angeles). After six decades, women are still not fully integrated into the nation's police agencies. They are given "feminine" responsibilities; clerking, typing, attending juvenile offenders or female prisoners. Only in a few cities do female officers perform functions equivalent to those of their male counterparts. Sherman argues that there are numerous benefits accruing to police agencies from the integration of women into all aspects of police work and provides some evidence and some theory in support of his claim.

First the evidence: In those cities in which women are given the opportunity to perform all kinds of police work, they have generally proved themselves to be fully as capable as men. In Indianapolis, women ride patrol, work as plainclothes narcotics investigators, and handle complaints of family disputes. Miami employs women in supervisory work, undercover work, and homicide investigation, as well as on patrol. In Peoria, women have proved themselves in handling lines of angry male pickets, rioting teenage girls, and, in those most common police activities, aiding victims of crime, accidents, illness, or emotional distress. They also patrol Peoria in all areas of the city, including high crime areas.

Sherman asserts that women are fully integrated into the Washington, D.C. department. That a female officer was killed in the line of duty there some years ago substantiates this claim.

The success of women in foreign police departments is also cited by Sherman in support of his thesis. In England and in Israel, the work of female officers is highly regarded. He reports that the Israeli traffic police, 90% of whom are women, are widely recognized as the best in the world.

One objection voiced by many male police officers is that women cannot cope with violence as well as men. Sherman counters that female officers are less likely to *stimulate* violence, that their femaleness itself inhibits violent behaviors among males and reduces the likelihood that a police–civilian encounter will require the use of force. A high-ranking police officer described to one of the authors an occasion on which a slim young female officer walked alone between two gangs of youths who were converging for a "rumble." The sight of her so confused or amused the would-be combatants that their anger turned to laughter and the threatening confrontation failed to materialize. So far, in our culture, there is nothing very daring or masculine about starting a fight with a woman, even a police woman.

Another experienced officer commented to us that male *criminals* he has known have not been inhibited from violent behavior by the presence of a female. The response of the young woman's peers was that she was just lucky, very lucky. Luck may not be the whole story, however.

Sherman describes a psychiatric hospital housing disturbed and violent male patients and prisoners. For years no women were allowed on their wards. Over the last decade women have gradually been introduced: first a nurse, then a social worker, later dietitians, and so on. No female worker has ever been attacked or struck. The behavior and grooming of the male patients have improved, and several believe that the women understand their problems better than the male staff does. In short, by their presence, women seem to have had a calming effect on the patients.

The fact, shown time and again, is that while police work carries with it potential for danger, 80% or more of an officer's time is devoted to service activities that do not require great strength or agility; and even where there is physical danger, the officer rarely relies on physical strength to cope with it. He or she must *think* clearly, says Sherman, and this ability is not an exclusively male function.

Sherman discusses notions from the literature of social psychology and sociology that are, at least, thought-provoking, if not totally convincing. A series of studies by Rosenthal has shown that our expectations about another's behaviors cause us to approach that person in a particular way; and the manner of our approach often evokes the very behavior that we had anticipated. A person expecting to be liked, for example, will approach the other in a friendly manner, smile, make eye contact, perhaps say a friendly word or two. It is unlikely that the response will be hostile. Similarly, if "cop" means bully, tough guy, threat, or enemy to a person, his approach or response to a police officer will be one of fear or defensiveness, or, if his self-esteem is threatened, he may attempt to buttress it by an abusive or "put-down" remark. This is likely to cause the officer to respond more or less in kind. In fact, Sherman cites a study by Chevigny in which it is demonstrated that some police officers want deference from civilians, perceive its absence as defiance, and view defiance as a provocation which justifies the use of force.

The point of all of this is that human beings often establish for themselves a self-fulfilling prophecy. That is, a belief that something is true causes one to act as though it were true, and that action makes the prophecy come true. It is this cycle which the neighborhood police teams and family crisis intervention units were designed to offset, and it is this pattern which the employment of policewomen may short-circuit. Society has, as yet, no clear-cut expectations (stereotypes) about female police officers. Since we do not know what to expect of them, perhaps we approach them with more open minds.

It was indicated above that Sherman envisions numerous benefits from integrating women into police departments. Some are implicit in what has already been written. Others follow.

If, in fact, women provoke less violence than men, the public image of the entire department stands to benefit from their activities. Police officers will increasingly be seen as providers of service to the public rather than as occupying troops. Second, the community is likely to be more adequately represented in a department which recruits women. For one thing, women do constitute more than half of the civilian population; for another, minority participation in police work can be increased more rapidly if women are hired as well as men. Third, the use of arbitrary and inappropriate recruitment standards will be reduced to the extent that women fail to meet them. It is likely that these standards will be replaced by standards more linked to the requirements of the job, and that job performance will be measured not only in terms of number of arrests but in terms of number of civilians assisted or other less narrow criteria of excellence. Fourth, the presence of women can enhance the ability of a department to fight crime, particularly in light of the rapidly growing crime rate among females. Finally, women may find themselves helped by civilians more readily than men are. If this proves to be the case, it will greatly enhance police–community relations. This is no small consideration, inasmuch as the nature of police work tends to set the police and the public apart.

The resistance of many male officers to the presence of females on patrol is, to some degree, motivated by concern for the safety of those whom they regard as the "weaker sex." It also reflects their concern for the safety of the woman's partner, who might be endangered by what they view as a woman's lesser capacity to cope with physical threat.

Resistance to female officers on patrol also comes from the wives of policemen, who know the intimate nature of the relationship between partners on patrol and fear for the safety of their marriages.

Finally, it seems likely that some of the resistance is to the intrusion of women into what has historically been a male preserve. If a woman can do the job, then the job cannot be a means of defining one's identity as a man. If a woman can carry a gun, a male officer's gun loses some of its symbolic significance. If a woman can be a cop, the "fraternity" among officers is threatened, the camaraderie of the locker room is disrupted, and the macho status of the job[14] is undermined. In our society, until very recently, if a woman could perform a certain job, the job lost status in the eyes of many people. The officer who already feels unappreciated or looked down upon by the citizenry will be unlikely to welcome further evidence of the job's low status.

One could speculate, too, that the "intrusion" of female officers may exacerbate feelings that persons removed from police work are determining the fate of the police department and its personnel. Many police officers, probably most, share a sense of estrangement and alienation from civilians, researchers, and, to a lesser extent, the "brass." The feelings of group cohesiveness that result are illustrated by the rush to donate blood for an injured brother officer, by the massive turnouts of officers from all over the country for the funeral of one killed in the line of duty, and the loyalty of officer to officer which traditionally has made one protect another from shoo-flies as well as from the threats or actions of a civilian. The anger against officers Durk and Serpico, who reported on corrupt practices in the New York City Police Department, may be attributed as much to their flouting of this tradition as to the embarrassment their disclosures brought upon some of their fellow officers.

THE POLICE UNIFORM

The uniform, which is disliked by many who wear it, nonetheless symbolizes the fraternity among officers. While eager to remove it at the end of a tour so as to slip into the obscurity of civilian life, police officers will report that they feel "different" when they put it on. They are likely to stand straighter, walk more assertively, be more self-confident when in uniform; or so, at least, some have reported to the authors. They are conscious of being always in the public eye when in uniform, and vulnerable. Not only are they vulnerable to the potential assassin; they are vulnerable to the complaint that might be lodged against them unjustly by an irate citizen. This is especially true in larger cities, where police behavior can be a potent political issue. This fear is illustrated by the great opposition in certain departments to the requirement that individual officers wear tags bearing their last names. Officers have reported fear of reprisals against themselves or their families.

The uniform also functions as a symbol to the public. Its military styling, the obvious handgun, and the imposing appearance of the wearer can serve to intimidate or inflame as well as reassure the citizen. Some officers report, too, that some women find the uniform especially attractive.

Several theoretical and field studies have appeared in recent years concerning the police uniform, its significance to the wearer and to the public, its effects on behavior and reasons for these effects. Joseph and Alex offer a theoretical discussion of the significance of the uniform as a means of identifying the wearer as a member of a group (Boy Scout, soldier, police officer), as a means of providing immediate information about the wearer's relative status within the group (stars, chevrons, medals), and as conferring upon the wearer certain legitimate power over subordinates, or the public at large.

The social psychologist Bickman conducted a series of field experiments in middle class sections of Brooklyn to determine, first, whether or not the uniform does confer power, and, second, if it does, the basis of the power. Young men, dressed as civilians, milkmen, or private (unarmed) guards served as experimenters. More or less imperiously, each asked civilian passers-by either to pick up a paper bag, give a motorist a dime for a meter, or move from a bus stop to the other side of a "No Standing" sign. There was significantly more conformity with the experimenters' demands when they appeared to be guards. (One does wish that the sample sizes had been a bit larger, inasmuch as there seemed to be a tendency to obey the milkman more than the civilian.) Bickman related his inquiry to theories of *social power*. Some people have power over others because of their ability to reward or punish. Some have power due to their expertise on an issue or because they possess information needed by others. Some people have power by virtue of their place in the social system which grants them certain rights and duties to control others' behaviors. To the extent that the latter accept the power of the former over them, this power may be said to be legitimate. Bickman proposes that the guard's demands are perceived as more legitimate than those of a civilian or a milkman. The idea that a police or police-like uniform increases the perceived legitimacy of a directive given by the wearer remains plausible, at least where the officer is not perceived as a member of an occupying army.

Another aspect ought to be considered, however, one that was alluded to above. One of the authors found himself interacting, in informal circumstances, with a Catholic priest, who was wearing a short-sleeved shirt, open at the neck. It was a very hot summer day. A third party, joining us, said, "Good morning, Father." Automatically, the priest buttoned his collar! Cast suddenly in the role of priest, he found that the open collar did not feel right. Interestingly, he was unaware of what he had done until it was pointed out to him a little later. Shaw, a former actor, points out that donning a costume affects an actor's performance during rehearsal. Somehow, the costume seems to "flesh out" the role, increasing the performer's ability to enact the character. Zimbardo also describes the effects of clothing on the behavior and demeanor of undergraduates playing the roles of prison inmates and guards. In short, the other side of the legitimacy coin is that a uniform becomes "part of" the one who wears it. It changes *his* behavior as well as that of the person who responds to him. It is possible that there was something extra in the manner of Bickman's "guards," a more authoritative air, perhaps, that they did not have when clad as civilians or as milkmen. They may have been more convincing as well as more "legitimate."

The situation appears to be comparable to that of the experimenter in the laboratory whose mere status as an experimenter gives him the power to induce a nearly limitless variety of foolish, aggressive, or tedious behaviors on the part of subjects.[15] Like the police officer, the experimenter enjoys legitimate power. It seems likely that, as the experimenter interacts differently with subjects than with students, the police officer acts differently with civilians than with colleagues. Particularly when in uniform!

There is some evidence that police agencies are aware of this. A number of communities have begun to experiment with modifications of the typical police uniform, instituting what is called "career clothing" in an attempt to improve police–community relations, change the officers' perceptions of their roles, and enhance the process of professionalization. Tenzel and Cizanckas describe such an experiment in Menlo Park, California.

In Menlo Park, as in many other communities, the traditional uniform appears to have become a stimulus for fear and alienation. It signified a separation between the police and the policed, a hierarchical relationship in which the police were empowered to command the civilians. Tenzel and Cizanckas suggest, too, that it prevented police and civilians from discussing "novel" ideas about police work by maintaining an artificial barrier between them. The civilians felt inhibited about expressing these ideas, and the police about listening to them. It was hoped that by relinquishing the military-like uniform, and the symbols of authority it includes, flexibility would be encouraged in the interaction between police and civilians as well as among the officers themselves. Accordingly, a switch was made to olive-colored blazers worn over dark trousers with a shirt and tie. Instead of a shield, a name plaque was worn. The clothing bore no indication of rank. No night stick was carried, and the revolver was concealed under the blazer.

Not surprisingly, police of neighboring communities responded with ridicule. As has been shown, the standard uniform confers status; its modification may entail a loss of status in the eyes of those whose status depends upon the clothing. The ridicule, report Tenzel and Cizanckas, impelled the Menlo Park officers to seek support among themselves, a process that ultimately resulted in the restructuring of the department along egalitarian lines. Ranks were eliminated, attitudes toward professionalization and education became more positive, turnover dropped, and the number of applicants increased. It may be that the public benefited, too.

An important component of the uniform which in and of itself tends to set police officers apart from civilians is the revolver. Schlossberg discusses its significance for the officer, suggesting that for some it becomes symbolic of their manhood. To have one's gun taken away in the course of a disciplinary proceeding is to be symbolically castrated, at least as far as some policemen seem to be concerned.

JOB STRESSES OF POLICE WORK

Another source of the camaraderie among police officers is the peculiar working hours that the job entails. Typically, an officer works one of three shifts: 8 A.M. to 4 P.M., 4 P.M. to midnight, midnight to 8 A.M., rotating from one tour to another at fairly frequent and often unpredictable intervals. This wreaks havoc with the officer's life in several ways. Social life is virtually restricted to other police officers and their families, who share and understand the peculiar demands of the job. An officer's functioning as spouse or parent is disrupted. The officer frequently does not see the children for several days at a time, and one spouse is sleeping or working while the other is doing the opposite. Digestive processes and other biological rhythms are constantly being rearranged. Lunch time one week is sleep time the next. The spouse whose mate is assigned to patrol in a high crime area is under additional strain. Such problems place a great stress on the police officer's marriage. Some departments are now helping their members cope by means of orientation and other programs for spouses or fiance(e)s. Nevertheless, divorce is very frequent, an ironic fact in view of the practice of many departments that, until recently, disqualified divorced applicants.

Police officers also suffer from alcoholism to a greater extent than other occupational groups. Police agencies are increasingly, but not yet commonly, offering counseling and other services to the alcoholic officer.[16]

Finally, police officers are, more often than other groups, victims of heart disease and suicide. It makes sense, perhaps, to attribute all of these ills and difficulties to the nature of police work. Lefkowitz suggests, however, that occupational hazards of this type may have several different determinants which may relate either to the job itself or to the personality or background of persons attracted to the job. The role of police officer itself defines certain behaviors and circumstances (e.g., tour changes, public scrutiny, and vulnerability). Certain attitudes of those on the job become part of the officer's belief and behavior systems (e.g., there is pressure to pretend self-assuredness, which may be false). Those less suited to or happy in the job drop out, leaving an increasingly homogeneous body of personnel as seniority increases. Most officers are drawn from segments of the population whose attitudes are consistent with those of the police. Finally, there is some self-selection independent of socioeconomic factors such that individuals with certain personality characteristics are drawn to police work.[17]

Lefkowitz' paper, incidentally, deals with many of the issues considered in this chapter from the perspective of an industrial psychologist concerned with matters of personnel selection, job satisfaction, occupational choice and status, and assessment of job performance. His work is comprehensive and is recommended.

There remain to be considered a few examples of the work of other psychologists on the psychology of police work and police officers. One such instance is the research of an undergraduate student of one of the authors, who was an officer in a good-sized police department.

Police trainees are taught in academies to maintain a polite, nonthreatening demeanor when dealing with the public, and that such behavior will improve the relationship between police and policed. The image of the "tough cop" is giving way to that of the professional, and the assumption is that this transformation will, in time, reduce hostility toward the police and enhance cooperation with them. The assumption may be correct; adequate data have not yet been collected. For a term paper in a social psychology class, this student, who was assigned to traffic control, worked out a research design with a friend and colleague. Operating in two widely separated precincts in their city, the two officers systematically varied the approach they made to motorists whose driving required that they be stopped. Every second motorist so detained was exposed to a tough cop; the others saw a polite one. The two officers rode scooters, small motorized vehicles that enabled them to move freely even in heavy traffic. While riding they wore helmets and goggles and were equipped with a radio on which to receive calls.

In the "polite cop" treatment, the errant motorist was signaled to pull over in the usual fashion. When he did so, the officer dismounted, placed his helmet on the scooter, removed his tinted goggles, turned the radio's volume down, and approached the motorist. He said something to the effect that: "It's too bad that I had to stop you but you went through a red light (or whatever the violation was). May I please see your license and registration? You may get out of the car or stay in it, as you prefer."

The "tough cop" kept the helmet and goggles in place, thus minimizing eye contact and exaggerating his size and impersonal manner. He kept the radio volume at a high and irritating level as he approached the motorist, to whom he said brusquely: "Let me have your license and registration!" He remained far enough from the car window that the motorist had to leave his car in order to comply, thus leaving the psychological "safety" it may have provided. He informed the motorist of the violation only when asked.

The dependent variable was the reaction of the motorist to being stopped.

When people are stopped by a traffic cop, some get very frightened and are quiet and respectful; some flirt and cajole; some are angry and abusive. The usual training program suggests that the polite approach will yield a respectful response and that an abrupt one will engender anger and resentment. This is what the experimenter predicted.

Because of the nature of the study it was not possible to assess how reliably the experimenter gauged the motorist's behavior. It could not be systematically witnessed by a third party. What the experimenter attempted to do was to specify seven levels of behavior ranging from very polite and respectful to hostile and threatening to the point of risking arrest for disorderly conduct. The intervening five levels each were described in terms of specific types of behaviors to assist the experimenter in categorizing the motorist's behavior. (The experimenter insisted that whether or not a summons was issued was independent of the manipulation or the response of the motorist.)

The results were clear-cut. With a sample of over 300 motorists of many ethnic groups, both sexes, and all ages, the pattern was consistent: the "tough cop" was reacted to docilely, politely, and respectfully. The polite cop was taunted, verbally abused, and threatened. The results were the same for both experimenters, for all ethnic groups, for both sexes, and for all age groups. The degree of consistency was significant and high. Why?

One possibility concerns social perception and expectations. Most civilians, as has previously been suggested, have an image of police officers as judgmental, brusque, and punitive. If they are stopped for a violation, they do not expect to be greeted with a warm smile or even with polite indifference. They expect to be made to feel guilty, to be ticketed. The tough cop meets the expectation, and the civilian responds in the stereotyped way: polite, remorseful, and so on. The polite cop confronts the driver with an ambiguous situation. He is not behaving as the driver has learned to expect. Perhaps the motorist thinks: "He's stopped me, but he's being very nice. If I had really done something wrong, he'd be mad at me. Therefore, his polite manner is masking uncertainty about whether I, in fact, did do something wrong. He's got some nerve! Besides, if he's polite that must mean he's uneasy about stopping me. Maybe he's afraid of me (or trying to 'pick me up'). If he weren't, he wouldn't be behaving like this. How do you like that!"

The result is the abuse to which the polite officers were subjected.

The fact that these findings suggest that brusqueness tends to reduce the amount of abusive behavior directed at police officers should not lead the reader to the unwarranted conclusion that police training programs should avoid stressing politeness in dealing with the public. The function of a police officer is to enforce the law, not to produce submissive behavior on the part of citizens. The public has a right to courteous treatment by public officials under all circumstances. Even if consistently replicated, these data would not justify the conclusion that courteous treatment of the public by police officers is a poor policy. Regardless of individual reactions, courtesy may still result in improved police–community relations.

Is it true that most police officers fit the stereotype of the "tough cop"? It is hard to say. Most studies are interested in the characteristics of the very effective or very ineffective police officer, not in the great majority in between. Lefkowitz does offer a description of the "successful" officer, which he gleaned from a number of studies by listing those characteristics that appear more or less consistently. They include:

1. High intelligence
2. High scores on civil service examinations
3. High grades in recruit training
4. Stable previous work history in skilled occupation
5. Stable family life
6. Conventional life style
7. Self-assurance and sense of independence
8. Good health and emotional adjustment[18]

One area of study that is related to personality but is of special interest because it is pertinent to the nature of the interaction between the police and the public, concerns values. Values are attitudes of a general nature having to do with what one regards as important in life, as the "right" or "wrong" way to live, think, or behave. A social psychologist who has long been interested in values as objects of study is Rokeach.

Rokeach came to the study of values from a long-term concern with the ways in which attitudes operate as part of a system of personality. Some people are open to conflicting ideas and are able to confront discrepancies among their beliefs and, in some instances, to tolerate them. Others do not permit themselves to recognize contradictions among their beliefs; they maintain a closed system, segregating inconsistent beliefs from each other rather than confronting and resolving the inconsistency. One example in an extreme form is the delusional system of the paranoid schizophrenic.[19]

Values are beliefs or attitudes that are particularly long-lasting and pertinent to the way one chooses to live or to one's objectives in life. Rokeach refers to these two types of values as, respectively, one's preferred mode of behavior or "instrumental value" and one's preferred end-state of existence or "terminal value." Examples will make this clear. One may value ambition or cheerfulness, logic or obedience as modes of behavior in oneself or in others. These are among the instrumental values listed by Rokeach. Similarly, one might value a world at peace more than wisdom, or self-respect more than freedom. These are examples of what Rokeach calls "terminal values."[20]

The Rokeach Value Survey consists of two lists of such values: 18 terminal and 18 instrumental ones. Respondents read a brief description of each value and are instructed to arrange them in order according to their importance to them as guiding principles in life.

Theory and data prompted Rokeach and his associates to predict that police officers will have different values from those of the civilians they serve. The nature of their job suggests that they will value conserving property, order, and the status quo. A number of studies are cited which, indeed, indicate that policemen are relatively conservative, moralistic, and less tolerant than the general public. If this is so, the average rankings that they assign to the 36 values should differ somewhat from the rankings of civilian respondents.

The police respondents in the study by Rokeach et al. were 153 white male officers in a middle-size, Midwestern department. They represented more than 80% of the white males in the department. Their responses were compared with those of 561 white and 93 black males drawn from a nation-wide sample.

Certain values were shared by all three groups. All valued highly a world at peace, family security, and freedom; all rated low an exciting life, pleasure, and a world of beauty. These are terminal values. Similarly, among instrumental values, all three groups gave high ratings to being honest, responsible, and ambitious, and low ratings to being obedient and imaginative. Despite these similarities, some of the rankings of values were significantly different between groups. Police rated the following more highly than the civilians did: an exciting life, a sense of accomplishment, family security, and mature love. They also valued more highly being: capable, honest, intellectual, logical, obedient, responsible, and self-controlled. In the other direction, the police assigned lower average rankings than did civilians to: a world at peace, a world of beauty, equality, national security, and social recognition. Among instrumental values, police gave lower rankings to being: broadminded, cheerful, forgiving, helpful, and independent.

The difference that is most interesting, however, concerns the valuation of equality. It was ranked fourteenth by the police, twelfth by the white civilians, and *third* by the black civilians. Rokeach et al. contend that this difference helps us to understand why many blacks feel that the police are unsympathetic to them. Data from other research have shown that the ranking of equality is the best predictor of conservatism. To the extent that conservatism characterizes the police and not the policed, the possibilities for discord between the two are numerous.

A popular stereotype of police officers involves a propensity to react with undue force, especially against members of minority groups. Data exist pertaining to the matter, so that we need not resort to stereotypes for our information.

Inn, Wheeler, and Sparling investigated the effects of race of the suspect and whether or not he was armed and/or firing, on the shooting behavior of patrolmen in a large police department. Records of shooting incidents (which must be filed whenever a gun is discharged by accident or by intention) were examined for the period January 1, 1970 through October 31, 1972.

One clear finding is that officers shot more often at suspects who were armed and firing than they did at unarmed suspects. Blacks, who comprised about one-fourth of the city's population, were the targets of shots in nearly two-thirds of the incidents. Does this mean that the police were biased? Not necessarily. It is possible, although pertinent data are not provided, that police have more contact with blacks, that blacks commit more street crimes or are more likely to flee or to resist than whites. Unraveling such data is a very convoluted process. No single or simple explanation is possible.

Perhaps the situation has changed in the last 15 years. Perhaps, in light of the revolution in race relations that is in progress in this country, police are being more cautious about shooting than they once were, particularly about shooting blacks. In any event, it should be noted that in a 1963 paper Robin showed that during an 11-year period in Philadelphia, 28 of 32 civilians slain by police were black (87.5%), although the percentage of blacks in the city was 22%, and the percentage of major crimes attributed to blacks was 31%.

Rightly or wrongly, police fear that public reaction to use of firearms by police may cause them to "freeze up" in an emergency with perhaps fatal consequences. It is for this reason that they resist civilian review boards so strongly. Many police officers, already feeling unappreciated, are reluctant to have actions taken during emergencies subjected to "Monday morning quarterbacking" by civilians who, they believe, cannot appreciate the risks their job entails. There are citizens' groups which argue that this indicates the wish of the police to protect themselves at all costs from the scrutiny of the public. As in many other issues in the criminal justice system and in human interaction in general, there are legitimate concerns on both sides.

NOTES AND REFERENCES

1. For details of their procedures see Baehr, M. E., Furcon, J. E., and Froemel, E. C. *Psychological Assessment of Patrolman Qualifications in Relation to Field Performance.* Washington, D.C.: U.S. Department of Justice, Law Enforcement Assistance Administration, 1969, pp. 22–30.
2. Ferretti, F. Recruiting police: Standards vary widely; some are being relaxed. *The New York Times* October 21, 1973, IV, 8:1.
3. Janson, D. Philadelphia enrolls teen-age police. *The New York Times* January 26, 1970, 20:5.
4. Richardson, J. F. *Urban Police in the United States.* Port Washington, N.Y.: National University Publications, Kennikat Press, 1974.
5. Delaney, P. Recruiting of Negro police is a failure in most cities. *The New York Times* January 25, 1971, 1:2,14.

6. E.g., Alex, N. *Black in Blue: A Study of the Negro Policeman.* New York: Appleton-Century-Crofts, 1969; Bannon, J. D. and Wilt, G. M., Black policemen: A study of self-images. *Journal of Police Science and Administration* 1973, 1(1), 21–29; and Stevens, W. K. Black policemen bring reforms. *The New York Times* August 11, 1974, 1:4,35.
7. Rubin, J. G. Police identity and the police role. Chapter 6 in J. G. Goldsmith and S. S. Goldsmith (Eds.) *The Police Community: Dimensions of an Occupational Subculture.* Pacific Palisades, Calif.: Palisades Publishers, 1974.
8. Treaster, J. B. Neighborhoods: 'Cop of the Block' project is calming Bedford-Stuyvesant's tension. *The New York Times* January 29, 1975, 37:1,40.
9. Allport, G. W. *The Nature of Prejudice.* Cambridge: Mass.: Addison-Wesley, 1954.
10. Sherif, M., Harvey, O. J., White, B. J., Hood, W., and Sherif, C. *Intergroup Conflict and Cooperation: The Robbers Cave Experiment.* Norman, Okla.: University of Oklahoma Institute of Intergroup Relations, 1961.
11. Freedman, J. L. and Fraser, S. C. Compliance without pressure: The foot-in-the-door technique. *Journal of Personality and Social Psychology* 1966, 4, 195–202.
12. Bem, D. J. Self-perception: An alternative interpretation of cognitive dissonance phenomena. *Psychological Review* 1967, 74, 245–254.
13. Schlossberg, H. and Freeman, L. *Psychologist with a Gun.* New York: Coward, McCann & Geoghegan, Inc., 1974, Chapter XVII; Prial, F. J. City's hostage unit had genesis in Munich. *The New York Times* June 13, 1974, 48:5–8.
14. Sherman, L. J. A psychological view of women in policing. *Journal of Police Science and Administration* 1973, 1(4), p. 383; see also, Women effective on police patrol. *The New York Times* May 21, 1974, 38:4–6, an account of a Police Foundation study by P. B. Bloch and D. Anderson of The Urban Institute.
15. See, respectively, Orne, M. T. On the social psychology of the psychological experiment: With particular reference to demand characteristics and their implications. *American Psychologist* 1962, 17, 776–783; Milgram, S. Behavioral study of obedience. *Journal of Abnormal and Social Psychology* 1963, 67, 371–378; Festinger, L. and Carlsmith, J. M. Cognitive consequences of forced compliance. *Journal of Abnormal and Social Psychology* 1959, 58, 203–210.
16. Schlossberg and Freeman, *Psychologist with a Gun,* Chapter XI; Cassese, S. Inside help for police alcoholics. *Newsday* February 20, 1977, 9:1; Cunningham, B. The cop and the psychiatrist: How much mental illness? *New York Post* October 20, 1976, 3:1,17.
17. Lefkowitz, J. Industrial-organizational psychology and the police. *American Psychologist* 1977, 32(5), p. 358.
18. Ibid., p. 357.
19. Rokeach, M. *The Three Christs of Ypsilanti: A Psychological Study.* New York: Random House Vintage Books, 1967.
20. Rokeach, M., Miller, M. G., and Snyder, J. A. The value gap between police and policed. *Journal of Social Issues* 1971, 27(2), 155–171.

7
Lawyers, Psychologists, Psychiatrists, and Social Workers

The characteristics of offenders, victims, and police officers having been considered in the preceding three chapters, it remains for this chapter to deal with the training and characteristics of those professional people who are most influential in determining the actual structure and functioning of the criminal justice system and who must originate any significant improvements or changes in it.

LEGAL EDUCATION

The legal profession is the one primarily responsible for the creation and maintenance of any criminal justice system. Its members not only function within the system in the roles of defense attorneys, public prosecutors, and judges, but they also contribute to its development in their capacities as legislators and politicians, for the most common professional background of either legislators or politicians is the law. Thus we will first deal with the selection and training of lawyers.

The trend in legal education over the years has been toward increasing the amount of graduate education required. During Lincoln's time few lawyers attended a formal law school. In fact the first law school in the United States was not even established until 1817. Instead, lawyers acquired their training by "reading law" in an attorney's office under the tutelage of the practitioner. Many eminent attorneys of an earlier era, such as Clarence Darrow, never attended law school. Until quite recently it was still possible to take this route to be admitted to the bar in New York, although only a very small number of candidates availed themselves of it in recent years.

Early law schools tended to require two years or less of study and did not require a college degree for admission. Today most law schools require three years of study, and all are graduate schools, although, as in the case of medical schools, it is still possible for the rare student to be admitted after only three years of college. The recognition of the graduate nature of law school was symbolized by the change in the 1960s of the first professional degree in law from the old LL.B. (Bachelor of Laws) to the new J.D. (Juris Doctor).

Law schools differ in the amount of elective work permitted. Some have a totally prescribed course of study, and others provide for a substantial amount of elective work. In most cases, the program consists almost totally of legal coursework with few, if any, offerings from related disciplines. Some law schools are national in orientation in that they do not teach the law of any particular jurisdiction, but instead consider the minority and majority views of the major legal questions that occur in *any* jurisdiction. Others teach the law of a particular jurisdiction. There is some conflict in legal circles as to which approach is better. Proponents of nationally oriented law schools take the position that while graduates of the other type of school may do better on the bar exam of the jurisdiction studied, they are not as broadly educated as graduates of a national law school. Others view it as better to illustrate abstract legal principles by considering the law of a particular jurisdiction as an integrated entity. The national accrediting agency for all law schools is a committee of the American Bar Association.

The major teaching method employed in most law schools is the case study method in which the students recite on assigned cases, and the operative principles of law are derived from those cases. This method is very similar to what practicing lawyers will be doing for the rest of their professional lives as they research cases to find the law applicable to the causes entrusted to them. The reader will recognize this as an example of inductive reasoning, which was described earlier.

A typical law school program will include courses in the following major areas of substantive law: Contracts, Suretyship, Bills and Notes, Sales, Bailments, Corporations, Partnerships, Wills and Estates, Real Property, Personal Property, Trusts, Constitutional Law, Torts, Administrative Law, Domestic Relations, and Taxation. It will also include such courses in adjective law as: Pleading and Practice, Evidence, Conflicts of Laws, and Equity.

The emphasis is predominantly in the civil area, and the average law school graduate may have no training in the criminal law beyond a three-credit course which may include both substantive and procedural aspects. Thus, attorneys wishing to specialize in criminal matters must rely for their training on elective and graduate courses or, more commonly, upon on-the-job training in district attorneys' offices, in legal aid societies, or with law firms that specialize in criminal matters.

Incidentally, unlike the medical profession, the legal profession has never had certifying boards to attest to competency in a specialty, and attorneys who do specialize in certain areas of the law have been restrained from holding themselves out as specialists. To do so has been considered an unethical form of self-aggrandizement and advertising. The exception to this is the patent attorney (who is certified), who may describe him- or herself as a specialist in this area. Some jurists, e.g., Chief Justice Burger, have been critical of the performance of many lawyers in court, particularly of those whose principal practice consists of office work, and who have relatively little experience in litigation. These critics would like to see a system of specialization in trial work analogous to the British system of solicitors (non-trial lawyers) and barristers (trial advocates). In such a system only specially qualified lawyers would be permitted to try cases in court. At present, any person admitted to the bar may try a case in court even if that person has not tried a case in 20 years. In fairness to the profession it must be pointed out that even with a system of trial specialists there will always be young lawyers needing experience in trial advocacy, just as there will always be young surgeons needing experience in surgery. Furthermore, there are ethical constraints against lawyers performing services for which they are not qualified, and most lawyers honor these constraints. A system that limits appearance in court to a special subgroup of lawyers may or may not speed up the work of the courts, although the authors are inclined to doubt that it will. It would almost certainly result in increased costs to the criminal defendant and might preclude many persons from obtaining private legal representation.

Because of their special type of training, lawyers as a group tend to think more "legalistically" than their social scientist colleagues. That is, they are more inclined to think in terms of legal precedents and principles than in terms of such abstract and essentially undefined concepts as "justice" or "social good." Also, they recognize that because of the doctrine of *stare decisis*, what may appear to be a just or reasonable ruling in a particular case may ultimately work great mischief when it becomes a general legal principle.

For example, if an illegal, warrantless search is conducted against a major figure in organized crime, and it turns up substantial incriminating evidence, nonlawyers are not as likely as lawyers to see such police action as a threat to the civil rights of all law-abiding citizens and to support the suppression of such illegally obtained evidence.

Lawyers have often been described as being more conservative than social scientists, presumably because they have more at stake in the maintenance of "the system." It is probably true that they are more opposed to change than members of other professional groups because of their commitment to precedents, but it should be pointed out that conservatism or opposition to change in legal matters is often motivated not by self-interest but by a desire to protect hard-won principles of human and constitutional rights. Nonlawyers concerned with human welfare or rights typically consider themselves to be liberal and seek government aid in attaining their objectives. Lawyers with the same goals are more likely to be wary of government intervention, as they have learned by hard experience that with government aid usually comes government control and the erosion of personal liberties.

Since there are no uniformly prescribed sets of prerequisites for admission to law school, the training and education of lawyers in the social sciences, in general, and in psychology, in particular, is extremely variable. This does not make it likely that an attorney or a judge will have the optimum background for evaluating the reports of psychologists in such matters as sentencing or probation. In recent years students have been seeking admission to law schools in unprecedented numbers, and, in response to these admission pressures, these institutions may begin to require formal prerequisites. The authors hope that they will not. Forcing college students to make career decisions before they are ready to, as is the present unfortunate result of medical school admission requirements, will probably do much more harm than the failure of a judge to have had a course or two in any subject, even psychology.

There was a time when lawyers were required to serve a clerkship in a law office for a year before being eligible for admission to the bar. The purpose of this requirement was to assure that the academically trained young lawyers would get the needed practical experience that their counterparts of a generation earlier got in the offices in which they read law. It soon developed that this requirement turned into a form of peonage, and candidates for the bar were being forced either to work for nothing or even to pay their "employer" to meet this requirement. Therefore, the requirement was discontinued. Neither the medical profession nor the profession of psychology has taken the same step. Indeed, in psychology the tendency at present is to increase internship requirements. In medicine, the tendency has been to pay interns more realistic salaries, but in psychology the longer internship period has had the effect of increasing the financial hardships for persons entering the profession.

Eligibility to take the bar exam is contingent upon graduation from an approved law school. If the law school is approved by the American Bar Association, the candidate may take the bar examination in any state in the union. If it is not so approved, he may take it only in those states which approve the school. Upon passing the bar examination the candidate is subjected to the close scrutiny of a character committee and, if found qualified, is required to take an oath of office before finally being admitted to practice law.

Some states require additional experience before permitting an attorney to practice in the highest court in the state. Admission to practice in the federal courts must be obtained by application after admission to practice in the courts of a state. Admission to practice before the United States Supreme Court requires the candidate to have been admitted to practice before the highest court of a state for three years. Many states will admit a candidate to practice without a bar examination if he has been admitted to practice in another state for more than five years and has been in active practice.

The legal profession is the only one to be mentioned in this chapter that subjects its candidates to an investigation of their characters in spite of the obvious importance of this factor to all of these professions. The success of this investigation in maintaining the standards of the profession is not easy to measure and will probably never be known. However, the profession does provide machinery for rectifying errors made in the admission process. These procedures can result in the censuring, suspension, or disbarment of offenders guilty of professional misconduct. Unlike analogous procedures in medicine or psychology, which are either under the control of state licensing agencies (which can revoke a license or certification) or professional societies (which can merely expel a member), these procedures are under the control of the profession itself. Thus, in New York, the Appellate Division of the Supreme Court controls both the admission of attorneys to practice and disciplinary proceedings against them. Nonlawyers have often criticized this arrangement as making it likely that offenders would be dealt with lightly. If anything, the opposite seems to be the case. Several U.S. Supreme Court decisions were necessary before lawyers accused of professional misconduct were accorded the same basic rights in disciplinary proceedings (such as the right against self-incrimination) as those routinely accorded to defendants in criminal actions.

PSYCHOLOGICAL EDUCATION

The requirements for certification or licensing as a psychologist usually include the holding of a doctoral degree in psychology (or sometimes in a related field), some professional experience under supervision, and the passing of a state examination.

A Ph.D. degree in psychology requires three full years of formal course work beyond the bachelor's degree, the completion of a doctoral dissertation involving original research (typically taking about two years to complete), and, in some programs, such as clinical psychology, a one-year internship in an institutional setting.

The courses required during the three years of course work are likely to include many of the following: Experimental Design, Statistics, History of Psychology, Psychological Testing, Methods of Psychotherapy and Counseling, Psychology of Personality and Behavior Pathology. The Psychology of Learning, the Psychology of Perception, Physiological Psychology, and Social Psychology are other frequent requirements or electives.

The few people opposed to internship requirements argue that working in a profession will give the same type of experience that an internship can provide without the attendant financial hardship. Another objection to the requirement of an internship is that it tends to obscure the difference between education and job experience. A good internship may, of course, provide a candidate with a greater diversity of case material than one is likely to come into contact with in private practice, but internships are too variable in their scope and quality to be counted upon to do this. Often the intern will learn the procedures used in a particular clinic or office but little else, as the quality of supervision is often not as high as in an educational institution.

Unlike the situation in law where there are no recognized specialties, or medicine where specialization training occurs after the attainment of the M.D. degree, psychology programs tend to be in special areas. Often there is very little difference between two specialized Ph.D. programs other than in the names. The authors are concerned about what they view as an unwarranted attempt to create a plethora of nominally specialized programs instead of a basic and general preparation in all areas of the subject. The major division in psychology is between experimental and clinical programs. The difference between them is largely one of emphasis, the former stressing research methodology somewhat more than the latter, and the latter stressing diagnostic and therapeutic procedures.

The American Psychological Association certifies only Clinical, Counseling, and School Psychology programs. New York State, possibly in recognition of the realities of the situation, does not certify psychologists as specialists. In view of this, the State Department of Education, which certifies psychologists, has stated that it considers it unethical for a psychologist to advertise as a specialist even under the new court rulings that restrictions against professional advertising are unconstitutional.

Like many states, the State of New York does not license psychologists; it certifies them. This means that the state does not restrict the right to practice as a psychologist. Anyone, even with no training at all, can legally do that. The law merely restricts the right to call oneself a psychologist. For a long time, psychological associations have been advocating legislation to restrict the right to practice psychology, but the legislature has failed to act for a variety of interprofessional political reasons. Currently psychotherapy is being practiced by some physicians, psychiatrists, social workers, and psychiatric nurses, in addition to psychologists. There is another group of totally unqualified faddists, faith healers, and laymen doing the same thing. These latter groups have exerted very effective political pressure on legislators in the past. This influence has been complicated by the existence of interprofessional rivalries among the professional people involved. Some psychiatrists would like the public to believe that the practice of psychotherapy is really the practice of medicine, not psychology, and that somehow a psychologist is just another type of medical technician, not an independent professional. Because of the influence of organized medicine, few legislators would be willing to declare that a general practitioner in medicine is unqualified to practice psychotherapy. In addition, a certain amount of what might properly be called psychotherapy is an unavoidable concomitant of the work of such diverse groups as physicians, clergymen, and even lawyers. To complicate matters further, many psychologists do not feel that social workers are as well trained as they are, and so are reluctant to agree to any legislation giving social workers the same rights to practice as they seek. This puts organized psychology and organized social work into conflict.

The result is a ludicrous form of anarchy in which people doing the same things are trained in radically different ways, each with its own unique advantages and disadvantages, but no training program exists that combines the best features of each.

In addition to the conflicts between psychologists and other professions that are alluded to above and elsewhere in this book, there is much conflict within psychology itself between experimental and clinical psychologists. Many clinical psychologists take the position that those trained in experimental psychology do not have adequate training in working with patients and should not be permitted to do so. Experimentalists, on the other hand, generally take the position that clinicians are not adequately trained in scientific psychology or methodology, and some even express regret that they call themselves psychologists. It is the opinion of the authors, one of whom has been trained in both areas, that this conflict is really a characteristic of a young science and will die out over the years. As long as psychotherapy was based on theory and dogma rather than on applied psychological knowledge, there was really very little, if any, connection between the science of psychology and clinical practice. Today, as the findings in the psychology of learning are beginning to be applied to developing new methods of treatment (such as behavior modification), people who are essentially experimentalists are becoming involved in clinical areas. A generation from now the artificial dichotomy between experimental and clinical psychology may well have disappeared and young Ph.D.'s will, of necessity, be adequately trained in both areas. Thus, degrees in experimental or clinical psychology will be replaced by degrees in general psychology which signify the graduate's readiness for specialized training if it is required.

MEDICAL EDUCATION

The degree of M.D. (Doctor of Medicine) is awarded after from three to four years of medical school training following the bachelor's degree. As in the case of law schools it is theoretically possible to enter medical school after only three years of college, and there are a few programs that combine both college and medical school in six years (two of college and four of medical school). All American medical schools require courses in organic and inorganic chemistry, biology, physics, and mathematics for admission; however, because of the inadequate number of American medical schools, many American students are forced to attend foreign medical schools that have different requirements and standards.

The first two years of medical school typically consist of formal courses in the classic medical sciences, such as: Anatomy, Physiology, Histology, Bacteriology, Pharmacology, Pathology, Embryology, and Medicine.

The remaining years are served in the form of clerkships in the different medical specialties, such as: Obstetrics and Gynecology, Medicine, Pediatrics, Surgery, Urology, and so on, with the student assuming some responsibility for the care of patients and receiving practical instruction and supervision from the staff.

National licensing examinations must be taken in sections after the first and last two years of medical school and after serving an internship, as opposed to the single sitting required for bar examinations.

Following graduation from medical school and before licensing, the candidate must serve one or two years in a hospital setting as an intern. Here the practical training of his or her clerkship years is continued with a greater level of responsibility for patient care.

Internships may be one of two types: a rotating internship, in which the intern serves in each of the various services of the hospital and continues general medical training, or a free-standing internship, in which the intern remains in a particular department, and which may be counted toward the first year of residency or specialization training. With the advent of more specialization in medicine, the rotating internship seems to be declining. Physicians desiring to specialize in some subfield of medicine will take additional hospital training as residents for from three (psychiatry) to five (surgery) years, depending on their specialty. They are then eligible to take examinations given by specialty boards, successful completion of which permits them to list themselves as specialists.

Both clinical psychologists and psychiatrists who desire to specialize in the subspecialty of psychoanlysis conventionally take additional training in this field in a psychoanalytic institute. This training requires additional course work in psychoanalytic theory and methods, case seminars, and supervised treatment of patients. It also requires a personal or training analysis, and most institutes today require at least 350 hours of such a personal analysis. This is interesting in view of the fact that most of Freud's disciples, the first generation of psychoanalysts, generally had only about 200 hours of a training analysis. It tends to support the view that governments and politicians are not the only institutions or people that tend to centralize power and overregulate. Psychotherapists and educators do it too!

SOCIAL WORK EDUCATION

Social workers are involved in several ways in the criminal justice system. They may serve as probation officers responsible for assisting convicted persons to meet the demands of society for law-abiding behavior, employment, and so on. They may be involved in investigations of the backgrounds and family life of convicted felons so that, through their pre-sentencing reports they can assist the judge in determining appropriate sentences. They help to find facilities to care for persons who commit minor offenses, and who, for one reason or another, are not capable of maintaining themselves outside an institution.

Most social workers have a Master of Social Work (M.S.W.) degree. Unlike master's degrees in other fields, it has, until recently, been the highest degree that could be earned in this field. Currently, the degree of Doctor of Social Welfare (D.S.W.) is beginning to be offered. The M.S.W. requires as many as 70 credits beyond the bachelor's degree, more than twice the number required of master's candidates in other fields. Hence, the M.S.W. is by no means a typical master's degree.

Courses are usually required in human development and behavior, group process, family interaction, the nature and delivery of social services, culture and ethnicity, interpersonal relations, and the like. In many graduate programs in social work a thesis is a degree requirement. Course work in statistics may also be required, since social workers must be able to evaluate research in this field whether or not they engage in it themselves.

Like psychologists and psychiatrists, social workers are generally required to complete internships during their training, although the term employed is field work or field placement. A substantial portion of the student's time (from one-third to one-half) is spent under the supervision of experienced social workers, who are certified in a number of states just as psychologists are. In field work, students acquire firsthand experience in the methods, values, and ethics of the social work profession by working on the job.

Social workers may specialize in such areas as social casework, group work, psychiatric social work, community organization, or research on the delivery and use of social services. These areas require skills in interviewing, counseling, group dynamics, and other general skills, as well as some that are more specialized (e.g., alcoholism counseling).

Social workers generally view clients' problems in the context of their circumstances in life as well as in terms of psychodynamics, although psychiatric social workers may stress a psychodynamic approach in assisting their clients to cope with emotional stress. The social worker's orientation is to provide services to those who need them or to direct the clients to persons or agencies that can provide the required aid. Such services include assisting individuals to secure benefits due them from government agencies, directing them to private sources of assistance where their needs and resources make the latter appropriate, providing counseling to individuals or families in the throes of crisis, and so on. The orientation is usually different from that of the psychologist, who may be primarily concerned with diagnosis or therapy and less concerned with helping the client to find someone to care for an aging parent.

The approach which is taught the social work student and which guides his or her activities may be eclectic, borrowing from several disciplines, or it may stress one or another way of viewing the matter at hand (e.g., a psychoanalytic approach or a systems theory orientation). One well-known school of social work has included in its curriculum such diverse areas as: ego psychology, organization theory, role theory, group dynamics and other approaches drawn from psychology and sociology, all integrated into a systems approach in which the clients and their social context are taken into account.

8
Overview of Criminal Procedures in a Typical State

In this and the next two chapters we are going to be concerned with the procedures involved in criminal prosecutions or the adjective criminal law. As a starting point, the judicial structure of the State of New York as it relates to criminal matters will be described, since it is a typical example of criminal court structure.

The State of New York is divided into 62 counties. Each county has a court called the Supreme Court, a somewhat misleading name as it is neither the highest court in the state nor even an appellate court. It is, in fact, a trial court, which has unlimited trial jurisdiction both in law and equity and in civil and criminal matters. Most counties have a County Court, which has both criminal and some limited civil jurisdiction. The Criminal Procedure Law defines the Supreme and County Courts as Superior Courts, and they have exclusive trial jurisdiction over felonies. They also have trial jurisdiction over misdemeanors concurrent with that of the local criminal courts. If a petty offense, i.e., a traffic infraction or a violation, is charged along with a crime, these courts may also try such offenses in the same trial as the crime.

In addition to trial jurisdiction, superior courts have preliminary jurisdiction over all offenses, but they exercise this jurisdiction only through the agency of their grand juries.

There is a diversity of lower courts in the various counties of the state, such as county-wide district courts, the New York City Criminal Court, or city, town, and village courts. These are collectively referred to in the Criminal Procedure Law as Local Criminal Courts to distinguish them from the Superior Criminal Courts. (The somewhat pejorative term Inferior Courts is no longer used.)

Local criminal courts have trial jurisdiction over all offenses except felonies. They have exclusive trial jurisdiction over petty offenses except when these are tried together with a crime in a superior court. They have concurrent trial jurisdiction over misdemeanors with the superior courts, subject to divestiture by the latter. They also have preliminary jurisdiction over all offenses, subject to divestiture by the superior courts and their grand juries.

A criminal action is commenced by the filing of an accusatory instrument in a criminal court. Usually the instrument is filed in a local criminal court. The only way for a criminal action to be commenced in a superior criminal court is by the filing of a grand jury indictment against a defendant who has never been held by a local criminal court.

There are several types of local criminal court accusatory instruments: an information, a simplified information, a prosecutor's information, a misdemeanor complaint, and a felony complaint.

An information is a written, verified (sworn) accusation by a person called a complainant charging one or more persons with the commission of one or more offenses, none of which is a felony. It serves to commence an action and as the basis for prosecution for a misdemeanor or less in a local criminal court. Statutes provide for simplified forms of information in cases of traffic infractions, parks department violations, and violations of the environmental protection laws. A prosecutor's information is prepared by a district attorney at the direction of a grand jury or a local criminal court or on his or her own initiative.

A misdemeanor complaint is an instrument that serves to commence a criminal action for a misdemeanor, but it is not sufficient to form the basis for a prosecution unless the defendant has waived the right to be prosecuted by an information. A felony complaint is similar to a misdemeanor complaint in that it starts a criminal action involving a felony charge, but it is never sufficient to form the basis for a prosecution. A prosecution for a felony must be based on a grand jury indictment or, with the defendant's consent, a superior court information in lieu of indictment. Informations, misdemeanor complaints, and felony complaints must all contain an accusatory part and a factual part.

The accusatory part must designate the offenses charged. Two or more offenses may be charged in separate counts, and two or more defendants may be charged, but every defendant joined must be charged with every count in the instrument.

The factual part of the accusatory instrument, to which the complainant swears, must contain facts of an evidentiary nature tending to support the charge. It is in the requirements of the factual part that an information differs from the other two types of instrument. The factual part of an information must provide reasonable cause to believe that the defendant committed the offenses charged in the accusatory part *and* non-hearsay allegations which, if true, establish each and every element of the offense charged and the defendant's guilt, as well. This latter requirement is what lawyers refer to as a *prima facie case*; it means that, if the evidence is taken at face value, each element of the *corpus delecti* of the crime is established. The former requirement is merely a statement of reasonable cause. The two are not equivalent. It is possible to have a very weak or unconvincing *prima facie*, or legally sufficient, case. On the other hand, there may be a strong basis for the belief that a defendant has committed a crime although the elements of a *prima facie* case are missing, and the defendant could not be convicted on such evidence. For example, a young man stopped while running away from an appliance store with a television set in his hands may claim that he had the store owner's permission to enter the store and take the set to work on it. If the store owner is not presently available to contradict this story, there is no *prima facie* case even though there is reasonable cause to believe that a crime has been committed and that the accused probably committed it. In this case, a misdemeanor complaint would be filed until the store owner could execute the information, as misdemeanor and felony complaints are not required to have their factual parts allege a legally sufficient case. They need only set forth facts to indicate a reasonable cause to believe the defendant guilty. It is for this reason that these instruments, while adequate to commence a criminal proceeding, are inadequate to form the basis for a prosecution.

If the factual part of a local court accusatory instrument is inadequate, it may be supplemented with additional sworn statements or affidavits by other witnesses. Simplified informations do not have factual parts, but the defendant may demand supporting depositions prior to entering a plea or going to trial. If this material is not supplied, the information must be dismissed. The filing of a proper accusatory instrument not only sets in operation the legal machinery that will ultimately result in the defendant's conviction or discharge, it also stops the statute of limitations from running.

A statute of limitations prescribes a period of time from the commission of an offense during which a prosecution must be commenced. The idea behind this limitation is that, as time goes by, witnesses become harder to locate, and their memories become weaker. Hence, it becomes unjust to require a defendant to defend him- or herself against an accusation after a long delay in prosecution. There is no statute of limitations on a Class A felony, and prosecutions for them may be commenced at any time. A prosecution for any other felony must be commenced within five years of its commission and, for a misdemeanor, within two years. A petty offense must be prosecuted within one year. There are special circumstances under which these limits are extended. For example, the statute for a larceny committed by a fiduciary may be extended for one year from the time when the facts were discovered or should have been discovered. In offenses involving misconduct in public office, a prosecution may be commenced at any time while the defendant is in office and five years thereafter, but the statute can never be extended for more than five years from the basic limitation. There is one interesting anachronism left over from the time when a criminal prosecution was deemed to commence with an arrest rather than with the filing of an accusatory instrument. If a defendant is continuously out of the state, or the defendant's whereabouts remain unknown and unascertainable despite a reasonably diligent search, then the statute is tolled, i.e., stops running. Here again the basic statute can be extended for no more than five years.

In addition to the right to a timely prosecution, a defendant in a criminal action has a right to a speedy trial after a prosecution has commenced. A criminal action is entitled to a preference in trial or hearing over all civil actions or special proceedings. If a defendant is in the custody of the sheriff pending trial, the defendant is entitled to a preference over all criminal actions (except those in which the defendant is out on bail or his or her own recognizance for 180 days or longer).

Following the filing of an accusatory instrument in a local criminal court, the defendant must be brought before the court for an arraignment to the charge.

The purposes of the arraignment are:

1. To give the court jurisdiction over the person of the defendant.
2. To advise the defendant of the nature of the charges against him and of his rights, and to effectuate these rights.
3. To issue a securing order or set bail pending further proceedings.
4. To chart the course of future proceedings.
5. To permit motion attacks on the legal sufficiency of the accusatory instrument.

The defendant is brought before the bar of the local criminal court in one of two ways. He may be arrested either with or without a warrant, or he may be invited to appear either by an appearance ticket issued by a police officer or a summons issued by the court. The details of these devices will be considered in the next chapter.

If the defendant is charged with a misdemeanor in an information, he may enter a plea at this stage. If charged by a misdemeanor complaint, the defendant may waive his right to have the complaint replaced with an information and consent to be prosecuted on the basis of the complaint. If he is well advised, however, he will demand that this instrument be replaced with an information before entering a plea. If the defendant is charged by a felony complaint, he cannot enter a plea, as there is no prosecutory instrument to plead to. The entire purpose of the felony complaint is simply to hold the defendant pending the action of the grand jury. At the arraignment stage, however, the defendant may demand a preliminary hearing on the felony charge. The purpose of this hearing is not to establish guilt or innocence, but simply to test whether the people have enough evidence to justify holding the defendant for the action of a grand jury. The people are no longer required to present a legally sufficient or *prima facie* case. They merely must prove reasonable cause to believe that a crime was committed and that the defendant probably committed it.

As a result of the preliminary hearing: (1) the defendant may be held for grand jury action on the original charge, (2) the charges may be reduced, or (3) the charges may be dismissed and the defendant discharged. If the last situation occurs, it does not mean that the district attorney cannot still present the case to the grand jury, or that the defendant cannot be tried and convicted of the original charge. It simply means that the defendant cannot be rearrested for the same charge until a grand jury has acted. No jeopardy attaches to the defendant as a result of a felony hearing within the meaning of the constitutional prohibition against double jeopardy. For jeopardy to attach, a defendant must appear before a court of competent jurisdiction to acquit or convict (which a local criminal court lacks in a felony case), and a trial must have proceeded at least to the stage where a jury has been impaneled or a witness has been sworn. As a practical matter, however, if the local criminal court dismisses a case, the people are unlikely to pursue it further unless there is a lot of publicity associated with it. Most prosecutors' offices are busy enough.

While the people are not required to present their full case at a felony hearing, they must disclose enough to establish reasonable cause to hold the defendant. That is why many defense attorneys routinely demand a preliminary hearing. It allows them to get information about the people's case. This strategy results from the adversary nature of the criminal procedure and from the fact that neither side is willing to give the other any more information about its case than is required. Often, to get around the need for this disclosure, a district attorney will try to present the case to a grand jury before the date set for the preliminary hearing. If this is done, the defense is deprived of the opportunity for this hearing because it has become moot. For this reason defense attorneys try to get preliminary hearings as soon as possible.

In the City of New York, misdemeanors were formerly tried in a court called Special Sessions, while arraignments were conducted in the old Magistrate's Court. Hence, in New York City, preliminary hearings were conducted in misdemeanor cases to see if the evidence warranted holding the defendant over for Special Sessions. When the new Criminal Procedure Law was under discussion, the right of a defendant in New York City to a preliminary hearing in a misdemeanor case was retained. This was done, in spite of the fact that the same court (the New York City Criminal Court) now had both preliminary and trial jurisdiction, in order to get the support of the criminal bar for the new law. The fact that there are differences in procedures within the same state should cause no surprise to the reader. Often the standards of justice vary enormously from one part of a state to another. A defendant charged with a serious felony in a city with a congested criminal calendar may have the charge reduced to a misdemeanor and ultimately get an adjournment in contemplation of dismissal. In a less crowded rural area, a defendant charged with the same offense may ultimately draw a 20-year prison term.

If, following a felony hearing, the local criminal court does not reduce or dismiss the charge, the file is forwarded to the superior court for the action of its grand jury. The defendant is continued either in custody or on bail. In the case of a misdemeanor, after the entry of a plea of not guilty, the case is scheduled for trial.

If a grand jury finds that the evidence presented *both* provides a reasonable cause to believe that some crime was committed and that the defendant committed it, *and* is legally sufficient to establish each element of the crime and the defendant's guilt thereof, it issues an accusatory instrument called a "true bill." When filed with the superior criminal court, the true bill becomes an indictment. An indictment charges at least one crime and may charge several in separate counts.

If a grand jury refuses to indict, no jeopardy attaches to the defendant, but the case may not be presented to a grand jury again without the court's permission. If permission is granted, and the grand jury refuses to indict a second time, the case cannot be presented again. If a grand jury fails to return a true bill, the defendant must be discharged and any bail exonerated.

Following an indictment, there is a second arraignment of the defendant, to the indictment, this time in the superior court.

Again the defendant must be advised both of the charges against him and of his rights, and, as in an arraignment in a local criminal court, must be provided with a copy of the accusatory instrument. A securing order or bail must be set, and the defendant may make motion attacks on the indictment, or on any parts of it that he contends are illegal. Unless the indictment is dismissed pursuant to these motion attacks, the defendant must enter a plea to the indictment, and the case is scheduled for trial.

In most misdemeanors and in all felonies, the defendant is entitled to a trial by jury. He may waive this right and be tried by the court alone. In general, it is the function of juries to decide on all contested issues of fact and the responsibility of the court to decide on all questions of law, and on preliminary questions of fact relating to the admissibility of evidence. If the defendant waives a jury trial, the judge sits as the trier of both the facts and the law. Such a waiver must be in writing and signed by the defendant in open court before the commencement of a trial. If they feel that their case is strong, many lawyers prefer to try a case before a judge rather than a jury, particularly if they are familiar with the judge's attitudes toward the issues involved in the trial so that they can predict how the judge is likely to react to the case. Even an unfamiliar judge reacts more predictably than a jury of laymen in that the judge is likely to think about the issues as a lawyer does. Often lawyers will seek adjournments solely for the purpose of getting the case heard by a particular judge or to avoid another. This is called "judge shopping." If the case is weak, or counsel fears it will be heard by a judge unfavorably disposed to his or her arguments, then counsel will prefer a jury. Some trial lawyers feel very confident with juries and would prefer them in any event. A very skilled trial lawyer once told one of the authors that he could make a jury cry and laugh at the same time, and he probably can. In any event the final decision about waiving a jury trial must be made by the defendant with the advice and recommendations of the lawyer. The details of the procedure in a criminal trial will be discussed in Chapter 10. For now we will merely list the sequence of the major events.

The first step in a jury trial is the examination and selection of jurors and their swearing in. This is followed by preliminary instructions from the judge to the jurors concerning their duties.

The next step requires the people to make an opening statement to the jury outlining the case against the defendant and stating what the people intend to prove. In turn, the defense is given an opportunity to make an opening address to the jury if it chooses. Often defense attorneys either waive an opening or merely ask the jury to keep open minds until all the evidence is in. They do not wish to disclose their case in advance. If the defense is going to trial simply because a satisfactory plea bargain could not be arranged, it may have no case to present. The defense may waive an opening because it has no burden of proving anything in a criminal trial. The people have the burden of proof and must make an opening statement offering to prove at least a *prima facie* case. If they fail to do so, the action will be dismissed.

After the opening addresses, the people, having the burden of proof on all issues, must present their direct case first. This is done by calling their witnesses to testify. After each prosecution witness testifies under direct examination by the assistant district attorney, the witness is subjected to cross-examination by the defense attorney. Following this a re-direct examination by the prosecutor is permitted. Technically, it is limited to matters brought up under cross-examination, but the trial judge has discretion to permit new material to be introduced. After presenting all of their evidence, the people rest, and the defendant routinely makes a motion to dismiss the action on the grounds that the people have failed to prove a *prima facie* case. The defendant may also move to dismiss on other grounds. Usually the trial judge will reserve decision on this motion because a trial order of dismissal, while not an acquittal, cannot be appealed by the people if this would necessitate the taking of new trial evidence if the appeal was successful. If this motion is granted after the verdict is in, then a new trial will not be needed if the people are upheld on an appeal.[1]

Unless the motion attacks are summarily granted, the defense presents its direct case in the same manner as the people did and subject to cross-examination by the assistant district attorney. Following the defense's direct case, the people may present rebuttal witnesses to respond to the defense's evidence; the defense may then present its rebuttal witnesses. This procedure may continue for as long as the trial judge deems proper.

When all of the evidence is in, the defense sums up its case to the jury. This is followed by the people's summation. Since the people have the burden of proof, they have the right to make the opening and closing arguments.

After the summations, the judge charges the jury as to the law applicable to the particular case, instructing them to apply the law to the facts as they find them and advising them concerning the manner of their deliberations and the possible verdicts that they may render. Each side is then given an opportunity to object or take exception to specific instructions in the court's charge and to submit requests for points to be included in the charge. At last, the jury retires to deliberate and reach a verdict.

If the jury's verdict acquits the defendant of all charges, the court must immediately discharge him from custody and exonerate his bail. If he is convicted on any charge, a date is set for sentencing, and bail is either continued, revoked, or increased. The reason for revoking or increasing bail at this point is that it is the function of bail to assure the defendant's attendance at subsequent proceedings. Since he has now been convicted of a crime and is in greater peril of incarceration, there is a greater risk of his absconding. This is especially so when the defendant has neither roots nor property in the area.

Cases tried before a judge without a jury follow basically the same order except that opening and closing statements are briefer. It is considered bad manners to make the same type of argument to a judge that would be appropriate for a jury, since the judge is presumed to be a highly skilled lawyer capable of following the most complex legal arguments without the prompting of counsel. There is, of course, no charge given in a non-jury case. The court simply retires to consider its verdict. In simple cases that are unlikely to be appealed, the court may render its verdict immediately following the motion made for an acquittal by the defense after the closing of its case. This is particularly likely if the court feels that there is some reasonable doubt of the defendant's guilt because the people cannot appeal an acquittal.

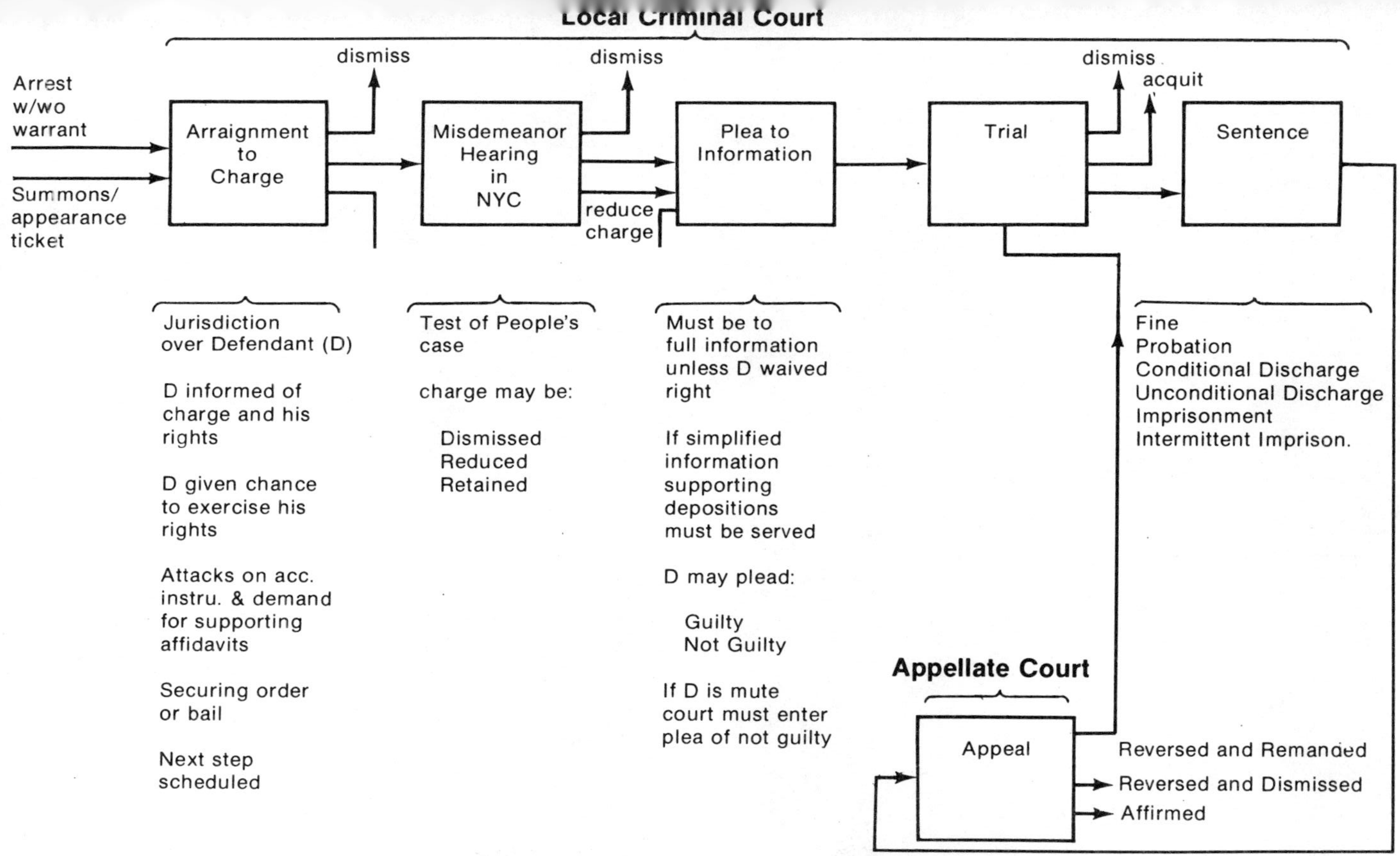

Local Criminal Court

Arrest w/wo warrant → **Summons/ appearance ticket** →

Arraignment to Charge
- Jurisdiction over Defendant (D)
- D informed of charge and his rights
- D given chance to exercise his rights
- Attacks on acc. instru. & demand for supporting affidavits
- Securing order or bail
- Next step scheduled

dismiss →

Misdemeanor Hearing in NYC
{ Test of People's case
charge may be:
- Dismissed
- Reduced
- Retained

dismiss →
reduce charge →

Plea to Information
- Must be to full information unless D waived right
- If simplified information supporting depositions must be served
- D may plead:
  - Guilty
  - Not Guilty
- If D is mute court must enter plea of not guilty

Trial

dismiss
acquit →

Sentence
- Fine
- Probation
- Conditional Discharge
- Unconditional Discharge
- Imprisonment
- Intermittent Imprison.

Appellate Court

Appeal
- Reversed and Remanded
- Reversed and Dismissed
- Affirmed

Fig. 8-1   Procedural steps in a misdemeanor prosecution.

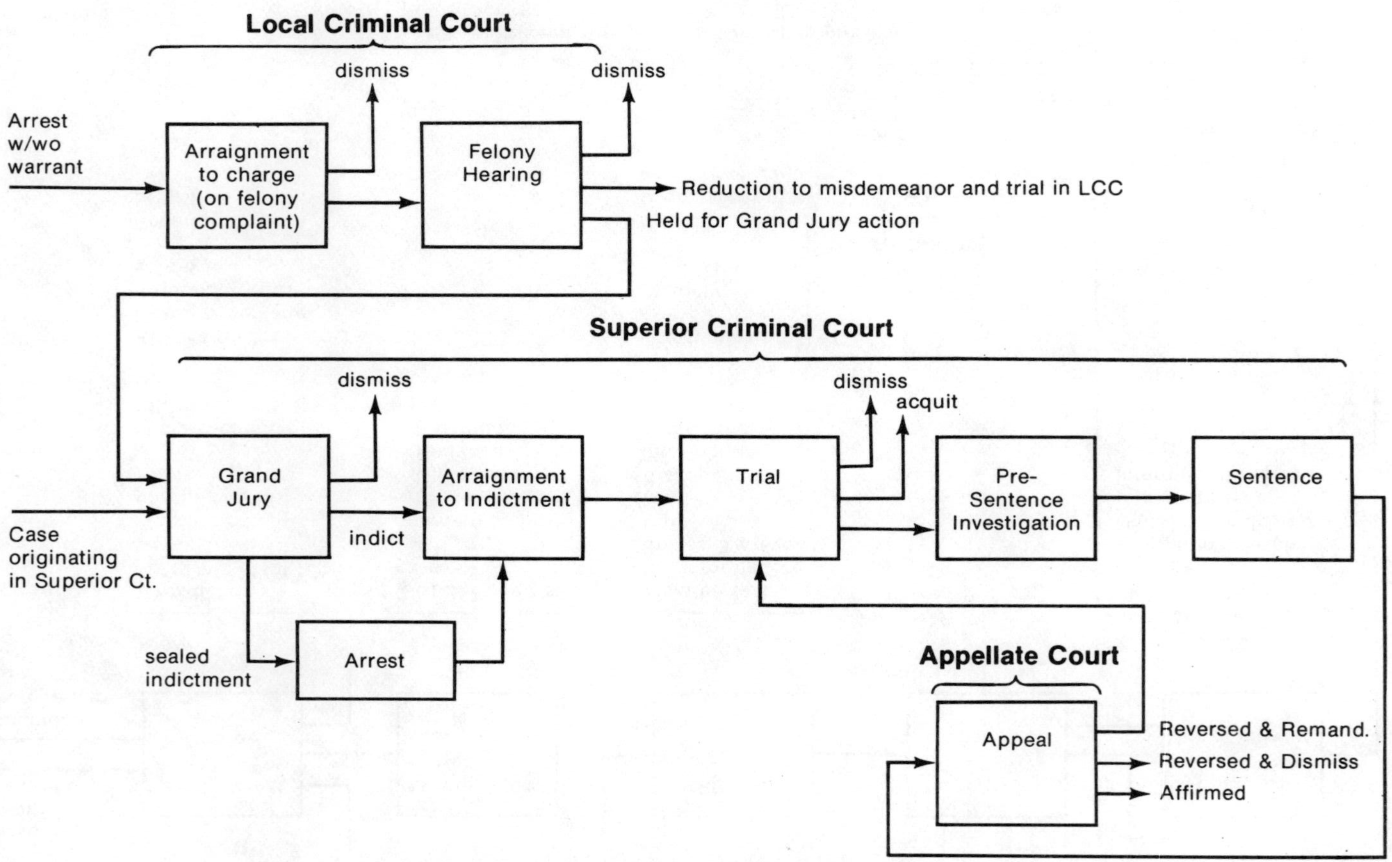

Local Criminal Court

Arrest w/wo warrant

Arraignment to charge (on felony complaint)

dismiss

dismiss

Felony Hearing

dismiss

Reduction to misdemeanor and trial in LCC

Held for Grand Jury action

Superior Criminal Court

Case originating in Superior Ct.

Grand Jury

sealed indictment

Arrest

dismiss

indict

Arraignment to Indictment

Trial

dismiss

acquit

Pre-Sentence Investigation

Sentence

Appellate Court

Appeal

Reversed & Remand.

Reversed & Dismiss

Affirmed

Fig. 8-2   Procedural steps in a felony prosecution.

Figure 8-1 summarizes the procedural steps involved in the prosecution of a misdemeanor, and Figure 8-2 illustrates the procedure for felony prosecutions. The details of each of these steps will be expanded upon in chapters 9, 10 and 13.

The overall plan that emerges from a study of these charts is that the criminal procedures are like a set of progressively smaller sieves. A certain number of defective prosecution cases are eliminated at each step. Many potential cases are lost because the offenders are never detected or apprehended. Of those arrested, some will be dismissed at the arraignment to the charge because of defective informations. Other cases may be dismissed later at preliminary hearings because, while the felony complaint is suffcient on its face, the evidence elicited at the hearing does not support it, or the interests of justice require a dismissal. If the case proceeds to a grand jury, it may now be dismissed because, for the first time, a *prima facie*, or legally sufficient, case, is needed to proceed, and it may be lacking. Finally, a case may be dismissed after the people's direct case if the court feels that the people's case is too weak. The effect of this series of sieves is, first of all, to protect an innocent person by providing a series of reviews before he or she is required to go through the expense, risk, and mental anguish of a criminal trial. Second, it is designed to assure that the people will only go through the expense of a trial where they have the strongest cases and the highest probability of success.

REFERENCES

1. *People v. King Brown*, 40 N.Y. 2d 381.

9
Pre-Trial Procedures

ARRESTS

The various types of accusatory instruments that are used to initiate the prosecution of all types of offenses were described in a general way in the previous chapter. The appropriate instrument must be filed with the court at or prior to the defendant's arraignment to the charge as it is the basis of the arraignment and must be read to him and a copy furnished either to him or to his attorney. However, this instrument may not be in existence at the time of the defendant's arrest on the charge. In cases in which the instrument has been filed prior to the defendant's arrest, the local criminal court will issue a warrant of arrest addressed to some police officer or a class of police officers directing that the defendant be taken into custody and brought before the court for arraignment without unnecessary delay. A warrant of arrest may be executed on any day of the week and at any hour of the day or night. Unless the defendant's resistance or attempt to escape makes normal procedures impractical, the officer is required to state his authority for making the arrest and to show the defendant a copy of the warrant upon request if he has it with him (which is not required). The officer may use reasonable force, if necessary, in effecting an arrest. He is also authorized to enter premises in which he has reasonable grounds for believing that the defendant may be, but he must first state his authority. If he is denied permission to enter, or if the normal procedures might allow the defendant to escape, destroy evidence, or risk harm to the officer or someone else, the officer may enter by breaking in.

If a police officer discovers a person committing an offense, the officer may make an arrest without a warrant and will file the accusatory instrument with the court when he brings the defendant in to be arraigned. Most large district attorney's offices have complaint bureaus where incoming complaints are screened and private complainants and police officers are aided in the preparation of the required accusatory instruments. A police officer may arrest a person for a *petty* offense which he reasonably believes that the person has committed in his presence, and for any *crime* which he reasonably believes that the person has committed whether in his presence or not. As in the case of an arrest with a warrant, he must inform the detainee of the reason for the arrest, if it is practical to do so. The officer has the same right to use force and enter or break into private premises without a warrant as he would with one under the appropriate circumstances. The somewhat archaic practice of arrest without a warrant by a private citizen is still permitted, but in this case the private citizen will be liable for a false arrest suit if the suspect is not, in fact, guilty of the offense charged. This is so regardless of how reasonable the grounds for suspicion were.

A novel legal concept that New York has enacted is its "Stop and Frisk" Law. This law gives a police officer the right to stop a person in a public place when the officer reasonably suspects that such person has committed or is about to commit a felony or a misdemeanor defined in the Penal Law. He may demand of him: his name, address, and an explanation of his conduct. Further, if the officer suspects that he is in danger of physical injury, he may search such a person for any dangerous weapon not ordinarily carried in public by law-abiding citizens. If a search discloses such a weapon, the officer must either arrest the detainee or, if the possession of the weapon was legal, return it, following his inquiry. The courts, in accordance with the principle that statutes are to be interpreted in such a manner that they are constitutional, if possible, have held this search permission to be limited to a "pat down" and not a full body search. It should be noted that while reasonable grounds to suspect the person are required, this is considerably less restrictive than the requirement of probable cause to believe that the person has committed a crime, which is necessary to authorize an arrest without a warrant.

If an arrest is legally made, the officer has the authority to search the defendant and his immediate vicinity (grabbing distance) without a search warrant, both to secure evidence and to protect himself. If an arrest is made illegally, without probable cause, no evidence turned up as a result of a post-arrest search will render the illegal arrest legal. In such a case, the defense may move at the trial to suppress the use of evidence obtained as the result of an illegal search and seizure. This new remedy was made available on the theory that law enforcement agents should not violate the law, and that if they are permitted to use the fruits of their illegal conduct, they are in fact being motivated to do so.

Prior to bringing the arrestee before the local criminal court for arraignment, the arresting officer is required to have him fingerprinted. This is mandatory if the charge is:

1. A felony.
2. A misdemeanor defined in the Penal Law.
3. A misdemeanor defined outside of the Penal Law if it would become a felony given a previous conviction.
4. Loitering for the purposes of soliciting deviant sexual conduct.

The officer is not required, but is permitted, to fingerprint an arrestee if unable to ascertain his identity, or if he reasonably believes that the identification given is not accurate or that the person may be sought by other law enforcement officials for some other offense.

These fingerprints are forwarded to a Central Criminal Justice Services Department, which will return information to the police officer concerning the defendant's prior criminal record, if any. The officer must then supply copies to the district attorney and to the court. At the arraignment, the court must supply a copy of this "rap sheet," as it is called, to the defendant or his attorney. This record is part of the information that the judge has available for making decisions about bail.

If a defendant is charged with any crime or offense less than a felony, it is not necessary that he be arrested to be brought before the court for arraignment. If an accusatory instrument has already been filed in a local criminal court, the judge may cause the defendant to be served with a summons requiring his appearance at a specified time and place in order to be arraigned to the charge against him, instead of issuing a warrant of arrest. If the judge believes that the defendant will comply with a summons, then the judge must issue a summons instead of an arrest warrant. This requirement is designed to protect the public from an unduly abusive enforcement of legal processes, such as the arrest and handcuffing of a citizen on some relatively minor and possibly spurious charge.

In spite of this law, abuses still occur. In a recent case, a respectable middle-aged woman with no prior criminal record was arrested and subjected to the degrading experience of a full body search by a matron on a charge of not answering a few parking tickets. In another case, a conviction was set aside when it was shown that the prosecutor deliberately withheld evidence that would have exonerated the defendant. In neither of these abuses of power could the judge or prosecutor be held accountable, for their actions were privileged. This privilege is granted because if public officials could be sued for every mistake in judgment, it would be impossible for them to function. Perhaps this thinking needs to be replaced with the notion that with power ought to go responsibility. The greater the power exercised over others, the more, not the less, accountability is needed.

If a police officer arrests a suspect without a warrant for an offense less than a felony, it is not necessary to keep him in custody or bring him before a local criminal court for an arraignment. The officer may instead issue him an "appearance ticket" directing him to appear for arraignment. If there are doubts about the defendant's compliance, the officer may require him to post pre-arraignment bail at the local police station prior to his release. The amounts of such bail that may be required are limited to $500 for a Class A misdemeanor, $250 for a Class B misdemeanor, and $100 for a violation. If the defendant fails to post such bail, then he must be brought before the local criminal court without unnecessary delay. Unlike judges and prosecutors, police officers are both civilly and criminally liable for illegal arrests and detentions. That is, they can be sued or prosecuted. This offers the citizen some protection; it might make officers more cautious than the public would like them to be.

ARRAIGNMENTS TO THE CHARGE

In general a defendant must appear in person at an arraignment, although the court may agree to permit his counsel to stand in for him if his appearance was procured by a summons or an appearance ticket.

The first thing done at an arraignment is to inform the defendant of the charges against him. Either the court or someone in the presence of the court must read the accusatory instrument to the defendant and provide him or his lawyer with a copy of the instrument. When the defendant is represented by counsel, the attorney will usually waive the reading of the instrument to save time. The requirement that the reading must be either by the court or in its presence was put into the law to legalize the once illegal practice of having a bridgeman (court attendant) read the complaint instead of the judge. In any event, it must be read so that the defendant can understand it, rather than in the *pro forma* fashion of a tobacco auctioneer. If the defendant does not have counsel with him, the judge will usually ask the defendant on the court record if he does understand it. If the defendant does not speak English, an interpreter must be supplied to translate the complaint to him.

Next, the court informs the defendant of his rights. It must advise him that he has a right to the aid of counsel at the arraignment and at every subsequent stage of the action, and that if he appears without a lawyer, he has a right to an adjournment in order to obtain counsel. He has the right to communicate free of charge by phone or letter for the purpose of obtaining counsel and to inform a relative or friend that he is being charged with an offense. He is not, as the media would have it, limited to a single phone call. In fact, he may make as many calls as necessary to locate his lawyer, since once the defendant has demanded counsel, the proceedings cannot go on until his lawyer is present.

The defendant is then asked if he wants an adjournment to obtain counsel or to call family or a friend.

Except in cases where the offenses charged are violations or traffic infractions only, he must also be told that if he cannot afford counsel, he will be furnished one free of charge by the court.

The court is not only required to advise the defendant of his rights and give him an opportunity to exercise them, but it must also take whatever affirmative action is necessary to see that these rights are effectuated.

All of this may not seem like much to a reader with little experience in criminal matters, but there are some countries in which a person can be held for years without any charges being preferred against him and without any means of notifying family or friends that he is a prisoner.

If a defendant says that he cannot afford private counsel, the court will assign to him either a Legal Aid Society lawyer or a private lawyer who has volunteered to handle such cases. The lawyer has the responsibility to inquire into the defendant's ability to pay private counsel. If he finds that the defendant can afford such counsel, he will ask the court to be relieved; if not, he will represent the defendant. In the past, assigned counsel were not paid except in capital cases. Young lawyers would volunteer to handle these cases to get experience, often at the expense of their clients. Today court-appointed counsel are paid, however inadequately. This makes it more likely that an indigent defendant will have a lawyer who can afford to take the time to prepare a proper defense.

Legal Aid Society lawyers are probably more experienced in the operation of the criminal courts than any other lawyers except assistant district attorneys. A defendant represented by a Legal Aid Society lawyer usually gets excellent counsel. People often say that there are two systems of justice, one for the rich and one for the poor, but, in our opinion, this is not really true. The two systems of justice are for the rich and poor, as opposed to the middle class. As in the case of medical or psychological care, both the rich who can afford the best and the poor who get it free usually get good-quality legal representation. Members of the middle class who have to pay for these services themselves and cannot afford to, usually wind up with something less.

Another public service performed by some Legal Aid Societies is the training of young lawyers through internship programs. Inexperienced lawyers can gain trial experience under the supervision and guidance of more experienced counsel. One of the authors was the beneficiary of such a program conducted by the New York City Legal Aid Society's Criminal Courts Division. Some 20 years later he still regards it as the most valuable part of his legal education.

If the defendant advises the court that he wishes to proceed *pro se*, i.e., without counsel, and the court is satisfied that he has made this decision with knowledge of its significance, it must permit him to do so. If not so satisfied, the court may not proceed until the defendant has counsel, either of his own choice or assigned. If the court does permit the defendant to represent himself, it must inform him that the right to counsel cannot be waived, that the defendant retains the right to counsel at any stage of the proceeding and is always entitled to an adjournment for the purpose of securing counsel. If the defendant does later choose to obtain counsel, the proceedings do not start over *ab initio*, and the attorney will be bound by any mistakes that the client has made.

It is difficult to conceive of any circumstances under which a defendant, even if he is an experienced criminal lawyer, can rationally elect to proceed in a criminal matter without the aid of counsel. There is an old saying in the law that one who tries his own case has a fool for a client. Nowhere is this truer than in a criminal action.

Having informed the defendant of the charges against him and of his rights, the court will entertain any motion attacks that the defense may make against the accusatory instrument in cases of misdemeanors or less. A motion is an application for a court order, and the defense may move for an order dismissing the charges on the grounds that the accusatory instrument is insufficient on its face to comply with the statutory requirements, or that it shows that the court lacks jurisdiction, or that the law under which the offense is charged is unconstitutional. If the court finds these objections well taken, and the people neither move to amend the complaint nor to correct the defect, or are not able to, the court will dismiss the charges. A dismissal is not an acquittal and does not bar future prosecution of the defendant on the charge if the people are later able to draft a satisfactory accusatory instrument. As a practical matter most cases do terminate upon such a dismissal.

At this stage of the proceedings the defense may also move to dismiss an information or misdemeanor complaint on the grounds that:

1. The defendant has received immunity from prosecution.
2. The defendant has been placed in double jeopardy, or there has been a previous prosecution on the same or similar charges.
3. The statute of limitations has expired.
4. There is some other legal impediment to prosecution.
5. The defendant has been denied his right to a speedy trial.
6. Even though there are no legal grounds for dismissal, the interests of justice would require a dismissal.

The defendant must raise every one of these objections that he can in the same motion (except number 5), for if he seeks to add one later, the court may dismiss it summarily on the grounds that it was not made at the appropriate time. The court has, however, the discretion to consider such a motion on its merits at a later time if good cause can be shown for the delay.

The sixth of these objections provides the court with authority to dismiss an otherwise legally sound case if some compelling reason demonstrates that a prosecution would result in an injustice. Such a motion will be granted only in very unusual circumstances.

If the motion attacks on the complaint fail, and the offense charged is not a felony, the court, with the consent of both the people and the defense, may grant an "adjournment in contemplation of dismissal" (ACOD). This is an adjournment *sine die* (without a day set for further proceedings) made with a view toward the ultimate dismissal of the charges. On issuing such an order the court must release the defendant on his own recognizance (ROC). Upon the application of the people within six months of such adjournment the case must be restored to the calendar; otherwise it is deemed dismissed in the interests of justice. This treatment is much more likely to be afforded in relatively minor offenses, particularly if the defendant has no prior record. Much less common is a dismissal in the interests of justice because here if the defendant gets into any further trouble within six months, the people cannot reinstitute the case.

In the case of a misdemeanor, either the people or the defendant may request an adjournment, at any time prior to the entry of a plea of guilty or the commencement of a trial, for the purpose of making a motion in superior court to prosecute the case by indictment. If such a motion is made and granted, the local criminal court loses jurisdiction, and the case proceeds in the superior court. If the motion is not timely made or is denied, the case proceeds in the local criminal court.

Preliminary Hearing

If the charge is a felony, the defense may now demand a preliminary hearing to determine if there is enough evidence to hold the defendant for the action of the grand jury.

The district attorney must conduct a preliminary hearing for the people and provide reasonable grounds to believe that a crime was committed and that the defendant committed it. At this time, it is not necessary to prove a legally sufficient or *prima facie* case. The defendant has the right to be present at this hearing and to cross-examine the people's witnesses. He does not have the right to call his own witnesses at this stage, but the judge has discretion to permit him to do so. The defendant does have the right to testify in his own behalf if he wishes. All witnesses, including the defendant, must testify under oath and be subject to cross-examination. The former practice of permitting the defendant to make an unsworn statement has been eliminated on the theory that his testimony should be tested like that of any other witness and that he should not have a license to commit perjury. Only non-hearsay legal evidence is permitted at the hearing. On the application of the defendant, not the people, the court may exclude the public and direct that there be no disclosure of the proceedings. This step is designed to protect a possibly innocent defendant from harmful publicity.

If the court finds at the conclusion of the hearing that there are reasonable grounds for believing that the defendant committed a misdemeanor or less but not a felony, it may reduce the charges, and have the felony complaint replaced with an information, and continue the case in the lower criminal court. The court may reduce the charge even if the evidence does provide reasonable grounds for believing that the defendant did, in fact, commit a felony if the felony is not an armed felony or a listed class A felony, and if the court believes this to be in the interest of justice. In this case, though, the people must agree to the reduction. If there is insufficient evidence that the defendant has committed *any* offense, he must be discharged and any bail exonerated. If none of these happens the defendant is held for grand jury action, and his file is forwarded to the superior court. (A misdemeanor hearing in New York City is disposed of similarly except if the action is not dismissed, it continues in the local criminal court.)

Even if the defendant waives a felony hearing, the court has the authority to inquire into the charges to determine whether they should be reduced or dismissed.

If the defendant is charged with a misdemeanor or less and the accusatory instrument is a simplified information, he may demand at the arraignment that supporting depositions be filed prior to the entry of his plea. If the instrument is a misdemeanor complaint, he may demand that it be replaced with an information before he pleads to it. Both of these rights may be waived. If they are not, failure of the people to supply depositions supporting a simplified information renders the information insufficient on its face, and a defendant held in custody for over five days on a misdemeanor complaint not replaced by an information is entitled to be released on his own recognizance unless the people can show some compelling reason to the contrary. The judge at the arraignment must inform the defendant of his right to have these preliminary accusatory instruments perfected. He must also warn the defendant if a conviction will or may result in a license revocation, and advise him that a plea of guilty is equivalent to conviction after trial.

When all of the other matters at an arraignment have been completed, and a misdemeanor hearing, if available, has been held, a defendant charged with a misdemeanor or less is required to enter a plea to the information. There can be no plea entered in a local criminal court to a felony charge, since the basis of a felony prosecution is an indictment, and the defendant has not yet been indicted. There are two pleas available to a defendant, guilty or not guilty, and usually a plea must be made by the defendant personally. If the defendant stands mute, the court must enter a plea of not guilty on his behalf. The effect of a plea will be discussed in more detail under indictments, since the same principles apply to pleading to misdemeanor or felony charges. For now it suffices to point out that a plea of not guilty places each and every allegation in the accusatory instrument in issue. This is very different from a civil action. There the plantiff serves a pleading called a complaint, which alleges certain ultimate facts that constitute his cause of action. The defendant then serves a pleading called an answer, in which he either admits or denies each separate allegation in the complaint. The only issues in a civil trial are those allegations in a complaint that the defendant denies. Thus, the issues to be tried are narrowed. In a criminal action, the defendant may not admit any of the allegations in the accusatory instrument unless he admits them all by pleading guilty. Unless he does so, the people must proceed to prove each and every element of their case beyond a reasonable doubt.

SECURING ORDERS AND BAIL

The last step at an arraignment to the charge is the issuing of a securing order to assure the appearance of the defendant at the next step of the proceedings. The court may order the defendant remanded to the custody of the sheriff, set bail in a certain amount, or discharge the defendant on his own recognizance without security. The alternative it selects and how much bail, if any, is required depend upon how likely the judge feels the defendant is to appear when required to. Some of the factors that the court will consider in this regard are:

1. The seriousness of the offense charged and the penalties the defendant may be facing. (The protection of the public or the punishment of the defendant may be related to this factor, but they are not proper considerations despite the pressure from some sources for "preventive detention." The purpose of bail is to assure the defendant's appearance, not to punish him in advance of a judicial determination of guilt.)
2. The defendant's prior arrest record and reputation in the community.
3. The defendant's roots in the community, e.g., how long he has lived in it, his owning a home, his having a family in the community, his employment record.
4. The probability of conviction, i.e., the strength of the people's case.
5. Recommendations by counsel. District attorneys' recommendations tend to have more influence on judges than defense attorneys' simply because the former are a form of buck-passing. If the people recommend a very high bail and the judge refuses to go along, he is more vulnerable to criticism if the defendant absconds. Also the people cannot appeal a bail determination, while the defense can.

The incarceration of a defendant without bail being set has been upheld, as the Constitution only prohibits the setting of excessive bail, not the setting of no bail at all. In many states, certain serious crimes, usually capital ones, are not bailable on the theory that no amount of bail will assure the appearance in court of a defendant likely to be executed.

Psychological Factors in the Setting of Bail.   The bail decision is an important one, which has been the subject of a few studies by social scientists. Ebbesen and Konečni summarize several and add two of their own.

A 1960 study of 114,653 people under pre-trial detention for inability to make bail showed that only 27% were convicted and jailed. A study of 1,000 detainees in Philadelphia in 1954 showed that two-thirds were acquitted or, if convicted, were not jailed; yet they were detained an average of 33 days. In other words, many of those who are detained before trial would not be incarcerated at all but for the setting of bail at a figure too high for them to post. One might point to the numerous bail bondsmen in and around courthouses and argue that anyone can borrow what is needed to make bail. Since the borrower must pay the lender up to 10% of the bail figure, however, it is clear that the cost is too great for many. When one adds to that the finding that very few defendants flee to avoid trial,[1] it appears that justice requires that the bail-setting procedure be carefully scrutinized. Ebbesen and Konečni employ information integration theory in attempting to determine how judges arrive at bail figures with the ultimate hope of making recommendations for increased fairness in these decisions.

Information integration theory is concerned with the ways in which we put together information from various sources in forming impressions of people or groups and in making decisions about them. Some sources are more influential than others. The theory weights each bit of information according to its significance to the perceiver so that the net impression or decision is a kind of weighted average of the various inputs. Ebbesen and Konečni performed two studies, one a simulation, the other involving unobtrusive observation of actual bail hearings. The results of the two were different, presumably because while the first was better controlled, the second had greater external validity (i.e., was a more accurate picture of the way things really are).

In the California city in which the studies took place, bail hearings are generally brief and involve limited types of information. Essentially, the judge receives a file on the case that indicates the allegations and a bail recommendation made by the probation department. In addition, arguments are offered by the prosecution and the defense to support their respective recommendations for bail. The first study was designed to determine the weight each of these inputs was assigned by the judge and the rules the judge followed in integrating them.

Eighteen municipal and superior court judges were presented with simulated versions of such information. In this factorial design there were two levels of prior record, two of local ties, three levels of D.A. recommendations, and three levels of defense attorney recommendations. Each judge was given eight such records.

Judges were told that the cases came from the city's archives. Each record was printed on a separate sheet. The judges were asked to indicate the amount of bail they would set.

In all cases the accused was an unmarried male Caucasian between 21 and 25 years of age who was pleading not guilty to a charge of robbery. While the nature of the robbery differed slightly from case to case, the stolen property was always valued at between $850 and $950.

The D.A.'s recommendations were in the neighborhood of $1600 bail (low), $2250 (moderate), or $6250 (high); the defense's were $0 (i.e., release on own recognizance) (low), $550 (moderate), or $1100 (high). The accused was described either as having no prior record or as having a prior record for which he was now on probation. His local ties were either strong or weak; i.e., he had lived in town for more than four years or only a month or two, he was employed or unemployed, and he had or did not have family in the area.

In general, the first study showed that the judges averaged the information they were given, setting bail lower than the D.A. requested but considerably higher than the defense recommendation. With respect to the independent variables, bail was lower as ties were higher, and was higher where there was a prior record and where the D.A.'s recommendations were higher. The judges' decisions were unrelated to the recommendations of the defense. Which variables were most heavily weighted? The most important determinant of the decision was the strength of the local ties of the accused. Next in importance was the recommendation of the district attorney, and third in weight was the existence of a prior record. In short, the judges seem to have made decisions setting bail lower the more reasons the accused had for remaining in town. Experiment 2 inquired into decisions in real cases.

Judges are unlikely to be very different from other subjects in psychological research. Subjects generally like to be liked, respected, well thought of. One way to achieve this is to behave in a manner that the researcher will evaluate positively. In the present instance this means behaving judiciously, taking due account of all pertinent data, acting without bias, remembering that bail is to assure appearance, not to punish. In court, one might speculate, judges are less eager to impress another with their wisdom and fairness. To determine the degree of similarity between their on-the-bench behavior and their research-subject behavior, observers attended bail hearings conducted by five of the eighteen judges who had participated in the first study. They recorded data concerning the variables already mentioned as well as the severity of the crime at issue.

Nearly 80% of the variance of the actual decisions could be accounted for by the five predictor variables, each of which was significantly related to the decision. Of the five, the weakest predictor was the existence of a prior record and its seriousness. The strongest predictor was the D.A.'s recommendation (not local ties as in the first study). Severity of the crime, prior record, and local ties influenced the bail decision primarily indirectly, through their influence on the attorneys' recommendations. If cases of homicide are not included (bail practices differ for this crime), the amount of variance explained rises to 94.3%, and severity of the crime becomes a more significant predictor.

Judges seem to have weighed the D.A.'s recommendations most heavily although those recommendations were not always consistent with the purposes of bail. They sometimes called for higher bail for defendants with moderate or strong local ties than for those whose local ties were weak. In such cases, the D.A. seems to have weighed local ties less than other considerations.

The defense rarely suggested that bail be set (recommending release instead); when it did suggest bail, the judge was influenced by the suggestion. When the defense attorney urged that little or no bail be required, the judge was unlikely to be influenced.

The simulation study indicated that the judge added together local ties, D.A. recommendations, and prior record (listed in order of importance) in arriving at the bail decision. If we except murder cases, the observational study yielded a different picture. Further, both judges and D.A.'s actually average rather than add information in making their decisions. Judges averaged the severity of the crime and the attorneys' recommendations, assigning little weight to the defense's views unless it suggested substantial bail. The D.A. took account of both the severity of the crime and local ties, weighing more heavily the factor that would call for higher bail.

In a review of recent data concerning bail, Wald makes a number of pertinent points.[2] Pre-trial release appears to be closely related to a number of critical variables. If we control on local ties, prior record, the present offense, and the assignment or retention of counsel, we still find that persons released on bail are less likely to plead guilty, to be convicted, and to be imprisoned following conviction.

Although bail is a right of the accused, large numbers of men and women are detained, sometimes for very long periods, because they cannot raise the required money. In many instances, the conditions of detention are worse than the conditions of imprisonment. Since most of these detainees are very poor, their attorneys are likely to be court-appointed. One study of 1,000 such defendants showed that they had had little contact with their attorneys.

A related experiment in New York City showed that one in four detainees who could telephone family or bail bondsman freely were released; of those without this access, one in eight were ultimately released.

Bail practices were modified during the 1960s to the benefit of persons with community ties and personal resources. Reforms have helped the indigent or transient offender very little, if at all.

GRAND JURY PROCEEDINGS

At this point our discussion will be limited to felonies and misdemeanors prosecuted by indictment.

A grand jury is composed of not less than 16 nor more than 23 members who are selected in accordance with the Judiciary Law. Sixteen members constitute a quorum empowered to transact any business. A vote of at least 12 (a majority of 23) is required for any affirmative action. Neither the entire grand jury nor any individual grand juror may be challenged by either party, but the court has the authority to dismiss a grand jury and impanel a new one if it believes it was not selected in substantial conformity with the Judiciary Law. It may discharge or refuse to swear in any grand juror who it believes to be disqualified under the Judiciary Law or who is guilty of prejudice or misconduct.

The court appoints a foreman and an alternative foreman to serve in the foreman's absence. The grand jury members elect a secretary to keep material records.

Prior to the commencement of their duties, which usually last for a term of court, the court administers an oath of office and instructs the grand jurors in procedure. It also makes available to each grand juror a copy of the Criminal Procedure Law and such other material as it deems proper. If a grand jury's work will not be completed at the end of the term of court for which it was impaneled, the court has the authority to extend its term if requested to do so by both the grand jury and the district attorney.

Grand jury proceedings are secret. Neither the defendant nor his attorney has the right to be present during the presentation of evidence. The people's witnesses before a grand jury, therefore, are not subject to cross-examination as they were during a preliminary hearing and as they will be at any subsequent trial.

During grand jury deliberations no one except grand jurors may be present. During the hearing of evidence, in addition to the grand jurors and the witness, the district attorney, a clerk, a stenographer, and, if necessary, an interpreter may be present. A guard may be present to hold a witness in custody. Except for witnesses, all of these persons, as well as the grand jurors themselves, must be sworn to secrecy and are not permitted to disclose what occurred in the grand jury room. Witnesses may disclose anything they want to concerning the procedure.

The grand jury is the exclusive judge of the facts in any matter before it. The legal advisors to the grand jury are the court and the district attorney. The latter may rule on all questions of the competency of witnesses and the admissibility of evidence.

The secrecy of a grand jury proceeding, the lack of the right of cross-examination, and an adversary party acting as its legal advisor all prevent the grand jury from being a very effective screening device. In fact, grand juries often act as rubber stamps for prosecutors. Occasionally, they will refuse to indict so that they offer some, if not very much, protection for a defendant against whom the people have a very weak case.

There was a time when grand juries had the authority to fire the district attorney as their lawyer and to hire any lawyer whom they wished to advise them. This has been specifically prohibited by statute to prevent runaway grand juries who are out of the control of the district attorney's office. A grand jury still has a great deal of power to contravene the wishes and recommendations of a district attorney if it desires, as indeed it should have. If it were totally under the district attorney's control, it would be of no value as a screening device in the criminal justice system.

With certain specific exceptions all evidence presented before a grand jury must be non-hearsay and legal evidence, i.e., in accordance with the rules of evidence that will be described later.

A district attorney may subpoena to testify before a grand jury any person who he believes has relevant information or knowledge concerning the subject of the inquiry.

The grand jury may call any such witness on its own initiative by directing the district attorney to subpoena the witness. The district attorney must comply, but may ask the court to vacate such a subpoena on the grounds that it is in the public interest to do so. For example, if the issuing of such a subpoena will alert a potential defendant that there is a secret grand jury inquiry into his activities, it might be in the public interest to vacate (invalidate) it. Even if the court fails to grant the motion, a district attorney can require that such a witness be required to execute a waiver of immunity before testifying. If the witness refuses to execute such a waiver, he cannot be sworn as a witness.

A district attorney must submit to a grand jury evidence concerning a felony for which a defendant has been held by a local criminal court for grand jury action, and must do so, too, for a misdemeanor when a superior court has ordered that it be prosecuted by indictment.

The district attorney may submit to a grand jury evidence of any offense prosecutable in the county or evidence of misconduct or neglect in public office whether criminal or not. It is possible for a felony prosecution to be initiated by a grand jury. In this case the defendant has not been arrested or arraigned in a local criminal court. The people simply present their evidence directly to a grand jury. If the grand jury indicts the defendant, the indictment is sealed until the defendant is taken into custody under a superior court warrant of arrest and is brought before the court to be arraigned on the indictment. This type of procedure is common in extensive investigations of rackets or corruption, and is one of the reasons for the secrecy of grand jury inquiries.

A defendant has no right to call witnesses before a grand jury, but if he knows that he is under investigation, he may request that the grand jury call as a witness a person designated by him. The grand jury has the discretion to do so. As a matter of strategy, most defense attorneys would be reluctant to make such a request unless the testimony was almost certain to exculpate the defendant. They would otherwise be unwilling to give away part of their case to the people and even more reluctant to have the people cross-examine the defense witness in their absence.

In considering witnesses before a grand jury, the issue of immunity is an important one. We will consider it first in general and then specifically in grand jury proceedings. There is a constitutional prohibition against compelling a person to be a witness against himself. This has been held to be limited to criminal liability and also to testimonial compulsion as opposed to the required submission of a person's books or records. The latter is permissible. Because of this constitutional prohibition, any witness in any trial (or other proceeding involving the taking of testimony) may decline to answer any question put to him on the grounds that the answer may tend to incriminate him. He cannot decline to answer on the grounds that the answer might result in an admission of civil liability. If a witness can no longer be prosecuted for his crime because of the statute of limitations, he cannot claim self-incrimination and decline to testify. Asserting the privilege against self-incrimination is not an admission of guilt; it is simply the exercise of a constitutional right.

A problem for law enforcement arises from this privilege. If there is a criminal conspiracy and each member of the conspiracy invokes this Fifth Amendment privilege, it will be impossible to convict any of them. Thus, by statute, a judge is authorized, with the consent of the district attorney, to order a witness who raises the objection of self-incrimination to answer the questions asked of him while advising him that if he does testify he will have immunity from prosecution for anything to which he testifies or which flows from leads given the people by his testimony. The witness who is given this protection must then answer all questions or be in contempt of court. If the witness chooses to answer all questions without asserting his Fifth Amendment rights against self-incrimination, he has no immunity. His testimony may then be used against him in a criminal case, since he has, in effect, waived his privilege by answering voluntarily.

The situation in a grand jury is somewhat different. Every person who testifies before a grand jury without first executing a waiver of immunity automatically acquires immunity from prosecution for anything that he testifies to unless: (1) his testimony was knowingly given gratuitously rather than in response to a question, or (2) his evidence consisted solely of physical or documentary evidence without any testimony.

The reason for this greater protection of witnesses before a grand jury is that, unlike the situation in a trial or a hearing, the witness is not allowed the protection of having counsel present. The automatic immunity conferred on a witness is the reason that a district attorney can require a grand jury witness to execute a waiver of immunity prior to giving testimony. If the district attorney could not do so, a runaway grand jury could completely destroy the district attorney's case simply by calling all of the potential defendants as witnesses. Their testimony would automatically endow them with immunity from prosecution.

While a defendant may not be compelled to be a witness before a grand jury, if he is aware that a grand jury is investigating him, he may serve a notice on the district attorney that he wishes to testify. The district attorney is not required to notify a defendant that a grand jury will be considering his case unless the defendant has been held for grand jury action in a local criminal court. The people may thus conduct secret criminal investigations and obtain sealed indictments.

Once such a notice is served on the people, however, the district attorney must inform the grand jury of this demand and serve the defendant with a notice of the time and place at which his testimony will be heard by the grand jury. Any indictment found after the service of such notice by the defendant and before he is given the opportunity to testify is defective, and will be set aside on motion. The defendant must execute a waiver of immunity before he will be permitted to testify, and his attorney may not be present with him in the grand jury room, either during his direct testimony or under cross-examination by the people. For this reason most defense attorneys are very reluctant to have a client appear before a grand jury unless the client is extremely personable and convincing and has a good, believable story. Basically the decision as to whether or not to testify before a grand jury is the client's, but his attorney must advise him of the risks involved and, in a proper case, must exert considerable persuasive pressure on him. It is the authors' personal view that there are many more persons who make a case for the prosecution by trying to explain their way out of an arrest than the people could ever convict if defendants simply asserted their right to stand mute following an arrest. Similarly, there is very little reason for a defendant to expect much good to come out of a grand jury inquiry dominated by the prosecution. So, in the absence of some very cogent reason for a contrary course of action he should decline any opportunity to testify before a grand jury.

The deliberations of a grand jury may result in:

1. the voting of a true bill or indictment against the defendant for any offense supported by the evidence presented whether or not the offense was among the original charges in the local criminal court. To find an indictment the legal evidence presented must both:
   A. be legally sufficient to establish both the commission of the offense charged and the defendant's guilt thereof, *and*
   B. provide reasonable cause to believe that the defendant committed the offense.

   If the evidence does not meet *both* of these requirements the charge in question must be dismissed;

2. the directing of the district attorney to file a prosecutor's information in a local criminal court and prosecute the defendant there for any offense less than a felony;

3. a dismissal of all charges;

4. a request by the grand jury to remove an action against a juvenile offender to the Family Court;

5. a grand jury report relating to the conduct of public office.

INDICTMENTS AND WAIVERS OF INDICTMENT

An indictment is a pleading on which all superior court prosecutions for any offense must be based. The only exception to this is that a defendant not charged with a Class A felony may, with the prosecutor's consent, execute a waiver of indictment and consent to be prosecuted by a superior court information prepared by the district attorney in lieu of an indictment. Such a waiver must be signed in the presence of both the court and the attorney for the defense and the court must advise the defendant that: (1) he has a constitutional right to be prosecuted by indictment for a felony, and (2) that the superior court information will have the same force and effect as an indictment and will charge the offenses listed in the waiver. Such a waiver will eliminate the need for grand jury action, but has no advantage for the defendant unless it is part of a plea bargaining arrangement by which the defendant agrees to save the people the time and expense of procuring an indictment in exchange for his being charged with a less serious crime than he might have been. Most of what will now be said concerning indictments also applies to superior court informations.

An indictment is a written accusation by a grand jury accusing one or more persons of one or more offenses, at least one of which is a crime. Two offenses are joinable in a single indictment if:

1. They are based on the same act or criminal transaction.
2. They are based on different criminal transactions, but the proof of one offense would be material and admissible evidence of the other.
3. They are defined by the same or similar statutory provisions.
4. Even though the two offenses are not joinable with each other as above, each is so joinable to a third offense in the indictment.

If the sole basis for joinder is the third one, the court may choose to grant a motion either by the people or the defendant for a severance, and direct separate trials on each offense. If two or more separate indictments against the same defendants include charges joinable as above, the court may grant a motion by either side to consolidate the charges for a single trial.

Duplicious counts in an indictment are prohibited. This means that each separate offense charged must be stated in a separate count of the indictment. For example, if a statute defines a crime and then, in subsequent paragraphs, describes different ways in which the crime may be committed, such as different ways of committing fraud, then each such paragraph defines a different crime and must be charged by separate counts in an indictment. This is to make it easier for the defense to determine exactly what the charges are and to prepare an adequate defense. Lesser included offenses need not be stated in separate counts if they are necessarily included in the offense charged, but they may be. Thus, if a defendant is charged with criminal solicitation in the first degree, this necessarily includes criminal solicitation in the second degree.

Each count in an indictment must accuse the defendant of a separate charge, allege that it was committed in a designated county (to establish jurisdiction), and allege that it was committed at a designated time or period of time (to establish that prosecution is not barred by the statute of limitations). Each count must also contain a clear and concise statement of ultimate facts supporting every element of the offense charged and the defendant's guilt. The indictment is signed by the foreman of the grand jury.

An indictment for a crime may not allege the commission of and conviction for a previous crime even if it is a necessary prerequisite to the present charge. For example, as a first offense drunken driving is a misdemeanor in New York. On a second offense, it is a felony. An indictment cannot accuse the defendant of "drunken driving as a second offense" as this would be prejudicial, and the trial jury would be more likely to convict him simply on the basis of the past conviction rather than on the evidence in the present case. Some other way of describing the offense such as "drunken driving as a felony" must be used, not the language of the defining statute.

The rules governing the requirements of a good indictment are very technical and are designed to protect the rights of the accused. In general, the function of an indictment, like any accusatory instrument on which a trial may be based, is to inform the defendant clearly as to the nature of the charges against him in order to permit him to prepare his defense. If, after reading the indictment, the defense feels that the allegations of facts are inadequate to enable a proper defense to be prepared, it may move for what is called a Bill of Particulars. If this motion is granted, the people will be required to answer certain specific questions concerning the allegations being made. In no event will the court require the people to answer questions concerning the evidence to be used to support these allegations at the trial.

Under certain circumstances the court may permit the people to amend a defective indictment with respect to matters of form, time, place, names of persons, or the like; it will not permit an amendment that changes the theory of prosecution as reflected in the grand jury evidence or that will otherwise prejudice the defense on the merits of the case. An indictment cannot be amended to correct a failure to charge an offense, legal insufficiencies of the factual allegations, or misjoinder of offenses or parties. If an amendment to an indictment is permitted, the defense is entitled to a reasonable adjournment so that it may have time to modify its case.

Any number of defendants may be charged in the same indictment, but all must be accused of every offense charged in the instrument. The court has discretion to order a separate trial for any defendant in the interests of justice or to consolidate trials of defendants charged with the same offenses in different indictments. Either the defense or the people may move for separate trials, but only the people may move for a consolidation, as the defense is unlikely to be prejudiced by a separate trial.

ARRAIGNMENTS TO INDICTMENTS AND PLEAS

Everything that occurs at an arraignment to the charge in a local criminal court also occurs at an arraignment to an indictment. A defendant named in a sealed indictment now makes his first appearance in court. In the case of a defendant held for grand jury action by a local criminal court, much of this may be repetitious. Thus, the indictment is read to the defendant, and he or his attorney is given a copy of the instrument. The defendant is informed of his right to an attorney at this and all subsequent stages of the action, and if he appears without an attorney, he is informed of his right to an adjournment to get one and to communicate free of charge by phone or mail for the purpose of getting an attorney or of informing his family or friends that he is being charged with an offense.

If, on behalf of the defendant, a lawyer has filed a notice of appearance with the court prior to the arraignment (or if one was filed in the local criminal court), the lawyer must be given at least two days' notice of the arraignment, as must the defendant and his bail bond surety.

Again, if the defendant elects to proceed without counsel, and the court is satisfied that he understands the consequences of what he is doing, it must permit him to do so. But it must advise him that the right to counsel cannot be waived and that he may assert it at any time in the future. Most judges, especially in felony cases, will try to convince the defendant that he should either get private counsel or have one assigned if he cannot afford one. If the court is not convinced that the defendant understands the significance of proceeding *pro se*, than it must see that he has either assigned or private counsel before proceeding further.

The reader will recall that a defendant arraigned in a lower criminal court on a felony charge is not able to make motion attacks on the accusatory instrument (as are people charged with misdemeanors and less) as there is no accusatory instrument in existence at that time for him to attack. A felony complaint is not a sufficient basis for a prosecution; it is merely a legal device to hold a defendant prior to grand jury action. It is after the arraignment to the indictment in superior court that the defendant first gets the opportunity to attack the legal sufficiency of the accusatory instrument or indictment. The defendant may move to dismiss the indictment on every ground available to a defendant attacking an information in a local criminal court plus two additional grounds: that the evidence presented to the grand jury was not legally sufficient to establish the offense charged, i.e., no *prima facie* case was presented; or that the grand jury proceeding was legally defective, e.g., a meeting was held without 16 grand jurors present, or fewer than 12 concurred in the indictment. The problem for a defense lawyer seeking to attack an indictment on one of the latter two grounds is finding out about a defect in a grand jury proceeding or the evidence before it. How can the defense do this if the proceedings are secret? The answer is that the defense makes a motion requesting the court to inspect the grand jury minutes to see if there is a basis for the proposed motion to dismiss the indictment. In making this motion the defense must allege some basis for believing that the grand jury proceedings may have been defective. One usual method is to say that the people failed to present a *prima facie* case at the felony hearing, and that if the same evidence was presented to the grand jury, it was not enough to justify an indictment. Also, witnesses before the grand jury may properly be interviewed by the defense as to their testimony or anything else that went on in their presence.

These motions must be in writing, on notice to the people, within 45 days of the arraignment. The defendant will be required to enter a plea to the indictment at the arraignment, and a securing order for his custody pending trial or the posting or continuance of bail will be made. Bail may also be increased because the likelihood of ultimate conviction is becoming stronger as the people's case by now has survived many of the preliminary screening devices, e.g., a felony hearing and the grand jury.

The defendant may as a matter of right enter a plea of not guilty to the entire indictment. He may also as a matter of right enter a plea of guilty to the entire indictment or change a plea of not guilty to one of guilty at any time up until a jury verdict. Where an indictment charges more than one count or offense (as they usually do) the defendant may, with the consent of both the court and the district attorney, enter a plea of guilty to one or more but not to all offenses charged or to one or more lesser included offenses in satisfaction of the entire indictment and, if specified on the record of the court, certain other pending indictments. This is the practice known as "plea copping" or plea bargaining.

The practice of plea bargaining has been much maligned in the press, but without it the criminal courts would be so bogged down with old cases that they would be unable to function. A plea bargain is basically a deal made by the defendant with the people to save the people the expense, time, and uncertainty of a trial in exchange for some consideration in the form of a reduced charge. How much of a charge reduction a defendant can get depends on how unsure the people are of a conviction, how serious the offense is, and the defendant's prior record. Some district attorneys who are very sensitive to potential criticism in the press have established rules to guide the bargaining, e.g., a reduction of more than one degree of an offense requires a bureau supervisor's approval, and so on. The really serious problem with plea bargaining is not the one that the newspapers have been much concerned with, namely the escaping of punishment by a defendant guilty of a serious crime, but rather the situation in which an innocent defendant opts to plead to a lesser crime because he fears a conviction on the more serious charge lodged against him. He may be particularly prone to accept such a "bargain" if he is unable to afford an adequate defense to the charges.

The practice of most district attorneys' offices of using multiple-count indictments which charge the defendant with every offense that could conceivably be inferred from the incident in question has a two-fold purpose. First, it makes it more likely that an indecisive jury will compromise and convict the defendant on at least one of the lesser counts. This counts as a conviction for the district attorney's record regardless of how many spurious counts the accused was acquitted on. Secondly, it gives the people some bargaining power in negotiations. Often the defendant winds up pleading guilty to what he should have been charged with originally.

As a result of newspaper accounts of dangerous criminals being permitted to plead to trivial offenses, the legislature has limited the power of the courts to accept lesser pleas. For example, if an indictment includes a charge of a class A III drug felony, the bargaining defendant must plead guilty to at least a class C felony. In other cases persons charged with class A or B felonies, and all second felony offenders, must plead to at least one felony charge. Also under a recent change in the law a person indicted for a violent class B or class C felony must plead to a violent felony charge. If an indictment does not charge a class A or a violent felony it can not be pleaded to in satisfaction of another pending indictment charging one of these offenses.

DISCOVERY PROCEEDINGS

Due to the adversary nature of a trial and the concern of both sides with keeping their strategy secret, one often loses sight of the fundamental purpose of the trial which is to secure a just outcome. In an effort to ameliorate this problem certain procedures have been set up in both civil and criminal cases by which one side is forced to disclose part of its case in advance of trial in order to give the other a reasonable chance to avoid surprise and to prepare to respond adequately. This attempts to assure that the whole truth will be brought out at the trial. These procedures, called discovery procedures, are both technical and involved and will not be dealt with in this book except for two examples applicable to a criminal trial.

If the defense intends to rely on a defense of mental disease or defect, evidence of such condition is not admissible in a trial unless the defense serves written notice on the people that it intends to rely on such a defense, doing so before the trial and not more than 30 days after the entry of a plea. This is to protect the prosecution from surprise and to permit it to prepare to disprove the defense. The people also have a right within 20 days of the arraignment to serve a demand on the defense attorney that they be furnished with a list of the names and addresses of any witnesses the defense intends to call in establishing the defense of alibi; and the defense attorney has a right to receive from the people not later than 10 days before the trial a similar list giving the names and addresses of witnesses that the people intend to use to disprove the alibi. The defense of alibi claims that at the time of the alleged crime the defendant was somewhere else. Each party has the obligation to inform the other of any new witnesses located after the filing of the original lists, and the court may exclude the testimony of any alibi or rebuttal witness not listed. On the other hand, it may, for good cause, permit such a witness to testify. If it does permit this testimony, it must grant the other side a three-day adjournment should it be requested. A witness testifying that he saw the defendant at the scene of the crime is not, by statute, considered a rebuttal witness to the defense of alibi.

REFERENCES

1. Ebbesen, E. B. and Konečni, V. J. Decision making and information integration in the courts: The setting of bail. *Journal of Personality and Social Psychology* 1975, 32(5), 805-821.
2. Wald, P. M. The right to bail revisited: A decade of promise. In S. S. Nagel (Ed.) *The Rights of the Accused*. Beverly Hills: Sage Publications, 1972.

10
Trial Procedures

A defendant must be present at the trial of an indictment and is generally required to be present at the trial of lesser offenses unless the court permits him to be represented by counsel. There can be no trial *in absentia* without the presence of the defendant or his counsel, nor can a defendant be denied the right to be present at a criminal trial unless he conducts himself in so disorderly a manner that the trial cannot proceed with him present. If he persists in this behavior after being warned by the court, he may be removed and the trial conducted by his counsel. In the past, disorderly defendants have been physically restrained, tied in their chairs, or gagged to prevent them from disrupting trials, but it would appear that such methods are more likely to prejudice a jury than is the act of simply removing the defendant. Some courts have provided facilities for disruptive defendants to view the proceedings through closed circuit television and to communicate with counsel electronically, but such devices are not required, since the defendant, by his own conduct, has waived his right to be present and assist counsel.

The first step in a jury trial is the examination of potential jurors and the selection and impaneling of a petit or trial jury. It is interesting to note that today jury members are required to be strangers both to the parties in an action and to their counsel. Originally jurors were supposed to be local people who knew both the litigants and the witnesses and thus would be more likely to know who was telling the truth. A trial jury is the final and supreme judge of all questions of fact in a trial except for those preliminary questions of fact determined by the court in deciding whether evidence is admissible or a confession is likely to have been voluntary. The people cannot appeal a verdict of acquittal by a jury under any circumstances although a defendant can attack a conviction on the grounds that there was no evidence in the record to justify the verdict or even that the verdict was contrary to the weight of the evidence. As far as a verdict of acquittal is concerned, the jury is supreme, and no court may challenge its findings regardless of how overwhelming the evidence of the defendant's guilt may have been. Indeed, this is one of the reasons that the Constitution retains a jury trial for felonies.

The legal profession has often been criticized as being the only profession in which experts ask a group of laymen to make a final decision, often in very complicated and technical matters. However, having a group of average citizens use their own good common sense and basic ideas of justice in rendering a verdict is a very powerful safeguard for an accused citizen against the all-too-frequent overzealous prosecution and abuse of power on the part of unprofessional prosecutors. Juries not only do justice on occasion in spite of the law's inflexibility; they probably do as good a job as the average judge would do in deciding the cases before them. A very experienced trial judge once noted that in all of the thousands of cases that he had presided over, he disagreed with the jury's verdict in only a very small percentage of the cases, and there was no special reason to believe that he was right and the juries were wrong in those cases.

The panel from which a trial jury is drawn is selected in accordance with the Judiciary Law, and potential jurors are summoned to appear before the Commissioner of Jurors to answer questions concerning their qualifications before being assigned to a panel from which jurors are selected for trials.

Trial jurors must be U.S. citizens and residents of the county in which the trial is to be conducted. They must be between 18 and 75 years of age, in possession of their faculties, with sound judgment and of good character. They must be able to read and write English and not have been convicted of any felony involving moral turpitude. Elected officials and civil officers are disqualified.

While not disqualified, certain groups of people are given an exemption if they choose to exercise it. They include: clergymen; doctors, and people in certain related professions; firemen and police officers; ships' officers; editors and reporters; persons over 70; and practicing attorneys. These exemptions are designed either to avoid disrupting vital public services or to prevent people from being called for jury duty whom no lawyer would permit on a jury. In general, unless they have a special reason for having some type of expert on a jury, lawyers will try to keep such a person off on the theory that the prestige of his or her profession will confer on that person undue influence over the rest of the jury. Also, no lawyer is likely to let another lawyer or even a law student sit on the jury for the same reason. Formerly, women were exempt from jury duty, but because of pressures from women's liberation groups for equal treatment they are now exempt only if they are responsible for the care of a young child.

There are two kinds of challenges that may be directed against a petit jury. One is a challenge to the array, i.e., to the entire panel. Such a challenge can only be made by the defendant and must be on the grounds that the panel was selected contrary to the judiciary law and that the method of selection has resulted in substantial prejudice to the defendant. If the motion is opposed by the people, there will be a trial of the issues of fact and law raised. If the challenge is allowed, the panel must be discharged and a new one selected.

Challenges to the array are useful in situations where the selection method systematically excludes certain ethnic minorities. Whether or not it is desirable from the point of view of the defense for a jury to contain members of the defendant's ethnic group is a matter of trial strategy. If a defendant has a sympathetic case, it may be wise to seek jurors of the defendant's group; but if he is charged with a despicable offense (e.g., child molesting), and the people have a strong case, it might be wiser for the defense to try to keep members of his ethnic group off the jury. They may be especially angry at the defendant's conduct if they feel it has put their entire group in a bad light. If so, they can be expected to treat him far worse than jurors of other ethnic backgrounds would. In the Rosenberg treason case, for example, it was a Jewish judge who sentenced the Jewish defendants to death and labeled the offense a crime worse than murder. At the time many in the American Jewish community were very upset over the conduct of these defendants and felt that it reflected on and threatened all Jewish Americans. One can only wonder whether the sentence would have been different had the judge been Italian or Irish, for there was a question at the time of the sentencing as to whether it was possible to commit the crime of treason during peacetime, since the Constitution specifically defines treason as levying war against the United States or lending aid or comfort to their enemies. Later, in a very unpersuasive decision, the U.S. Supreme Court held that all foreign powers are potential enemies and that treason can therefore be committed in peacetime.

The second kind of challenge that may be made is to the poll or the challenge of an individual venireman. This challenge is made after any challenge to the array is disposed of and the first 12 persons have been called to sit in the jury box. There they are sworn to answer questions truthfully and are examined by counsel for both sides. This examination is called the *voir dire*. The potential jurors may be questioned individually or collectively, first by the people and then by the defense. The scope of the examination permitted is within the discretion of the court. In general, the more serious the offense charged, the more care there will be in selecting a jury. In the federal courts, potential jurors are examined by the court instead of by counsel, although the judge may allow counsel to participate. The latter procedure has some advantages as well as disadvantages. The court is likely to seek unbiased jurors, while the lawyers each would prefer to select jurors likely to favor their case. Their competing efforts tend to cancel out, however, and probably result in juries that are just as unbiased as those the court would select. But in examining a potential juror, the attorney gets his first chance to develop a rapport with this juryman, and this is probably the most important function of the jury selection process. There is an old saying among lawyers that it is more important to have the judge than it is to have the law on your side. This statement is equally true with respect to jurors. While it is considered unprofessional for a lawyer to attempt to curry favor with a juror, a lawyer who gives the juror the impression that he is fair and wants only to see justice done is off on the right foot in the trial. Jurors may take out their dislike of a particular lawyer on the lawyer's client, and for this reason some lawyers are reluctant to let any potential juror whom they have questioned at length remain on the jury. If the extended questioning reveals no valid cause for a challenge, they will therefore challenge him peremptorily.

After both sides examine the jurors, each, commencing with the people, may challenge prospective jurors for cause. If the challenge is allowed by the court, the juror is excused. After both parties have challenged for cause, each, commencing with the people, may challenge peremptorily. As in the case of challenges for cause, the people must challenge first. The district attorney cannot "play games" and hold back on a peremptory challenge until he is sure that the defense will not challenge the venireman. No reason need be given for a peremptory challenge. When the challenges are finished, the remaining jurors are sworn in immediately. If necessary, an additional group of names is called to replace those veniremen who were excused, and the process of examination is repeated until a full jury of 12 is sworn in. The first juryman called and selected becomes the foreman of the jury. He is not appointed by the court as is the foreman of a grand jury. (In some jurisdictions the jurors elect their foreman.)

A potential juryman may be challenged for cause if:

1. He does not have the qualifications required by the judiciary law.
2. He has a state of mind that is likely to prevent him from rendering an impartial verdict based on the evidence at the trial, e.g., he has read about the case in the papers and thinks the defendant is guilty or is prejudiced against members of the defendant's ethnic group.
3. He is related "within the sixth degree of consanguinity" to the defendant, the victim, one of the attorneys, or a witness, or was an adverse party to any such person in a criminal or civil action, or he bears some other special relationship to such party that is likely to prevent him from rendering an impartial verdict based on the trial evidence.
4. He was a witness at the preliminary hearing, the grand jury proceedings, or is likely to be a witness at the trial.

5. He served on the grand jury that found the indictment or on a prior civil or criminal petit jury involving the same incident charged in the indictment.
6. There is a possibility of the death sentence, and the potential juror has conscientious convictions for or against the death penalty.

An erroneous ruling by the court in allowing a challenge for cause by the people is not a reversible error (i.e., an error that would require an appellate court to reverse a conviction) unless the people had exhausted all of their peremptory challenges before the jury was selected. The same is true of an erroneous denial of a challenge for cause on the part of the defense.

A jury for the trial of a felony consists of 12 jurymen and from one to four alternates, at the discretion of the court. If the trial is likely to be a long one, the impaneling of alternate jurors will prevent the need for declaring a mistrial should a regular juror become ill or disabled during the trial.

Each party in the trial of a Class A felony has 20 peremptory challenges plus two for each alternate juror to be selected.

For a Class B or C felony each party has 15 peremptory challenges plus two for each alternate juror to be selected. In all other felonies there are ten peremptory challenges for each side plus two for each alternate juror selected.

The jury trial of an information is with a six-member petit jury selected as above except that there may only be up to two alternate jurors, and each side is allowed only three peremptory challenges.

If there is more than one defendant on trial, a majority of the defendants must agree to the exercise of each peremptory challenge, but the defense is allowed no more such challenges than if there were only one defendant. The defense lawyers are thus compelled to cooperate, a requirement that may be unfair as there is often considerable conflict of interest among co-defendants.

Alternate jurors must be kept apart from the regular jurors during deliberations but are present at all of the trial proceedings. At any time until the jury retires for its deliberations a regular juror who becomes unable to continue may be discharged, and the first alternate juror selected takes his place. After the jury has retired for its deliberations, the court may make such substitution only with the written consent of the defendant signed in open court in the presence of the judge. Unless the defendant gives such consent, a mistrial must be declared. This has the effect of returning the indictment to its original state at the opening of the trial (restoring any charges that may have been dismissed during the trial) and requires a new trial. Other grounds for a mistrial include those situations where, through no fault of the moving party, something has occurred that prevents the moving side from getting a fair trial, or where it becomes physically impossible for the trial to continue.

A jury having been selected, the court will advise the members as to their duties. These instructions will include an admonition not to discuss the case among themselves or with anyone else until they retire to deliberate and not to read or listen to media accounts of the trial. They will also be told not to visit the premises at which the offenses charged were alleged to have been committed, and to report promptly to the court any improper attempts to influence them. If the court feels that a viewing of the premises involved would be helpful to the jury, it may have the jury brought *en masse* to the scene, but the judge must accompany them there. Both lawyers have a right to be present, but neither may make any comment or argument at the scene. The jury is brought to the scene simply to view it. Following the instructions to the jury, the people are required to make an opening statement.

OPENING ADDRESSES

The legal purpose of the people's opening is to offer to prove a *prima facie* case. The practical purpose from the point of view of the prosecution is to develop a rapport with the jury as well as to help it in following the evidence about to be presented. There are enormous differences in styles of opening among prosecutors. Some will outline their cases logically; others will emphasize the heinous nature of the offense; some will try to do both. Most will emphasize to the jury its responsibility to base its verdict solely on the evidence and not on sympathy (unless, of course, they feel the defendant is not likely to evoke much sympathy from the jury anyway). In any event, the district attorney will have to outline at least a *prima facie* case and, at the same time, try to avoid giving the defense any more information about the case than is necessary at this stage. If the district attorney succeeds in informing the jury about the major thrust of his case and gives the impression of being a fair-minded person whose only interest is in seeing justice done, he has accomplished nearly all that can be expected of an opening statement.

The defense, having no burden of proving anything in a criminal trial, may simply waive an opening statement to avoid giving the people any information about its case or strategy. On the other hand, it is not desirable to give up this chance to establish rapport with the jury. Most defense attorneys will make short opening addresses that advise the jury that the defense has no obligation to prove anything and that the people must prove each and every element of the offense beyond a reasonable doubt. They will then ask the jury to keep their promise to keep an open mind until all of the evidence is in, at which time the defense will contend that the people will have failed in their promise to prove their case, and the jury must then remember its duty to acquit the defendant.

In their opening, both sides frequently give the jury some idea of what procedures to expect. They try to make it easier for the jurors to follow events as they unwind, but it is extremely important that the lawyers do not give the jury the impression of talking down to them. The lawyers' major job at any trial is to persuade a jury; so they should go to any lengths to avoid antagonizing its members. If the people's opening is lengthy and complicated, the defense can often start off on the right foot by a simple, short opening statement. This is a lot easier for the defense as, unlike the prosecution, it does not have to outline a case at this time. It is important for trial counsel to be both fair and courteous, not only to the court, but to opposing counsel and especially to witnesses who are laymen like the jurymen, and with whom the latter will identify. One of the best things that can happen to a lawyer in a jury trial is to have an adversary who is rude to counsel and witnesses. It is not necessary or even desirable to do much to defend oneself against such an adversary (although it may be necessary to protect a witness from abuse) because the jury will do this themselves when they retire to deliberate. Rudeness and abusive tactics on the part of counsel are not only poor trial strategy and a sign of bad manners, they are also unprofessional conduct that will ultimately damage the perpetrator's reputation as well as his cause. One of the authors remembers conducting a felony examination as a young lawyer against a very abrasive and arrogant assistant district attorney, who kept interrupting his cross-examination with such exclamations as: "The witness has already answered that question. What's the matter with you? Don't you listen to him?" The author didn't respond to these interruptions primarily because he was too inexperienced and taken aback at the time to know what to say, but the magistrate conducting the hearing knew what to say. At the conclusion of the evidence, in response to a *pro forma* motion to dismiss based on very tenuous grounds, if any, he said, "Granted." It seems unlikely that this decision was based as much on the weakness of the people's case as it was on the judge's pique at the unnecessary abuse heaped upon a poor, neophyte attorney who was obviously too incompetent and confused to defend himself.

When the opening statements have been completed, the people present their direct case and must do this by putting their witnesses on the stand.

THE RULES OF EVIDENCE

In order to understand the testimony of witnesses and how it is elicited in a trial, it is necessary to know something concerning the rules of evidence. In general all rules of evidence are exclusionary. In other words, anything that is probative, i.e., tends to prove or disprove a fact in issue at a trial, is admissible unless there is some rule of evidence that excludes it. Evidence is anything that tends to prove or disprove a fact in issue. In a criminal case, the accusatory instrument defines what the facts in issue are, i.e., what it is, specifically, that the people must present evidence to prove beyond a reasonable doubt. There are three types of evidence:

1. Real or autoptic evidence, e.g., a physical object such as a weapon.
2. Documentary evidence, e.g., a firm's books or a bank statement.
3. Testimonial evidence, e.g., a witness's report of what he saw or heard.

Since this book is concerned with the psychology involved in the criminal justice system, we will limit our discussion to testimonial evidence.

The rules of evidence were designed to protect the constitutional rights of defendants and also to avoid confusing juries with irrelevant or unreliable forms of evidence, thus making it easier for them to arrive at the truth. With certain exceptions the same basic rules of evidence apply in both civil and criminal cases. In general, any evidence offered at a trial may be received unless the opposing party objects to it. Objections may be made generally or on specific grounds. If an objection is made on specific grounds and overruled, the appellate court will only reverse if the grounds stated in the objection are sound. If an objection is made and overruled on general grounds, the appellate court will reverse if there is any sound basis for the objection. Thus, lawyers often object on general grounds that the testimony is irrelevant, incompetent, and immaterial.

"Irrelevant" means that the testimony offered is not probative, i.e., it does not logically tend to prove or disprove a fact in issue. "Incompetent" means that the evidence offered violates a rule of evidence. Incompetence may refer either to the witness offering the testimony or to the testimony itself. Thus, what the defendant told his psychologist may be very relevant to the issues in the trial, and the testimony itself may be admissible, but the witness is incompetent to give such evidence because of the privileged relationship of psychologist and patient. "Immaterial" means that the evidence, while tending to prove or disprove a fact in issue, does not do so to any substantial degree.

Evidence may be direct or circumstantial. Direct evidence is testimony by a witness directly concerning a fact in issue. Circumstantial evidence is testimony by a witness to an observation that is not directly in issue, but which logically tends to establish a fact in issue. Direct evidence may be very weak, while circumstantial evidence may be extremely strong. For example, a hesitant identification of the defendant as the person who committed a robbery may be unconvincing, while the fact that the ground is covered with snow in the morning is extremely convincing circumstantial evidence that it snowed during the night. If the people's case is based solely on circumstantial evidence, then, in addition to the normal instructions to the jury concerning the meaning of the requirement that the people must prove every element of their case beyond a reasonable doubt, the defendant is entitled to have the court instruct the jury that unless they are convinced of the defendant's guilt to "a moral certainty," they must acquit him.

One of the most important rules of evidence is the rule against hearsay testimony. Hearsay, as its name implies, is testimony by a witness that he heard somebody else say something, and this testimony is offered as evidence of the truth of what the other person said. If what the other person said is the fact in issue (e.g., a witness reporting that the defendant threatened the life of the victim), then this is not hearsay but direct testimony. The rule against hearsay is often stated as the requirement that an ordinary witness (as opposed to an expert witness) may testify only to facts that he has observed with one of his "five" senses. The reason for the prohibition against hearsay evidence is that admitting it would deprive the other side of its right of cross-examination. If witness A were permitted to testify as to what B said, then B, not A, would have to be cross-examined to test the truth of this statement. But A, not B, is on the witness stand. Cross-examination is a basic right because it affords a party an opportunity to inquire into both the ability of a witness to observe and recall and his propensity and motivation to tell the truth. It also permits the whole truth to be brought out, rather than just the part that helps the party's case. There are many exceptions to the hearsay rule which permit the introduction of evidence that would otherwise be excluded as hearsay, but in each case there is always some special reason to believe that this evidence is more than ordinarily likely to be the truth.

For example, a "dying declaration" made by a murder victim, limited to the identification of the perpetrator, will be admitted into evidence provided that the people can show that the victim knew he was dying and had no hope of recovery. This is admitted on the somewhat shaky reasoning that if one knows that he is about to come into the presence of his Maker, he is not likely to lie. Sometimes police can be quite callous in informing a victim that he is dying in an effort to get a dying declaration. If the victim recovers, the declaration is not admissible, and he must testify personally.

The *res gestae*, or a verbal act, is another exception to the hearsay rule. If a party to an action makes an immediate and spontaneous verbal exclamation before there is time to think, so that the words are an involuntary verbal act, a report by a third party of what he said is admissible.

Records kept in the normal course of a business where the business involves keeping such records are also admissible on the theory that the business purposes of the records are some assurance of their accuracy.

A special type of testimony permitted in a criminal case is called character, or reputation, testimony. A character witness is permitted to testify to the defendant's reputation in the community for certain relevant character traits. Hence, if the defendant is accused of assault, his reputation for peacefulness would be relevant; if the charge is larceny, his reputation for honesty would be admissible. By its very nature, character testimony must be hearsay. Technically, the witness is not permitted to give his own opinion on these issues, but must testify as to what others in the community think about the defendant. Often the courts are quite liberal in this regard and permit such direct testimony, particularly if the people do not object. The theory behind character testimony is that people usually behave consistently, so it is less likely that a person with a good reputation for integrity would commit a dishonest act. If, and only if, the defendant offers character testimony, the people can put rebuttal witnesses on the stand to prove his bad character. They may also introduce evidence of prior convictions for this purpose, provided that such convictions are relevant to the character trait the defense is seeking to establish and their mention will not unduly prejudice the defendant in his trial. Thus, defendants with prior criminal records are effectively precluded from introducing character testimony; for if they did so, the jury could be told of the prior conviction, which, even if it was for an unrelated crime, might prejudice the jury.

If an element of a crime charged is a previous conviction, such as a charge of a second offense of drunken driving, the defendant must be given the opportunity to admit or deny the predicate conviction before the court and in the absence of the jury. If he admits it, that element of the present offense is deemed proven, and neither evidence nor even mention of the conviction may be made in the presence of the jury. If the defendant denies the conviction or stands mute, the people may present evidence to establish the prior conviction as a necessary part of their case. The entire purpose of this procedure is to avoid prejudicing the jury in its consideration of the present charge by telling it of a prior conviction for the same offense.

A defendant is never required to testify in a criminal case, but if he elects to do so, he may be cross-examined and impeached like any other witness. The only exception is that any evidence of prior convictions offered to impeach his credibility as a witness cannot be of a nature that would unduly prejudice the jury against him. Thus, the people would be permitted to ask a defendant charged with rape about a prior conviction for perjury, and if such conviction was denied, offer proof of it. They would not be permitted to ask him about a prior conviction of rape or sodomy because not only would it be unduly prejudicial, but it would not be logically related to the likelihood that the defendant could be expected to testify truthfully. The decision as to whether or not to testify on his own behalf must ultimately be made by the defendant with the advice of counsel. Not only must the guilt or innocence of the defendant be considered, but also the impression that he is likely to make on the jury and what prior criminal record may ultimately be exposed should he testify.

As to the issue of whether or not it is proper for a lawyer to put on the stand a defendant whose story he does not believe, the dilemma is that unless the lawyer was a witness to the crime (in which case he should not be representing the defendant), he is never in a position to know how accurate anything that his client tells him is. The client may well be telling the truth in spite of the attorney's opinion. If a defendant has a story that he wants to tell on the stand, he has a right to do so. If his lawyer does not believe the story, he has a duty to tell the client so and to tell him that the jury probably will not believe it either, and that his testimony may hurt his case. The decision, however, is up to the client not the lawyer. The client, not the lawyer, is the one who faces prison if the case is lost. It is not the function of an attorney to usurp the duties of a jury and decide upon his client's guilt or innocence. His job is to present his client's side of the case as effectively as possible, consistently with the facts as he knows them.

A different situation is presented if the client candidly advises the lawyer that he intends to commit perjury on the stand. Here the lawyer must either elect to go along with the defendant, as advocated by Freedman, on the theory that if a defendant is told he must be completely honest with his lawyer he ought not be penalized for being so, or must ask the court to relieve him from the case without violating the defendant's confidence by advising the judge of the reason why he seeks relief.[1] The best way to resolve this situation is for counsel to convince his client that perjury, in addition to being a crime, is an extremely poor trial tactic and is rarely, if ever, successful in the face of a skillful cross-examination.

Often a client will tell his lawyer that he is guilty of an offense when he is, in fact, not guilty. Such a defendant may have tried very hard to commit the crime in question, but, through ineptitude, may have neglected to commit a vital element of its *corpus delecti*. Hence, lawyers must be on guard against the client who is ready to plead guilty to crimes he technically did not commit. Guilt is a matter of law not merely intent!

While it is clearly improper for a defense attorney to tell or even to suggest to a defendant what to say on the stand, it is both proper and necessary to prepare him like any other witness. Whether or not the defendant is to take the stand, he will be the focus of the jury's attention during the trial, and the attorney must instruct him as to dress and deportment so as to assure making as good an impression on the jury as possible.

All evidence in a criminal trial must be given under oath except that, if a witness is younger than 12 years of age, the court must first inquire if he has the capacity to understand the nature of an oath. If the court finds that he does, then he must testify under oath. If the court finds that he lacks the capacity to understand the nature of an oath, but he has sufficient intelligence and capacity to testify, it may permit him to do so without an oath. No defendant may be convicted solely on this unsworn testimony without corroboration.

A court may exclude any witness who it believes lacks capacity to testify because of infancy, mental disease, or mental defect.

An accomplice is a person who may reasonably be assumed to have participated in the offense charged or in some other offense based on the same or some of the same facts. No person can be convicted on the uncorroborated testimony of an accomplice. The corroboration required must tend to connect the defendant with the commission of the offense.

Today, most sex crimes require corroboration of the victim's testimony for each element of the offense. Because of pressures from women's liberation groups this corroboration requirement was dispensed with for rape on the argument that, unless there was a witness present, it was impossible to get a conviction. This was, of course, not true. The victim's story of a sexual assault could be corroborated by the report of a medical examination. Even the defendant's false denial that he was at the scene of the crime has been held to be corroboration of the offense. What the corroboration requirement sought to do was to protect an innocent defendant from being charged with the crime of rape when all he was guilty of was having an illicit relationship with a woman who got angry at him or who tried to protect her reputation after the relationship was discovered and decided to prosecute for rape.

In real rape cases, even if the corroboration for a rape conviction were lacking, the defendant could still have been convicted of the underlying assault and usually a host of other offenses that required no corroboration. This is not to understate the seriousness of the crime of forcible rape. In addition a rapist is often a sadist or a psychopath and is a potential murderer, who ought not to be dealt with lightly. However, spurious rape charges are all too common in the courts for society to be complacent about the removal of this safeguard against the conviction of innocent defendants.

The same political groups were displeased with the activities of defense counsel in the cross-examination of complainants concerning their previous sexual conduct. They felt that this was done for the purpose of abusing or humiliating complainants so that they would be less likely to prosecute rapists rather than to ascertain the likelihood that the allegations were true. As a result, there have been restrictions placed on what defense counsel can ask rape victims concerning their prior sexual behavior. There is some possibility that these restrictions may ultimately result in helping rather than hurting guilty defendants in rape cases as the issue may be raised on appeal as to whether these restrictions violate the constitutional right of the accused to defend himself at the trial.

An admission is a statement by a party to an action that is contrary to the position which he takes at the trial. Admissions are another exception to the hearsay rule, and a witness may testify to any statement he heard the defendant make that would tend to inculpate (but not exculpate) him for the offense charged.

A confession is not evidence, but something that makes the taking of evidence unnecessary. It is a written statement signed by the defendant admitting his guilt of the crime. A statement made by the defendant may be less than a confession and may admit or deny part or all of the charges. No defendant may be convicted on the basis of an uncorroborated confession. This is due to the interesting psychological fact that many people suffer from such guilt feelings and have such a pathological need for punishment or attention that every time a major crime is reported in the papers dozens of such people come forward to confess to it. The corroboration required must tend to prove that the crime has been committed.

No confession or statement by the defendant may be received in evidence unless it was voluntarily made. It is not voluntarily made if it was obtained by the threat or use of physical force on the defendant or a third person or under pressure that has impaired his ability to choose whether or not to make a statement. It is not voluntarily made if it was in response to a promise or statement of facts by a public servant which created a risk that the defendant would falsely implicate himself, or if it was obtained in derogation of his constitutional rights. Whether a statement is voluntary or not is a question of fact for the jury, but before admitting the statement into evidence the trial judge must conduct a preliminary investigation to determine if there is any reasonable view of the circumstances involved that would permit a jury to find that the statement was voluntary. If there is no such possibility, the court will not admit the statement.

Until the case of *Miranda v. Arizona* there was no requirement that an arresting officer inform a defendant of his right to remain silent or to consult a lawyer, before making any statement.[2] In this decision Mr. Chief Justice Warren did an extensive review of police practices used to coerce or trick defendants into making incriminating statements. He quoted extensively from police texts concerning current law enforcement techniques. The Court concluded that, as a matter of law, any statement made by a defendant while in police custody and at a tremendous psychological disadvantage (because he is isolated from friends, family, and any source of help) is involuntary and inadmissible unless (1) he was informed immediately on being taken into custody and before any questioning: (2) that he had a right to remain silent, (3) that anything he said could and would be used against him, (4) that he had a right to be represented by counsel, and (5) that he had the right to talk to counsel before making any statement.

This rule has been criticized severely by many who have claimed that it would cause a breakdown in law enforcement. Evidentally it has not, nor has it done so in England where a similar rule has always been in effect. It does not appear sensible to say that a defendant has a right against the state unless there is some assurance that he knows of this right and is in a position to exercise it. The need for such a rule can be seen clearly in the case of *Escobedo v. Illinois*, which preceded *Miranda*.[3] Here a defendant requested an attorney, and the attorney was present in the station house, but was not permitted to see his client until after a confession had been obtained. There is a simple principle involved here, namely, that if a law enforcement agency can violate a constitutional right of a defendant and then use the product of this violation in a subsequent trial, it will violate the right, and, in fact, the right is nonexistent. The *Miranda* decision is quite lengthy, but ought to be read in its entirety by anyone involved with the criminal justice system. It ought to be required reading, too, for commentators who criticize it.

When a witness is called, he is required to take an oath, and the party that calls him conducts what is called the direct examination. The witness's testimony is elicited in the form of answers to questions. Except in preliminary matters, the witness may not be asked leading questions on direct examination. A leading question is a question that suggests an answer. Most questions that call for a yes or no answer are leading questions. The reason that leading questions are forbidden on direct examination is that, if they were permitted, the attorney would be testifying, rather than the witness.

If the attorney has done his trial preparation properly, he will have reviewed the witness's testimony prior to the trial so that he knows what to expect. Counsel will also be able to advise the witness concerning the procedures that he may expect, his demeanor on the stand, and what is likely to be asked on cross-examination. Among other things, the witness ought to be instructed to think before answering all questions, particularly when under cross-examination, and to confine himself to answering the question asked. A witness should avoid volunteering any information. He should be told to pause before answering a question on cross-examination to give his side's lawyer a chance to object before the jury hears his answer. The witness should be instructed to refrain from conflict or fencing with opposing counsel. Finally, it is a good idea to tell the witness to be sure to answer all questions accurately and truthfully and not to worry about the effect this has on the case.

There is nothing wrong with this type of pre-trial preparation of witnesses. In fact, it is a breach of professional responsibility to fail to do it. The purpose is not to manufacture evidence or suborn perjury, but to ensure adequate preparation. Often, however, the opposing lawyer will ask a witness, "Isn't it a fact that you rehearsed all of your testimony with Mr. Doe?" This question is usually asked in a manner which implies that there was something improper involved. If the witness denies this consultation, he has committed perjury and may easily be impeached. If he readily admits it, and opposing counsel, not knowing when to quit, goes on to ask him, "And what did Mr. Doe tell you to say?", a devastating reply is, "He told me to tell the truth as accurately as I could."

Not only will a trial counsel interview all of his own witnesses prior to a trial, but if the witnesses that the other side is likely to call will talk to him, he will try to interview them as well. A good rule for a trial lawyer is to try to avoid asking a witness a question when he does not know what the answer to it will be. Pre-trial preparation can help prevent embarrassment.

It is not ethical for an attorney to talk directly to the opposing party in a lawsuit when that party is represented by counsel. He must deal with the opposing attorney and not the party. However, the district attorney is not the complainant's but the people's lawyer, and it is perfectly proper for a defense attorney to interview a complainant. He may wish to inform the district attorney in advance or even request that there be an assistant district attorney present to protect himself from a charge that he attempted to intimidate the witness. In an age of tape recorders, however, this is probably not necessary.

If a witness surprises the attorney who called him and testifies differently from what he said during the pre-trial investigation, a special problem is created. There is a rule that one cannot impeach one's own witness. This simply means that an attorney calling a witness vouches for the witness's veracity (at least in theory) and therefore cannot try to prove that he is lying even if his testimony hurts the attorney's case. There is one exception to this rule. An attorney may impeach his own witness if, before his testimony, the witness had made a contrary statement either under oath or in a writing signed by him. This evidence is admissible only for the purpose of impeaching or discrediting the witness; it is not admissible as proof of the facts stated. It is not even admissible to impeach the witness unless his testimony tends to disprove the case of the party who called him.

CROSS-EXAMINATION

After the party calling the witness has examined him, the opposing attorney is given the opportunity to cross-examine the witness either to impeach his credibility or to bring out the whole truth. The credibility of a witness is always in issue so that questions relating to his ability to observe and remember and his opportunity to do so are proper. Also, his character and his motivation to tell the truth may be examined. If he is an accomplice, he may be asked what kind of promises he was given by the people in exchange for his testimony. A witness can also be asked about prior criminal convictions (not arrests), and if he denies them, evidence of such convictions may be introduced. This is an exception to the general rule that a cross-examiner is bound by a witness's answer to any collateral issues and cannot go beyond such answers by introducing additional evidence. If it were not for this rule, trials could be extended into all kinds of secondary issues. Leading questions are permitted on cross-examination, and a good cross-examiner will rarely ask any other kind. If a party must call a witness who will probably be hostile toward him, for example the people calling a close relative of the defendant as a witness, the party may ask the court for permission to examine the witness "as a hostile witness." If granted, this means that he may ask leading questions on direct examination, but he may still not impeach the witness except as described above. By calling the witness, he has made him his own and is bound by his answers.

After the cross-examination, the party calling the witness is given an opportunity for a re-direct examination to attempt to rehabilitate the witness if his testimony was thrown into doubt during cross-examination.

The jury is permitted to consider not only what a witness says but how he says it, and his manner on the witness stand. If they feel that the witness has lied in any part of his testimony, they have the right to disregard all of his testimony. One of the problems that the people have in many criminal prosecutions is that the witnesses whom they have to rely on are fairly vulnerable to impeachment, either because of their past criminal records, because they were involved with the present crime, or because, if they are law enforcement officers, they obviously are motivated to testify in such a way as to justify their action in arresting the defendant.

Until now we have been discussing the testimony of ordinary witnesses who have directly observed something that is relevant to the proof or disproof of some fact in issue in a criminal trial. Such a witness may only testify as to what he has directly observed, not to his opinions, except in certain very limited and commonplace areas. Questions requesting an opinion of an ordinary witness are often objected to "on the grounds the question calls for the operation of the witness's mind."

Often, however, juries are called upon to decide questions of fact that the average layman is not qualified to decide. In these cases, the parties may call an "expert witness," who may or may not have any firsthand knowledge of the facts in the case. He will be asked to express his opinion as an aid to the jury in rendering its decision. However, this expert testimony is merely advisory; the jury is free to disregard this expert opinion and substitute its own. Often the jury is forced to do just that, since, in most instances, the experts on each side of the case directly contradict each other.

In calling an expert witness to the stand, the party offering his testimony first asks him questions designed to establish his credentials as an expert and thus permit the party to ask him for his opinion on the facts in issue. This process of qualification will cover such matters as the witness's education and degrees, professional experience, publications, teaching posts, awards, and other credentials. Being an expert in a field is a matter of fact not of degree although the presence or absence of a degree is some evidence to establish such fact. If the witness has very impressive credentials, the opposing attorney may concede that he is qualified, to avoid letting the jury hear of all those impressive qualifications, but the attorney calling him may still insist that the jury be permitted to hear them. Having qualified the witness, the attorney calling him will then ask him questions concerning his opinions in the case. If the opposing attorney thinks the witness has not been qualified as an expert, he will object at this point on the grounds that the witness is not qualified. The federal courts have finally gotten around to discovering that psychologists are experts in psychology, and, over the opposition of an *amicus curiae* brief filed by the American Psychiatric Association, concluded that psychologists are competent to testify as to the mental condition of a defendant raising an insanity defense.[4]

The opinion of an expert who has no personal knowledge of the facts of the case is usually ascertained by asking him a hypothetical question that incorporates certain assumed facts about which the expert then gives his opinion. Every fact to be assumed must be stated in the hypothetical question because the jury has the right to determine if these assumed facts have been properly proved in considering the weight to be accorded the expert's opinion on the hypothetical case, in deciding the actual case.

Cross-examination of an expert witness may involve attempts to impeach him like those used against an ordinary witness (e.g., by inquiring into his motives in testifying). It also may include attempts at impeachment by demonstrating that the expert is not, in fact, an expert. An example of the former type of question would be "Doctor, how much are you being paid for your testimony here today?" A proper response to such a question is that the witness is being paid nothing for his testimony as that is not for sale, but he is being paid X number of dollars for his time. Attempts to overemphasize the amount of a witness's fee may backfire. They may make the jury feel that the witness must really be an eminent authority to command such a high fee. Incidentally, the reason that expert witnesses are paid a fee for their testimony is that they usually have no personal knowledge of the case and so cannot be subpoenaed like an ordinary witness. They must be hired to testify by the party calling them. If an expert has firsthand knowledge of the facts, he may be subpoenaed, but is entitled to a fee if qualified as an expert and asked for his opinion. If an expert has testified often in court, then he may be impeached on the grounds that he is not really a doctor or other expert, but a professional witness. Clarence Darrow made such an attack on one of the people's psychiatrists in the Leopold-Loeb Trial.[5]

An example of an attack on the expert's expertise is the confrontation of the witness by the cross-examiner with a book that contradicts his testimony and the request that he explain the discrepancy. Before counsel can do this, however, he must get the witness to admit that the book is authoritative; thus the witness would be well-advised to consider carefully what works he considers authorities in his field. On the other hand, a physician who disputes the authoritativeness of *Gray's Anatomy* may be in for a rough time. Incidentally, this type of impeachment can be a risky business because if the witness can explain the apparent discrepancy between his testimony and the book satisfactorily, he will have scored very heavily with the jury. In cross-examining an opposing expert, the attorney would do well to consult with his own experts for help in framing the proper questions.

A very important area involving expert testimony which is germane to the subject of this book involves the defense of insanity. We will first consider the substantive law involved and then the practicalities of proving or disproving the defense.

The law concerning the effect of mental illness or defect on criminal responsibility in New York is basically a restatement of the M'Naghten rule, set down in 1843 in England in the case of Daniel M'Naghten, who shot and killed the prime minister's secretary while suffering from what we would now call paranoid delusions of persecution. This rule states that a person is excused from criminal liability for his actions if at the time of their commission he suffered from a mental disease or defect such that he lacked substantial capacity to know or appreciate *either*: (1) the nature or consequences of his action, *or* (2) that such action was wrong.

If he passes this test, it is irrelevant that he was unable to control his conduct. Hence the doctrine of irresistible impulse has no application in New York, and a kleptomaniac (who cannot resist the impulse to steal) is criminally liable in spite of having a "mental disease," as he is aware of both the nature and quality of his actions and that they are wrong. The term "wrong" means morally, not legally, wrong. Otherwise this rule would be contrary to the general principle that ignorance of the law is no defense. Not only does the M'Naghten rule hold some mentally ill defendants criminally liable while it excuses others, often it treats differently defendants suffering from the same mental illness. Thus, a paranoid who believes that a person was following him and therefore kills the person will be held responsible, while another paranoid with the delusion that the victim was trying to kill him will be excused for the homicide. The reason is that the first knows that it is wrong to kill a person merely for following him, but it is justifiable to kill in self-defense. Hence the second paranoid had no grounds for believing his action was wrong.

This situation involving paranoids is often referred to among lawyers as a case of partial insanity of "a sane man with an insane delusion," and the rule is set down that to determine criminal liability one must look to see whether the defendant's conduct would be legally justifiable if the assumptions of the delusion were true. If it would be, his conduct is excused; if not, he is criminally liable. This rule however is nothing more than the results obtained from the application of the M'Naghten rule. The reason for referring to a paranoid as "a sane man with an insane delusion" is that, apart from their delusions, paranoids are generally able to function quite well and give the impression of being normal. They are one of the few types of psychotics who rarely require hospitalization. Psychologically speaking, such designation is nonsense. There is no such thing as a partial psychosis. A person is either psychotic or not, and merely having the symptom of a delusion is enough to classify a person as a psychotic. Paranoia is a condition characterized by a logically closed system of delusions typically involving delusions of persecution, grandeur, reference (everything refers to him), or influence (someone has control over his mind). If the truth of the delusions is assumed, the average paranoid's behavior appears as reasonable as anyone else's.

The way in which an insanity defense is proved in court is for the defense to put an expert witness on the stand who has examined the defendant and testifies to his opinion concerning the defendant's mental state at the time of the commission of the alleged crime. The expert is usually a psychiatrist rather than a clinical psychologist because, rightly or wrongly, most attorneys feel that a medically qualified witness will be more impressive to a jury. The profession of psychology is not only younger than that of medicine; it has evidently not done the kind of public relations work that physicians have done. One result is that the New York Penal Law makes no mention of psychologists in its section on psychiatric testimony to establish or contest an insanity defense. The law requires that a psychiatrist testifying in connection with a defense of mental disease or defect must be permitted to make a statement concerning the nature of the examination that he conducted, his diagnosis, and his opinion of the defendant's capacity to understand the nature and consequences of his actions and their wrongfulness. He may be cross-examined on his competency and credibility as well as on the validity of his diagnosis or opinion. It would appear that, in spite of the unfortunate wording of this statute, it would apply to a clinical psychologist or any other expert in the area of mental illness or defect. It is doubtful whether this section would apply to a non-psychiatrist physician, since, in most cases, his training in mental illness would be insufficient to qualify him as an expert in court.

The reader should be aware that there has been and probably will continue to be much controversy between psychologists and psychiatrists over clinical psychologists practicing independently. Often this is more of an economic battle than a scientific one. The classical psychiatric position was that the diagnosis and treatment of mental illness is the practice of medicine and should be restricted to physicians or people working under their supervision. The psychologist's position has been that the treatment of what is called mental illness is the practice of psychology, not medicine, and that the reason that this area was originally the exclusive province of physicians was that there were mentally ill people needing treatment long before there was any science called psychology on which to base a scientific method of treatment. It was natural for medical doctors to fill this vacuum and attempt to treat these people. When physicians entered the area of mental illness, they brought along concepts and styles of thinking from medical practice such as the term "mental illness" itself. Many psychologists dispute the assumption that a so-called mental illness has any similarity to a physical illness. They prefer such terms as "behavior disorder," which they feel are more descriptive of what these conditions really are. Some even object to the term "patient" and would prefer to use the term "client" in an effort to get away from the medical model.

It should not be assumed that there is necessarily any homogeneity of thinking in regard to these issues within these two professions. Many psychiatrists, like Sigmund Freud, have felt that their medical education was irrelevant to the treatment of psychological conditions, and that psychotherapy is not the practice of medicine.[6] On the other hand, many psychologists feel that a psychologist's unique training in research is somehow being wasted if he spends his time practicing psychotherapy (which, at present, is more of an art than a science) instead of doing research.

Certainly there are physical (or organic) conditions that produce deranged behavior, and their treatment is the proper province of psychiatry. The treatment of the more common behavior disorders that have no demonstrable organic etiology is the proper province of either psychologists or psychiatrists who have been trained in this area. Many psychologists and psychiatrists are not so trained, and the question of whether a prospective expert witness ought to be allowed to testify about a defendant's mental state is a preliminary question of fact for the trial judge to decide before permitting opinion testimony by the witness. It depends on more than the presence or absence of an M.D. or Ph.D. degree.

One of the problems in expert testimony about a defendant's mental state at the time of the commission of an alleged offense is that the expert typically has examined him either after the event, which is the more usual case, or before it (if the defendant was in treatment prior to the offense or for some reason previously had a psychological examination). The witness, however, must testify to his opinion of the defendant's mental state *at the time of the crime* not before or after (which is difficult enough for any expert to be able to do accurately). This is normally accomplished by the expert testifying that the defendant was suffering from a chronic or progressive condition, and, based on his condition at the time of the examination, the defendant could not have had the mental capacity to appreciate the nature and consequences of his actions or that they were wrong at the time of the commission of the alleged offense.

Following the cross-examination of the defense witnesses, the people will call and qualify their rebuttal experts. If they have not had an opportunity to examine the defendant personally, or if he was not cooperative with them (and it is hard to think of any good reason why he should be), they may testify in response to hypothetical questions based on the facts brought out by the evidence in the case. It is improper to ask a witness to base his opinion on "all of the evidence presented in the case," as the jury is then unable to know what facts the expert's decision is based upon. In effect, this permits the expert to usurp the jury's role as the exclusive judge of what the defendant's mental state was at the time in question, and the witness is no longer aiding them in their decision; he is making it for them.

Often the testimony of the experts on both sides of the case is completely contradictory, and the jury is forced to decide the issue on its own. Of course, the jury has the final responsibility for this decision in any case.

The spectacle of two experts directly contradicting each other does not reflect much credit on either themselves or their profession, and gives the impression that their testimony is for sale. This is usually not the case. The contradiction typically results from the inexactness of the present state of the art of the behavioral sciences, coupled with the unfortunate tendency of most expert witnesses to state conclusions of law rather than professional conclusions and how these conclusions were arrived at. If the proper explanation were given by mental experts for their conclusions, many of the apparent contradictions in their testimony would disappear, and the jury would be aided in its search for the truth. Judge Bazelon of the U.S. Court of Appeals has taken psychiatrists to task for testifying to conclusions of law that are the proper province of the jury (i.e., that the defendant was or was not criminally liable). This is probably more the fault of examining lawyers who have failed to explain to their witnesses what is necessary in the way of effective testimony than it is the fault of the witnesses themselves. It is not fair to expect a layman to understand the nature of the judicial process without such preparation.

In 1954, in the *Durham* case, the U.S. Court of Appeals, for the District of Columbia, pronounced a new test of mental capacity in an effort to solve the problem of psychiatrists testifying to ultimate legal conclusions concerning the defendant's liability for a crime rather than to their opinion of the defendant's mental state so that the jury might assume its proper role.[7] It was also intended to correct some of the apparent injustices of the M'Naghten rule.

Durham held that in the federal courts of the District a defendant was not criminally responsible if his actions were the product of a mental disease or defect. The rule was much broader than M'Naghten, which was the law in these federal courts prior to Durham. It would excuse people with irresistible impulses to commit crimes who would not have been excused under the old rule. However, in spite of the hopes of the Court, it did not stop psychiatrists from testifying to the conclusion that the defendant was (or was not) criminally responsible. In 1972, in the case of *U.S. v. Brawner*, the Durham rule was set aside in favor of a new rule for the federal courts based on an insanity test proposed by the American Law Institute.[8] This rule holds that a person is not criminally liable for his conduct if, at the time of such conduct, he lacks substantial capacity either to appreciate its wrongfulness or to conform his conduct to the requirements of the law.

PRIVILEGE

Certain relationships require free communication between the parties for the relationship to be effective. The law regards these relationships as of greater importance than securing the conviction of any defendant; thus communications between the parties to such relationships are privileged. They may not be testified to without the consent of the party for whose benefit the relationship is established. These special relationships include:

1. The husband–wife relationship
2. The clergyman–penitent relationship
3. The attorney–client relationship
4. The doctor–patient relationship

and more recently:

5. The certified psychologist–client relationship
6. The certified social worker–client relationship.

Only the last four relationships are relevant for our purposes. In order for an attorney–client relationship to exist and the privilege to attach, the client must consult the attorney in his professional capacity. Something more than advice between two friends must be involved, but a fee need not be charged. The subject matter of the communication must involve a legal matter, not business advice or a tip on the stock market. Once the privilege attaches, the attorney cannot be compelled or even permitted to testify about his communications with the client without the client's consent expressed or implied. The privilege belongs to the client not to the attorney, and only the client can waive it. If it were not for this privilege, no one could consult an attorney with security, and the constitutional right to be represented by counsel would be meaningless. In short, this is a constitutional privilege, and the legislature probably cannot erode it. The only exception to the coverage of this privilege is that if the client tells the attorney that he intends to commit a crime in the future, such disclosure is not privileged. If the attorney cannot talk him out of it, he is required to warn the potential victim.

The doctor–patient privilege is not a constitutional privilege and is in derogation of the common law. It has been the subject of attack by many legal writers on the grounds that, in most cases, it is not necessary for the proper functioning of the doctor–patient relationship. The average patient would not be inhibited in going for medical treatment for an ulcer if his communications with his physician were not confidential. Since the privilege is not constitutionally required, the legislature may whittle away at many of its areas of coverage, and in fact has done so. For example, a physician is required to report if his examination discloses that a child under the age of 16 has been the victim of a crime. He is also required to report to the authorities all cases of gunshot or stab wounds and certain communicable diseases including venereal diseases. Thus in those areas where there is some legitimate need for confidentiality of communication between doctor and patient, there is in fact no effective privilege. In the case of psychiatrists there is a clear-cut need for both confidentiality and privilege; without it, few patients would be rash enough to make the kind of revelations required for effective psychotherapy. (Confidentiality refers to an ethical obligation on the part of the professional person to refrain from discussing his client's or patient's case with third parties; privilege is the legal principle that makes his testimony on such matters inadmissible in evidence.) The privilege covering communications between attorney and client, or doctor and patient, also extends to employees of the attorney or doctor.

For a doctor–patient privilege to exist, the patient must consult the doctor for purposes of treatment. If he consults him in order to get a medical opinion for use in litigation, no privilege attaches to the communications. In one case an appellate court sustained the introduction into evidence of the testimony of a psychiatrist hired by the defense to establish an insanity defense who believed that the defendant was criminally responsible and had therefore refused to testify for the defense. He was called instead by the prosecution. The defense's claim of doctor–patient privilege was clearly inadequate, as the psychiatrist was not consulted for the purposes of treatment. The argument that the doctor was in fact an agent of the attorney and should have been prevented from testifying on the basis of the attorney–client relationship seems to us to be more compelling than the court found it to be.[9]

The N.Y. Civil Practice Law and Rules states that the certified psychologist–client privilege is identical to the attorney–client privilege, while it creates a separate privilege for social workers and their clients.

It is interesting to note that clinical psychologists and psychiatrists doing exactly the same thing in psychotherapy have different privileges. We suspect that the reason for this state of affairs is that the psychiatric societies objected to anyone other than a physician having a privilege labeled a physician-patient privilege. Whatever the reason, the psychologist–client privilege is the broader one afforded to attorneys and their clients. Unlike the attorney-client relationship, this privilege is not a constitutional requirement, and could be changed by the legislature. However, a privileged relationship is an absolutely essential requirement for the ethical practice of any form of psychotherapy.

SUMMATIONS

After both the people and the defendant have presented all of their evidence, each side sums up its case to the jury. The defense speaks first.

The purpose of the summation is to help organize and clarify all of the evidence presented during the trial and to put the speaker's case in the most favorable possible light. Evidence in a trial is often presented in what appears to be the most confusing manner imaginable. Instead of there being a clear narrative account of a situation, the facts have to be brought out in a question-and-answer format, often from several different witnesses testifying at different times. The testimony is interrupted with objections, court rulings, and other distractions. Furthermore, if the trial is lengthy, the jury may have forgotten little things that seemed unimportant when testified to, but which, in the light of later testimony, become vital. The summation is counsel's chance to connect the facts in order to present the picture most favorable to his case. The defense may also point up those extralegal factors that may win the jury's sympathy for its cause.

Often lawyers will use this opportunity to advise the jury of the procedures to follow. For example, a defense attorney ought to inform the jury that this will be his last chance to address them so that if the people raise any questions in their summation and he remains silent, the jury will know that it is not because he has no answer, but because trials have to end at some point. Often the lawyer will say something to the effect that if such questions are raised, he will rely on the jury to come up with the answers for him. He will also usually tell them that neither his nor his adversary's statements are evidence, and that only the judge can tell them what law to apply to the case at hand. Juries should also be reminded that they always have the right to acquit the defendant and not to let the people fool them into thinking that they have no such right by statements about what their sworn duty is. In fact, the defense will urge that, based on the quality of evidence presented, the people have failed to prove their case beyond a reasonable doubt, and it is not only the jury's right but its duty to acquit. Often, in such matters as the meaning of the term "reasonable doubt," lawyers will define terms subject to the court's charge on the law.

A good defense lawyer will try to take the punch out of the people's summation by saying things that he knows the district attorney will say or by responding to such arguments in advance. A defense attorney cannot mention the sentence that may be imposed if a conviction occurs, since this is not a proper part of the jury's consideration. He may, and will, make general remarks about the seriousness of the consequences of a conviction to the defendant and his family. He will certainly point out how the evidence presented is not inconsistent with the defendant's innocence, and will attack the credibility of key witnesses against the defense if he can. Finally, remarks may be in order concerning the defense's confidence in the good judgment and common sense of the jury and the importance of the institution of jury trials in the protection of the innocent against false accusations.

In the people's summation there may also be appeals to sympathy, but they are for the poor, defenseless victim, not the defendant. The defendant and his alleged conduct may be the subject of a scathing attack, but any reference to a prior conviction not properly introduced into evidence during the trial will result in a mistrial; so, too, will any comment concerning the defendant's exercising his right not to take the stand and testify in his own behalf. Both sides must limit themselves to the evidence presented and avoid talking about the law except subject to the court's charge.

It is a good idea for opposing counsel to keep a poker face during summations and to avoid taking notes unless he is later to have an opportunity to address the jury, for any reaction on counsel's part will have the effect of making the argument seem more important to the jury. Summations are rarely interrupted except for the most cogent of reasons, such as counsel referring to evidence not presented or making extremely prejudicial and unfounded remarks. Summations are not evidence that can be objected to, but merely arguments. If a defense summation is unduly abusive, the people will have an opportunity to point out to the jury that the defense really had nothing cogent to say relative to the case. The district attorney may even choose to quote the old bit of advice to a neophyte trial lawyer to this effect: "When the law is on your side, but the facts are against you, hammer away at the judge; when the facts are on your side, but the law is against you, hammer away at the jury; when both the law and the facts are against you, hammer away at the counsel table."

THE COURT'S CHARGE TO THE JURY

When the summations are completed, the court will deliver its charge to the jury. The purpose of the charge is to inform the jury of the law applicable to the case at hand, which they are to apply to the facts as they find them. In addition to advising the jury of the elements of the charges that the people must prove, the court must advise them of certain general principles of criminal law, such as the presumption of the defendant's innocence and the meaning of the term "reasonable doubt." The latter does not mean that the people must prove the defendant's guilt to a logical certainty. Such a result is manifestly impossible. It does mean that all of the believable evidence presented must be inconsistent with the defendant's innocence. The jury must be advised that in their determination of guilt or innocence, they may not speculate on the sentence that may be imposed and that they may not go beyond the evidence presented or speculate on matters not in evidence. The court need not marshal or summarize the evidence presented, but it may. Upon the request of a defendant who did not testify at his trial, the court must advise the jury that no inference adverse to such defendant may be made from the fact that he did not choose to testify on his own behalf.

The court must specifically inform the jury of which counts in the indictment it is submitting to them for a verdict, and the verdicts that they may find on each of these counts. Some counts in the original indictment may have been dismissed on motion following the people's direct case; any remaining counts not submitted to the jury are deemed dismissed by a trial order of dismissal. A court need not submit a count of an indictment if no reasonable view of the trial evidence would support it, and if a verdict of guilty on such count would have to be dismissed as not supported by legal evidence. When a court submits a count to the jury, it must submit either the count charged or the greatest lesser included offense supported by legally sufficient evidence. In submitting a count to a jury, the court may, in addition to submitting the greatest offense it is required to submit, submit any lesser included offense if a reasonable view of the evidence suggests that the defendant may have committed the lesser, but not the greater offense. Two counts are inconsistent if a verdict of guilty on one count necessarily requires a verdict of not guilty on the other. At least one of such inconsistent counts must be submitted, but if some reasonable view of the evidence would sustain a conviction on either charge, both inconsistent counts may be submitted. The court must then instruct the jury that they may find the defendant guilty on only one or neither of these charges. A court need not submit a count to a jury if the people consent that it not be submitted, and the defense does not insist on the submission of a lesser included offense that it is entitled to. The dropping of some counts may be desirable if the indictment contains many counts which would tend to confuse a jury. A count is consecutive with another if consecutive sentences could be imposed upon conviction on both counts; counts are concurrent with each other if concurrent sentences would be required. In general, if there are groups of counts that are concurrent with each other but consecutive to other groups of counts, the court will submit one count from each consecutive grouping.

To each count submitted the jury must find a verdict of either guilty, not guilty, or, in an appropriate case, not guilty by reason of mental disease or defect. There are no special verdicts in criminal cases. A special verdict in a civil case is used in a situation in which, because of the complex legal issues involved, the jury renders a verdict answering specific questions of fact submitted to it, and the court then applies these facts to the law. In a criminal case, the jury must decide on guilt or innocence. Thus, it is not only the trier of the facts, but, in a sense, a trier of the law. For, while a conviction may be set aside if the jury disregards the court's instructions as to the law, or goes beyond the evidence, no one can question a verdict of acquittal, no matter how contrary to the evidence or law it may be. In effect the jury has decided that, in this case, at least, the law is wrong; it ought not to apply here if justice is to be done.

Prior to their summations, the parties must be informed by the court as to which counts it intends to submit to the jury so that the summations can be addressed to the charges that the jury is to consider. Both before and after the court's charge to the jury, either side may submit requests to the court either orally or in writing to charge the jury in some specific manner. If a party feels that the court has charged the jury erroneously, he may object to that portion of the charge. If he believes that the court has omitted something from its charge, he may request that such an instruction be added. If an attorney requests the court orally, in the presence of the jury, to charge the jury on a particular point of law, and the court says "I so charge," the attorney may request the judge to repeat the charge so that the jury may hear the words from the judge. It is likely to make more of an impression when spoken from the bench than when spoken from the counsel table.

Following the court's charge, the jury retires to the jury room to deliberate and arrive at its verdict (literally its "true saying").

Often during the trial when motions are made to dismiss, or arguments are made concerning the admissibility of evidence offered, either the moving party, his adversary, or the court on its own motion will ask that the jury be excused before such motions are argued. This is to assure that the jury not be prejudiced by material ultimately deemed inadmissible or lose respect for the attorney whose motion is denied. Denial of a *pro forma* motion to dismiss the case may be viewed by the jury as indicating that the judge feels that the people have proved their case, or at least that the judge feels they have a strong case. Neither conclusion is necessarily correct. Juries are instructed by the court that the court has no opinion concerning the defendant's guilt or innocence, and if the court has done or said anything to give the impression that it has such an opinion, the jury may not properly consider it in arriving at its verdict.

The jury may take into the jury room any exhibits received in evidence that the court in its discretion permits, as well as a written list prepared by the court of the counts submitted to the jury in its charge and the possible verdicts on each count. If, in the course of its deliberations, the jury requests further instructions or clarifications of the court with respect to the law, or wishes to review the testimony, the court must order the jury returned to the courtroom and, after notice to both the defense and the people, and in the presence of the defendant, give the jury whatever further instructions and information it deems proper.

THE JURY'S VERDICT

The jury's verdict must be given in the courtroom in the presence of both the court and the defendant. The prosecutor has the right to be present, but his right may be waived. Before reading the verdict the foreman must be asked if the jury has agreed on a verdict and must answer in the affirmative. If a jury renders a verdict not in accordance with the court's instructions, the court must explain to the jury members why the verdict is defective and require them to retire and render a proper verdict. If a jury persists in rendering an improper verdict, the court may elect to treat the verdict as an acquittal or discharge the jury and order a retrial, unless it is clear that the jury intended to find a defendant not guilty on a particular count. In such a case, the court must order that the verdict be recorded as an acquittal on that count. If a jury has deliberated for an extended period of time and reports that it cannot agree on a verdict, and the court is convinced that further deliberations would be futile, or if both parties consent, a mistrial may be declared. In that event the case will be retried on the original indictment, including any counts that may have been dismissed by a trial order of dismissal or which were not submitted to the jury. If a jury is unable to agree to a verdict on all counts but does agree on some, the court may accept the partial verdict. In such a case the defendant may be retried on any offense on which the jury did not agree, unless a conviction on such an offense would be inconsistent with the partial verdict rendered. In a criminal case the jury verdict must be unanimous for guilt or innocence, a situation contrary to the civil rule, in which verdicts may be rendered on a ten to two or five to one vote for juries of twelve and six members respectively.

When a defendant is convicted of a particular degree of an offense, this verdict is deemed an acquittal of all counts submitted charging a greater degree of the same offense and a dismissal of all counts charging a lesser degree. The people can appeal a dismissal only if no new findings of fact would be required. They cannot appeal an acquittal.

After a verdict is read, it must be entered in the court minutes and read to the members of the jury, who are then asked collectively if it is their verdict. Either party may then move to poll the jury, and if such motion is made, each juryman must be asked individually if the verdict is his in all respects. If, on either the collective or individual questioning, any juror answers in the negative, the court must refuse to accept the verdict and direct the jury to go back and continue deliberating. If the jurymen all agree that the verdict is theirs, they are thanked by the court and discharged. If the defendant has been acquitted on all charges, he must immediately be discharged by the court and his bail, if any, exonerated. If he is convicted on any charges, the court will set a date for sentencing and will either continue the defendant on bail or on his own recognizance or increase or revoke bail. In all convictions for a felony and in the case of some misdemeanor sentences, the court must order a pre-sentence report, and time must be allowed for the preparation of these reports and for pre-sentence conferences. Even in cases involving misdemeanors or less when the court can impose a sentence immediately, it is required to ask the defendant if he desires an adjournment and, if so, for what purpose. The defendant having requested such an adjournment and stated the purpose for which it is sought, a reasonable adjournment for such purpose must be granted.

It is both proper and customary for both counsel to discuss the case with the former jurors after they are discharged, as this enables the lawyers to ascertain the effects on the jury of their arguments and strategies and prevents them from repeating tactical errors in the future. It is, of course, grossly improper to criticize a former juror for his verdict, and post-trial discussions with jurors are best conducted in the presence of opposing counsel. On some occasions jurors with guilt feelings have come forward and informed counsel of improprieties that occurred during their deliberations. These revelations have later provided the basis for attacking convictions on appeal.

In cases of acquittal it is customary for defense counsel to thank the jury on behalf of his client before the jury is dismissed. In a trial before a judge, the court is never thanked for a verdict of acquittal. The theory here is that it has not done a favor for the defendant but has merely performed its duty to acquit the innocent.

REFERENCES

1. Freedman, Monroe H. *Lawyer's Ethics in an Adversary System.* Indianapolis: Bobbs-Merrill, 1975.
2. *Miranda v. Arizona*, 1966, 384 U.S. 436, 86 S. Ct. 1602, 16 L. Ed. 2d 694.
3. *Escobedo v. Illinois*, 1964, 378 U.S. 478, 84 S. Ct. 1758, 12 L. Ed. 2d 977.
4. *Jenkins v. United States*, 1962, 307 F. 2d 637.
5. Weinberg, Arthur. *Attorney for the Damned.* New York: Simon & Schuster, 1957.
6. Freud, Sigmund. *The Question of Lay Analysis.* New York: W. W. Norton & Co., 1950.
7. *Durham v. United States*, 1954, 214 F. 2d 862.
8. *United States v. Brawner*, 1972, 471 F. 2d 969.
9. *People v. Edney*, 39 N.Y. 2d 620.

11
Psychology and
Jury Selection

Psychologists have been interested in the workings of juries at least since the work of Münsterberg near the turn of the century. Among the issues that have been considered over the years are: How persuasible are the jurors? How do they proceed to deliberate? Are some types of jurors more influential than others? Are jurors more readily influenced by appeals to emotion or by appeals to reason? Do jurors attend closely to the evidence that is presented in court? Are they influenced by the penalties that they assume attach to the crimes in question? Are jurors influenced by the appearance, social class, ethnicity of the defendant and the victim? Do juries follow instructions to disregard inadmissible evidence? Do juries arrive at decisions similar to those at which the judge in the case arrives? Are some laws more amenable than others to jurors' understanding? What kinds of people make the best jurors from the points of view of the opposing sides? Can a jury of six render verdicts as just as juries of twelve? Can nonunanimous decisions be as just as unanimous ones? To what extent do extraneous motives intrude themselves into deliberations? To what extent do jurors truly represent the communities from which they are drawn? Are most defendants tried by juries of their peers? How do attorneys select their jurors? Can social scientists help to select unbiased juries? In this chapter, we will consider some of the factors that lawyers and psychologists believe are predictive of juror performance.

JURY SELECTION

Plutchik and Schwartz considered some of the beliefs of lawyers and others about the selection of jurors. They cite a 1936 article by Clarence Darrow, who viewed trials as contests between the haves and the have-nots. The former, he said, will convict any defendant except other haves who stand accused of financial double-dealing. He expressed strong feelings, too, about ethnicity. Irishmen and Jews would be predisposed to acquit, as would Unitarians and other liberal Protestant denominations. He did not want women jurors but felt that a juror who laughs easily would be loath to convict.

While the relationship between income and verdict appeared plausible to other writers, that between sex and verdict enjoys less consensus. Some argue that women know too little of life, others that they are too much subject to their spouses' influence, still others that they are likely to be especially sympathetic to emotional appeals.

Stereotypes about the relative emotionality of different ethnic groups have led lawyers who plan emotional appeals to seek jurors of Irish, Jewish, Italian, French, Spanish, or Slavic backgrounds. Those whose appeal will be to logic, to facts rather than to feelings, are led by similar stereotypes to seek jurors whose backgrounds are English, German, or Scandinavian. Plutchik and Schwartz rightly point out that there are prison inmates in Ireland and that defense attorneys have not emigrated to the Emerald Isle *en masse*.

Many lawyers claim the ability to size up a prospective juror's attitudes, openness, and mode of thinking. They consider such elements as appearance, response to questions, and reactions to authority, and extrapolate from them to the candidate's behavior in the jury room. How helpful these clues may be will be seen shortly. As far as sex and income are concerned, an unpublished study by Mayer (cited by Plutchik and Schwartz) suggests that the factors just mentioned are not very good predictors. In ten hypothetical accident cases in which a corporation was the defendant and an individual the plaintiff, men and the more wealthy made significantly more decisions in favor of the plaintiff than did women and the less wealthy, but the difference was small.

Surely successful lawyers know what they are about. How is it, then, that they operate on premises which are demonstrably untenable? Plutchik and Schwartz offer one plausible suggestion. If the lawyer selects jurors whom he likes or who he expects will favor his side of the case, he will feel more comfortable and is likely to be better able to establish rapport with them. The better the rapport, presumably, the more attentive the jurors will be to that advocate's side. The more attentive they are, the more influenced they should be. To a layman it may be unnerving to think that the outcome of a criminal trial may depend upon the mutual attraction of jurors and attorneys.

There has been exploration in recent years of the feasibility of using personality tests in the screening or selecting of jurors. Golden reports the use of a variety of personality tests in attempts to predict the votes of real jurors and college students serving as mock jurors. Such traits as authoritarianism (a tendency to respect authority and status), dogmatism (a tendency to maintain a mind closed to unfamiliar or contradictory information), Machiavellianism (a tendency to regard people as appropriate targets of manipulation), and acquiescence (a tendency to "go along with" others) have been investigated. Golden cites a paper by C. D. Emerson in which it is proposed that such tests be given to prospective jurors and the results be made available to the court, the attorneys, and a psychologist. Such tests, Emerson seems to imply, would permit the discrete excusing of those whose scores on standard tests are such as to suggest their inability to function as conscientious, unbiased jurors. Pathology and prejudice might be revealed without the need for public questioning. (Emerson also considers some ethical concerns raised by his suggestion.)

V. R. Boehm was the author of a much-cited study that reviews research and court cases involving jury bias and examines psychological measures of bias. She finds that the measures usually used are inappropriate for use with juries because:

1. Few of the items pertain to the activities of jurors.
2. Correlations between attitudes and preliminary verdicts do not, in and of themselves, indicate that the verdicts are false.
3. Persons who are demonstrably biased may not actually serve on juries.

Accordingly, Boehm developed a Legal Attitudes Questionnaire, whose items are framed in legal terms, correlate with the Authoritarianism and Dogmatism scales, and predict the behavior of mock jurors. Subjects indicate agreement or disagreement with items that can be classed as Authoritarian (right wing, punitive, unequivocal acceptance of constituted authority), Anti-Authoritarian (left wing, society to blame for criminal acts, unequivocal rejection of constituted authority), or Equalitarian (liberal, nonextreme, suggesting shades of gray among the black and white). Using college student "jurors" who responded individually to information adapted from a real case, Boehm found that those who voted to convict the defendant who seemed, objectively, to be innocent, had higher authoritarianism scores. Similarly, although it was less clear-cut for younger subjects, judging a case in which there was abundant evidence against the accused, those who acquitted had higher anti-authoritarianism scores. Viewed differently, authoritarians were more likely to err on the side of the prosecution; anti-authoritarians were more likely to err on the side of the defense.

Asked to give reasons for their verdicts, subjects appeared to respond to impressions that were consistent with their own attitudes. Authoritarians tended to blame the defendant or his character for the crime; anti-authoritarians tended to blame society.

Boehm herself points out that a paper-and-pencil test may not be a fully accurate representation of real jury deliberations. One would hope, too, that real jurors are more careful to confront and consider all facts before reaching a verdict.

If psychological testing is one approach to selecting the jurors most favorable to a party's cause, another more costly and controversial approach is that of R. Christie, J. Schulman, and their associates.

In a number of recent trials the defendants have been confronted with the task of defending themselves in the face of strong negative public opinion within the community from which the jurors have been chosen. Complications have included political bias (e.g., the trial of the Harrisburg Seven, the Angela Davis case), racist attitudes (Joan Little), or a combination of the two (the Wounded Knee trials). The Watergate defendants also were subject to many of the pressures previously experienced by the Berrigan brothers and their followers.

The legal remedy for a defendant in such a situation is to move for a change in venue or trial site. However, if a case has received an enormous amount of publicity, it may not be possible to find a site where potential jurors have not been contaminated by press accounts of the crime.

In any case, a team of social scientists volunteered to assist the defense in selecting a jury to try Philip Berrigan, Elizabeth McAlister, and their five co-defendants on, among other things, charges of conspiracy against draft boards, Henry Kissinger, and heating tunnels in Washington. An account of the techniques used is given by Schulman et al.; here is a brief summary of it.

The first task was to determine the degree to which the potential jurors were, in fact, representative of the community of Harrisburg, a conservative, Protestant, Republican city, located near several military facilities in central Pennsylvania. If it were representative, the panel of jurors would have resembled the community-at-large in key demographic variables: age, sex, race, education, and occupation. From lists of registered voters (potential jurors) a sample of 1,236 people were selected, of whom 840 were successfully interviewed by telephone. Results showed that the panel tended to be older than the telephone respondents. Judge Herman accordingly agreed to selection of a new panel from which the trial jury would be chosen.

With the help of 45 volunteers it was possible to interview at greater length 252 of the 840 previously contacted. The 252 had characteristics similar to the new jury pool and were interviewed concerning a number of matters that Schulman et al. felt might be pertinent to a juror's attitudes and bias. Respondents were asked to indicate their exposure to the mass media, printed and electronic, what they had heard about a number of public figures, including the two most prominent defendants, and to identify the greatest American in recent years. Three questions tapped respondents' trust in government. In addition, they were asked about their children's activities and ages, their own religious attitudes and commitment, their leisure time activities, memberships, several pertinent attitude questions, and their view of antiwar actions.

From these data several conclusions were drawn which guided the defense in its selection of jurors. It seemed wise to avoid Episcopalians, Presbyterians, Methodists, and Fundamentalists and to select Catholics, Brethren, and Lutherans. Unlike their counterparts in other areas, college-educated people, especially those over 30, tended to be conservative in this region. But jurors who had little trust in government were likely to be "good" for the defense. From the defense standpoint, in short, the ideal juror would be a female Democrat, employed in a white-collar or skilled blue-collar job, having no religious preference, somewhat sympathetic to antiwar views, and willing to accept nonviolent resistance to government policies.

The judge, who in federal cases controls jury selection, allowed the defense considerable latitude during the *voir dire*. They were permitted 28 peremptory challenges, while the government had 6, and were permitted to question prospective jurors directly and at length. Daily, after each session, the defense team jointly rated the prospects on a five-point scale ranging from 1, a very good defense juror, to 5, an undesirable defense juror. Good defense jurors as seen by *both* sides were under 30, black, related somehow to the counter-culture, opposed to the Vietnam war, and related to someone near draft age.

But jurors do not work individually. The team attempted to envision how the possible combinations of people would function as a problem-solving, decision-making group. Who would be the likely foreman? Should all the jurors, or most of them, be of the same sex?

The jury finally selected by this technique convicted some defendants on the relatively minor charge of smuggling letters, and were deadlocked on the more serious charges with a 10–2 vote for acquittal. Schulman et al. claim neither credit nor blame for the outcome. As they point out, there having been no trial *without* their procedures, it is not possible to attribute the outcome *to* their procedures. That is, there was no "control group." On the other hand, the efforts of the social scientists did seem to help influence the judge to order a new panel or "jury wheel." They provided the defense with information about the community that gave rise to several defense motions, and suggested criteria to the attorneys for the selection of jurors.

Schulman et al. conclude with several recommendations and some questions:

1. Attitudes toward the defendants and their alleged crime should be explored in each case. They may differ from one place to another (cf. *infra*).

2. Ratings of jurors should be based on standardized and reliable procedures.

3. The defense should consider how the individual juror conceives of his role. A juror who perceives himself as deciding whether or not the government has presented enough evidence is better for the defense than one who thinks in terms of guilt or innocence.

4. The relative dominance of the jurors should be taken into account. Who will give support to whom? A defense-prone juror who will not speak his mind is not as helpful as one who will.

5. Nonverbal cues can be very helpful. Although they were not examined systematically in the Harrisburg case, they were by the Angela Davis defense team, as we shall see.

While Schulman and his colleagues see no ethical problem in taking sides as they did, they do acknowledge ethical qualms about two aspects of their activities. First, in interviewing respondents they told only part of the truth. They said they were researchers interested in the area because a major trial was to take place there. They did not say that their data would be used to assist the defense. An ethical principle for psychologists is that subjects should be informed of the uses to which their information will be put. Schulman et al. feared that they would get little cooperation if they revealed their true purpose and concluded that their interview could not harm the respondent in any way. Whether these are sufficient justifications is an open question. They argue that the techniques which they employed are available to the government and that the defense must have equal access to these methods.

Survey research and interviewing are not the only skills which psychologists have brought to the process of jury selection. Sage describes a famous case in which their participation was limited to observation of, and advice during, the *voir dire*.

Angela Davis, a black Communist militant, was accused of conspiracy, kidnapping, and murder in connection with an attempted escape involving defendants in a California courtroom. Because the trial was to take place in a county whose population included fewer than 2% blacks (motions for change in venue having been denied), Davis's attorneys enlisted the services of a team of psychologists. Their goal was to identify the prospective jurors who would be able to evaluate the evidence without filtering it through ethnic or political prejudices. They tried to pick up subtle behavioral clues to attitudes, an inclination of the head or a stammer which revealed attentiveness or tension, as prospective jurors responded to questioning by the opposing attorneys. They hoped to be able to infer accurately how objectively the candidate would assess the testimony that would be presented.

The lawyers were urged to ask questions that would require fairly lengthy responses rather than yes or no, with which they might otherwise have been content. The more a person talks, the more he reveals about his style of thinking and his open- or closed-mindedness. Accordingly, jurors were asked their reactions to Afro hairstyles, to Communism, to certain newspapers, and so on. The defense's task was facilitated by the fact that one of its attorneys appeared to be white and the other black. Differences in the nature of responses to questions asked by each attorney offered some clues. More valuable were differences in responses to the opposing attorneys. A juror who was expansive in answering the prosecution questions and succinct in answering the defense was conveying more information than his spoken words were. Eye movements were watched, too. Did the would-be juror glance approvingly toward an attorney's or the defendant's hair when asked about Afros? Or did he look away, perhaps betraying uneasiness or dislike? Was the individual equally able to understand questions asked by both sides, or was one side compelled to explain the question or to repeat it?

Another concern was the ultimate interaction of individuals selected for the jury. When a group of people meet together to deliberate or to solve a problem, they can proceed in an infinite variety of ways. One juror may seek to dominate the discussion; there may be subgroups within the jury consisting of those who approach the task in one way and those who prefer another. Hence, the psychologists attempted to discern leadership qualities among the candidates and to anticipate the relationships that would develop among the 12 people finally selected. Were there instances of meaning-laden eye contact between the waiting veniremen? Did there occur matching gestures, e.g., did two jurors fold their arms at the same time, indicating some unspoken communication between them? Who stood with whom during breaks? Who sat together at meals? After three-and-a-half weeks, before the panel became irritated by the process, the defense moved to accept the 12 persons then in the box. The psychologists also warned the defense that some favorable predispositions which they believed they had picked up might be revealed to the prosecution if the process continued much longer. Each day's observations were reviewed in a meeting during which the psychologists compared what they had seen and inferred. They found themselves in agreement to an encouraging degree.

Without presenting the details of the people's case, suffice it to say that the jury found it hard to accept. After 13 hours of deliberation they acquitted the defendant on all charges. Not a single juror had voted to convict on any charge at any time! A remarkable indication of the jurors' feelings for Angela Davis was the appearance of nine of them at a victory celebration the evening following the trial. Ten of them appeared at a private party a week later.

Like Schulman, Christie, and their colleagues, the psychologists in the Davis case view their activities as righting an imbalance that they believe penalizes the poor, minorities, and the unpopular in many jury trials. Sage concludes his interesting article with the suggestion that a jury of one's peers does not mean one's ethnic, social, or economic equals. He suggests that psychologists can help in the selection of jurors who can understand the circumstances of one's life, and that in the pursuit of justice this is a worthy goal.

The survey and the observation of behavior methods were combined in another well-known trial at the other end of the political spectrum. Marty Herbst (a research and media analyst, not a psychologist) conducted a telephone survey in order to assist the defense in the trial of John Mitchell and Maurice Stans for conspiracy. Interestingly, some of the liberal press reacted to this news with abhorrence.[1] In addition, Herbst observed the jurors throughout the trial, noting reactions to the various developments in the case.

H. Zeisel and S. Seidman Diamond examined the jury selection procedure in that case in some detail. Veniremen were examined initially in groups of 48. The number examined totaled 196, of whom the court excused 138 for cause: 85 because of hardship (the jury was to be sequestered), 38 because they were not impartial, and 15 for miscellaneous reasons.

Zeisel and Seidman Diamond discuss the grounds for attorneys' challenges to the jurors. The defense used all 20 of its peremptory challenges; the government used 6 of the 8 allowed it by the court. What effects did these challenges have? Jurors with college experience were reduced in number from 45% to 8%, largely as a result of defense challenges. White-collar workers with some high school education increased in proportion from 36% to 76%. The government did not challenge liberals; the defense did not challenge conservatives. But the proportions of conservatives and of Republicans increased after challenges had been made. The defense reduced the number of readers of The New York Times and New York Post from 32% to 8%. Of the six excused by the government, four were relatively uninformed about Watergate, and two felt themselves to be incapable of serving.

Of some importance to the outcome was the impact of a single prestigious juror, originally an alternate, upon the remaining 11. Research by Kalven and Zeisel had shown that a jury's first ballot is a very good predictor of the final verdict. Ten weeks after the start of the trial the jury began deliberations and balloted informally to see where they stood. They stood 8 to 4 for conviction. Data drawn from 225 cases had shown that where there are from 7 to 11 votes to convict on the first ballot, the verdict is guilty in 86% of the cases. Yet Mitchell and Stans were acquitted. What happened?

In the middle of the trial a juror became ill. She was replaced by the alternate, a prominent man whose education and position caused him to be regarded with caution by the defense. For various reasons, enumerated by Zeisel and Seidman Diamond, he became suspect to the government before very long and eagerly sought by the defense. In time, he joined the other jurors. He quickly established himself as the jury's "social director" during the long sequestered weeks of the trial. His position enabled him to secure films for private screenings. He made it possible for the jury to view a parade from a branch office of his company. In short, his activities during the trial made the entire jury more comfortable. At length, the jury began to deliberate.

A female bank teller was elected foreman. Most of the other jurors were skilled wage earners. The prominent alternate voted initially to acquit and, according to reports cited by Zeisel and Seidman Diamond, was very influential in the deliberations, so influential that the eight convicting jurors changed their minds. The issue of relative influence during deliberations will be examined in due course. This case is mentioned here in order to emphasize that jury selection can make a difference. In other countries (e.g., England) no *voir dire* is conducted. The authors of the paper under discussion suggest that the heterogeneous nature of American society makes the *voir dire* desirable.

Be that as it may, what is the verdict concerning participation by social scientists in the process? Several writers have had their say on this question.

Journalist Edward Tivnan reviewed a number of cases in which methods of the sort described above were employed. Lawyers whom he interviewed differed in their assessment of these procedures. Some reported that they had been employing essentially the same techniques throughout their careers and that there is nothing new in this approach. Others felt that "psychoanalyzing jurors" was a waste of time and energy, that high-risk jurors can be screened by means of a few good questions. A third group appears still to function by folklore or old attorneys' tales, e.g., fat jurors are jolly and will resist convicting, thin-lipped jurors convict easily, and accountants will want all the facts to fit perfectly. Several well-known lawyers are quoted expressing views ranging from "Psychological jury selection is bunk," to the view that you only need two or three strong personalities who, like the man in the Mitchell–Stans jury, will be able to persuade the other jurors.

Tivnan discusses the Joan Little case. She was a young black woman accused of stabbing her white male jailer to death while allegedly fending off his sexual advances. The trial was scheduled to be held in Beaufort County, North Carolina, a community that survey data showed to be high in racial prejudice and in assumptions of the defendant's guilt. Based on the survey data, collected with the help of Schulman and Christie, the judge ordered a change of venue. The defense team then undertook a second survey, of Wake County. The results are illuminating. Following essentially the same procedure as in the Harrisburg case, the researchers uncovered distinctly different relationships among certain variables. In Harrisburg, Episcopalians and Presbyterians leaned less toward the defendants than Lutherans and Catholics did. In the community from which the Joan Little jury was drawn, college-educated people younger than 45, living in Raleigh, who read *Harper's* or the *Atlantic*, were likely to be good for the defense; but if they read *Sports Illustrated* or *The Ladies' Home Journal*, they would be bad. Among rural people, those who were less educated but who read the right periodicals were better for the defense than more educated urban readers of the wrong ones. The search for the most potent predictors of jury leanings yields such complex relationships as to suggest that each case is likely to be unique unto itself and that the "science of jury selection," if one is to emerge, will be a science of methodology rather than of relationships predictable across cases.

In the Little case, Christie sought to identify jurors whose attitudes were consistent with the characteristics of the "Authoritarian Personality."[2] Such people were shown, in the 1950s, to have a predisposition toward prejudice, toward intolerance for ambiguous information or circumstances, and relatively rigid views of right and wrong. Throughout the 1950s and later, literally hundreds of studies were conducted by social psychologists in which this syndrome was shown to be related to many other variables, including amount of education, feelings about one's parents, attitudes toward foreigners, and political and economic conservatism. Christie looked for such people by having the lawyer ask items from the scale developed to measure these traits. Another of the defense team focused on body language. Potential jurors whose demographic characteristics, attitudes, and body language seemed to be consistent and favorable to the defense were especially sought as jurors. After three weeks of testimony, the jury acquitted the defendant in less than an hour and a half.

Some of those with whom Tivnan spoke justified such procedures on the theory that jurors' decisions are not based on the evidence alone, anyway. Some jurors are better able to distinguish between strong and weak evidence. Some jurors are better able to keep their feelings and attitudes under wraps as they deliberate. Proponents view the major purpose of this process as screening out potential jurors whose competence in these areas is weak. On the other hand, some lawyers object that the whole procedure takes too long, that it is little better than gambling, and that they can select juries as well without the help of survey researchers and translators of body language.

Schulman takes the position that jurors are predisposed to assume that where there is an indictment there is guilt, and that these techniques simply correct an imbalance in favor of the people. Others fear that the procedure can produce biased as readily as unbiased juries. It would be naive to believe that the goal of either side in a criminal side is to select an unbiased jury. Unbiased juries, in our adversary system, result from the conflicting efforts of the opposing parties to select jurors favorable to their own sides. It would also be naive to believe that the prosecution has never investigated potential jurors. Indeed, the Harrisburg site appears to have been selected by the government in order to maximize the chances of conviction in that case. It certainly was not the scene of the alleged offense. The FBI, State Police, and sheriffs' deputies have been used to look into the backgrounds of jurors in various cases, and, as a rule, they have at their disposal far greater resources for such purposes than the defense has.

Shapley, another writer, quotes a lawyer with the American Civil Liberties Union as noting that police and local law firms in many communities have files on the past performances of jurors; and, given the disproportionate power of the government to gather these data, this man urges legislation to mandate sharing of pertinent information by each side. On the other hand, in the same article, Shapley cites the views of another lawyer who feels that these techniques are not essential if the attorneys know the community. As a practical matter, an attorney trying a case in a strange jurisdiction will usually retain local counsel for assistance on the case. Lacking such assistance, an outsider might find the Schulman–Christie approach very helpful.

Psychologist M. J. Saks argues that social scientists could not stack the deck in a jury trial even if they wanted to. The evidence, he says, is of far greater significance to the outcome of a trial than are the characteristics of the jury. He points out that, in its run of successes, the Christie–Schulman team has not had its results subjected to comparison with a control group of juries selected in more traditional ways, and that the conspiracy trials (he omits the Little case) involved charges difficult to prove under any conditions. In fact, the Chicago 7 and the Panther 21 won acquittal without benefit of applied social science.

Saks conducted a study of his own in Columbus, Ohio. A total of 480 jurors viewed a videotaped trial and then deliberated in small groups. Twenty-seven predictor variables were measured and correlated with the verdict and the juror's certainty about it. Predictors included: attitudes toward criminals, values, education, socioeconomic status, even whether they were right- or left-handed. The single best predictor of their vote was their attribution of crime either to "bad people" or to "bad social conditions." Those who believed in the latter were more likely to convict! But this and the other most potent predictors (attitudes toward obedience, leadership, and politics) were, in fact, of little real significance. Together they accounted for only 13% of the variance in the verdicts.

Saks notes, too, a study by Mitchell and Byrne, who found that, among college students, high authoritarians were less certain of the guilt and more lenient in recommending punishment of an exam-stealing student whose attitudes were similar to theirs. Egalitarians were equally firm or compassionate regardless of the attitudes of the accused. Mitchell and Byrne imply that egalitarian (nonauthoritarian) jurors should be sought for juries because they can treat evidence more objectively. That is, they appear better able to ignore legally irrelevant information. This recommendation ignores the adversary nature of a criminal trial, in which each side seeks an advantage, not an unbiased jury.

Saks also cites a study by Buckhout, who examined demographic characteristics, values, and attitudes of jurors and found that the only variable which discriminated between acquitters and convicters was their attitude toward the prosecutor. The more they liked him, the more likely they were to convict.

Former jurors were interviewed by Saks, who described several hypothetical cases to them and then assessed their attitudes toward the defendant and their certainty as to his guilt or innocence. He systematically varied the degree to which the evidence was incriminating and found that variable to be a far more potent predictor of the verdict than jurors' attitudes toward the defendant. This is a very reassuring finding to believers in the jury system. Saks' study, of course, is subject to the same criticisms as other simulation studies; behavior under simulated conditions may not be the same as under real conditions.

The famous study of *The American Jury* by Kalven and Zeisel showed that, of thousands of jury trials, judge and jury concurred on the verdict more than three-fourths of the time, 64% to convict, 14% to acquit. It is Saks' view that this indicates that both judge and jury were responding to the evidence. He may be right. It is possible, though, that both were responding to a D.A.'s charisma or to the defendant's sullen or confident air, or that the jury had picked up cues from the judge.

Berman and Sales offer "A critical evaluation of the systematic approach to jury selection," pointing out the controversial nature of the issue. Some lawyers share Saks' view that the quality of the evidence is the key; some look to the persuasiveness of the arguments, and some feel that the system of juror challenges sufficiently safeguards both the people and the accused.

However valuable they may be, these procedures are costly in time and in money. Berman and Sales list questionnaire construction, interviewer training, sampling, key punching, data analysis, and interpretation of findings among the steps involved in "systematic jury selection." Nearly all these steps require the time and skills of professionals.

In addition to these practical problems, there are some conceptual difficulties. Systematic jury selection involves a sampling procedure. Studies are made of people similar to potential jurors, and, from the data, predictions are made as to the behavior of actual jurors. One immediate problem is the sample to be interviewed. It is selected from lists of registered voters, but such lists are not the same as jury panels. Not only do challenges and other circumstances exclude many voters from jury service, but also occupational status, age, or other characteristics make certain registered voters unlikely to serve as jurors. Lawyers, police officers, the elderly, and mothers of small children may be excused systematically if not automatically.

Several books and countless papers have been concerned with the relationship between attitudes and behavior. Going to great expense to select jurors with "good" attitudes may not be productive if these attitudes come into conflict with group pressure or with compelling evidence.

Investigation of members of the jury panel is another pitfall of the method of systematic jury selection. Of necessity, this procedure is limited to hearsay information. If members of the panel are drawn from a large geographic area, it may be hard to touch all bases. If the area is small, it is not unlikely that potential jurors will learn of inquiries made about them and react negatively to the news. Moreover, information gathered about one would-be juror may be of a different nature from, and so not comparable with, information gathered about another. In such a case it would be difficult to know how to evaluate either.

Ratings of responses during the *voir dire*, another critical part of systematic jury selection, have pitfalls, too. The judge may limit the questioning so much that there is little opportunity to form impressions. Where the judge asks the questions, even assuming he agrees to ask what the attorneys request of him, he may do so in a tone or with phrasing that cues the juror to make the socially desirable or "expected" response. In such a case the vigilant social scientist will learn little of value. If all veniremen are present for the *voir dire*, they will soon learn to anticipate the questions and to distinguish acceptable from unacceptable answers. Finally, since one generally cannot administer standardized tests to a panel of jurors, one is reduced to drawing inferences from partial, nonvalidated assessment procedures, a situation that does not gladden the heart of the scientifically trained observer.

Berman and Sales point out, too, that the way in which the accumulated data are evaluated and combined depends in no small way upon the evaluating team. Decisions must be made, but the amount of influence team members have, the accuracy of their insights, and the forcefulness of their presentations all may influence the recommendations ultimately given the attorney. To the extent that the team has a leader whose views are known and also has a high degree of cohesiveness, it may be especially vulnerable to what has been called "groupthink."[3] This is a process of decision-making in which assumptions are unchallenged, disagreement is discouraged, and decisions are, in all likelihood, other than optimal. It is ironic that so much effort goes into systematic information gathering while the employment of the information is so haphazard. The account of the Harrisburg proceedings discussed above is laudably candid about difficulties of this type.

In evaluating the efficacy of systematic jury selection, and in assessing whether it is worth the considerable expense involved, it is necessary to scrutinize those cases reported above in which it appears to have been used successfully. Unfortunately, those cases appear to be very atypical. They all involved issues subject to a great deal of newspaper publicity and were defended by unusually prominent and skillful attorneys. The situation is analogous to classical psychoanalysis in that even if it were proved to be 100% effective, the method would be of no value to the average defendant, who could not afford the procedures used and whose plight would fail to attract the attention necessary to inspire voluntary assistance.

Several of the ethical and legal issues commented upon by Berman and Sales have already been considered. A few still remain to be looked at.

If systematic jury selection by means of psychological assessment is effective yet too expensive for the defense, it could become exclusively a prosecution tool, which could prevent the defendant from having an unbiased jury. This, however, is but one more example of the advantage that the people have in a criminal prosecution by virtue of their vastly superior financial resources.

Sociologist Amitai Etzioni and Angela Davis's lawyer, Howard A. Moore, Jr., view the process, respectively, as "creating an imbalance" and "redressing the balance." Etzioni asserts that the jury's impartiality is at stake. Since the average defendant will not receive the free assistance, the wealthier defendant, who can purchase it, will have a relatively greater advantage. To minimize any advantage of the prosecution Etzioni argues for *fewer* rather than more challenges, fewer withdrawals from jury duty, a ban on out-of-court investigations of jurors, and restriction of questioning and removal of prospective jurors to the judge.

Moore, on the other hand, argues that juries as presently selected are predisposed to favor the prosecution; that, historically, America's juries have not been composed of cross sections of the community; in short, that such proposals as Etzioni's would fix the status quo and leave unchanged the injustices, which, in Moore's view, make assistance of social scientists necessary and just.

Finally, how should social scientists regard these potentially lucrative, attention-getting procedures of unproven value?

Time and data will be required to answer some of these questions. Thoughtful, conscientious exploration of our values as citizens and as social scientists will also be required.

A THEORY OF THE *VOIR DIRE*

One need not agree with Clarence Darrow's view that trials are contests between the haves and the have-nots in order to recognize that they are contests. The last contribution to be discussed views jury selection itself as a contest.

Fried, Kaplan, and Klein conceive of the *voir dire* process not from the point of view of one side or the other, but as part of the more general adversary proceeding that the trial is. They point out that the strategy of an attorney in deciding whom to challenge or accept depends on which side he represents and the quality of the case he is to present. Lawyers' actions and decisions reflect at least some of the following goals:

1. To learn what they need to know about each venireman in order to ascertain his suitability.
2. To begin to build rapport between attorney and jury.
3. To influence the manner in which jurors assess and perceive the arguments to be presented.
4. To sensitize the jurors to their own preconceptions and prejudices that might affect deliberations.
5. To stress the legal obligations and requirements of a juror.

The purposes of the prosecution and defense may not be compatible. At the very least, the prosecutor hopes to choose jurors who will view the people's evidence as weighty and will be inclined to convict. The defense will stress such issues as reasonable doubt in hopes of making jurors more ready to acquit. In short, these writers' basic thesis holds that: (1) opposing sides will follow different strategies in order to select people open to their efforts to influence; (2) attempts will be made to influence the ways in which jurors view and evaluate evidence and arguments, and assess possible verdicts. What means do the opposing attorneys employ?

Fried et al. assume that the prosecution prefers authoritarian, and the defense egalitarian, jurors. To the extent that the prosecutor is viewed as a representative of the government, his arguments should be seen as more "legitimate" by authoritarians. Further, authoritarians are likely to be less tolerant of people and behaviors that differ from the norm. To the extent that the defendant is "different" from most people, authoritarian personalities should be predisposed to perceive him as guilty.

This assumption is not supported by Mitchell and Byrne's data, and also runs counter to Saks' arguments, which ought to cause us to be cautious about its validity. The contrary evidence, however, is itself not very compelling. Additional factors, such as the defendant's characteristics, need to be considered. Prominent persons whose bearing or position suggest power or authority might win the support of authoritarian jurors; the prosecution might then be better off with egalitarian jurors, who would be less likely to distinguish between defendants who are like or unlike themselves.

A second assumption in the Fried et al. analysis is that the prosecution will favor jurors who are prone to conform with the views of others, and that the defense will seek individualists who are capable of withstanding pressures toward conformity. Two reasons are offered for this assumption. First, the consequence of dissent, a hung jury, is more costly to the prosecution than to the defense. The case might not be tried again; if it is, the charges will probably be reduced. Second, conforming personalities are likely, too, to be higher in authoritarianism than nonconforming people are. Conforming jurors are more likely to go along with someone who appears knowledgeable (an expert witness) or is in a position of authority (the jury foreman), regardless of the merits of the other's position. Similarly, conformity may take the form of openness to another's persuasive arguments, whether or not the other is of high status. Since the prosecution has the advantages of speaking first and last, suggestible jurors might be more influenced by these efforts than less suggestible jurors. The latter will be more likely to weigh the evidence objectively and, if there is room for reasonable doubt, will be better able to recognize that fact.

These theorists suggest that a homogeneous group of jurors will more quickly feel themselves to be part of a "group" and so will be better able to achieve agreement than will a more heterogeneous aggregate. For this reason, too, the defense might be well advised to seek a heterogeneous jury, especially if its arguments are weak. By the same token, the defense should avoid selecting someone whose status or expertise will make it possible for him or her to become the focus of the jury's attention during deliberations. Such a person will increase the likelihood of a jury's achieving consensus, and, unless the defense's case is strong, will work against the interests of the defense.

Another concept that psychologists have developed in recent decades is that of cognitive set. It refers to the tendencies people have either to be attentive to the variety of events and stimuli in their lives, responding to each in turn, integrating each into their funds of knowledge or views of the world, or, on the other hand, to be relatively closed to novel stimuli, changing perceptions of them so that they become consistent with what has gone before. The first approach makes one aware of the complexity of most things in this world; the latter shuts out the unusual, making new perceptions fit into old frames of reference, rather than modifying the frame of reference itself when the new information "doesn't fit." Consistent with their previous assumptions, Fried et al. assume that the prosecution will prefer jurors whose congnitive style or set is closed; the defense will prefer jurors who are capable of discerning bits of evidence that are inconsistent with an argument, who do not lose sight of the details of a case.

Of interest is the application made by Fried et al. of statistical decision theory to jury deliberations and the *voir dire*. Suffice it to say that the model constructed from this theory leads to some predictions: the greater one's tendency to side with authority and the more compelling the evidence, the more important it will seem to convict a guilty defendant and the more likely a vote to convict will be. The less one's tendency to side with authority and the less compelling the evidence, the more important it will seem to acquit the accused and the less likely a vote to convict will be. In other words, authoritarianism, conformist tendencies, and cognitive set combine (with other variables) to influence the jurors' readiness to perceive guilt. The probability of guilt is, in turn, weighed in the balance with the consequences of correct and incorrect verdicts. As the probability of guilt increases and the likelihood of reasonable doubt decreases, the probability of conviction rises. A juror's tendency to see a given level of doubt as "reasonable" is, in turn, related to the variables authoritarianism, conformity, and cognitive set. Since the defense and the prosecution seek to achieve different ends concerning reasonable doubt, adequacy of evidence, and the like, their strategies during the *voir dire* may be expected to vary accordingly.

REFERENCES

1. Defending Mitchell by the numbers. Editorial in *Newsday* April 2, 1974, 48:1; M. Chambers. A jury watcher advises Mitchell's defense on the reactions of panel members. *The New York Times* April 1, 1974, 20:1–6.
2. Adorno, T. W., Frenkel-Brunswik, E., Levinson, D., and Sanford, N. *The Authoritarian Personality*. New York: Harper, 1950.
3. Janis, I. L. *Victims of Groupthink*. Boston: Houghton Mifflin, 1972.

12
Psychological Factors in Trials

THE PSYCHOLOGY OF PERSUASION

The prosecution and the defense, respectively, open the trial with preliminary statements in a manner already described. Both attorneys will seek to establish rapport with the jurors and to prime them to attend to the evidence in a manner favorable to their sides. What are the effects of these opening statements?

A recent dissertation by Shaw addressed this question. Using videotaped versions of filmed trials, he found that his jurors made their first "decisions" about the case during the opening statements and that these initial decisions were not readily changed during group discussion (deliberations). He found, too, that the identical trial can lead to different verdicts, depending upon the way in which a given offense is viewed in different communities. That his experimental juries were composed of people of varied backgrounds who rendered consistent verdicts suggested to him that juries drawn by purely random means (rather than by the elaborate procedures described in Chapter 11) would render fair verdicts by a process of rational decision making.

Because of the impact of the opening statements and his view of the trial process as a means of evaluating propositions about facts, Shaw suggests that opening statements be replaced by a statement from the bench concerning the propositions which the people must prove in subsequently presenting evidence.

Needless to say, such a change is unlikely to win rapid approval. If so much can be accomplished in the opening statements, attorneys are unlikely to relinquish this tool willingly. Also, the U.S. Supreme Court has held that the parties have a constitutional right to make opening and closing arguments, and the elimination of these arguments can serve no purpose other than the interests of expediency. Accordingly, a closer look at opening statements is warranted. Some issues that are especially pertinent have been examined by psychologists studying the criminal justice system; others have not.

One-sided v. Two-sided Arguments. The first such issue has to do with the nature of one's opening statement. A district attorney about to present a good but not airtight case against a defendant has several choices to make. He can present himself as the avenging arm of society, heaping scorn and venom upon the accused, or he can take a reasonable stance and matter-of-factly present the major elements of his case while enlisting the cooperation of the jury in the determination of truth. In other words, he can appeal to the emotions or to reason. At the same time, he can present an overview only of his own case, or he can try to anticipate what the defense attorney will say in order to undercut the impact of those arguments. That is, he can make a one-sided or a two-sided argument.

Another choice, if he opts for a two-sided argument, is whether to present his own major points first followed by the other side's, or to present the expected defense position first and then knock it down point by point.

One area in which he has no choice is the order in which opening statements are made. The people make theirs first, followed by the defense. Psychologists have examined the effects of this and the prescribed order for summations on verdicts.

Lawson explored some of these issues in the context of the courtroom. While lack of prior familiarity with the issues makes juries' responses to opening arguments less predictable than when experimental subjects deal with commonplace matters, Lawson suggests that, in regard to closing arguments, a two-sided argument will be more effective than a one-sided one. He reviews two series of studies conducted during and after World War II in which arguments were presented on matters of controversy as well as on noncontroversial issues. In general, the data indicated that anticipating an opponent's arguments while making one's own makes the audience better able to resist the opposition's arguments when they are presented later. Very much as an inoculation enables the recipient to develop antibodies that help him or her to fight off a disease, prior exposure to an opposing advocate's views may help the hearer (juror) to marshal his or her own arguments (or doubts) and so be less persuasible.[1]

A closing argument differs from an opening statement in that the latter constitutes the juror's orientation to a case of which he is totally ignorant. A closing argument is made after a juror has had an opportunity to hear all of the evidence and to see all of the exhibits in a case. Despite this difference, Lawson found that a two-sided argument was more effective in the closing argument.

Primacy v. Recency Effects. Given this recommendation, the question arises as to *how* the two-sided argument should be organized. Miller and Campbell arranged a simulated jury trial, (not a criminal case). All of the plaintiff's arguments were presented together (testimony by the plaintiff's witness, cross-examination of the defendant, and the plaintiff's opening and closing arguments). Similarly, all defense arguments were grouped together. The independent variables were the interval between the reading of the second set and the rendering of a verdict and the interval between the reading of the two sets of arguments. Both primacy and recency effects were observed. A primacy effect (i.e., the position presented first was more persuasive) occurred when the interval between the arguments was brief, and when the verdict was not decided upon until well after the second set of arguments. A recency effect (in which the later, more recent, arguments carried the day) was observed when there was a lengthy interval between the two arguments, and when the verdict followed quickly after the second.

Does the law which mandates that the prosecution present its case first *and* last give the people an advantage? From the foregoing it would appear so, since a primacy effect is predicted for opening statements, and a recency effect is predicted for closing ones.

Walker, Thibaut, and Andreoli took a closer look at the issue. They began by distinguishing between "gross order" and "internal order." Gross order refers to the order of arguments in a trial; internal order refers to the sequence within each side's presentation. The gross order of arguments is fixed by law and was designed to provide the prosecution with an advantage to compensate it for having the burden of proof. Internal order is determined by the lawyer as a matter of trial strategy. For instance, in the opening statement, does the district attorney present the major points of the people's case first followed by what he expects will be the major points of the defense? Or are the defense arguments anticipated one at a time, each of them followed by an indication of what the people intend to say in refutation? According to Walker et al., most attorneys like to build their cases in a dramatic sequence, proceeding from the weaker to the stronger points in their favor. This internal order, they say, is justified as likely to have the most lasting impact on the jurors.

Until the paper of Walker et al., research had been concerned either with gross or with internal order. Since trials are adversary proceedings in which one side presents its case and the other side responds, however, both orders may be expected to have significant effects. Moreover, other factors may interact with the order of arguments in determining their persuasiveness.

Using a fictitious case of assault, the facts of which were either favorable or unfavorable for the defense and strong or weak in their persuasiveness, both gross and internal orders were varied. Either exculpatory or inculpatory facts were presented first, and within this gross order the individual facts were arranged in either climactic (weak to strong) or anticlimactic (strong to weak) order.

Undergraduate subjects were asked to indicate their assessment of the lawfulness or illegality of the accused's actions at intervals during and after the presentation of facts by opposing "attorneys."

Concerning gross order, the evidence is that the side that spoke second was more persuasive. That is, holding arguments constant and varying only the gross order of presentation, the second speaker was "the winner."

Results of varying internal order were more complex.

Within the first (opening) presentation, the prosecutor who argued in a climactic order had the more favorable results. The climactic order did not benefit the defense when it spoke first.

Within the second presentation, a climactic order was more effective than an anticlimactic order for both sides.

In discussing their findings, Walker et al. make several interesting observations. It appears that facts presented first have less effect in this quasi-legal situation than in other situations in which primacy and recency have been examined. Why? They suggest two reasons:

1. Initial impressions as usually studied concern relatively stable characteristics (attitudes, abilities, traits) rather than judgments of specific events as in their study. Because of their stability, such characteristics may be expected to describe an individual in whatever setting or circumstances he is found. Hence, the wise person will attempt to keep them in mind as more is learned about the one whose behavior is at issue. "Legal facts," in contrast, may have nothing to do with what *kind* of person the defendant is; rather they are concerned with whether or not he committed a particular act at a particular time and place. Thus, the earlier information may not provide a pertinent frame of reference within which to interpret later facts. They may, in fact, be directly contradictory. This leads to these authors' second point.

2. When fact-finders (the "jurors," in this instance) are aware from the start that there are two sides to the matter and that whatever information they hear first is not the whole story, the first facts are likely to be regarded as tentative, not as a scale on which subsequent information is weighed, or as a fabric into which new threads will automatically be woven. Jurors, in fact, may reserve judgment in anticipation of contradictory arguments. In fact, an earlier study[2] suggests that after hearing one side of a case, jurors are especially eager to hear the other, perhaps to learn how seemingly compelling facts will be refuted, perhaps to confirm doubts that were engendered by the first set of facts. This heightened interest may itself account for the gross order differences found by Walker et al.

In any case, they were willing to suggest "an optimal sequence for an adversary system." In the presentation of evidence the prosecutor should go first and should follow a climactic order in the presentation of his statement. Next, the defense should follow suit. This would give the defense the gross order advantage while preserving for the prosecution the internal order advantage.

If order effects were neutralized in this fashion, the merits of the statements would be more likely to be recognized by the jurors.

The foregoing studies might suggest that by performing such manipulations as were described, the extraneous effects of such factors as gross or internal orders and primacy and recency effects could be canceled out. It might appear that this would lead to more just verdicts based solely on the evidence. What may be less obvious is the fact that doing this would require replacing our present adversary system of criminal justice with an inquisitorial system in which the facts are elicited by questioning by a neutral party. A study of such a procedure has been reported by Thibaut, Walker, and Lind, who found in their data support for the adversary procedure as a means of combatting bias.

WITNESSES

Testimony to personal identity is proverbially fallacious . . . . A man has witnessed a rapid crime . . . and carries away his mental image. Later he is confronted by a prisoner whom he forthwith perceives in the light of that image, and recognizes or "identifies" as a participant, although he may never have been near the spot.[3]

If that was proverbial 90 years ago, statements of this sort are no less commonplace today. From the work of James's colleague Hugo Münsterberg through much more recent work to be reviewed in this section, behavioral scientists have devoted attention to perceiving, recalling, and testifying by witnesses in station house lineups, courtrooms, and psychological laboratories.

Following a burglary of his home, Münsterberg reports having testified under oath:

that the burglars had entered through a cellar window, and then I described what rooms they had visited. To prove in answer to a direct question, that they had been there at night, I told that I had found drops of candle wax on the second floor. To show that they intended to return, I reported that they had left a large mantel clock, packed in wrapping paper, on the dining room table. Finally, as to the amount of clothes which they had taken, I asserted that the burglars did not get much more than a specified list which I had given the police.[4]

Subsequent investigation and information proved all of these sworn statements to be wrong! Even this careful observer, who was reporting on a crime in which he had not been menaced, and in which he could peruse the crime scene at his leisure, did not know what he was talking about.

How is this possible? If we cannot trust our own senses, of what value is an oath "to tell the truth, the whole truth, nothing but the truth"? The problem is not the willful liar; the problem is the inadvertent one.

A Professor von Liszt is credited by Münsterberg[5] with originating a classroom demonstration that continues to be employed in one form or another: One person "shoots" another after a short, but violent argument. The perpetrator flees, and the instructor orders the class to write down a description of what took place, of what they saw and what they heard. These descriptions of the parties involved, their appearance, clothing, words, and actions always vary widely. Rarely do two or more witnesses report the same events. (One of the authors' professors who described this demonstration to his class was warned by a student not to do it. Showing his police shield, the student said, "I'd shoot first." *Caveat magister!*)

What are some of the causes of this unreliability of eyewitnesses?

James Marshall, an attorney and an astute participant-observer of the social sciences, points to the conflict between the rules of evidence and research findings on factors that affect the accuracy of witnesses' statements. The three points at which these factors may enter the picture are the perception of the incident, the recollection of what took place, and the articulation of the remembrance in testimony.

Perception.   Perception may be regarded as a process by which sensations are classified, interpreted, and given meaning by the perceiver. Most often one interprets events automatically, without pausing to think about the process by which a stimulus person is classified as drunk or sick, threatening or harmless, young or old. The classification is made on the basis of one's expectations, one's previous experience with similar stimulus objects, one's attitudes or values, and so forth. As Marshall points out, the witness to a crime is limited in his perception by the acuteness of his senses as well as by characteristics of the event itself. Some events are time consuming; others, including most crimes, are not. Some are everyday happenings; others, including most crimes, are unusual. Especially handicapped is the witness who is required to note distances or to estimate the duration of an event. Time that is filled with pleasant events seems to pass quickly.[6] Witnessing a crime is likely to be unpleasant, and one's estimate of the duration is likely to be excessive.

A number of studies have indicated that we attend to, learn, and remember events which are congruent with our attitudes and expectations and ignore those which are not. Psychologists call this phenomenon selective perception. In short, perceiving is a function of our past experience, our attitudes, and our expectations.

One of the authors walked in on a burglar rifling his desk drawer. The burglar simply walked out the door and up the stairs to the street before the author fully realized what had happened. The only description he could give to the university's security officer was of an ordinary-looking young Caucasian, neatly dressed. Not very helpful and perhaps not very accurate. The other author once came upon a violent fight between a rather large man and an equally large woman. Possibly fearful for his own safety, he perceived it as a battle between husband and wife and not his concern. Had he perceived it as a mugging or an assault upon a stranger, he would have felt obligated to intervene. Thus, unconscious motives may enter into the process of perception. When we are feeling anxious, we are more likely to be frightened of a harmless stranger than when we are calm; when we feel confident, we are more likely to be trusting.

Recollection and Articulation.   Perception is only one of the sources of unintentional "perjury." Recollection is another. Just as we perceive certain events and not others, we recall selectively, too.

An especially disquieting contaminant of a trial is the fact that testimony is usually given long after the events described. This leads to two sources of difficulty. On the one hand, a great deal is likely to be forgotten by an individual recalling events that occurred six months or more earlier. There is abundant psychological evidence that most forgetting takes place soon after events have transpired. Second, and related to what Marshall calls the articulation problem, is the fact that in describing events, we have a tendency to fill in gaps in the story, to dramatize the commonplace, in short to tell a good story rather than to give the facts alone. This situation is made worse by the fact that we tend to forget, with time, the distinction between what did happen and what we have said happened. Statements tend to be converted into "facts," and, in testifying, the witness remembers his statements more clearly than the events they describe. Worse still, the witness may be unable to describe just how clearly he does recall what he is describing with aplomb on the stand.

With a number of social psychologist colleagues, Marshall has conducted studies to assess the impact of several variables on the completeness and accuracy of witness testimony.

With H. Mansson he showed a 42-second sound motion picture to beginning law students, police trainees, and a small group of settlement house members, most of whom were on welfare. The film showed an action that could be interpreted in several ways, ranging from altruistic behavior to criminality. There were 115 pieces of information discerned by the experimenters, and subjects' reports of what they saw and heard were compared with those items. In addition, the major character in the film was described to half of the subjects as having a criminal record and to nearly all subjects as having been indicted for the behavior shown in the film.

Generally, the better-educated subjects demonstrated more accurate recall in their accounts of what was shown. They also tended to make more inferences (statements not directly supported by the content of the film). All groups overestimated the duration of the film, the law students most of all. Actions were more accurately described than persons, backgrounds, or signs.

The use of direct questions (e.g., "The man in the picture was dressed in (check one) a light jacket, dark jacket, wore no jacket") elicited responses about information rarely mentioned under conditions of free recall. But the responses were incorrect as much as half the time.

The status of the interrogator was manipulated, too. Some students and some police trainees responded to questions in the presence of a professor or police captain, respectively. The law students with their professor present made many more inferences than their peers or the police. The police with their captain present had more accurate recall than their fellow trainees. Marshall concludes that the witnesses' memories were a function of the circumstances of the interrogation as well as of their personal characteristics.[7]

In a later study, Marquis, Oskamp, and Marshall found that more specific questions elicited more complete testimony, although not necessarily more accurate testimony.

The psychological state of the witness was more strongly manipulated by Johnson and Scott, who staged a rather frightening performance for the benefit of their witness-subjects.

Reporting to an old, deserted dormitory for a "learning experiment," the subject was informed that the experimenter was busy in an adjacent room and was left to wait alone. He soon heard the sounds of an argument coming from that room, something about continuing with a shock procedure. The sound of breaking bottles and crashing chairs ended the argument as a confederate of the experimenter ran into the waiting room. He held a letter opener covered with blood, had blood on his hands, and had a wire attached to his arm. Saying "He wouldn't let me go," the confederate left. This was the high-arousal condition.

In the low-arousal condition, equipment failure precluded the continuation of the experiment and was followed by the appearance of a confederate with grease-covered hands, holding a pen. His parting remark was, "Too bad the machine broke."

After one or the other of these experiences, the subject was greeted by the experimenter, who was clad in a police uniform (in the high-arousal condition) or in a white lab coat (low arousal). The subject-witness was promptly informed of the true purpose of the experiment and, after completing a measure of his state of arousal, was asked to recall the details of what took place and to identify the confederate from an album of photographs. Half of the witnesses were questioned immediately after completing the arousal measure; half were questioned one week later.

What happened? Generally, more information was recalled accurately under high than under low arousal. Descriptions and identifications of the confederate, however, were more accurate under low arousal. Generally, immediate recall was more accurate than delayed recall. The exception to this was that female subjects in the high-arousal condition recalled more after one week than their male counterparts had who were questioned immediately. Finally, male witnesses were more accurate than females under high arousal, and females were more accurate than males under low arousal. One complicating factor was that females were more upset than males in the high-arousal condition.

Johnson and Scott interpret the outcome as due to the joint effects of females' lower stimulus threshold and their stronger feelings of vulnerability, on the one hand, and males' relatively inefficient information processing under low arousal, on the other.[8]

All of these findings notwithstanding, the witnesses did not do very well. Across conditions witnesses were as likely to identify the wrong person as not and to include in their testimony less than half of the descriptive information that they might have. The experimenters offer some recommendations on the basis of their findings:

1. Females' testimony in highly arousing circumstances and males' in less arousing circumstances should be treated with caution. Under stress females are more likely to make errors of commission than males are, and their estimates of time duration and distance from the suspect are especially questionable.

2. Interrogations generally should be prompt with the possible exception of the case of female witnesses to a stressful episode. The risk in this case is of more errors of commission (i.e., incorrect description of an item, event, person, or situation).

While these data are based only upon the behavior of 48 beginning psychology students, it should be noted that they essentially replicate an earlier study. Whether it is wise to generalize beyond Oklahoma college students in contemplating these data is a matter for further research.

The Witness's Task.   In a series of papers, Buckhout cites and employs experimental procedures, actual criminal procedures, and psychological theory in discussing the testimony of eyewitnesses.

The law appears to be based on the assumption that once a human being has "witnessed" an event, no matter how rapid or complex, it is engraved in some fashion upon his brain, to be recalled at will and with great accuracy. That, at least, is what the attorney whose side the witness is testifying for would like the jury to think. (Paradoxically, the attorney would like the jury also to think that the opposing witness is confused, mistaken, lying, or as unreliable as his own witness is trustworthy.)

This assumption, that all that was observed was permanently recorded in the mind of the observer, is consistent with an earlier view of the process of perception. It does not hold up today. As Marshall pointed out, we are limited in our ability to sense, to classify sensations, to remember what has been perceived, and to describe what we remember. At each step of the way, we make choices, decisions, selections, and amplifications.

The witness (perceiver) does more than simply record; he constructs events, makes sense of isolated bits of information, puts conflicting facts together in a coherent and meaningful, if sometimes inaccurate, way. Michotte has shown that the subjective impressions which observers have of the antics of geometric figures are determined by such factors as their speed of movement, the directions in which they move after making contact, and so on. We seem to attribute to inanimate objects (rectangles of different colors) motives and intentions that one might have thought we would reserve to living beings, if not solely to humans. Imagine, then, how much more readily we attribute motives and intentions to people purely on the basis of their actions, physical appearance, and the like!

Among the types of factors that Buckhout lists as restricting the accuracy of testimony are the following:

1. Sources of unreliability that are implicit in the original situation.
2. Physical and psychological characteristics of the witness himself.
3. Sources of unreliability inherent in the circumstances of the attempts at information retrieval.

We will consider each of these factors in turn.

The Original Situation.   In a television production, *"The Pallisers,"* one character testified that he saw another, wearing an unusual gray cloak, flee the scene of a murder. The event took place at night; the face of the becloaked accused was, admittedly, obscured. But a man owning such a cloak was known to have quarreled with the victim moments before the murder, and he was arrested. This fictitious near-miscarriage of justice provides an illustration of several points listed by Buckhout. First, the perception of the fleeing figure had no special meaning for the witness until later, when the body was found. The witness would have to have recalled seeing the suspect at a time when the event was of no consequence. Second, the elapsed time during which the accused was allegedly seen was very brief, as is usually the case in criminal acts. The less time one has to observe, the less information one can take in, and the fewer distinguishing characteristics one can note, let alone recall. Third, the conditions under which the behavior was witnessed were surely not optimal. Where there are other passers-by or a crowd, or the scene is poorly lit, or the focal act is a substantial distance from the witness, or the action occurs quickly, it seems indisputable that what is "seen" or reported is likely to be in error.

The Characteristics of the Witness.   Most crimes that involve the threat of violence take the witness by surprise, particularly when the witness is also the victim. In times of stress one focuses on what seems important—the hand holding the gun, the instructions to keep quiet. One is less likely to attend to the color of the assailant's trousers, or his height, weight, or complexion. When people are under stress, the sympathetic nervous system begins to work changes in their bodies. They breathe faster; their heartbeats accelerate; their blood pressure increases; and so on. They become, in theory at least, better able to fight or to flee the situation. At the same time, though, they become less alert to features of their surroundings that are not critical to their survival. Buckhout cites his own findings that memory for extraneous details is interfered with and that estimates of time are exaggerated even among highly trained individuals under stress.

Incapacitated people are often victims of crimes. Their age or physical infirmities make them especially vulnerable to society's predators. The same infirmities may make them poor witnesses. If they were sick or fatigued at the time of the crime, they are even less likely to be accurate or to be believed by a jury following a cross-examination. The ability of many aged people, particularly those in poor health, to remember recent events, has been shown to be less than that of younger, healthier people.[9]

Academic psychology illuminates another source of unreliability in the perceptions of a witness, that of *set* or *expectancy*. It has often been documented that we organize stimuli according to our previous experience with them or with similar stimuli, and according to what we *expect* to see, hear, taste, and so forth. A famous example of this phenomenon is the study by Hastorf and Cantril, who showed films of a particularly rough football game to students at the two colleges involved (Princeton and Dartmouth) and asked the students to estimate how clean or dirty the game was and "which team . . . started the rough play."

Nearly all the students at Princeton, whose star player had been injured early in the game, saw the game as rough and dirty. Eighty-six percent of them reported that Dartmouth had started the rough play. Half as many Dartmouth as Princeton students saw the game as rough and dirty, and only 36% felt that Dartmouth had started it. It was as though the students had viewed very different films.

Schlossberg and Freeman and Toch and Schulte, among numerous others, have made the point that police training and experience increase the probability that a given action will be perceived by police officers as violent or as criminal in nature.

In enlarging on the ways in which set or expectancy affects perception, Buckhout points out that prior experience may predispose a person to report that an event has occurred, although in reality it has not. A tragic event occurred in 1973 in which such a phenomenon may have been involved. A police officer, responding to a report of a robbery by two black males, spotted two people who appeared to him to be "suspicious." It was very early in the morning. The two were walking in an area near the robbery scene. The officer called to them to halt. Instead, they began to run. The officer shot (he claimed it was in response to a threatening movement) and killed one, an unarmed ten-year-old boy who had been walking with his grandfather. The survivor later said that the two ran because the policemen and his partner were dressed in civilian clothes and had not identified themselves as police officers. Having a substantial sum of money in his pocket, the man feared that he was about to be robbed and ran for safety. Because the two figures ran (and because one appeared to spin around with what seemed to be a gun in his hand), the officer shot at them.

Any ambiguous action may be interpreted by the perceiver in a manner consistent with his mood or motives. On a dark and lonely street one is likely to interpret shadows or noises as threatening, especially if one is uneasy about being there in the first place. If a person is carrying a large sum of money, his uneasiness may be noted by a robber and may mark him as a likely target. Thus this assumption of vulnerability becomes a self-fulfilling prophecy which precipitates the very outcome that he fears.[10]

Circumstances of Interrogation.   The third major source of unreliability of testimony pointed out by Buckhout inheres in the circumstances under which the witness is interrogated or otherwise asked to give information.

The longer the interval between the event and the testimony concerning it, the less accurate the witness is likely to be in recalling what was observed. Witnesses, as we have seen, have a way of filling in the gaps as they repeat their stories from the earliest preliminary investigations to the final testimony in court.

Buckhout has demonstrated that a lineup can be rigged to increase the likelihood that one or another person (or photograph) will be singled out. In theory, the actual suspect would be no more likely than anyone else to be identified by a witness if he were innocent, or if the witness did not see the event clearly enough. Those standing with him in the lineup should not all be taller or of a different race. They should all be looking straight ahead, or at least not all at the real suspect. The witness should not be told that "one of these guys is the mugger." The same principles should be followed when photos are shown for identification. But sometimes they are not. Buckhout describes the procedures used in the Angela Davis case. Of the nine photos used, three were candid pictures of the accused; two were police "mug shots" of other women, their names written on chalk boards on their chests; one was a picture of a 55-year-old woman; and so forth. Buckhout estimated that the probability of selecting a picture of the defendant, Davis, by a witness who had never seen her was about 75%.

Other ways in which circumstances can lead to biased testimony are through conformity pressures, the status of the interrogator, rewards for testimony, and perceptual set. Witnesses may wish to be approved, especially by an important attorney or police officer or by someone who is very attractive. They may be willing to be swayed, or to acknowledge agreement with such a person. Numerous cases have hinged on the credibility of a witness who received anything from a reduced charge to a bicycle in return for his testimony.

Buckhout concludes his provocative paper with a review of several laboratory studies on witness accuracy. Among other things he found that biasing instructions ("One of these men is a suspect") and biasing the array of photographs (by placing the critical one at an angle and depicting the suspect with a facial expression different from the others') increased the "correct" identification of the suspect from 40% to 61%. Even those who *never saw the staged attack* selected the distinctive photo! Buckhout does not report data in which the biased photo was of an "innocent" suspect. Under those circumstances one might expect witnesses to give the same response as non-witnesses, or at least to do so with a frequency sufficient to be distressing.

In any event, it is Buckhout's conclusion that eyewitness testimony is not superior to circumstantial evidence although it is commonly regarded as such in legal circles.[11]

Another psychologist, Loftus, reviewed several cases in which eyewitness testimony was proved false by the accused's alibi. One of these involved 17 witnesses!

Using college students as subjects, Loftus demonstrated that the testimony of an eyewitness, even of a *discredited* eyewitness, greatly increased the likelihood of a guilty verdict in the mock trials she studied. Specifically, she presented evidence of a shooting under three different conditions. In one, the witness claimed to have seen the accused shoot the victim, but the defense attorney argued that he was mistaken. In another, the same claim was made, but the defense argued that the witness had poor vision, was not wearing his eyeglasses, and could not possibly have seen the perpetrator's face from his vantage point. The third group was told that there was no eyewitness. The percentages of subjects who "voted" to convict the accused in each of these three conditions were, respectively, 72, 68, and 18%.

Loftus cites the Sacco-Vanzetti case as one in which witnesses were subjected to great pressure to identify the suspects although, in their original statements, most had denied their ability to identify anyone.

Using films of automobile accidents, Loftus demonstrated the importance of the wording of questions as a determinant of testimony. For some of the 100 students the critical questions included an indefinite article (e.g., "Did you see a broken headlight?"). For others, "the" replaced "a." When asked about events or things that did not appear in the film, 15% of the "the" group and 7% of the "a" group reported seeing them. Of those who said they did not know whether the event had occurred, many more were from the "a" group than from the "the" group. In short, the use of the definite article increased acquiescence and decreased indecisiveness among these witnesses to a filmed accident.

Loftus also showed that judgments of the velocity of cars moving toward a collision varied according to the verb used to describe their contact. The basic question was, "About how fast were the cars going when they hit each other?" Depending on the verb used to replace "hit," mean estimates of their velocity varied as follows: "smashed" (40.8 mph), "collided" (39.3 mph), "bumped" (38.1 mph), "hit" (34.0 mph), and "contacted" (31.8 mph).

In addition, a week after seeing the film and answering either the "hit" or the "smashed" form of the key question, subjects were asked whether there had been any broken glass shown in the film. Compared to the "hit" group, twice as many who had seen the "smashed" cars reported seeing the glass. There had been no broken glass at all.

Loftus's data also support the assertions made above that eyewitness testimony concerning speed, duration, distance, and time is not as accurate as one would like to think. In some proceedings, including one cited by Loftus, such estimates may be critical. In a recent case a young defendant had been convicted of killing his mother. His alibi hinged upon the times when he had left his friends, called an ambulance, and so on. Charges against him were dismissed following a successful appeal and prior to a new trial. The court decided, among other things, that he could not have done all that he was alleged to have done in the amount of time he had had.

Hypnosis and Memory.   In an effort to improve the memory of witnesses, some law enforcement agencies have resorted to hypnosis.

The evidence seems to suggest that, by age regression techniques, good hypnotic subjects can be helped to achieve clearer memory traces.

Only about one person in five is a very good hypnotic subject, and laboratory data, while showing some improved memory under hypnosis, do not support the popular notion that exact or total recall can be achieved.

While hypnosis may be a useful tool in criminal investigations, its use in a courtroom is a very different matter. There is no evidence for the proposition that a hypnotized witness can neither lie nor be mistaken. Also, hypnotized subjects are extremely vulnerable to suggestion and often cannot distinguish suggestion from reality.

Witnesses' Demeanor.   The demeanor of a witness probably affects his or her credibility in the eyes of the jury. Witnesses are coached as to how to dress, about what to expect from the opposing attorney, to answer only the questions they are asked, and so on. One policeman described to the authors the trial of a narcotics offender whom he had arrested while working under cover. Until the trial all of his contacts with the defendant had occurred while the officer was unkempt, unshaven, and sloppily dressed. Hearing this, the defense attorney waited eagerly to get this "slob" on the stand where, he anticipated, his very appearance would negate his testimony. Following the instruction he had received in the Police Academy, the officer arrived in court very well groomed, dressed in a well-tailored three-piece suit, his hair neatly styled. Upon seeing him walk to the stand, the defendant, who, at first, had not recognized him, asked to confer with his attorney and forthwith changed his plea to guilty.

Witnesses also convey information to the jury by their manner of gesturing while testifying. Psychologists have become increasingly aware of the nature and significance of nonverbal communication and have studied it extensively. Means and Weiss have studied the gestural behavior of the courtroom witness. They found that when being questioned by friendly counsel, witnesses made more expansive gestures than when being cross-examined. Other predictions about the relative openness of posture or about "small gestures" during stress were not supported. Subjects were actual witnesses who were observed during the first 15 minutes of their testimony.

CONFESSIONS

A number of writers claim that innocent persons have been convicted on the basis of questionable confessions that were contradicted by a good deal of other evidence. Zimbardo suggests the possibility that police (and judges) feel more comfortable and sure of their own actions if a confession is on the record.[12] In Renaissance Venice *all* trials began with a confession by the accused, a system similar to that employed in some totalitarian societies today. The authorities appear to need reassurance that they have the real offender in custody, and use the confession as a means of persuading the public of that, as well.

Despite the fact that it is well known that people confess falsely to crimes as a result of pathological needs for punishment or even as a desperate bid for respect or attention,[13] many police interrogators appear convinced that their procedures will not incriminate innocent people. That information "known only to the perpetrator" is sometimes allowed to slip from the interrogator's lips and may ultimately become part of a false confession is rarely acknowledged.

As previously noted, the *Miranda* decision of 1965 has been the object of bitter attacks. Police agencies have argued that their investigations would be impeded if they were required to warn a subject of his rights to remain silent and to consult an attorney. Proponents of the *Miranda* rule argue, on the other hand, that it requires better, more conscientious police work, precluding, as it does, interrogation through intimidation.

Those who feel compelled to confess by psychological pressures of their own are surely not going to be deterred by a *Miranda* warning. But why, the reader may ask, would innocent persons feel compelled to confess?

Münsterberg cited the case of a young man who was hanged for murder in Chicago in 1906 on the basis of a confession apparently uttered at a time when he was suffering from what was then called dissociation of personality. Before his execution the condemned man appears to have recovered from his fugue state and reasserted the innocence he had proclaimed when first arrested.

Even in 1906, police and press felt it was inconceivable that an innocent person would confess—this despite the numerous false confessions that follow any well-publicized crime.

Münsterberg suggested several conditions under which false confessions might be made. One such confession occurred when two innocent brothers feared that the evidence against them was sufficient to condemn them. They confessed in return for a less extreme sentence, and, much later, their supposed victim reappeared, alive. Münsterberg suggested that people confess from hope, from fear, out of cunning, and because of their passivity. Some confess in response to physical torture, others as a result of emotional stress. Consistent with major interests of psychologists of the time (1909), Münsterberg discussed the untrustworthiness of memory and the "power of suggestion," as well as dissociation of personality and melancholia (psychotic depression) as causes of false confessions.

Somewhat more recently, in 1925, Theodor Reik lectured on the compulsion to confess. He presented a hypothesis derived from the psychoanalytic treatment of neurotics. Neurotic symptoms are themselves a kind of unconscious confession, which relieve guilt feelings while unconsciously repeating the forbidden act, often through the medium of speech. Self-betrayal, or involuntary acts of confession, may take the form of slips of the tongue or the pen or, as in the famous Leopold-Loeb murder case, the inadvertent loss of eyeglasses at the scene of the crime. Such unconscious compulsions are the bases of conscious confessions, said Reik, particularly those that appear to bring to the confessor no such gain as might accrue in a plea bargaining proceeding or in an explanation of extenuating circumstances. Viewed as the product of general feelings of guilt, false confessions are understandable to the psychoanalyst. The confession may result from feelings of guilt related to imaginary or unrelated acts.

Reik wrote of the difference between external compulsions to confess (e.g., torture) and internal compulsions (e.g., guilt). He said that physical torture has been replaced by more subtle measures.

Other writers have viewed confessions as quests for forgiveness or, as in some cases noted by Reik, as reflections of pathological guilt of the sort observable in sufferers from psychotic depression.

The Miranda rule appears not to be totally effective in preventing police from exerting pressures, subtle or otherwise. One confession in a murder case was recanted because the defendant claimed that the police would not permit him to sleep until he confessed. Sleep deprivation, in fact, is a technique that was used to elicit a confession from Joseph Cardinal Mindszenty in Hungary 30 years ago when he was tried for treason.

Since a confession has questionable probative value, at best, why do police press so relentlessly for it? One reason is that the introduction of a confession into evidence is very likely to result in a conviction.

Interrogation Techniques. Social psychologists have repeatedly demonstrated that manipulation of physical or psychological environments can enable one person to gain considerable control over another. Such manipulations as well as techniques of persuasion have long been in the repertoire of police interrogators.

For one thing, interrogation of suspects is usually conducted in a police facility. The prisoner is in unfamiliar surroundings, perhaps frightened by stories of beatings, very likely frightened by the seriousness of his situation and by the absence of reassuring persons and objects.

He is likely to be seated in a straight chair, facing and very close to the interrogator. He may not have a light shining in his eyes, but the room is likely to be bare of decorations and empty of such distracting stimuli as windows, phones, or any objects which might help him to feel less tense. That is, there may be no ash tray, no surface on which to rest his arms, no small objects to handle or play with.

The interrogator is likely to be dressed conservatively in a manner designed to command respect, and to conduct himself authoritatively but with an approach sufficiently flexible that he can adapt to the suspect's needs, behaviors, and personal characteristics.[14,15]

For example, in interacting with a respectable, middle class suspect, the interrogator may address him by his first name, symbolically enhancing his vulnerability with the implicit message that his status counts for little under these circumstances.

A commonplace technique was illustrated by a young policeman-student who described his "foolproof way of picking up girls." He and his male friend would go to a singles bar where one of them would be surly and rude to an attractive young woman. His "partner" would intervene in a short while, "forcibly" removing the offensive man, apologizing for his behavior, and being friendly and charming. The contrast between the two led to his becoming the hapless woman's "friend and protector" for the evening. On alternate evenings the two rogues switched roles.

Police interrogators use a similar technique, known as the "Mutt and Jeff" approach. "Mutt," the first interrogator, relentlessly affirms his certainty of the suspect's guilt and his success in locking up others who have committed similar offenses. He behaves hostilely and displays growing impatience. "Jeff" observes all of this with quiet dismay, and, at the first opportunity, when Mutt steps out of the room, urges the suspect to confess because, while he doesn't like Mutt's tactics, he will soon be unable to keep him from behaving even worse. The victim of this ploy may be induced to confess out of gratitude for Jeff's concern.

Driver suggests that suspects may become accustomed to telling the truth in response to innocuous initial questions or to "large, kindly, persistent men" and, conditioned by this experience, may, in fact, believe false statements that they are subsequently induced to make. This would be consistent, at least, with a study by Bem, who showed that subjects told to lie when a green light was on and to tell the truth when the light was amber, in time believed false answers they were induced to make under the latter conditions.

Sometimes, if two persons are in custody under suspicion of committing a crime together, one will be removed from their cell for an hour. His (factual) insistence that nothing happened during his absence will be hard for the other to believe, and when he is later told that his partner confessed, he will be likely to believe that.

There have been instances in which lineups have been faked. Several bogus witnesses appear to identify the suspect in a lineup so that his confidence in his ability to avoid indictment or to win acquittal will be shaken, and he will be more likely to confess.

The very wording of the interrogator's questions will be designed to prevent the suspect's denying his guilt. He is not asked whether he committed the crime, but why he did so.[16]

In addition to manipulating the conditions of interrogation, persuasive efforts are generally made. Chief Justice Warren summarized one aspect of this in his opinion in *Miranda v. Arizona*:

> To highlight the isolation and unfamiliar surroundings, the manuals instruct the police to display an air of confidence in the suspect's guilt and from outward appearance to maintain only an interest in confirming certain details. The guilt of the suspect is to be posited as a fact. The interrogator should direct his comments toward the reasons why the subject committed the act rather than court failure by asking the subject whether he did it. Like other men, perhaps the subject has had a bad family life, had an unhappy childhood, had too much to drink, had an unrequited desire for women. The officers are instructed to minimize the moral seriousness of the offense, to cast blame on the victim or on society. These tactics are designed to put the subject in a psychological state where his story is but an elaboration of what the police purport to know already—that he is guilty. Explanations to the contrary are dismissed and discouraged.[17]

Thus there are appeals to reason as well as appeals to the suspect's emotions in interrogator attempts to elicit a confession. Repeated expression of confidence in his guilt, repetition to the defendant of his story, or repetition of it by him may lead to minor inconsistencies which can be stressed by the interrogating officer. The suspect may even come to believe statements he had not believed earlier. Exaggerating the charges or expressing compassionate understanding of such behaviors may serve to evoke a statement from the suspect.

An interrogator may try to exploit a suspect's embarrassment or shame by urging him to spare his family more grief by confessing and getting it over with, or by doing "the only decent thing." He may urge the suspect to turn his back upon his criminal past by making a clean breast of things. Inexperienced first offenders are said to be more susceptible to such emotional appeals, as are those whose crimes were the result of a moment of passion. More experienced offenders, or those whose crimes were premeditated quests for personal gain, are said to be more susceptible to rational appeals.

Driver summarizes variables that facilitate or impede the evocation of confessions. Among the former are a "confidential" relationship with the interrogator, an impression fostered by his manner and his physical closeness. Isolation from social support as well as the ambiguity and unpredictability of the situation are additional environmental factors. A prestigious or high-status interrogator who is skilled in playing different roles as the situation requires will be likely to facilitate confession. One who has only a professional manner and no other skills will be less successful. If the suspect is a passive person of low socioeconomic status and little experience with the police, he will be more susceptible to the pressures described here than a more self-confident, assertive person or an experienced criminal will be.

The suspect will also be likely to resist confessing, says Driver, if he perceives or defines the situation as illegitimate or coercive rather than as a standard investigatory procedure in which his cooperation is being enlisted. By the same token, an interrogator to whom the suspect takes an instant dislike will be unlikely to elicit a confession, since he will have difficulty establishing a relationship that encourages the suspect to trust or even to identify with the interrogator during the course of their interaction.[18]

Zimbardo points to the demand characteristics of the situation, noting the attention given to every detail of the environment within which the interrogation takes place. All of the stimulus conditions are designed to convince the suspect of the officer's knowledge of the crime, the suspect's isolation, and the power of the police over the suspect. He notes, also, the attempt to encourage perceptual and judgmental distortion by telling the suspect that his crime was understandable or not really so terrible. The false lineup mentioned above may also be used to make the suspect think he has been identified in a far more serious crime so that he will eagerly confess to the present one to avoid the worse accusation. Manipulation of the relationship between suspect and interrogator, and the exploitation of the suspect's characteristics, constitute a somewhat different ploy. It is exemplified by the interrogator's being friendly or doing a favor for the suspect as well as by the pitting of one of a pair of suspects against the other, as described above.

The use of clinical and psychological phenomena is the last of the categories discussed by Zimbardo. This includes such acts as falsely calling attention to a twitch or a tremor, thus causing that quirk to appear, and then explicitly drawing an inference of guilt from it or asking the suspect to account for the fact that his carotid artery is pulsating or his mouth is dry. Not knowing that the simple calling of attention to a part of one's body can elicit a response there, the suspect may interpret the otherwise inexplicable response as evidence of his own guilty conscience.[19,20]

JURY DELIBERATIONS

Once impaneled, members of the jury are exposed to the arguments and evidence of the opposing sides, instructed by the judge, and then sent off by themselves to deliberate and decide upon a verdict. In most jurisdictions, they are permitted to make no notes and are barred from discussing the case, even among themselves, until the judge has completed the charge. While some evidence suggests that most jurors have made a tentative decision as early as the opening arguments, in theory, at least, they have not communicated their views. When at last they do so, it is not to one trusted confidante; they must reveal their views to 11 strangers whose agreement or disagreement is as yet unknown. This ambiguous and often intimidating circumstance doubtlessly affects individual jurors in diverse ways, and is a major reason that the wise attorney tries to anticipate not only the manner in which the individual juror will attend to the case, but also how the collection of jurors will influence one another once they undertake to decide.

Münsterberg saw great hazards in this process. He wrote that "it is not lack of general or logical training of the single individual which obstructs the path of justice. The trouble lies rather in the mutual influence of the twelve men."[21] Compelled to work in groups rather than alone, people become more persuasible or subject to pressures to conform, function less intelligently, and relinquish individuality, or so Münsterberg's data suggested. A group decision represents the absorption of individual judgment into a collective consciousness, which produces, or has the potential to produce, a unique verdict different from those which the jurors would have reached individually. Münsterberg feared that this outcome would be unpredictable and not based solely on the evidence.

He designed experiments to determine whether the need for cooperative discussion and repeated balloting helped or hindered persons attempting to arrive at a judgment about complicated information. Like most of his successors, he used a situation analogous to, but not identical with, a real jury. That is, he tried to assess responses in situations similar in some vital ways to the deliberations of a jury. As will be shown, more recent researchers have tried to develop procedures whose content includes the weighing of hypothetical evidence. Such procedures have not been shown to have greater validity than Münsterberg's, although they may be more interesting to read about and to construct.

His approach was very straightforward. Eighteen students were seated around a table where they were exposed to stimuli that had objectively verifiable characteristics. Specifically, they were shown two cards on which were printed 104 and 98 dots, respectively. The cards were exposed for 30 seconds, after which each observer wrote on a piece of paper his judgment as to whether they bore equal numbers of dots or, if not, which of the cards had more dots printed on it. The observers were next instructed to indicate their judgements by a show of hands, and then to discuss the matter. After five minutes there was another vote, followed by more discussion and then by a final vote. On the first ballot, 52% of the votes were correct, on the last 78% were. For these "jurors," then, deliberations led to greater accuracy. But these observers were males. With female suffrage in the offing and the prospect of women voters serving as jurors, Münsterberg repeated his study using female subjects. His worst fears were realized!

The percentage of correct votes by women was 45% on the first ballot. It was 45% on the last ballot, too. Münsterberg concluded that his female subjects were not consistently influenced by the discussion. Where 40% of the male subjects had changed their votes, most in the direction of greater accuracy, 19% of the females had changed but in no consistent direction. Münsterberg viewed his female subjects as stubborn, as willing to listen to but unwilling to be swayed by each other's arguments. Consequently he felt that they were unfit to serve as jurors!

During the last 15 years, social psychologists have found that researchers who fail to take adequate precautions are very likely to signal their hypotheses unwittingly to their subjects. That is, the subject learns by means of an experimenter's subtle (and unintended) cues what response is expected. It seems likely that Münsterberg's view of differences in the mental processes of the sexes preceded his study. If it did, he might well have conveyed to the males his expectation that they would be open to one another's influence and to the females that they would "stick to their guns." If this was the case, those undergraduates, wishing to be "good" subjects, very likely responded as they perceived it was expected they would. Two things, in any case, are clear. First, these findings cannot be accepted without suitably controlled replication. Second, deliberations can change judgments, if only where the number of dots per card is at issue.

A more recent study was undertaken to investigate the issue of juror's sex. Nemeth et al. reviewed a series of studies dealing with stereotypes about women jurors. Some appeared to conclude that women are relatively passive in the role; that they are more emotional than men; that some, at least, are more sympathetic than men to a housebreaker but more punitive than men where incest was the charge. Suffice it to say that any relationship between the juror's sex and the juror's opinion is a very complicated one, and, more important, that the changing roles of women in our society suggest that such patterns of juror behavior as there may once have been, may exist no longer.

From an initial sample of 753 undergraduates, Nemeth organized 28 groups of 6 to serve as juries. Each of the juries had at least two persons of each sex and were predisposed, as shown by a pre-test, either to acquit or to convict a fictitious murder suspect by a vote of 4 to 2. The juries deliberated for up to two hours, half having been instructed to reach a unanimous verdict and the remainder to reach a 2/3 majority verdict. Deliberations were surreptitiously videotaped. While males were more likely to seat themselves at the heads of the table, the sexes did not differ in their verdicts. There were some differences in their behavior during deliberations. For example, males were more likely to give opinions and information than females were; females more readily showed agreement. They differed in no other categories of interaction. The sexes were equally likely to stand by their initial decisions.

In a second study reported at the same time, Nemeth et al. transported

242 The Criminal Justice System and Its Psychology

undergraduate volunteers to a Federal District Court where they witnessed a "trial" conducted by law school students. Once again the sexes did not differ in their verdicts. Moreover, in this study, they did not differ in seating, or in any of the 12 interaction categories into which their behavior was coded. The jurors themselves perceived some differences in the relative confidence, aggressiveness, and leadership of the sexes, however. Perceived differences were also a function of sex: males felt that females spoke more freely, while females viewed males as more free to express their views.

In short, Nemeth et al. found no differences in verdicts but some differences in deliberations. They speculate that in an actual jury, each juror has something unique to contribute, namely his or her own perception of the evidence and the arguments. In the first study, all jurors had equal access to a written description of the case, and so the inputs of each were less crucial. Only opinions differed in this case, not information, and men more freely expressed their opinions. Where information was important, men and women gave it equally often. During deliberations the sexes did not differ in persuasiveness, persuasibility, passivity, or sympathy.

We turn now to a more microscopic consideration of what goes on during a jury's deliberations. More specifically, what do social psychologists investigate in contemporary studies of small groups in general and of juries in particular?

Many kinds of groups are studied by psychologists. Some are primarily work groups. The focus of study might be upon their working relationships and the relative openness of their channels of communication. Others are concerned with participants' feelings about themselves or their awareness of the world about them and the effects of these factors on group behavior. Here the focus of study might be upon the participants' receptiveness to feedback and their willingness to disclose "personal" feelings or to risk new and unusual ways of relating or behaving. Whatever the primary focus of a small group, certain variables can be studied as they affect its functioning. A noteworthy difference between juries and other groups is that with *very* few exceptions real juries deliberating real cases cannot be studied directly. Inferences must be drawn from the behavior of simulated juries or of groups whose activities have other purposes. Some studies have even involved individuals playing the role of juror and not "deliberating" in conjunction with others at all. This last is not a very helpful analogue of the jury system. Aside from this important difference, the tools and theories of the social psychologist can be applied to juries as to any group.

Psychologists and other social scientists may view the small group as a social system in miniature, in which various roles are played by the members as the group works at its task. Researchers in the tradition of the sociologist

Bales analyze the processes by which small groups operate. They observe small problem-solving groups at work and note the nature and frequency of interactive behaviors that take place. The categories into which behaviors are coded include: asking for or giving suggestions, opinions, and information, and showing solidarity or antagonism, tension or tension release, and agreement or disagreement. These 12 behaviors occur with greatest frequency at different stages in a group's life. Requests for information may be relatively commonplace when the group is new to its task, and displays of antagonism may not appear until later. Moreover, in such groups two types of leader typically emerge: (1) the "task specialist," whose primary concern is for accomplishing the group's goal, and (2) the "social-emotional specialist," who is concerned that the personal needs of the members be met by the group even if at the expense of achieving the group's goal.

The latter type of leader will often take responsibility for encouraging reluctant members to speak, for easing the tension with a witticism, and for expressing appreciation of a member's contribution. Some research on jury deliberations stems from this approach.

Other theorists are especially interested in the norms that a group develops. Norms, or standards of acceptable behavior, establish expectations as to what group members will probably do. Behavior outside the range of acceptability established by the norm is said to violate expectations or to be deviant. The lone juror who "holds out" against the views of all of his colleagues is likely to be the target of considerable pressure to conform and of strong negative feelings if he persists in his deviance. Some jurisdictions permit nonunanimous verdicts; others require unanimity. The effects of these decision rules on deliberations and on their results have been examined in a few studies.

The ways in which information is processed by members of groups has been another focus of interest of social psychologists. For example, persons in ambiguous circumstances will be likely to seek one another out for help and reassurance in defining the situation and the actions appropriate to coping with it. Very often the task confronting a jury is ambiguous, if not in the eyes of the law, then surely in the eyes of the jurors. The quest for "social reality," the clarity provided by the opinions of others in the same predicament, may often be an implicit component of jury deliberations.

A fourth concern of the social psychology of small groups has to do with styles of leadership (e.g., democratic, autocratic, and laissez-faire) and their effects on members' morale, productivity, and independence. There appears to be no research to date on the behavior of the jury foreman *per se* or on the ways in which foremen can facilitate or impede effective deliberating.

The seriousness of the jurors' task, the implications of their decisions for people's lives, may materially alter the relationships among variables from what they are in artificial or more frivolous settings. It is probably a good thing that jurors deliberate in secrecy, removed from some of the more intrusive contaminants which would otherwise impinge upon them. This very secrecy, however, requires that research on juries be artificial, using simulation rather than direct observation of deliberating juries. Hence, most of the data are only suggestive of what really goes on. Ironically, lawyers, who have much to gain from knowledge of real jury deliberations, are barred by their profession from participating on juries.

One recent helpful survey of small group research pertinent to jury deliberations is that of Kessler. She distinguishes between the product of a jury's deliberations, the verdict, and the process by which the product comes to be. She points out that earlier research generally focused on the verdict rather than on the means by which it is reached. More recent research has considered some issues concerning the process of deliberating: the effects of jury size and the requirement of unanimity, the selection of foremen, characteristics of jurors, the effects of the judge's charge, and the effects of pre-trial publicity and of videotaping deliberations. None of these studies employed real juries, but, in a number of communities, judges have permitted researchers to recruit subjects from among persons called to jury duty but not seated on a jury. This has permitted studies of subjects having more varied characteristics than college students. Kessler finds that college students talk less about themselves and comprehend judges' instructions better than other subjects, but the differences in their practices are not sufficient to justify the greater temporal and financial costs of employing "real" jurors.

Kessler also compares studies in which "jurors" read testimony or arguments, with studies in which stimulus materials are enacted on audio or videotape. Kessler feels that the latter situation makes for greater reality and motivation among participating subjects, and reports a few instances in which actual criminal trials have been videotaped (with the consent of both sides and the bench) for purposes of research. More common is the use of a videotaped reenactment of parts or all of a trial.

A Michigan doctoral dissertation led its author to the conclusion that live mock trials, audio tapes and printed, but edited, transcripts all are useful stimulus conditions.[22] Probably a videotaped trial is the most effective compromise between the requirements of realism and economy in research.

Consistent with the work of Janis on "groupthink," Kessler suggests that the greater the cohesiveness of the group, the greater the pressure is to conform with the group's dominant opinion. Group size, which has become a focus of concern with respect to juries since *Williams v. Florida* in 1970, affects the group product in any of several ways. Larger groups may lend themselves more readily than smaller ones to subgrouping and thus have greater difficulty achieving consensus. In the *Williams* case the U.S. Supreme Court upheld the use of six-member juries. Research using statistical models has shown that the smaller juries are less likely to fail to reach agreement. On the other hand, a number of studies suggest that the differences between six- and twelve-member juries in verdicts are negligible. Several of these studies, however, involved civil rather than criminal proceedings, as well as subjects who were not actual jurors. In 1978 the U.S. Supreme Court unanimously fixed the minimum jury size in a criminal case at six. While the Justices differed in their reasoning, some of their opinions made the point that very small juries are inadequately representative of the community. Justice Blackmun questioned the adequacy of the deliberation process in very small juries.[23]

There is some evidence that larger groups are more ready to take risks than smaller ones. There is a body of research in the field of social psychology concerning what is called the "risky shift" phenomenon. Under certain conditions people seem to be more willing to make bold judgments in cooperation with others than when they are alone. It is also well documented that conditions of anonymity, the presence of similarly behaving others, and unclear expectations enhance people's tendencies to behave in unusual, even antisocial, ways. To the extent that participation in a jury establishes such circumstances, one might predict that twelve jurors will take greater risks as a group than six. The question is what constitutes the greater risk: convicting someone about whose guilt one has doubt, or acqutting a defendant when one is all but convinced of his guilt? If one takes the position that most people in our culture would consider it a more serious error to convict an innocent defendant than to acquit a guilty one, the foregoing theory might predict that larger juries would be more likely to convict in questionable cases than smaller ones. As shown above, this prediction is contrary to the data.

Another issue which aroused the interest of researchers following a Supreme Court decision pertains to the requirement that verdicts be unanimous. Four Justices concluded that unanimity is not required at all in criminal cases; four concluded that it is, and one, Mr. Justice Powell, concluded that the Constitution calls for unanimity in federal cases but not in state trials. His view upheld a series of convictions made by votes of 9–3, 11–1, and 10–2.[24] Several researchers are studying the ramifications of this decision using mock juries. One of them, Nemeth, reports a series of three studies designed to test theories of inter-juror influence. Earlier studies had concluded that verdicts are similar under conditions of both unanimity and a 2/3 majority rule. Juries instructed to seek unanimity, however, are more likely to be "hung" than juries in which a 2/3 majority is sufficient for a verdict. Having reviewed these studies, Nemeth proceeded to test *how* the juries deliberate, a necessary step in order to test the validity of assumptions about inter-juror influence. Her first two studies employed groups of six undergraduates who were given accounts of the testimony in a fictitious murder case and, after privately indicating an initial vote, were assigned to deliberate. Some of the "juries" were instructed to reach unanimity; some were told that a 2/3 majority was sufficient for a verdict. Based on the initial votes, the juries were arranged so that in some four of the six initially favored conviction, and in others four of the six initially favored acquittal. Deliberations were videotaped and subjected to a Bales-type analysis of the interaction. Several findings are worth noting.

As in previous studies, there were no differences in the frequency of convictions or acquittals as a function of the unanimity requirement, although unanimity-seeking juries "hung" more often. Also, when the initial majority favored acquittal, acquittal was the verdict (eight out of nine times); when the initial majority favored conviction, the minority appears to have swayed them successfully often enough to make the ultimate verdict unpredictable. That is, the defendant was acquitted as often as he was convicted, despite the 2/3 majority initially favoring conviction.

One of the concerns of the dissenting Justices in the cases mentioned above was that under less than unanimity conditions, the arguments of the minority would be given short shrift. The majority, they feared, would ride roughshod over the minority. Nemeth found that when the majority was for conviction, deliberations did last longer under the unanimity requirement than under a majority requirement. Where the majority originally favored acquittal, deliberation times did not differ under the two rules.

What was the nature of the interaction among jurors? Based on the Bales categories of interaction process analysis, Nemeth found that groups working to achieve unanimity were more likely to show friendly behaviors, to give opinions and information, *and* to disagree and interrupt than groups working to achieve a majority verdict. These differences tended to be greater where the majority initially favored conviction. Majority and minority members spoke about equally often, although behaviors directed at them differed.

Where the minority favoring acquittal succeeded in converting two others to their point of view, they tended to stop the deliberations and rendered a verdict without considering the views of the hold-outs favoring conviction.

Asked to indicate the degree to which they felt that "justice had been done," jurors who sought unanimity were more likely to feel that way than those who operated under the 2/3 rule. Regardless of the outcome of deliberations, those initially in the minority were less content with the fairness of the deliberations, the openness of the group to opposing views, and the justness of the outcome than were those initially in the majority.

All of these findings were with juries of six undergraduates reading brief transcripts of a fictitious trial. Nemeth rightly wondered whether these results could be replicated under more realistic conditions. Accordingly, she presented to juries of twelve undergraduates a series of seven criminal and civil cases enacted in a courtroom by law students. As in the earlier studies, jurors indicated an initial vote and then were assigned randomly to deliberate under a requirement of either unanimity or a 2/3 majority. In this study the proportions favoring acquittal and conviction were not systematically varied. Once again the deliberation time was greater under the unanimity requirement. In addition, more people changed their votes under unanimity conditions. In this study, unlike the previous ones, there were no differences observed in the interaction processes. While they felt less comfortable deliberating, those who were required to reach unanimity felt more confident that they had reached a just verdict. Unlike the previously described experiments in which an acquittal-prone minority sometimes prevailed, in the simulated trials the initial majority remained the majority throughout.

The upshot of Nemeth's work seems to be that both groups of Justices were right. Mr. Justice White, writing the opinion favoring nonunanimous juries, expressed the view that the verdicts would not have been different if unanimity had been required. This may, in fact, be the case. Mr. Justice Douglas, who staunchly supported the unanimity rule, argued that nonunanimous juries would not debate as vigorously and that dissenters would be ignored. This, too, may be the case. Justice White had argued that reasonable dissent would surely be persuasive, and that discussion would continue as long as it was effective. Unlike Justice Douglas, he seems to have overlooked the fact that power is taken away from the minority juror if his vote is not needed for a verdict, and where one lacks power, one is likely to have less ability to influence. Schachter showed years ago that members of a discussion group will make several attempts to convert a deviant, but, in time, they will seek to oust him if he does not come around.

A comparable fate seems to have been experienced by some of those in the minority in Nemeth's juries. Such an outcome is important, but Nemeth is even more concerned about the effects on the community and its faith in jury trials if jurors leave the courthouse feeling uncertain that they have rendered a just verdict.

Like studies discussed above, an investigation by Davis, et al. suggests that jurors permitted to decide a case by a 2/3 majority appear to give relatively little attention or weight to the views of minorities equal to 1/3 of the jury or smaller. This study also suggests that jury size (6 or 12 persons) does not affect verdicts significantly although jurors assessing the evidence individually were more inclined to convict than jurors working in groups.

Valenti and Downing found, as had Davis et al., that jury size had no effect when apparent guilt was low, but smaller juries were substantially more likely to convict than were 12-person juries when apparent guilt was high.

Despite the existence of a number of studies and theoretical concepts pertinent to jury deliberations and persuasibility, Kessler concludes that we have as yet no unifying theory about small groups, let alone about juries.

Thus far we have considered some of the group dynamics issues in jury deliberations. Group dynamics refers to the ways in which a group's members interact and go about their tasks. The deliberations of a jury may be viewed from other perspectives, as well. Some of the things that happen in the jury room are affected by the way the trial itself is structured; others are the result of the structure of the jury. Finally, the members of the jury bring to their task ways of thinking, prejudices, assumptions, and values that have their impact on the jury's deliberations. We will examine some of these influences.

PRE-TRIAL PUBLICITY, INADMISSIBLE EVIDENCE, AND SPEECH PATTERNS

A trial's outcome is not necessarily determined only by what transpires in the courtroom. A number of psychologists have begun to explore extrinsic factors in jury deliberations and decisions.

Two Columbia University researchers, Padawer-Singer and Barton, conducted one of the few studies involving members of real jury pools. They reenacted a murder trial on audio tape and presented it to volunteer jurors in two New York State Supreme Courts. They had several purposes: one was to determine whether or not pre-trial publicity does intrude itself into a jury's deliberations and, if it does, to what extent. A second was to attempt to identify the characteristics of jurors who are most susceptible to such influence, and to assess the *voir dire* as a means of counteracting it.

Jurors who agreed to participate were first given either prejudicial or nonprejudicial news stories to read about the case. They then listened to a three-hour tape-recorded version of a murder trial, after which they retired to deliberate for up to six hours (until they had reached a verdict or had to be allowed to go home). The case was selected because the evidence against the defendant was circumstantial and because the defendant had declined to take the stand. The latter condition meant that information about any prior criminal activity was inadmissible as was his retracted confession. Reference to these things appeared in the bogus prejudicial news clippings.

In two studies that followed essentially this procedure, more than two-thirds of the jurors (78% and 69%, respectively) who had been exposed to the prejudicial news items thought the defendant guilty. Those exposed to neutral stories were much less predisposed to convict (55% and 35%, respectively).

In the second study another independent variable was introduced.[25] Some jurors were screened by a *voir dire* procedure (with the help of two volunteer attorneys); others were assigned to juries on a random basis. Some demographic differences were noted between juries selected by *voir dire* procedures and those selected at random. Fewer Catholics and fewer occupants of high-status positions were selected by *voir dire*. More important, though, are the data pertaining to the jurors' verdicts as they relate to exposure to prejudicial news items and to *voir dire* questioning. As hypothesized, jurors who were not subjected to the *voir dire* were much more likely to be influenced by prejudicial information. More than three-fourths of these jurors found the defendant guilty. Of randomly assigned jurors not exposed to the information, only 11% voted guilty. The experience of the *voir dire* caused a substantial reduction in the guilty verdicts of those who were given a prejudicial news item. Only 60% (as opposed to 78.3%) found against the defendant. Interesting, and not thoroughly discussed by these authors, was the finding that of the jurors who were *not* exposed to the prejudicial news item, those selected by *voir dire* found against the defendant 50% of the time; that is, they were nearly five times as likely to convict as their counterparts who had not been exposed to *voir dire* questioning.

These authors' concern was primarily with the interaction between exposure to prejudicial information and exposure to *voir dire* proceedings. The finding that conviction was less likely where those two conditions obtained than it was among randomly assigned jurors who were exposed to prejudicial information is interpreted by them as having several kinds of significance. They infer from the data that experiencing *voir dire* primes jurors to consider all of the evidence in a case and all of the arguments, and to be more alert to the importance of legal principles (i.e., to follow the law even when it seems unfair, to ignore inadmissible evidence, and so on).

Padawer-Singer et al. urge that the *voir dire* be conducted by opposing counsel in order to eliminate the more blatantly prejudiced, to reduce the effects of such extraneous information as recanted confessions and pre-trial publicity, and to establish a public commitment of jurors to adherence to legal procedures. In any case, it appears that jurors who are screened for bias before trial are less likely to be affected by prejudicial news stories.

Hoiberg and Stires also investigated the effects of pre-trial publicity. Using high school students who were instructed to imagine that they were actual jurors, these writers presented evidence concerning a charge of murder against a 24-year-old ex-marine. Pre-trial publicity was manipulated along two dimensions: heinousness and prejudgment, as follows. High heinousness subjects were given a spurious newspaper article that presented a grisly and detailed description of the crime. Low heinousness subjects read an article written in an objective, nondetailed fashion. Prejudgment was manipulated by including in the article statements that the accused had confessed (high prejudgment) or that a suspect was being questioned but that the investigation was continuing (low prejudgment).

After reading the article, subjects listened to a 15-minute tape summarizing the salient evidence. Following this, each subject indicated on a rating scale the degree of his or her certainty as to the defendant's guilt or innocence. Data were analyzed not only in terms of the independent variables but also in terms of the sex and approximate I.Q. (above or below 113) of the subjects.

Among female subjects both independent variables had an impact regardless of I.Q. Both heinousness and prejudgment were positively related to judgments of guilt. Among male subjects neither variable produced an effect, but the higher-I.Q. males were more likely to decide against the defendant than the lower-I.Q. males.

It would be interesting to see more studies of the effect of juror I.Q. on verdicts, as all simulated studies suffer from a very serious defect—the evidence is summarized in a manner much easier to follow than the chaotic sequence of events in a real trial.

That the female subjects rated the *victim* as less likable under the high heinousness condition (which included the information that she had been "brutally raped" as well as murdered) than under the low heinousness condition is cited by the authors as consistent with the "just world" theory, which suggests that we defend ourselves psychologically against the threat that an unjust world would pose by attributing to the victim responsibility for any serious misfortune. Many people like to believe that one gets what one deserves in life, whether good or ill. The heinousness variable was unrelated to the males' ratings of the victim. It is interesting and consistent that females rated the crime as less heinous than males. Both of these findings are interpreted by these authors as reflecting a defensiveness among the female subjects, who had to contemplate the terrible fate of a young woman like themselves. Males, being less threatened by the situation, did not have to rely upon such coping mechamisms. One might predict that a study in which a male was the victim of a brutal crime would yield findings in the opposite direction.

An earlier paper by Simon reaches a relatively optimistic conclusion.[26] Since restrictions on the press are not to be imposed lightly in a free country, she points out the need to determine whether pre-trial publicity does prejudice juries, and her study was intended to illuminate that issue. She employed a systematic sample of voters in Champaign and Urbana, Illinois, writing to every fortieth person on the voter registry lists. Of the 825 people contacted, 97 agreed to participate. Like Padawer-Singer and Barton, she found that a prejudicial story *did* influence these people to believe the defendant guilty. Having made this first judgment, however, the "juror" listened to a recorded admonition by the judge to put aside any opinions that he might have formed and to consider only the evidence presented. The jurors listened next to the evidence and indicated, as before, their opinion as to the defendant's guilt. Three-fourths of them at this point found the defendant to be innocent, where two-thirds had previously been inclined to convict on the basis of the pre-trial publicity. Her tentative conclusion was that the dangers of pre-trial publicity have been exaggerated and can be controlled by a judge's instructions.

This study suffers from three defects, two of which are rather serious. The first problem is that the sample selected was not random and therefore is not amenable to several statistical techniques. This criticism could be directed at a majority of the studies cited in this book or, indeed, in the entire psychological literature. The attempt at a representative sample, although frustrated by the small proportion willing to participate, is admirable. The second, more serious defect is that responding or not responding to a mailed inquiry is related to personality variables, so that selecting subjects in this manner can introduce bias into a sample. The effect of this bias on the dependent variable in this study is unspecifiable, but where persuasibility is a factor, as here, it could be substantial. Finally, like a number of other studies discussed here, this one seems likely to have been high in "demand characteristics." That is, the procedures employed probably provided clues to the subjects as to what the experimenter's hypothesis was. Seeing a prejudicial news story and then hearing a recorded warning to set aside any opinions he may have formed would seem likely to alert the subject that he was specifically to ignore the news story in considering the case. Wishing to be a "good subject," particularly after being singled out to serve and agreeing to do so, the subject would probably wish to comply with what he took to be the researcher's expectations.

Several other studies have been concerned with the impact of inadmissible evidence and the judge's instructions to disregard what jurors have heard in court. This issue also involves the effects of judges' instructions, but in a different area from pre-trial publicity.

One such study was that of Sue and his co-workers, who examined whether jurors in deliberating will, on instructions from the court, disregard evidence that, if not disregarded, would seriously impair the defense position.

It sometimes happens that a jury must confront a serious moral dilemma,[27] that of acquitting a defendant because of a technicality versus convicting him on the basis of evidence which the judge has ruled inadmissible.

Using a fictitious case that contained some incriminating evidence, Sue et al. required undergraduate psychology students to read an account of a crime and the subsequent trial, arrive at a decision, indicate their confidence in it, and, if they found the accused guilty, propose a sentence. There were two independent variables: the incriminating evidence was ruled admissible or inadmissible by the judge, and the remaining evidence was either compelling or unconvincing.

The stronger the people's basic evidence, the greater was the likelihood of conviction, and the greater was the students' confidence in their judgments. This, of course, had been predicted. Also predicted was the finding that additional admissible incriminating evidence increased the proportion of guilty judgments (from 24% to 47%).

If the primary case was strong, the additional evidence had no effect. If it was weak, the additional evidence was quite influential. And it was influential regardless of whether or not it was ruled admissible. With weak evidence alone, no juror voted to convict. If additional incriminating evidence was added to the weak evidence, however, it raised the proportion for conviction to 26% when it was admissible and to 35% when it was not. (The difference between these results was not statistically significant although the differences between the control group and these groups were both significant.)

Feneck recently completed a dissertation in which she related the characteristic of dogmatism to mock jurors' compliance with instructions to disregard inadmissible evidence. She found that dogmatism was unrelated to compliance with instructions, and that subjects given exculpatory inadmissible evidence did consider it and "acquitted" the accused despite the judge's instructions. Those for whom the inadmissible evidence was inculpatory did disregard it, as instructed. As indicated above, it seems that even in this role-playing study, jurors prefer to wrongly acquit a guilty individual when in doubt than to wrongly convict an innocent one.

Doob and Kirshenbaum investigated the effects of introducing a defendant's prior criminal record on individual judgments of guilt. They found that subjects were more likely to convict the defendant when, all else being equal, they were aware of his prior record (introduced to impeach his credibility as a witness, not—according to written instructions from the "judge"—to determine his guilt or innocence).

Hans and Doob raise several noteworthy questions and issues about this study, however. Individual judgments, they point out, may not be appropriately generalized to a jury's decision. All the factors discussed above that influence group decision making are clearly inoperable in individual decision making. Second, as one seeks to persuade others, some information may acquire greater importance. That is, persuasion efforts may influence both parties, the persuader as well as the target of his influence attempt. Moreover, an individual's decision-making process is private; a group's can be observed and recorded. Studies of individual jurors, therefore, cannot answer the question: *How* does the knowledge of a defendant's prior record affect the jury's decision making? Perhaps his credibility as a witness *is* reduced; perhaps the jurors generalize from one negative trait to others (the "halo effect"). The meaning or significance of evidence may be changed as the context is altered by the introduction or withholding of other evidence. Any or all of these factors could, conceivably, be the mechanism by which verdicts are effected.

Hans and Doob found that groups told of the previous criminal record deliberated 1.4 times as long as those not informed of it. Contrary to Doob and Kirshenbaum, knowledge of the criminal record had no effect on individuals, but it did have one on groups. That is, with the information that the defendant had one previous conviction (a weaker manipulation than Doob and Kirshenbaum's study, in which he had had seven), jurors working as a group were more likely to reach a guilty verdict than jurors working privately and alone. This may be because the probability that *some* juror will refer to the record is greater where there are more jurors discussing the matter.

More pertinent for present purposes are the ways in which awareness of a defendant's prior record actually influences the discussion. Hans and Doob tape-recorded the group discussions and coded each statement in terms of its content and its "valence" (for or against the defendant). Among other things they found that groups who were aware of the prior record made more initially damaging statements about the defense case, made more statements of respect for the people's case, engaged in more discussion of the incriminating evidence, and so on. Groups unaware of the record were more likely to dismiss the inculpatory evidence or at least to question its validity. When it was known that the defendant was a previous offender, the evidence was interpreted differently, and less favorably for the defense.

Anthropologists William O'Barr and John Conley have studied the nuances of language in the courtroom and attempted to relate them to verdicts.[28] From recordings of criminal trials they isolated various styles and mannerisms that they incorporated into a dramatized trial in systematic ways. One such trial included testimony presented in a narrative style; another contained the same evidence recorded in the form of short answers. Differences between the sexes' habits of intonation were also systematically varied, a male actor portraying either "masculine" or "feminine" speech patterns. College students heard recordings of the dramatized trial and responded in writing to a series of questions concerning the case and their reasoning in reaching a verdict. The outcome included the finding that narrative descriptions of events are more persuasive than the same information given in response to a series of questions. Information presented in a "feminine" manner was less persuasive than the same information given in a "masculine" manner.

This is another area in which there seems to be room for considerable research. There have been studies of such variables as witness and defendant attractiveness. Studies have shown that attractive defendants fare better at the hands of juries than less attractive defendants. The major exception to this is that if the defendant is an attractive woman whose attractiveness facilitated commission of the crime, she tends to be treated more harshly than a plain defendant.[29] The authors know of no study which definitively confirms or disconfirms the feeling common to many trial lawyers that female jurors are biased against attractive female defendants. Perhaps speech patterns and accents are best viewed as a subcategory of the dimension of attractiveness. For example, few people would choose to be defended by an attorney whose accent marked him as a stranger to the community. This is one reason why trial lawyers retained in cases in distant communities typically retain local trial counsel.

To summarize, pre-trial publicity, inadmissible evidence, and speech patterns are uncontrolled variables affecting the impact of a trial's structure on the jury. The structure of the jury, too, affects its deliberations and thence its verdict.

SOCIAL STATUS AND STEREOTYPES

Social status is one pertinent factor in determining the amount of influence that an individual juror enjoys during deliberations. It can also affect how jurors view defendants.

Nemeth and Sosis point to the stereotyping of defendants as a function of their social attractiveness. A stereotype is a set of beliefs about the characteristics of a group, shared by a large segment of society. Such stereotypes are commonly used to make judgments about individual members of the group. The groups in question may be ethnic, political, professional, and so forth. Nemeth and Sosis suggest that the nature and degree of stereotyping depend on the personality, expectations, and social class (and so on) of the juror. They compared the judgments of two groups of "jurors." One group was composed of undergraduates at the University of Chicago, of middle and upper-middle class backgrounds, who were politically liberal and activist and who dressed casually (jeans, sweatshirts, long hair). The other group consisted of students at a southwest Chicago junior college, of working class backgrounds, who were politically conservative (relative to the first sample), and who dressed more formally (coats and ties, high heels, shorter hair).

Nemeth and Sosis suggested that the two groups might differ in their verdicts as a function of the defendant's race or general attractiveness. In fact, the junior college group gave harsher sentences, especially to the white defendant, but they were less likely to stereotype defendants as a function of general attractiveness.

The greater emphasis on punishment of the junior college sample compared with the stress on rehabilitation of the University of Chicago students, was attributed by the authors to differences in upbringing. Finally, they suggested, as we have before, that identification with the defendant leads to greater punitiveness (at least for working class jurors). If the defendant's guilt is ambiguous, however, the same identification might lead to sympathy and leniency.

Strodtbeck, James, and Hawkins explore the issue of social status and stereotypes from a different vantage point. Their concern is with the effects of social status on the interaction among the jurors themselves. They suggest that any status differences become important in the jury room because the jury's task calls upon the jurors' unique experiences and backgrounds, which relate directly to their statuses.

Selection as foreman (in jurisdictions where jurors elect their foreman), participation and influence in deliberations, satisfaction with one's role in deliberations, and performance of group-maintenance functions all appear to be related to social status. If a jury deliberates long enough, members may become sufficiently acquainted to see each other as individuals rather than as representative of a given class or ethnic group, a situation that will reduce stereotyping tendencies.

Sex roles also play a part in jury deliberations, as Strodtbeck and Mann suggest. Unlike Münsterberg's female subjects (and the majority of subjects in simulation studies ever since), Strodtbeck's and Mann's were not college undergraduates. They were "fully established in their sex and occupational roles." Middle-aged women, like young and old men, tend to be fairly active in jury deliberations. Are they active in the same ways?

It is well established that the best-liked person and the most task-oriented person in small groups are usually different people. There is some evidence (at least there was in 1955) that men are more frequently task-oriented and women are more apt to be social-emotional specialists.

Using jurors from Chicago and St. Louis panels deliberating about a recorded trial, Strodtbeck and Mann found that those who were most active in giving orientation were males of relatively high status. Women tended to be less active in giving orientation but did give their opinions about as often as the active males, if not more often. They were also much more likely to show tension release and a high frequency of agreeing responses.

Interestingly, men's questions caused them to be perceived as helping the group arrive at its decision. Women's questions made them less likely to be perceived this way.

These authors suggest that men start a relatively long sequence of events aimed at solving the problem, i.e., reaching a verdict, while women are more likely to react to others' efforts. One variable mentioned in passing is the nature of the case. In litigation concerning business matters or damages, men and women may assume (or may have assumed in 1956, when this study was done) that men are more knowledgeable so that both expect and permit men to behave in a manner consistent with their supposedly greater competence, and women press their presumptive strong suit, social-emotional behaviors.

These results have been disconfirmed, at least where sex is concerned, by the more recent study reported above of Nemeth, Endicott, and Wachtler. Whatever influence sex or status may have on how a jury deliberates, the task that confronts the jurors and the legal rules that control their deliberations have an even greater influence on their proceedings.

JUROR ATTITUDES AND MOTIVES

The processes of jury selection and the give-and-take of deliberations are intended to minimize the effects of individual juror bias on the verdict. The fact is that there are psychological processes which may still intrude themselves into the jury room. Jurors are, after all, human beings, not computers. Their goals may include objectivity and discerning the facts, but because the information to which they are exposed goes through human perceptual and evaluative processes rather than computers, it is subject to distortion despite their best efforts. In this section we will examine a few of the sources of distortion.

One of the major historical schools of psychology is known as the Gestalt school. Psychologists trained in this tradition are interested in, among many other things, how we perceive events, people, and objects. More specifically, their concern is with the ways in which characteristics of the stimuli affect our perception of them. Thus, we see things that are close together in time or space, or things that have similar characteristics (of shape, size, color, and so forth), as belonging together. We, automatically and without thinking about it, structure our perceptions in a way that minimizes the likelihood of a surprise or an unpredictable event by interpreting the unusual in terms of the familiar. A circular arc of 350° will be viewed as a circle although it is, objectively, a large arc.

Because we prefer to interpret stimuli in terms of familiar perceptual categories and to have our interpretations fit together coherently, we sometimes distort reality in perceiving. We fill in gaps (as with the 350° arc). We perceive things that have some characteristics in common as being similar in most ways (as in stereotyping). We perceive people we like as agreeing with us and like people who agree with us.[30]

Since the mid-1950s, a major interest of social psychologists has been the ways in which attitudes and perceptions are distorted in order to maintain consistency among them. A number of theories or models of attitude change have been proposed and tested which, collectively, make a strong case for the premise that we prefer that our feelings, attitudes, behaviors, and perceptions be mutually consistent, and that we will unwittingly distort any one or combination of them in order to establish consistency. A simple example may make this clear.

If a person believes firmly that he is a sensible, competent person of good judgment yet finds himself voluntarily undertaking a grim, onerous, thankless task and doing so for the weakest of reasons, he will experience tension arising from the inconsistency between what he perceives himself to be doing and the way he perceives himself to be. Because this tension is unpleasant, he will be motivated (perhaps unconsciously) to remove the inconsistency that produced it. This will require him to change either his self-perception or his behavior. Because his self-perception (sensible, competent, and so on) is itself rewarding and consistent with many other attitudes, feelings, and experiences, to change it would create more inconsistencies than it resolves. Accordingly, in these circumstances, he may be more likely to view his chosen task differently. He might perceive himself as having had no choice in undertaking it. More likely, he will see it less as something grim, thankless, and onerous and more as a challenge, an opportunity for growth, an opportunity to benefit others, or but a short-term commitment. The tension which evokes these changes is termed "cognitive dissonance," and is an important motivational concept.[31]

Derived from this way of thinking about attitudes and perceptions are several models which have been directly applied to the jury system. Equity theory, its derivative the "just world hypothesis," and attribution theory have stimulated a considerable amount of research. We will examine each of these theories briefly.

Equity Theory. Walster, Berscheid, and Walster combine Gestalt notions with concepts derived from psychoanalysis, learning theories, and social exchange theory in presenting four propositions about the perception of justice and injustice. This approach is known as equity theory.

The first of their propositions is that we seek maximum rewards at minimal costs in our activities and relationships. In their language, "Individuals will try to maximize their outcomes (where outcomes equal rewards minus costs)." Since the number or quality of rewards is limited, it follows that a certain amount of competition is inevitable. This can be a serious obstacle to group cooperation.

Therefore, the second proposition is that there evolve in groups systems which make it more rewarding to behave fairly (equitably) than to behave unfairly. That is, rewards and costs are shared by the membership consistently with some system accepted by them as fair. The system, then, provides the guidelines by which members can determine whether a given allocation of rewards (e.g., salaries) and costs (e.g., work or taxes) is fair. Having developed this system, the group applies sanctions by which those who are equitable in their dealings with others are rewarded and those who behave inequitably are punished.

In becoming socialized, people learn to anticipate fair treatment from others and to feel obligated to treat others fairly. But life is not always equitable. Some persons may be incapable of learning to play by the rules (see Chapter 4). Some take unfair advantage of a competitor. Some are mugged by a thug. Some allow themselves to be "doormats" to be used by others. In order to maintain their cognitive consistency, people have a need to believe that the person who behaves inequitably suffers consequences. The ignoble competitor will feel guilt or become an object of scorn. The mugger will be arrested. The doormat will be deprived of the respect of others. Walster et al. view the complex process of socialization as leading, ultimately, to our associating participation in an inequitable situation with punishment.

This leads to the third proposition, which is that people feel distressed when in an inequitable relationship and that this distress is a function of the degree to which the relationship is inequitable. The distress of a person who gets a "raw deal" may manifest itself in anger or disillusionment. The imposer of the raw deal may experience the distress as guilt.

The fourth proposition is that this distress leads the individual to try to restore equity. The greater the inequity the harder one tries because the greater the inequity the greater one's frustration or tension.

Equity can be restored in two ways: by restoring "actual equity" (returning the stolen wallet, asserting one's own rights), and by restoring psychological equity (perceiving the situation in a distorted fashion). As far as psychological equity is concerned, one does not adjust the actual outcomes, only his perceptions of them. One says, "He only got what was coming to him," or "I didn't hurt him as much as you might think." One may also dissociate himself from an inequitable relationship by saying, "I wasn't in my right mind," although that, in and of itself, may not be sufficient to restore equity. Guilt or contrition is likely to remain.

Walster et al. go on to consider the conditions under which a victim will be derogated, his suffering minimized, or the responsibility denied by the offender.

Equity theory has provided the basis for research in numerous areas that are pertinent to this book, among them exploitation of one person or group by another, altruistic actions, and interpersonal attraction.

The "Just World" Hypothesis.   Lerner, Miller, and Holmes examine the themes of deserving and justice, their meaning and how they are learned. One portion of their work, in particular, has led to research in the criminal justice field: the "just world hypothesis." The transition to it from the more general equity theory is a straightforward one.

Just as we learn to treat others fairly (most of the time) and to expect fair treatment from others (most of the time), we learn, too, to expect fair treatment from fate, from society, and from God. We learn to believe that self-restraint in the presence of temptation, while temporarily frustrating and unpleasant, leads in due course to reward.

Because this expectation or faith is so central to our lives and social behavior, any evidence that injustice occurs is threatening. In most religions such events are interpreted as being the product of the mysterious ways of the Almighty. Less religious people may require a more mundane explanation. They are threatened by injustice. More specifically, their "personal contract" is threatened. The result is that such people are motivated to protect this belief that the world is just.

Lerner et al. point out the critical role of what we earlier defined as social reality. What we feel we deserve in life depends upon what others, who are like us, seem to expect or get. This is because we learn to expect for ourselves what we find similar others expecting for themselves.

If we find that a person is suffering more than he "should" be, the notion of a just world is thrown into question and our investments in self-restraint, self-sacrifice, and so forth, are threatened. For this reason we seek to preserve justice for others, for doing so preserves it for ourselves.

Faced with an injustice, and being strongly motivated to believe in a just world, people try to eliminate the injustice which threatens that belief. They may try to change the unjust situation by aiding or compensating the victim or by harming or taking from the person who causes the injustice. If they cannot do that (as when an unknown assailant brutally murders an innocent victim), they try to restore justice psychologically. They may decide that the victim contributed somehow to his fate. If there is no clear way to assign responsibility to the victim because of his actions or carelessness, they will be likely to derogate the victim's character. Lerner et al. suggest that, at least for some period of time, most people who feel helpless to right a wrong will find a way to see the injustice as not totally inappropriate. A number of studies have related this position to the criminal justice system.

As applied to members of a jury, this theory provides a motivational concept for the jurors' efforts to reach a just verdict and gives legitimacy to their purpose. The notion of psychological rather than actual restoration of equity provides a theoretical basis for the effectiveness of a defense attack upon the victim's character or role in the causation of the offense.

Attribution Theory.   The third theoretical position that bears on how jurors, as people, respond to the facts of a case is attribution theory. Like equity theory it comes from the Gestalt tradition in psychology, but, unlike psychoanalysis, learning theories, or social exchange theory, it is an outgrowth of theories of person perception. Attribution theory is also more general than either of the other two theories. Its purpose is to account for how people understand and interpret behavior through exploration of the process by which they assign explanations to behavior.

Building upon the work of Heider, social psychologists have been attempting for 20 years to specify the conditions under which behaviors are likely to be attributed to intent as opposed to chance, compulsion, or other causes. More generally, they distinguish between environmental and personal causes of behavior. Some of the things people do, they do habitually. Spouses, for example, may bestow a perfunctory kiss on one another when leaving for work. Some of the things people do, they do involuntarily. Children may be compelled to kiss repugnant relatives. And some people's actions may be accidental. For instance, a driver may skid on a patch of ice, "causing" a collision with a neighboring car.

Psychologists are interested in intentional behavior because only intentional behavior makes possible a meaningful attribution, i.e., an attribution that tells us something about the actor. If his behavior is unintended, or if its effects are, we can make no inferences about what sort of person he is or what he is likely to do on some other occasion.

How is it decided whether or not an action is the product of intention? Heider noted three determining factors: equifinality, local causality, and exertion.[32] If the person takes several actions all of which lead to a particular goal (equifinality), if he is somehow present and directing events, intervening to keep them on the desired course (local causality), then we will assume personal causation. If, further, he is exerting himself in order to progress in his chosen direction, we tend to assume that his behavior is intended rather than accidental or compelled by circumstances.

Jones and Davis focus upon personal causation and define the principles by which a judgment is made that certain effects of a person's actions were intentional. Two requirements of such an inference are that the actor had the ability to perform the act and that he could have anticipated its consequences. If the person lacked the ability (e.g., to score two successive holes-in-one), the outcome would be regarded as a product of luck or chance, not intention. If the person could not have anticipated the outcome of an act, he could not have intended it.

Further, the individual who is perceived to have had several options open to him, will be assumed to have *chosen* the path he took, i.e., to have intended it. On the other hand, one whose behavior appears to have been coerced by restrictive or extremely compelling circumstances or by others, will not be perceived as intending his actions. The bank manager who withdraws and gives to a robber one million dollars because his family are being held hostage will not be assumed to have intended a theft.

An actor who has not been known to behave in any other manner may be perceived as acting routinely or habitually, not intentionally. This is why the perfunctory goodby kiss conveys little reassurance. In addition, the actor may be perceived as behaving compulsively, i.e., as being incapable of choosing an alternative course of action. Those jurisdictions that permit a defense of irresistible impulse implicitly recognize this principle.

A jury weighing evidence may decide that a theft was due to the criminal character or dishonesty of the accused or that it was precipitated by the dire circumstances within which an impoverished defendant found himself. Its verdict may well be influenced by the jurors' attributional propensities. Attribution of the act to the defendant's characteristics is likely to lead to conviction. Attribution to the situation or environment will enhance the likelihood of acquittal.

Myslieviec applied some of this theorizing to understanding the ways in which juries preserve equity when the facts in a given case might be expected to lead to an inequitable verdict.

It should be noted that the right of a jury to do this, as opposed to its clearcut power to do so, is controversial. Some argue that biasing factors of the sort just discussed confront us with the risk of capricious and unpredictable verdicts. Others reply that the jury represents a major safeguard against oppressive legislation. Laws involving homosexuality, marijuana use, and the like are regarded by some as excessively repressive and intrusive although they remain in effect. The jury's ability to take account of unique aspects of a case in its deliberations and verdict makes it possible to preserve equity.

Kalven and Zeisel found that juries differ from judges in certain types of cases. Jurors were less inclined to convict on minor offenses and took into account a victim's provocative behavior or a defendant's post-offense suffering. Myslieviec argues that jurors' shared sense of fairness (equity) minimizes the likelihood that they will decide a case incompetently or indiscreetly. The theories discussed in the preceding pages help to provide a frame of reference within which the jurors' equity-protecting action may be understood. They are stated by Myslieviec in the form of principles in order to facilitate that understanding.

The first principle states that a defendant will be punished less the more he suffered while committing the offense. A defendant seriously injured while committing a crime is likely to be punished less than would otherwise be the case.

Second is the principle that a defendant whose criminal behavior is uncharacteristic (he was drunk or extraordinarily provoked) will be treated more leniently because the offense will be attributed to the liquor or to the provocation rather than to the defendant *per se*.

The third principle relates the certainty of the defendant's guilt to the harshness of the punishment. The more ambiguous his guilt, the less the jury will wish to see him punished and, therefore, the lower the degree of the crime they will be likely to convict him for.

Fourth, the attractiveness of the victim and defendant may be expected to affect the jury. The more attractive the former, the more severe the punishment of the latter. The more attractive the defendant, the more leniently he is likely to be treated (with the exception mentioned above of the defendant whose attractiveness is one of his tools as a criminal).

The scapegoat defendant is the subject of the fifth principle. To the extent that he is seen as a "fall guy" who is "taking the rap" for others equally guilty, a defendant is likely to be treated leniently.

In this chapter we have tried to give an overview of research and theory pertinent to an understanding of the psychological factors involved in trial procedures and jury deliberations. At the present time new studies are appearing at a very high rate. Thus for the reader with professional interests in this field, this volume and similar books are doomed to be at least somewhat out of date even before they are in print. New research questions, new methodologies, and, of course, new and more refined results are to be expected.

NOTES AND REFERENCES

1. McGuire, W. J. and Papageorgis, D. The relative efficacy of various types of prior belief-defense in producing immunity against persuasion. *Journal of Abnormal and Social Psychology* 1961, 62, 326–332.
2. Sears, D. O. Opinion formation and information preferences in an adversary situation. *Journal of Experimental Social Psychology* 1966, 2, 130–142.
3. James, W. *The Principles of Psychology*, Vol. 2, New York: Holt, 1890, p. 97.
4. Münsterberg, H. *On the Witness Stand: Essays on Psychology and Crime*. New York: Doubleday, Page & Co., 1909, p. 39.
5. *Ibid.*, p. 49.

6. Cohen, J. *Psychological Time in Health and Disease*. Springfield, Ill.: Charles C. Thomas, 1967.
7. Marshall, J. *Law and Psychology in Conflict*. Indianapolis: Bobbs-Merrill, 1966.
8. Johnson, C. and Scott, B. Eye witness testimony and suspect identification as a function of arousal, sex of witness, and scheduling of interrogation. Paper presented at 84th Convention, American Psychological Association, Washington, D.C., 1976.
9. Arenberg, D. Cognition and aging: Verbal learning, memory and problem-solving. In C. Eisdorfer and M. P. Lawton (Eds.) *The Psychology of Adult Development and Aging*. Washington, D.C.: American Psychological Association, 1973, pp. 74–97.
10. Merton, R. K. The self-fulfilling prophecy. Chapter XI in *Social Theory and Social Structure* (revised and enlarged edition). Glencoe, Ill.: The Free Press, 1957.
11. Buckhout's papers include: Eyewitness testimony. *Scientific American* December, 1974, 231, 23–31; (with K. W. Ellison) The line-up: A critical look, *Psychology Today* June, 1977, 11(1), 82–88; and see *Social Action and the Law Newsletter* of the Center for Responsive Psychology, Brooklyn College, Vol. 2, Nos. 2 and 3, The Eyewitness.
12. Zimbardo, P. G. The psychology of police confessions. Paper presented at 74th Convention, American Psychological Association, New York, 1966, p. 29. See also P. G. Zimbardo. The psychology of police confessions. *Psychology Today* June, 1967, 1(2), 17–20ff.
13. Reik, T. *The Compulsion to Confess*. New York: Wiley Science Editions, 1966. Also see *The Unknown Murderer* and "Capital Punishment" reprinted in the same volume.
14. Inbau, F. E. and Reid, J. E. *Criminal Interrogation and Confessions*. Baltimore: Williams and Wilkins Co., 1962.
15. Zimbardo, The psychology of police confessions, p. 13.
16. *Ibid.*, p. 25.
17. *Miranda v. Arizona* 384 U.S. 436, p. 450.
18. Driver, E. D. Confessions and the social psychology of coercion. *Harvard Law Review* 1968, 82, p. 56.
19. Zimbardo, The psychology of police confessions, pp. 21–24.
20. Schachter, S. and Singer, J. E. Cognitive, social and physiological determinants of emotion. *Psychological Review* 1962, 69, 379–399.
21. Münsterberg, H. The mind of the juryman. Chapter V in *Psychology and Social Sanity*. New York: Doubleday, 1914, p. 184.
22. Forston, R. F. The decision-making process in the American civil jury: A comparative methodological investigation. Unpublished doctoral dissertation. University of Michigan, 1968. Cited in Kessler, *q.v.*
23. *Ballew v. Georgia*, 98 S.Ct. 1029, 1978.
24. Harris, R. Annals of Law: Trial by jury. *New Yorker* December 16, 1972, pp. 117–125. Cases cited include *Williams v. Florida* 399 U.S. 78; *Johnson v. Louisiana* 406 U.S. 356; *Apodaca et al. v. Oregon* 406 U.S. 404.
25. Padawer-Singer, A. M., Singer, A., and Singer, R. Voir dire by two lawyers: An essential safeguard. *Judicature* 1974, 57(9), 386–391.
26. Simon, R. J. Murder, juries, and the press. *Trans-Action* 1966, 3, 40–42.
27. Sue, S., Smith, R. E., and Caldwell, C. Effects of inadmissible evidence on the decisions of simulated jurors: A moral dilemma. *Journal of Applied Social Psychology* 1973, 3(4), 345–353; Kadish, M. R. and Kadish, S. H. The institutionalization of conflict: Jury acquittals. *Journal of Social Issues* 1971, 27, 199–217.
28. Verdicts linked to speech style. *The New York Times* December 14, 1975, Sect. 2, 88:1.
29. Sigall, H. and Ostrove, N. Beautiful but dangerous: Effects of offender attractiveness and

nature of the crime on juridic judgment. *Journal of Personality and Social Psychology* 1975, 31(3), 410–414.

30. Byrne, D. Attitudes and attraction. In L. Berkowitz (Ed.) *Advances in Experimental Social Psychology*, Vol. 4. New York: Academic Press, 1969.

31. Festinger, L. *A Theory of Cognitive Dissonance*. Stanford, Calif.: Stanford University Press, 1957; Brehm, J. W. and Cohen, A. R. *Explorations in Cognitive Dissonance*. New York: Wiley, 1962.

32. Heider, F. *The Psychology of Interpersonal Relations*. New York: Wiley, 1958; see also K. G. Shaver *An Introduction to Attribution Processes*. Cambridge, Mass.: Winthrop, 1975.

13
Post-Conviction Procedures

Following a conviction and before sentencing, the defense may move to set aside or modify the verdict on any of the following grounds:

1. There is something in the record of the trial which would require an appellate court to set aside or modify the judgment as a matter of law.

2. During the trial and outside the presence of the court there was some improper conduct on the part of a juror or some other person in relationship to a juror that may have prejudiced the defense, and such conduct was unknown to the defense prior to the verdict.

3. New evidence was discovered since the trial which (a) could not have been discovered by the defense with due diligence, and (b) which is such as to make it likely that, had it been available at the trial, the verdict would have been more favorable to the defendant.

If it grants such a motion, the court must take whatever action an appellate court would be required to take upon reversing or modifying a judgment on the same grounds. If it sets aside a verdict on the second ground, the court must order a new trial. If the motion is granted on the third ground, the court must either order a new trial or, with the consent of the people, reduce the verdict to an appropriate lesser offense.

The defendant must be personally present on sentencing except that, if he is convicted of a misdemeanor or less, the court has discretion to grant his motion to dispense with the requirement that he be personally present.

At the time of sentencing the prosecutor has the right to make a statement concerning anything relevant to sentencing. The counsel for the defendant has a right to follow with his recommendations. In addition, the defendant has a right to make a personal statement, and the court must ask him whether he desires to exercise this right. The court may, but is not required to, summarize the factors that it considers relevant to the determination of sentence and afford the defendant and his lawyer an opportunity to comment on such factors.

When a defendant is to be sentenced for any offense for which the arresting officer must have him fingerprinted, the court may not pronounce sentence until it has received a copy of the defendant's prior arrest record.

In the case of any felony conviction or a conviction for a misdemeanor for which the court intends to impose a sentence of probation or imprisonment in excess of 90 days, it may not impose sentence until it has ordered a pre-sentence investigation of the defendant and has received a written report of such investigation. Even where a pre-sentence investigation is not required, the court may order it performed before pronouncing sentence.

The scope of a pre-sentence investigation will include, but not be limited to, information concerning the circumstances of the crime, the defendant's criminal history, employment record, family status, economic status, education, personal habits, and such other topics as the court may direct be inquired into. If available, information relative to the defendant's mental and physical condition must also be included. In cases of felonies or Class A misdemeanors, any defendant under 21 years of age may be ordered to undergo a mental or physical examination. The report must contain an analysis of as much of the data collected as the collecting agency believes relevant to the determination of a sentence.

In addition to the pre-sentence investigation ordered by the court, the defendant has the right to submit his own pre-sentence memorandum setting forth any information which he thinks that the court should have in determining the sentence.

Upon receipt of the pre-sentence report the court has discretionary power to hold pre-sentencing conferences either in open court or in chambers. Their purpose is to resolve any difference between the pre-sentence report and the defendant's memorandum and to assist the court in setting the sentence. Such a conference may be with defense counsel alone or in the presence of the defendant, as the court elects. The district attorney has a right to be notified and to attend. Any person who has submitted information or who may be able to do so may be directed to attend. Some judges prefer to see each attorney or probation department staff member individually; some prefer a joint meeting. Often the defense attorney will be informed of the intended sentence at such a meeting, and, since the decision is being made at this stage, whatever arguments that defense counsel intends to make must be made at this time if they are to be effective. The arguments made in open court on sentencing are mainly *pro forma* and for the record. If the defendant is to be dealt with lightly by the court, counsel's arguments on the record will help to justify the court's favorable action. If the defendant is to be given a more severe sentence, the oral arguments are in the nature of a last ditch and usually fruitless attempt to get the court to change its mind and to give the defendant the feeling that his lawyer has vigorously advocated his cause. Since the defense attorney often knows in advance what sentence will be imposed, he can prepare his client for it.

If a defendant is to be sentenced as a second felony offender or as a second

violent felony offender, the people must file a statement with the court prior to sentencing alleging the dates and places of the earlier felony convictions. The defendant must be given a copy of this statement and the opportunity to deny any allegation made in it. Uncontroverted allegations are deemed admitted. If the allegations are not admitted, a hearing must be held to determine the issue and the burden of proof is on the people to establish beyond a reasonable doubt that the accused had, indeed, been previously convicted.

If the people seek to have the defendant sentenced as a persistent felony offender or a persistent violent felony offender, a hearing must be held in which the people must prove the existence of the prior felony convictions beyond a reasonable doubt with legally admissible evidence. Since sentencing as a persistent (non violent) felony offender is discretionary with the court (which may elect merely to sentence a defendant with two or more prior felony convictions as a second felony offender) the people may introduce evidence of the defendant's criminal history and character and of the circumstances of the present crime for the guidance of the court. This evidence need not be the kind that would be admissible at a trial. Here the people must only prove their case by a preponderance of the evidence, not beyond a reasonable doubt. In the case of a persistent violent felony offender the court has no such discretion; only legal evidence is permitted and proof must be beyond a reasonable doubt. The hearings described are before a judge without a jury. No previous conviction obtained as the result of violations of the accused's constitutional rights may be counted as a predicate felony conviction, nor may a conviction be counted if the defendant had been pardoned for the offense on the grounds of innocence.

Under the former Code of Criminal Procedure a judge could, if he chose, suspend either the imposition of a sentence or its execution. If he took the former course the defendant was not deemed to have been convicted of any crime as the sentence was a necessary part of the judgment of conviction. Today any disposition of the court, whether a conditional or an unconditional discharge, probation, or actual imprisonment, is deemed a conviction. The defendant, therefore, has a criminal record regardless of what happens at sentencing.

Once a sentence of imprisonment has begun, the court loses jurisdiction to change, suspend, or interrupt it.

AUTHORIZED SENTENCES

Following the pre-sentencing procedures the court has the power, subject to the restrictions contained in the Penal Law, to impose one of the following types of sentences:

Revocable sentences:
1. Probation
2. Conditional discharge
3. Intermittent imprisonment (e.g., weekend sentences, and so forth)

Nonrevocable sentences:
4. Unconditional discharge
5. Imprisonment
6. Fine (which may be combined with a sentence of probation, conditional discharge, or imprisonment)

The sentences labeled revocable are tentative in the sense that they may be modified or revoked by the court if the defendant violates a condition imposed in the sentence, but for all other purposes they are deemed a final judgment of conviction.

SENTENCE OF IMPRISONMENT

In an effort to assure the punishment of serious offenders, the New York State Legislature has taken away much of the court's discretion in imposing sentences on felony charges. It has set limits upon both the type of sentence authorized and the duration of imprisonment. Now every person convicted of a Class A felony, unless sentenced to death, must be sentenced to imprisonment. An exception is the individual convicted of a Class A III felony involving drugs who turns State's evidence. On the recommendation of the district attorney and with the concurrence of the administrative judge or the presiding judge of the Appellate Division, he may be given lifetime probation. Every person convicted of a Class B felony or specific serious Class C or D felonies must be sentenced to a term of imprisonment. A person convicted of a previous felony must also be sentenced to imprisonment. All sentences of imprisonment for felony convictions must be for an indeterminate term except that the court has discretion to impose a definite sentence of one year or less for first felony offenders convicted of a Class D or E felony. An indeterminate sentence means that a maximum and a minimum term is imposed. In cases of second felony offenders the minimum duration of the maximum term is increased as is the minimum term. If a defendant has been convicted of two or more prior felonies the court may elect either to sentence him as a second felony offender or as a persistent felony offender. If it takes the latter course it must set forth its reason for doing so in the record and may sentence the defendant for the term authorized for a Class A I felony.

In all cases of sentencing for Class A felonies, the court sets both the maximum and the minimum term in accordance with Table 13-1. For Class B, C

Table 13-1
Authorized Indeterminant Sentences

FELONY	FIRST OFFENDER			
	MAXIMUM TERM		MINIMUM TERM	
	NO MORE THAN	NO LESS THAN	NO MORE THAN	NO LESS THAN
Class A I	Life	Life	25 years	15 years
Class A II	Life	Life	8 years, 4 months	6 years
Class A III	Life	Life	8 years, 4 months	1 year
Class B	25 years	3 years (6 years)	1/3 maximum*	1 year (1/3 maximum)**
Class C	15 years	3 years (4-1/2 years)	1/3 maximum*	1 year (1/3 maximum)**
*** { Class D	7 years	3 years	1/3 maximum*	1 year (1/3 maximum)**
Class E	4 years	3 years	set by parole board	1 year

FELONY	SECOND OFFENDER			
	MAXIMUM TERM		MINIMUM TERM	
	NO MORE THAN	NO LESS THAN	NO MORE THAN	NO LESS THAN
Class A I	Life	Life	25 years	15 years
Class A II	Life	Life	8 years, 4 months	6 years
Class A III	Life	Life	8 years, 4 months	1 year
Class B	25 years	9 years (12)	1/2 maximum**	
Class C	15 years	6 years (8)	1/2 maximum**	
Class D	7 years	4 years (5)	1/2 maximum**	
Class E	4 years	3 years	1/2 maximum**	

* if set by court
** must be set by court
*** may be alternative fixed sentence of 1 year or less
( ) for "violent" felonies

and D felonies the court must specify the maximum term and may, if it chooses, set the minimum term. If it does so, it must set forth its reason for so doing in the record. Such a court-imposed minimum sentence may be no more than 1/3 the maximum term imposed. In no event may the minimum term of an indeterminate sentence be less than one year. If the court does not elect to set the minimum sentence, it is set by the State Board of Parole in accordance with the Correction Law. The Board of Parole must set the minimum term for a Class E felony.

As this book was going to press, the legislature modified the sentences to be imposed for certain listed "violent" felonies. Violent Class B, C, and D felonies all require mandatory prison terms with the minimum duration of the maximum term increased as shown in parentheses in Table 13-1. Minimum terms must be set by the court at 1/3 the maximum term imposed. Persistent violent felony offenders must be given a maximum term of life and a minimum term of 25–10 years for a Class B violent felony, 25–8 years for a Class C violent felony and 25–6 years for a Class D violent felony.

Persons imprisoned for misdemeanors or less must be sentenced to definite terms imposed by the court. The maximum term imposed for a Class A misdemeanor may not exceed one year. For a Class B misdemeanor the term may not exceed three months and for unclassified misdemeanors the term must be set in accordance with the statute creating the offense. Violations require definite sentences not to exceed 15 days. Definite sentences are served in county or regional correctional institutions; indeterminate sentences are served in state prisons under the control of the state Department of Corrections.

When two or more multiple sentences are imposed at the same time they either run concurrently or consecutively as the court shall direct. If two or more offenses are committed through a single act or if one offense was a material element of the other, the sentences must run concurrently.

If the court is silent about how the sentences are to run, indeterminate sentences will run concurrently with all other terms and definite sentences will run concurrently with any sentence imposed at the same time and consecutively with all others.

If sentences are concurrent, time served on any of the sentences is credited against the minimum period of all and the maximum terms merge and are satisfied by the completion or discharge of the longest.

If sentences are consecutive, minimum terms are added to arrive at an aggregate minimum term and maximum terms are added to arrive at an aggregate maximum term. If the aggregate term exceeds 20 years, it will be deemed to be 20 years unless the offenses included a Class B felony. In that case, the maximum aggregate term is limited to 30 years. In a similar fashion the aggregate minimum term is generally limited to 1/2 of such reduced aggregate maximum term. These possible aggregate maximum terms and the terms permitted for single offenses in Table 13-1 might profitably be compared with the recommendation of the President's Commission on Crime that no offense carry a sentence in excess of five years. This recommendation was rejected by the Nixon administration because of its concern for high standards of morality and its belief that criminals should be punished severely.

The minimum sentence is that part of the term that a convict must serve before he is eligible to be considered for parole. The maximum term is the longest period for which he may legally be incarcerated. Parole treatment is completely at the discretion of the State Department of Corrections and no convict has a right to be paroled. However, convicts are allowed "good time" credit for compliance with the rules of the institution in which they are confined. A certain amount of such credit is allowed each month up to a maximum of 1/3 of the maximum term of an indeterminate sentence and one-sixth the term of a definite sentence. A person serving one or more indeterminate sentences shall upon his request be conditionally released when his "good time" allowance equals the unserved portion of his maximum or aggregate maximum sentence. A person so released will be under the supervision of the parole board for the unexpired portion of his maximum term. Just like an inmate who is paroled, he is deemed to be serving his sentence on the outside under the supervision of the parole board. If such a person has violated the terms of his release and been declared delinquent, his sentence will stop running until his return to the institution.

A person serving a definite sentence of over 90 days may be conditionally released at his request if he has served over 60 days including credit received for jail time. Jail time is time incarcerated prior to conviction. It is credited against a definite sentence and the maximum term of an indeterminate sentence. This conditional release interrupts the sentence, and such person shall be under the supervision of the parole board for one year. Compliance with the conditions will satisfy the term; noncompliance will result in a return to jail for the remainder of the unserved portion of the term originally imposed.

"Good time" earned may be reduced for violation of institutional rules and is one of the most effective disciplinary holds most penal institutions have over convicts.

The service of any indeterminate sentence satisfies any prior definite sentence. For this reason convicts having both indeterminate and definite sentences imposed are immediately turned over to the custody of the state Department of Corrections to begin service of the indeterminate term.

FINES

Fines may be imposed for a felony if the defendant has gained money or property through the commission of the crime. The fine may be in any amount up to twice his gain from the offense. If it intends to impose a fine, the court must determine the amount of this gain. This is, in general, the amount of any money or property obtained less any amount returned to the victim or seized by law enforcement officials. In cases of misdemeanors or violations the court may also impose a fine of up to twice the defendant's gain or one up to $1000 for a Class A misdemeanor, $500 for a Class B misdemeanor, or $250 for a violation regardless of whether or not the crime resulted in a financial gain to the defendant. Unclassified misdemeanors may be fined in accordance with the statute that defines the offense.

INTERMITTENT IMPRISONMENT

A sentence of intermittent imprisonment is an innovation designed to be used in minor cases to prevent punishing the defendant's family by putting them on relief and to mitigate the damage to the defendant's employment status that usually accompanies a jail sentence.

The court may impose such a sentence upon a defendant other than a second or persistent felony offender if the present conviction is for a Class D or E felony or of any lesser charge provided that: (1) it is not imposing any other jail sentence at the same time, and (2) the defendant is not under any other sentence of imprisonment having more than 15 days to run.

The term may be for any length that could legally be imposed as a definite sentence. The court must specify what days or parts of days the defendant shall spend in confinement, and the overall term, measured in calendar not confinement time, can be for no longer than the court could have imposed for a definite jail sentence but without time off for good behavior.

This sentence can be modified if the defendant commits another crime during the course of the sentence, fails to report to the institution when required to, or violates a rule of the institution.

The court must give the defendant an opportunity to be heard before it modifies the sentence. The court may change the times of confinement, increase or decrease the periods thereof, or revoke the sentence and have the defendant confined for its term under a definite sentence.

PROBATION AND CONDITIONAL DISCHARGE

In some cases the court is not required to impose some term of imprisonment. If, after considering the nature and circumstances of the crime and the history and character of the defendant, it finds: (1) that imprisonment of the defendant is not necessary to protect the public, (2) that the defendant is in need of the kind of guidance or training that can be provided through probation supervision, and (3) that such a sentence is consistent with the requirements of justice, the defendant may be sentenced to a term of probation. Unless terminated sooner, the term of probation for a Class A III felony shall be life and for any other felony shall be five years. For a Class A misdemeanor a term of three years is authorized, and one year is prescribed for a Class B misdemeanor. Unclassified misdemeanors that carry sentences of over three months may be punished by probation periods of up to three years. Those carrying lesser sentences may be dealt with by probation of up to one year.

If the defendant in a Class B misdemeanor (or in an unclassified one with a maximum sentence of less than three months) is found to be a narcotics addict, he may be placed on probation for up to three years. This situation is reminiscent of the old New York Penal Law. It prescribed a maximum sentence of one year for a misdemeanor in general; but if the defendant was found to be "reformable," he was eligible for a sentence of up to three years. That law was inspired by some foggy thinking on the part of the "social scientists" who urged it, and who evidently failed to realize that nobody is given any treatment in a penal institution. They apparently believed that if a convict was reformable, the system should be given enough time to do an effective job on him! This statute led to the ludicrous spectacle of a defense lawyer arguing in court at sentencing that his client was a worthless bum totally beyond redemption and so not subject to the longer sentence. It also led to one sentence of three years, imposed by a judge who excoriated the defendant, being set aside as illegal when the appellate court held that the record clearly showed that the judge considered the defendant beyond rehabilitation, and hence the sentence should have been a maximum of one year.

A sentence of probation is different from parole, which is granted by the state Parole Board after a convict has served his minimum sentence. Unlike parole, probation is imposed by a court on sentencing.

If, in a case which would be suitable for a sentence of probation, the court finds that the defendant is in no need of supervision by the department of probation, it may impose a sentence of conditional discharge instead of probation. In this case the defendant is not placed under the supervision of a probation officer. The periods for a conditional discharge are three years for a felony and one year for a misdemeanor.

In cases of probation or conditional discharge the court will impose conditions with which the defendant must comply, and which it may modify from time to time. If such conditions are violated, the probation or conditional discharge may be revoked and a prison term imposed at any time prior to the termination of the revocable sentence. The conditions that the court may impose are those that, in its discretion, it deems necessary to ensure that the defendant will lead a law-abiding life. They may include, but are not limited to, those requiring that the defendant:

1. Avoid vicious or injurious habits.
2. Refrain from frequenting unlawful or disreputable places or consorting with disreputable persons.

3. Work faithfully at some suitable employment, or pursue a course of academic or vocational study.
4. Undergo available medical or psychiatric treatment.
5. Support his dependents and meet his family responsibilities.
6. Make restitution of the gain from his offense, or compensate the victim for the damages that it caused in a manner which he can afford (if the court requires this it must specify the amounts to be repaid and the manner of repayment).
7. If under 21, live, attend school, or attend certain residential or nonresidential youth facilities, or contribute to his own support, as directed by the court.
8. Post a bond for the faithful performance of any conditions imposed.

If the defendant is placed under probation supervision, the court shall require him to:

1. Report regularly to his probation officer, and permit the officer to visit him in his place of abode or elsewhere.
2. Remain within the jurisdiction of the court unless granted permission to leave by the court or by the probation officer.
3. Answer all reasonable inquiries by his probation officer, and notify him of any change in address or employment.

UNCONDITIONAL DISCHARGE

If a case meets all the requirements for a court to authorize a sentence of conditional discharge, and the court believes that no useful purpose would be served by imposing conditions on the defendant's release, it may impose a sentence of unconditional discharge. This sentence is not revocable and is analogous to the former practice of suspending a criminal sentence. The only difference is that an unconditional discharge is deemed a final judgment of conviction, i.e., the defendant has a record of conviction.

APPEALS

The rules and procedures governing appeals are extremely complex, and only the general principles of criminal appeals will be outlined here. There are four Judicial Departments in the State of New York. Each department contains an Appellate Division of the Supreme Court, which hears both civil and criminal appeals from the County and Supreme Courts as well as other lower courts. The Appellate Division is comprised of at least five Justices. Five are necessary for a quorum, and three for a decision. The appellate court above the Appellate Division is the highest court in the state and is called the Court of Appeals. It is comprised of seven Judges. Five are needed for a quorum, and four for a decision.

As a matter of public policy it is not deemed desirable for criminal cases to be tied up in appeal procedures for prolonged periods of time. Hence a maximum of two appeals is allowed in a criminal case. Wherever the first appeal is heard, the second appeal, if any, is always to the Court of Appeals. The only time that the Court of Appeals is the first court appealed to is when the case involves the death penalty. All other courts of appellate criminal jurisdiction are referred to as intermediate appellate courts.

An appeal from a judgment, sentence, or final order of the Supreme Court is always taken to the appropriate Appellate Division. An appeal from the County Court is usually to the Appellate Division, except that in certain cases involving less than felonies, it may be heard in an appellate term of the Supreme Court. In most cases appeals from a local criminal court outside of New York City are taken to the County Court of the county involved. This is done unless the Appellate Division directs that such appeals be heard in an appellate term of the Supreme Court. In New York City, appeals from the criminal court are taken to the Appellate Division.

Appeals may be taken in some cases as a matter of right; in other cases they require permission. Appeals involving a death sentence are taken to the Court of Appeals by either party as a matter of right. Appeals to the Court of Appeals from an adverse or partially adverse order of an intermediate appellate court require permission from either a judge of the Court of Appeals or a judge or justice of the intermediate appellate court whose order is being appealed. An appeal to the Court of Appeals may be taken only if the intermediate appellate court expressly states that its reversal or modification is based on the law alone, or if the petitioner contends that the corrective action taken or ordered by the intermediate appellate court is illegal.

Except in death cases, going directly to the Court of Appeals appealing a judgment, sentence, or order does not automatically stay its execution unless either the trial judge or one of the appellate judges so orders.

The defendant may appeal to an intermediate appellate court as a matter of right from a judgment of conviction, other than one including a sentence of death; or a sentence, other than one of death; or an order setting aside a sentence granted upon motion of the people.

The defendant may appeal to an intermediate appellate court by permission from an order denying a motion to set aside or vacate a judgment, other than one including a sentence of death, or the denial of a motion to set aside a sentence other than death.

The people may appeal to an intermediate appellate court as a matter of right:

1. From an order dismissing an accusatory instrument or a count thereof.
2. From a trial order of dismissal (if no subsequent trial is needed).
3. From an order setting aside a verdict.
4. From a sentence other than one of death.
5. From an order setting aside a sentence of death.
6. From an order denying a motion by the people to set aside a sentence other than death.
7. From an order suppressing evidence at the trial.

It should be noted from the foregoing that the kind of court orders which appellate courts will review are not intermediate orders, but final orders in the sense that they finally dispose of the matter in question.

The scope of the review in an intermediate appellate court may include the consideration and determination of any issue of fact or law involving an error or defect in the criminal trial that may have adversely affected the appellant (party appealing). Based on its determination, the appellate court will either affirm or modify the lower court judgment, sentence, or order appealed. It may partially affirm and partially reverse a judgment. For instance, if the reviewing court finds there was not sufficient legal evidence presented at the trial to support a conviction on one of the charges of which the defendant was convicted, but there was enough evidence to support the other, it may reverse the conviction on the first and sustain it on the second. If the evidence would not support a conviction for the crime of which the jury found the defendant guilty but would support a conviction on a lesser count, the court may change the conviction to one for the lesser count. It is customary for a court reversing a judgment or part of one to remand the case to the trial court for proceedings necessary to conform with the higher court's ruling. If the higher court set aside a conviction on some of the counts charged, or reduced the grade of the offense of which the defendant was convicted, the trial court must re-sentence him accordingly. If a judgment of conviction is set aside because of some error committed during the course of the trial, the case will be remanded to the trial court for a retrial unless this cannot legally be done. In a reversal on the grounds of double jeopardy or the unconstitutionality of the law defining the offenses charged, no new trial may be held. In such a case the appellate court will order the case dismissed. The retrial of a defendant who has successfully appealed a conviction is not a violation of his constitutional protection against double jeopardy, as he is deemed to have waived this protection by filing an appeal. In the days when there was not so much uncertainty about the constitutionality of any kind of death penalty as there is now, defense attorneys appealing Murder 1 convictions (in which the defendant received a life sentence in lieu of death) made it a point in order to protect themselves from a claim of malpractice, to have the defendant sign a statement to the effect that he understood that if the appeal were successful, he could be retried, and, if he were convicted again, the death penalty could be imposed.

A reversal or modification of a judgment by an intermediate appellate court may now be made based upon the law, the facts, or the interests of justice. This is considerably more leeway than appellate courts had in the past when they were restricted in their decisions to questions of law.

The Court of Appeals can base its decision on any of the grounds available to an intermediate appellate court except that it may not reverse a death sentence on the grounds that it is too harsh "in the interests of justice." It is no longer restricted to deciding solely on issues of law, nor is it limited in its scope of review to legal questions passed on by the intermediate appellate court.

The procedures necessary to initiate and perfect an appeal are beyond the scope of this book, but they include the filing of a number of copies of the record of the trial court. This is the word-for-word transcript of everything that was said during the trial. The court recorder charges a per-page fee for this transcript. The expense of this transcript prevents some defendants with worthy cases from appealing. In fact, it transforms a trial court into a court of last resort for them. It is interesting that in an era of tape recording and electronic transcription devices, which are far more accurate than the best of court stenographers, these devices have not yet found their way into the courts, and that indeed such introduction has encountered considerable opposition. It would seem that a videotape record could provide an appellate court with a far more accurate account of what the court's instructions actually conveyed to a jury than an unduly expensive written transcript of the words without a record of the tone or inflection with which they were uttered or the concurrent facial expressions or gestures.

14
Imprisonment

Historically, imprisonment has been a means of punishing criminals or isolating them from society. The problem is that, while it retains these purposes to the present day, psychologists and other social scientists with limited or no experience with the criminal justice system or penal institutions persist in thinking of it as capable of reforming inmates or of changing their behavior patterns to conform with society's requirements.

As a matter of fact, the prison system in the United States was regarded as a humane innovation in the treatment of criminals when it was first introduced. During colonial times there were no prisons to house long-term convicts. Indeed, the Declaration of Independence refers to liberty as an inalienable right. Defendants awaiting trial were held for short periods in local jails. Upon conviction they were either executed, or whipped, pilloried, or branded, and released. When the Constitution prohibited placing a defendant twice in jeopardy of "life or limb," the words were intended to be taken literally. The interpretation of the Constitution has, as envisioned, changed with the times so that today any attempt to reinstate such forms of corporal punishment would probably be held unconstitutional on the grounds that it is "cruel and unusual." It appears to the authors that the present practice of confining convicts for long periods of time, often out of all proportion to the gravity of their offenses, and under conditions which destroy feelings of self-respect and human dignity, is even more cruel and inhuman. More important, from the point of view of society, it is also likely to be counter-productive. Imprisonment generates so much hostility in inmates and so strong a sense of being wronged that prisons probably *cause* rather than prevent recidivism. It is a rare defendant in a criminal court who does not have a previous arrest record testifying to the failure of the system to reduce crime.

When prisons were introduced as a method of dealing with convicted criminals, many of them functioned on the theory that people were sent to prison *for* punishment rather than *as* punishment. Most prison sentences included such terms as "to be confined at hard labor," and prisoners were, and often still are, required to work long hours at such physically exhausting tasks as road construction. In some states convicts were kept in chains while working and chained to each other at other times. Prison officials have always been primarily concerned with custodial control and preventing escapes.

At the prison at Auburn, New York, the silent system was introduced in 1821 and was widely copied by other institutions. Prisoners were forbidden to talk to each other even at meals. This rule had its roots in the Quaker idea that if he were required to be silent, the prisoner would have to think about his misdeeds and repent them. Further, if prisoners could not communicate with each other, there was less danger of escape plots being hatched. In many cases prisoners were confined in small cells except for an hour or two per day, with no facilities for exercise and nothing to do. Even today, because the walls of the older prisons were made of solid concrete without plumbing pipes (to preclude escapes and communication), prisoners may be locked in cells without toilet facilities other than a slop bucket.

Convicts are subject to having their persons and their cells searched at the whim of prison officials for contraband which may range from weapons or drugs to innocuous items that the prison officials have arbitrarily decided that prisoners may not have. These searches may include rectal and vaginal searches. Having been convicted of a crime, the inmate has no Fourth Amendment protection against such warrantless searches. Therefore, they need not be based on probable cause. They may result merely from the prison administration's constant concern about custodial security or even from the whim of a guard.

The American Civil Liberties Union publishes paperback books listing the rights of various classes of people such as women, teachers, mental patients, and so on. The slimmest volume among them deals with the rights of prisoners.[1] Even what the reader might believe to be basic human rights, like the right to medical care or to receive mail, have not been enunciated by the courts. Following a scandal in the Arkansas prison system, prisoners brought an action in the Federal District Court for the Eastern District of Arkansas contending that the conditions in the prison were unconstitutional and constituted "cruel and unusual punishment."[2] The contention was also made that the inmates were, in fact, slaves in violation of the Constitution. While the court agreed that the conditions in the prison amounted to cruel and unusual punishment and ordered some changes made, its statements concerning the allegation of slavery are more interesting. It held that even if an inmate were a slave, that would not violate the Constitution, as the proscription against slavery in the Thirteenth Amendment specifically excepts the case in which it is imposed as punishment for a crime. The court further found that there was a technical distinction between a slave and a convict, in that the state did not contend that it owned the body of a convict. This technical distinction is an example of a distinction without a difference. The real status of a convict is that he is a *de facto* slave with few, if any, human rights available to him. In some institutions he may be treated fairly well; in others the conditions may resemble a concentration camp. Whatever treatment the convict receives is determined primarily by the wishes of his master, the state Correctional Department.

There are reasons other than the excessive sentences and the harsh conditions of confinement that would prevent any reasonable person with or without training in psychology from expecting any reform in behavior patterns to result from a term of imprisonment.

Most prisons are run, in a real sense, more by the inmates than by the staff. Prison budgets have the lowest priority in the legislatures (inmates do not vote). Hence, prisons cannot afford to hire adequately trained personnel or, for that matter, enough guards to maintain proper security.[3] In the Arkansas case, the institution was literally guarded by armed inmate trustees! Since the administration cannot adequately protect an inmate, his physical safety, indeed his life, may depend on his adherence to a set of antisocial mores. Prisoners are often placed in a position where they are helpless to protect themselves from assaults, homosexual attacks, or other crimes, often far worse than those crimes of which they were convicted. Not infrequently, these crimes are committed by agents of the state, as when insufficient funds require the hiring of inadequately trained custodial personnel or persons who may be sadistic, emotionally ill, or unusually aggressive. The random killing of Attica inmates by state troopers assaulting the facility is an example of the state being a party to such criminal activity by failing to control its agents adequately. It is not being suggested that most, or even a sizable minority, of prison guards fall into this category. Most are probably decent people trying to do their jobs under very trying conditions.[4]

Zimbardo's famous study of a mock prison, which is discussed below, while replete with methodological and ethical difficulties, nevertheless is suggestive of how college students, randomly assigned to the role of inmate or guard, rapidly begin to act and think appropriately to the assigned role. Thus, students assigned to the role of guards began to think of the inmates as nonhuman and displayed a variety of sadistic behaviors towards them. Zimbardo's student guards were not in constant fear for their lives or safety as most actual prison guards are. If they had been, this effect might have been even more pronounced. An important point is that both inmates and guards (correction officer is their euphemistic title these days) are locked up. While the officer may leave at the end of the shift, perhaps half of his waking life is spent behind bars, steel doors, and high walls.[5]

Another destructive aspect of prison life is the enforcement of the institution's disciplinary rules. The problem faced by most penal institutions in enforcing discipline is that having taken away a convict's liberty, self-respect, and human dignity, there is little else one can do to punish him for breaking a rule. The usual procedure, in addition to taking away any good time credits or privileges, such as visitation rights or mail, is to impose solitary confinement on restricted rations in "the hole" or, more euphemistically, "administrative confinement." Solitary time is often out of all proportion to the seriousness of the offense charged. If the convict has committed a crime in prison, he may, of course, be criminally prosecuted for it; but if the rule infraction is less than a crime, his guilt is determined and his punishment administered by the prison authorities. It is interesting to contrast a disciplinary hearing in a prison with the trial of a criminal charge. The defendant in such a hearing has no rights at all. He cannot call witnesses in his behalf or cross-examine his accusers. He need not be proven guilty beyond a reasonable doubt. Indeed, the presumption is not of innocence but of guilt, as the prisoner will have been charged by a guard, and the administration will always take the guard's word over the convict's because it fears that any other policy would weaken the control of the guards over the prisoners. When corporal punishment occurs in prison administration, it is usually unofficial or *sub rosa*. Even if a convict has a clear-cut right that the courts will enforce, such right is often meaningless, as convicts usually have no access to the legal assistance necessary to vindicate such right effectively.

Certain public officials like judges and the attorney general have the right to inspect prisons and the conditions within them. Most of them fail to exercise this right, however, except in the most *pro forma* manner on due notice to the institution. The public, including convicts' families and counsel and the press, are generally either excluded entirely or admitted under very controlled circumstances. Unless and until these institutions are open to public scrutiny, it is not realistic to expect much improvement in the conditions under which their inhabitants must live.

In addition to punishing the defendant, a prison term also punishes his family although they have not been convicted of any offense. They are automatically deprived of a breadwinner and generally must seek public assistance. Children are deprived of a parent during their formative years, and marriages are subjected to severe stresses that destroy many of them. A sentence to a state prison, which may be hundreds of miles from the defendant's community, may make it impossible for his family to visit even when it is permitted. The convict or his spouse may be unwilling to have the children visit in the prison environment, where, in most instances, they have to talk to the inmate through screening or view him through a glass wall while talking by telephone. This arrangement is designed to prevent the smuggling of contraband into the institution. Some prisons are beginning to experiment with contact visits during which convicts are permitted to embrace or kiss family members, but even here guards may be present to prevent privacy in communication. To prevent the smuggling of contraband, visitors may be subjected to degrading search procedures. It is interesting to note that when attorneys visit clients in jail, the client is usually searched before and after the visit rather than the attorney.

When prison reformers and social scientists began to think about prisons as agencies of reform rather than as facilities for the administration of punishment, it was suggested that one of the causes of crime was the criminal's lack of marketable skills by which he could earn an honest living. This led to the development of vocational training or educational programs within prisons. The Nassau County (New York) Jail, for example, has a high school program that enables inmates to complete their high school education. A growing number of institutions have study-release programs which enable trusted prisoners to pursue college studies on campus, returning to the prison in the evening. For the most part, however, such training programs are inadequately funded. Convicts are generally being trained in trades or on machines that were out of date 20 years ago, and there are very few positions available in private industry for people skilled in the manufacture of automobile license plates.

A criminal record, in and of itself, makes it more difficult for an ex-convict to secure an honest job. How many potential employers would hire a cashier who had been convicted of larceny? If the potential job requires bonding by a surety company, a driver's license, or government security clearance, an ex-offender's record will bar him from it outright.

Another problem associated with a conviction for a felony is the loss of certain civil rights such as the right to vote. While there are procedures available to secure the restoration of such rights after a period of good conduct, the loss of these rights really serves no useful purpose. It merely harasses an ex-convict who has served his sentence, and alienates him further from the community.

A former professor of one of the authors was a high-ranking official in a state Department of Corrections. He once said that one of the most frustrating problems in prison administration is to secure inmates' release before they begin to deteriorate. Often this is impossible because other states have filed hold notices on the inmates, whom they will seek to extradite upon their release from prison.

Severe mental deterioration may result from the conditions of prison life, particularly in the more sensitive, younger, or casual offender. All prisoners undergo personality changes as a result of their incarceration. This phenomenon is usually called "prisonization" by criminologists.[6] It is a helpless, resigned acceptance of a subhuman role. It might better be called a form of regression, as prison life offers the inmate no opportunity to make the simplest decision for himself. With a few recent exceptions, he has no choice as to how he will dress or when and what he will eat. This regimentation has the effect of reducing him to a state of childlike dependency on the prison officials.

In the light of such effects, the psychologically interesting question is not why so many ex-convicts become recidivists, but how, in view of this type of debilitating treatment, any of them manage to survive in the outside world following release. Another interesting question is, why, in view of its manifest failure, do we retain the prison system?

We believe there are several reasons for this anomaly. First, prisons are a major source of jobs and patronage in most prison communities, and there are vested interests in preserving them.[7] Pharmaceutical companies test numerous compounds on prison "volunteers" before applying to the Food and Drug Administration for permission to market new products. Armies of probation and parole personnel help to maintain themselves and the system via their activities with ex-inmates and probationers.

Second, the public is often frightened by newspaper stories concerning crime waves and violence in the streets, and has been taught by the movies and the press that the way to stop crime is to arrest criminals and put them in prison, where they will "pay their debt to society." Many so-called adults have never progressed beyond this childlike mode of thought.

Perhaps the most important reason for maintaining prisons is that most voters are abysmally ignorant of both the operation of prisons and the results produced by them. Most really could not care less about the matter. That prisons are training schools for crime and that most inmates "graduate" so that they return home more skilled criminals does not seem to penetrate the public consciousness.

Thus prisons are maintained while breeding more crime and more skilled crime. In fact, one expert views the amount of violence that occurs nowadays in prisons as unprecedented.[8] That many of those involved in violent incidents in prison had had no record of violent behavior when free, suggests that prisons do more than *house* violence; they *create* it, while simultaneously sharpening the criminal skills of their inhabitants.

One of the effects of prison violence has been the emergence of self-protective gangs of inmates. They are generally organized, says Sommer, along racial lines. These gangs, which are blamed by authorities for much of the violence in prisons, do not only offer protection to their members; they also impose obligations upon them. Initiation rites, sexual services, thefts, and other behaviors that run counter to the prison program are organized by these gangs.

For economic, social, historical, and other reasons, not everyone who is convicted of a crime goes to prison. Similarly, not everyone who is incarcerated goes to the same sort of prison. If the crime in question was tax evasion, or some such "respectable" offense, or if the perpetrator had no history of violence or prior arrests, and is a white middle-class person with firm roots in the community, he is unlikely to be incarcerated in a maximum security institution. He may go to a prison where he will have considerable freedom to see visitors, palatable, even good, food, and even fine recreational facilities. If, on the other hand, the crime was a burglary or an assault, and if the offender has previously been arrested, and if he is poor, urban, and nonwhite, he is likely to be placed in a maximum security prison. One result of this pattern is that many such prisons have far fewer white than nonwhite inmates and they are guarded by a white, rural staff.

Sommer cites the Attica statistics for 1971: "70 per cent black and brown inmates . . . 100 per cent white staff."[9] He adds that the number of black and Hispanic staff has increased in New York to nearly 15%, while the proportion of black and Hispanic inmates is about 75%.

For identical crimes, blacks tend to receive longer sentences than whites, a fact that accounts in part for the high probability that a given inmate will be black.

Sommer alleges that prison staff may cause racial conflicts between prisoners in an effort to maintain control by means of a "divide and conquer" approach.

In short, some of the violence so prevalent in prisons is attributed to racial antagonisms which are fanned by the prison situation itself, by the vulnerability and alienation it fosters, and by the prison staff, who expect it and help to create conditions that promote it although they may not do so intentionally.

The violence can be understood in quite different terms, however. The deprivations of the prison inmate are many, pervasive, and constant. He has no privacy unless he is in solitary confinement. He is constantly vulnerable to abuse, harm, or insult from guards and fellow inmates. He must restrain himself, apologizing if he brushes accidentally against another inmate (particularly if his race is different). He must never respond to a guard's provocation. He has no territory that he can call his own or on which he can feel safe. He has no power except as it relates to physical force or allies. If he appears to be gaining undue power, or threatens somehow to use it in a manner unacceptable to the authorities, he may expect a prompt transfer to a different institution.

Skelton describes three phases that he, as a prison psychiatrist, has been able to observe in the development of coping mechanisms of prison inmates. The first phase includes active coping. The new inmate is alert to, and may seek from older or more experienced inmates, information about what he may expect in terms of treatment by officials, food, medical care, and living conditions. He may try to suppress feelings of fear and anxiety and fantasize a relationship with someone outside. This may involve lengthy correspondence, even with a total stranger who has altruistically answered a request for mail that appeared in a college newspaper. For the inmate this may become a very important relationship, perhaps his only contact with the outside world, and, as release nears, the contrast between reality and the idealized relationship may create new difficulties for the inmate.

While the early phase involves a need to maintain relationships with family and friends and to hold onto some identity outside the walls, in fact, a frequent occurrence is the dissolution of friendships and marriages. Feelings of abandonment, worthlessness, and loneliness are present in the best of circumstances for the prisoner. If a letter is not received, these feelings are strengthened. If a marriage ends, despair may be a consequence.

In this early stage, says Skelton, the inmate may look to authority for support—i.e., to the corrections officer. He may seek a guard's friendship. He may even turn informer (a role that brings with it the contempt of the officer and danger from other inmates).

Fantasies about, or attempts to, escape may assist one to cope, but escape attempts may also be disguised attempts at suicide. Some prisoners request solitary confinement or segregation from others in order to control the strong urges to attempt escape.

In general, the initial phase (which, typically, lasts from 1½ to 2 years) is that in which the prisoner comes to accept the fact of his incarceration. Longer sentences bring with them more severe problems of adaptation, deeper depression, and extended attempts to secure a legal release through endless writs and appeals. Indeterminate sentences may induce the inmate to join various rehabilitative or therapeutic programs in an effort to convince the authorities of his contrition, growth, and suitability for release. When release is denied, the results may be anger, depression, and self-defeating behavior.

Following the initial phase in which he is preoccupied with winning release and maintaining ties with home, the inmate enters a second phase in which his concerns turn more to the prison community.

In most prisons, inmates, particularly untested newcomers, are in constant fear. They may be harassed by others, threatened, stared at, assaulted, or raped. Increasingly, assaults in prisons involve the use of weapons, usually knives fashioned from bedsprings or eating utensils. Fear for one's physical safety combined with fear of the unknown, and sexual demands, may compel the prisoner to adopt a role with which to present himself to his peers and keepers.

Some assume the role of the incorrigible: the fighter, the tough guy. In part this is a way of defending oneself against assault, homosexual anxiety, feelings of inadequacy or resentment. But it has self-evident drawbacks. Fights, challenges, and arrogance reduce one's chances for parole and lead to confrontations with other "hard rocks." Further, once such a reputation is acquired, it becomes difficult to convince a parole board or psychologist that one has changed to a more acceptable mode of behavior.

Other inmates, says Skelton, assume the role of chump. These men purchase survival at the cost of their self-esteem. They become the errand boys for others, the sources of food or cigarettes, which they must give up on demand.

Homosexuality may also be a mode of gaining protection, but it is often accompanied by anxiety and, if the partner is released or loses interest, may lead to depression.

One of the most oppressive aspects of prison life is the lack of privacy, of the opportunity to be alone, even for a few moments. Some inmates seek jobs of relatively low status that permit them to work alone. Others "tune out" their peers as a means of achieving psychological privacy.

Some inmates, more likely those to whom incarceration is not a new experience, deliberately "cause trouble" in the early weeks or months of their terms, and, as their parole hearings near, abruptly change their behavior to make it appear that they have learned their lessons. The premise is that this pattern is more highly regarded by the parole board than a record which shows no change or improvement.

The prison experience produces anger and boredom as well as the fear, shame, and embarrassment that may come with sentencing. Boredom may lead to harassment of others or to gambling. Guilt, particularly for crimes against people, may give way to anger rather than be expressed directly. Depression and feelings of helplessness are not likely to be voiced but may lead to physical complaints. Anger is most often displaced against weaker inmates. It may produce insomnia, however, since the aggressive inmate must remain on constant combat alert. Anger, like other feelings, is rarely expressed verbally by prisoners.

Some inmates have been observed to engage in compulsive behaviors, even compulsive fighting, as a way of distracting themselves from their anxiety.

Since the vast majority of prisoners are ultimately released to return to their homes and neighborhoods, there comes to most prisoners a period of preparation for release. This is the third, or terminal, phase described by Skelton.

Release from prison does not come with fanfare or praise. The fortunate inmate may be greeted by family and friends, but they have not shared his experience and do not understand his fears. Anticipating this, and having

heard from peers of their own failure to remain free, the inmate in this terminal phase may feel increasingly helpless as the time of his release approaches
and may, in fact, develop a syndrome that includes anorexia (loss of appetite),
insomnia, headaches, anxiety, and hypochondriasis. This reaction has been
found to be especially common among those who will be unsupervised after
their release.

Release may also confront the ex-inmate with conflicts about his sexuality.
If he was active in a homosexual relationship while incarcerated, he may feel
guilt or shame about it to a degree that interferes with his resumption of
heterosexual relationships, or he may feel so attached to his prison sex partner
that he elects not to resume a heterosexual orientation.

In short, the time just before release may be a period of considerable stress
for the prisoner.

A social psychological variable that has been studied in connection with
incarceration sheds additional light on these phases of adjustment to prison
life. Levenson administered questionnaires to 145 inmates of a large state
prison to measure the degree to which they attribute events of their lives to
their own efforts or abilities, to chance, or to powerful other people. She
found that inmates who had been imprisoned five years or more believed
themselves to be controlled by powerful others more than those who had
served six months or less. That it was the prison experience which brought
this about is suggested by additional analyses of her data. Whatever the
original sentence, men who had served more than half of their term scored
higher on the Powerful Others scale than men who had served less than 10%
of their sentences. Among convicts who had served equal amounts of time
in prison, those who had been in solitary confinement were more likely to
score high on the scale.

Who the "powerful others" were is not measured by Levenson's scale. They
may have been guards, judges, or inmate "bosses." But, to the extent that one
feels governed by others, one may be expected to be, at best, ambivalent about
release which will throw one upon his own resources and require that he make
his own decisions.

Prisons need not be designed in ways that produce the effects just described,
although the tradition in the United States suggests that most will continue
to have these effects. Sweden, in contrast, has a very different system, in which
the prisoner (who is referred to as the "client") is likely to be incarcerated for
no more than four months and, in many cases, with fewer than 100 fellow
clients in an open institution near his home. The escape rate is high, and the
escapee is likely to be returned to a closed institution for a short time. Whether
recidivism is lower is unclear. What is clear is that the cost to the government
is considerably less when the sentence is short than when it is long, and that

most clients are given help prior to release and are permitted to remain in close contact with family and friends throughout the period of incarceration. Feelings of abandonment and hopelessness and homosexuality are quite uncommon. Swedish prisoners may be granted vacation periods in a civilian-like community. They may participate in work programs or schooling and, in some institutions, have what amounts to a therapeutic community.[10] It should, of course, be noted that Swedish prisons are not disproportionately inhabited by members of a visible ethnic minority.

We alluded to the lack of privacy of the prison inmate. A recent study indicates that crowding in prisons is increasing in 44 states, and that prisons are already overcrowded in 40 of them.[11] Prisoners are sleeping in corridors and basements for want of cell space. Some writers argue that reformers' efforts to end prison construction will leave those whom they intend to help worse off than they are at present.

Sommer points to the cultural and individual differences which determine the amount of space that an inmate requires and adds that those who design prisons have shown little concern for these differences. There are some minimal standards in some jurisdictions, however. Prisons run by the U.S. Army require 55 to 72 square feet per inmate. Juvenile dormitories in California require only 50 square feet (not including the toilet). Maximum security institutions tend to be overcrowded, while minimum security prisons often have room to spare.[12]

Most prisons offer little that is stimulating. They are drab, uninteresting places, isolated from people and communities and, to the extent that interpersonal trust is lacking (as is generally the case in prisons), from sustaining relationships with fellow inmates. Inmates who are in isolation or who remain locked in their cells for lengthy periods find themselves unable to concentrate or read (if, indeed, they know how to read). Some report enhanced sensitivity to noise and odors.[13]

The third matter discussed by Sommer is privacy. Some prisons have tried to increase privacy by using small dining rooms and cell blocks and by giving some privileged inmates keys to their own cells or lockers. Whether society is willing to bear the cost of these innovations on a large scale is questionable. Yet, as Sommer points out, privacy is not a luxury in prison any more than it is at home. Assault, homosexual abuse, exploitation of the weak by the strong are all less likely where one has some measure of privacy, particularly where one cannot freely leave the situation and go off by himself.

Sommer quotes an essay by one San Quentin inmate who likens the arrival of a new cell mate to the arrival of the spouse in a parentally arranged marriage. One has never seen the person before but must share his life in its most intimate details with the other from then on.[14]

THE STANFORD PRISON EXPERIMENT

Prisons, prisoners, and ex-prisoners are very difficult to study psychologically, even for those working within the walls. Penal institutions have for many years been entities unto themselves, surrounded not only by walls and towers, but by regulations as to who may enter, for what purpose, for how long, and so on.

In more recent times some institutions, most commonly jails or detention facilities, have been opened to outsiders who come in to teach classes, counsel, or offer some contact with the outside world. The Fortune Society, an organization of ex-offenders, has, with difficulty, won the right to enter some institutions to counsel inmates about to be released, to help them find jobs, and to be available to them during the first trying weeks after release. This Society has been one of the more effective means of publicizing the evils of prison life.[15]

Because of the secrecy and security that surround prisons, virtually no research has been conducted within prisons on their effects on the incarcerated. Further, any such research would be very difficult to interpret, since prison populations are not random samples of the general public or even of the criminal public, and the particular cause of any observed effect would be impossible to distinguish amid the myriad facets of prison life.

One way to approximate such a study might be to fashion a mock prison, populate it with randomly selected volunteers, and subject them to facsimiles of some of the routines and less frightening aspects of prison life. Zimbardo and his students did just this in a well-known study of the "Stanford County Jail."

More than 75 young men answered an advertisement placed in campus and city newspapers offering $15 per day for participation in a "psychological study of prison life." The applicants were given a series of psychological tests, and from among them 21 were selected who were middle-class, of college age, Caucasian (with one Oriental exception), law-abiding, healthy, emotionally mature, and stable. They were warned that there would be little privacy, that other civil rights might be violated, and that they could anticipate some degree of harassment during the two weeks that they were to be involved in the study. All agreed to these conditions.

The prison in which they were to be confined was built in the basement of the Stanford University psychology building. A corridor was converted into a "yard," lab rooms were made into cells and offices into guards' quarters. A closet became "the hole" in which inmates who caused disciplinary problems would be confined.

Video and audio tape facilities made possible the recording of what was to occur.

The 21 participants were randomly assigned to the role of prisoner or the role of guard by a flip of a coin. No differences were found between the two groups on any of the psychological tests that they had previously taken.

The guards were given a brief orientation during which they were instructed to maintain order but were told little more. The prisoners, who had been asked to remain at home on Sunday, August 15, were arrested at their homes by members of the Palo Alto City Police Department (the result of a remarkable feat of persuasion by Zimbardo, it would seem). Each was brought to the station house in a radio car whose lights and sirens were, respectively, flashing and wailing. Each was "booked," fingerprinted, and then, blindfolded, conveyed to the "Stanford County Jail." Carlo Prescott, an ex-offender who worked closely with the researchers in the planning and execution of this study, had described the helpless, emasculated, dehumanized feelings of the average prison inmate. Zimbardo et al. sought to create conditions that would have similar, if less intense, effects. Accordingly, they required prisoners to wear shapeless smocks on which were stenciled their prison numbers. The prisoners wore stocking caps to conceal individual differences in hair style (and to approximate the shaven heads required in many real prisons). Inmates were deloused upon arrival by means of an insecticide spray. They wore no underclothing beneath the smocks and a chain was bolted around their ankles. Each prisoner shared his cell with two others.

Upon arrival at the jail, they were given a list of 16 rules with instructions to memorize them so that they might be recited on demand. Among the rules were the requirements that they address one another only by number and that they address the guards as "Mr. Correctional Officer."

The guards were clothed in a manner designed to stimulate feelings similar to those of real guards. They wore khaki uniforms, reflecting sun glasses (which eliminated eye contact with each other and with the prisoners), and carried a billy club loaned to them by the police. They also carried handcuffs, whistles, and keys and were instructed to take their roles seriously and to be alert to danger and trouble.

Since watches had been taken from the prisoners and the prison was in a basement, their sense of time was disrupted. Periodically, including at night, the "prisoners" were awakened and removed from their cells for a "count." This permitted interaction between prisoners and guards and also a great deal of harassment to take place.

On the second day the prisoners staged a rebellion. The guards quelled it with force and retaliated by using "psychological" measures including selective granting of special privileges, which was used to sow dissension among the prisoners and to break down whatever solidarity was beginning to develop among them.

Several prisoners had to be released, the first within less than 36 hours. He was crying hysterically, and screaming with rage and frustration. Two others were released with similar reactions, and a fourth was released with a psychosomatic rash. Zimbardo was informed by staff and inmates at Rhode Island State Prison that these are not unusual "first offender" reactions.[16]

A parole hearing conducted by Prescott led to the surprising result that prisoners agreed to forfeit their pay in return for their release, and then returned docilely to their cells when parole was denied. They had lost sight of the fact that they were volunteers submitting to all of this for pay! A visiting former prison chaplain invited to assess the verisimilitude of the jail lost sight of his mission, too, and urged the inmates to contact a lawyer so that they might win their release!

By Thursday, the prisoners were demoralized and isolated from one another. The guards' harassment had reached the point of extending prisoner counts for hours, requiring push-ups and the cleaning of toilets by prisoners with their bare hands. They shouted threats at one inmate who refused to eat, and confined prisoners to "the hole" for much longer periods than the guards' own rules permitted.

Zimbardo and his associates, who had become as caught up in their roles, as prison officials, as the participants had in theirs, felt forced to end the experiment after only five days. The prisoners had, indeed, become passive, depressed, helpless, and dependent. The guards had viewed the situation as a "job" but one which most enjoyed because of the power and status it conferred. The effects of the simulation were so strong, in fact, that it became clear that ethical simulations of the effects of prison life would be hard to conduct.

Critics have assailed the researchers' loss of objectivity and have suggested that tougher, more "street-wise" young men would have responded differently from these middle class college boys. Others have argued that even this simulation is not adequate to recreate the torments of the jailed. There was no racism, no homosexual assaults, no fear for one's life as in real prisons. Yet the effects are compelling in one sense, at least. The study provides strong support for the position that one's behavior in this and perhaps in most restrictive situations is determined more by the situation within which one finds oneself than by the personal characteristics or predispositions with which one enters it. Circumstances, it suggests, can make even good people behave in cruel ways. Further, it would not be surprising in the light of other social psychological research[17] if the majority of us were to behave more consistently with situational demands than with the demands of our own consciences.

On the other hand, Banuazizi and Movahedi offer an alternative explanation for Zimbardo's results. They suggest that subjects were responding to demand characteristics of the situation, i.e., behaving as they thought the experimenters wanted them to behave. In view of the fact that four subjects had to be released prematurely, three with emotional breakdowns, this explanation hardly seems tenable, particularly where the prisoners were concerned.

PRISON REFORMS

Over the years, well-meaning people have attempted to reform the prison system by various methods. With all such reforms the problem is that they are designed to correct deficiencies caused by the very nature of the system and that their premise is that the system is somehow worth salvaging.

Conjugal visits, which permit prisoners and their spouses to be alone together in some suitable private facility, were originally introduced in Mexican prisons. They have recently been experimented with in the United States, Sweden, and other countries. These visits are intended to help keep a marriage intact during the incarceration of one of the spouses by permitting the parties to maintain some type of normal sexual relationship. In prisons where conjugal visits have been instituted on a trial basis, the staffs usually support the program. It tends to reduce problems of homosexuality and makes the inmates more cooperative lest they lose these visiting privileges. Whether middle class American morality will permit such visits by non-spouses seems questionable, but they may be possible at some point in the future.

The intermittent sentence, by which convicts are incarcerated on weekends or evenings so that they can maintain their regular jobs or attend study programs, makes it possible for nondangerous offenders to maintain their family, community, and vocational ties while serving their sentences. The fact that society considers it safe to release these convicts during certain periods of time suggests that there is little reason, as far as the protection of the public is concerned, to keep them locked up at any time. In any event, permitting a convicted felon to support himself and his family also has the beneficial effect of reducing the cost of his confinement to the taxpayer.

One very important area of penal reform is the attempt to provide psychological treatment for those inmates who need it, either to change their criminal behavior or simply to help them adjust to the stresses of life in prison. In theory, this approach is commendable. In practice, such psychological treatment is nonexistent for several reasons. In the first place, no penal institution can afford an adequate staff of psychiatrists or psychologists. Psychotherapy is, at best, an expensive and time-consuming process. Patients may have to be seen one or more times a week for several years in private sessions before any benefits can be noted. Even then, not all patients benefit from treatment. Second, to survive in a prison a prisoner must learn what it is that the authorities expect of him and then must comply or at least pretend to comply. There is no such thing as a volunteer in prison. A convict's whole future depends on doing what the authorities want him to do. If the warden wants volunteers for a psychotherapy program, he will volunteer. Thus it is often difficult to gauge the success of any therapy undertaken, since the patients do not come to it for help with their problems; they really come for help in obtaining an early parole.

In his book *The Right to be Different*, Kittrie notes the increasing tendency of states to assume parental functions for the protection and "well-being" of its citizens. The mentally ill, addicts, alcoholics, sex offenders, and other deviants are more and more the subjects of civil rather than criminal proceedings. Kittrie refers to this state of affairs as "the therapeutic state." Instead of ascribing antisocial acts to a criminal mentality, the state now views these behaviors as evidence of immaturity, illness, or mental deficiency. From this standpoint, society's task becomes that of curing or, at least, treating these offenders.

Kittrie expresses the view that our penal system is moving in the direction of a therapeutic state and asks whether such a shift is desirable. Surely it is not if therapeutic procedures employed are as costly as the traditional methods alluded to above.

In an effort to deal with the undue amount of time required by the conventional methods of therapy, experimental work has been attempted in prisons using the newer techniques of behavior modification. If successful, such methods could shorten the treatment process and reduce its cost substantially.

Behavior Modification.   The major premise underlying behavior modification is that mental illness and deviant behavior are learned and that psychotherapy is properly viewed as a process of extinguishing maladaptive behavior and replacing it with behavior that is more appropriate. The extinction and re-learning processes follow the laws of learning developed in psychological laboratories. Ayllon mentions three distinguishing characteristics of the behavior modification approach:

1. The patient's behavior is treated as unique and is related to his immediate environment.
2. Treatment is tailored to the individual and is evaluated in terms of predetermined criteria.
3. If ineffective, the treatment is restructured. That is, the process is self-correcting.

There are several techniques of behavior modification. One, systematic desensitization, helps those who, like neurotics, suffer from anxiety. It works by the systematic elimination of the anxiety response through the pairing of anxiety-provoking stimuli with a response incompatible with anxiety, e.g., deep relaxation. In other words, since anxiety and relaxation cannot co-exist, the state of deep relaxation will extinguish an anxiety response previously associated with a stimulus.

A second technique is the token economy. Here a quasi-economic system is established, usually within an institution, and the behavior that one hopes to make more frequent is rewarded with tokens. These tokens may be accumulated and used later to purchase certain rewards, privileges, or merchandise. In corrections, this approach has been used with delinquents as well as with youthful and adult offenders. It has also been used to induce improved educational and vocational performance and to control disciplinary problems in youngsters with delinquent propensities living in home-style settings.

A third major technique is aversive conditioning. Because of the difference between treating a voluntary patient in his office and treating a helpless inmate who cannot truly consent to treatment, the therapist employing aversive conditioning in a prison faces ethical problems. These problems cause some people to think that the treatment is worse than the disease. An example of such a treatment would be attempts to treat homosexuality by showing a male homosexual pictures of nude men while simultaneously administering a painful electric shock. The termination of the shock occurs when the stimulating but "bad" picture is replaced by one of a female. Thus anxiety is conditioned to previously erotic stimuli, and this anxiety is incompatible with sexual excitement. Also, positive feelings, namely relief from pain and anxiety, are being paired with stimuli that would be erotic to a heterosexual male.

The authors have a fairly positive attitude toward the methods of behavior therapy when used in a private-practice setting on adult patients who consent to their use and expect to benefit from them. Behavior therapy is one of the few current treatment methods to have been derived from experimentally validated principles of scientific psychology and, used properly, may materially reduce the duration and expense of treatment. When used on involuntary subjects in a prison population, however, the situation is quite different. If there is any difference between guards torturing a helpless prisoner with shocks from a telephone set generator and a psychologist applying electric shocks in order to aversively condition a prisoner to homosexual stimuli, the difference escapes us. In both cases pain is being inflicted on a nonconsenting and defenseless person in an effort to get him to conform to the type of behavior desired by the person in power. Under these circumstances, what would ordinarily be psychotherapy becomes a morally reprehensible abuse of power. Such abuse of power is not rendered ethically acceptable because the therapist involved does so with what he considers good motives. During the middle ages people burned witches in the belief that they were thus saving their immortal souls. The goal of real psychotherapy is to help the patient become whatever he wishes to become, not what the therapist thinks he should become.

The film "The Clockwork Orange" dealt with the use of aversive conditioning by presenting a violence-prone convict scenes of violence paired with a drug that made him nauseous. This conditioning caused stimuli that had previously excited the man to violence to make him physically ill, instead. The question is, does this really represent a cure for antisocial behavior or does it make the convict (more properly, the victim) sicker than before but in a manner that poses less risk to society? If the goal is simply to convert a dangerous person to a nondangerous one, it could be accomplished more readily by simply physically incapacitating the criminal permanently, as is presently done in some Arab countries.

Behavior modification has been employed for various goals and in various forms. Some programs are "total programs," in that the entire institution is designed for purposes of behavior change among prisoners. One such program was the ill-fated START program, to be described below. Others, less inclusive and intrusive, have focused more upon research or treatment. These programs include token economies, which are in operation during only part of the prisoner's day, and aversive therapies, which are designed to deal with specific behaviors that trouble the prisoner or, more likely, the institution or society-at-large.

All of these approaches are presently matters of legal, philosophical, and empirical controversy. Each has its supporters and detractors, but the reasons for support and detraction vary from instance to instance. There are those who fear that any attempts to focus change efforts on the individual inmate are oblivious to the social ills and environmental conditions which led to his criminal behavior. What must be changed, they say, is not the felon, but the social system which made his crime his most accessible method of coping. There are others whose concern is for the penal institution. For them, the inmate is not the client; the prison authorities are to be helped by the program to change the behavior of aggressive or unruly prisoners. Others in the debate are primarily concerned with legal safeguards. They view attempts to change the minds or behaviors of prison inmates as unconstitutional and illegally punitive. No judge ever sentenced a convicted felon to aversive conditioning or to a token economy. Such writers (e.g., Morris) argue that any treatment must be totally voluntary *and* totally unrelated to the terms of one's sentence, lest extraneous and illegitimate pressures intrude upon the few rights the inmate has. There are those, too, who assert that an inmate under a fixed rather than an indeterminate sentence, who knows his release date and has ready access to such privileges as telephone or reading matter, can only be *punished* for misbehavior. There is no way to *reward* him for good behavior or to hold over him the promise of early parole. His only rewards, therefore, come from other inmates, who thus acquire the power to secure conformity with *their* values, goals, and interests.[18]

The procedures which are collectively labeled behavior modification techniques include some that certain psychologists would rule out of the category and others that psychologists, not being physicians, could not legally employ if they wished to. Some psychologists strongly oppose such procedures as electric shock, psychosurgery, and use of vomiting-inducing drugs, and argue that they are not properly classified as psychological behavior modification techniques.[19]

START. The Federal Bureau of Prisons undertook a program at the United States Medical Center in Springfield, Missouri for the purpose of training disruptive prisoners to behave themselves. The program was regarded as a prototype of a far more extensive program to be introduced at a new federal prison at Butner, North Carolina, which was to employ a number of behavior modification techniques.[20]

Fifteen "special offenders" identified as trouble-makers by their guards were assigned to this Special Treatment and Rehabilitative Training Program (START). These men had had histories of noncompliance with prison regulations, and START was supposed to change their attitudes and behavior. The behaviors to be changed included assault, bad language, agitation, manipulation of others for personal gain, and disregard for rules or orders. The ultimate objective was the return of the inmate to the institution from which he had come! In short, trouble-makers were to be returned to their previous institutions as passive, obedient prisoners.

START was organized as a system of three stages, each with nine levels. Each level brought with it different deprivations and required different criteria for promotion to the next higher level.

Upon entering the institution the prisoner gave up all of his personal property, and was placed in isolation with virtually no privileges. He did have a bed, a mattress, a pillow, and minimal toilet articles. He was permitted to shower and change his clothes twice a week but was required to eat in his cell, in which he was generally locked. He had no visitors, no personal reading matter, no television or radio, no commissary privileges, and no cigarettes. From this level of privation he was required to earn his way to the next level.

Level two allowed limited commissary privileges and three showers a week.

At the higher levels the prisoner could visit the library and was given a full-time job in the prison industry. He was permitted to receive approved magazines and newspapers and, depending on the points he had earned, might be given up to $15 per *month* commissary privileges. He could also shower and change his clothes daily.

He could use tokens to purchase items, or to rent a radio or books. He could earn points for his personal appearance and hygiene and for participation in individualized learning programs. He also could earn points for his work in the prison industry and for social interaction involving obedience and passivity.

Another criterion for promotion to higher levels was his "good day" score. Completion of a specific number of good days made it possible for one's eligibility for promotion to be reviewed by the program's staff. A good day was one in which the prisoner had been suitably submissive to the guards, had done what he was told to do without persuasion, had followed directions willingly, had obeyed all rules, had talked in a "reasonable tone of voice," and had been willing to take "No" for an answer.

One aphorism about prison life and, perhaps, about such programs as this is that "Anything that can be abused will be abused."[21] START was no exception to this rule. A. G. Saunders, Jr., an attorney with the National Prison Project of the American Civil Liberties Union, reports having seen two of the inmates shackled to their beds, their arms and legs secured by leather and metal straps, their meals eaten with both hands shackled. Neither man had been charged with a violation of the rules; neither had appeared before a disciplinary committee. Four others had been placed in "segregation" for failure to cooperate and had been deprived without hearing or warning of the minimal rights their more agreeable peers enjoyed.[22]

The START prisoners brought suit charging violation of due process and equal protection rights in the involuntary transfer to START, which had been based on neither charges nor hearing. They questioned whether an untested program, one not proven to be consistent with principles of behavior modification, might be imposed upon them against their wills, and whether, in theory *or* practice, START constituted a valid program of treatment.

Eight months later the Federal Bureau of Prisons ended the program, claiming economic reasons and insufficient numbers of eligible inmates. At about the same time the Law Enforcement Assistance Administration terminated its funding of "medical research," clarifying its position, after protests by psychologists, to exclude from the ban behavior modification procedures that do not involve medical procedures.

With START stopped, the Bureau of Prisons claimed the inmates' suit was moot, but, in *Clonce v. Richardson* Judge Oliver ruled that START constituted a major change in the conditions of confinement to which the men were subjected and that, as such, required due process before a transfer could be imposed. The changed conditions included denial of access to spiritual leaders and religious services, continuous monitoring of conversations and actions, and denial of privileges freely available to other federal prisoners. Finally, the procedures were designed to change the individual's mind and behavior and to do so to assist him in adjusting not to society's standards, but to the requirements of prison life.

Clonce v. Richardson was one of a series of suits brought by prisoners during this period that have, collectively, required corrections, legal, and psychological personnel to evaluate the efficacy, legality, and ethics of programs such as this.

In *Knecht v. Gillman*, two inmates of the Iowa Security Medical Facility successfully sued to prevent the use of Apomorphine, a vomiting-inducing drug, as an aversive stimulus. The drug had been injected into inmates who did not get up in the morning, or who violated rules by giving others cigarettes, talking, lying, or swearing. The court ruled that the involuntary treatment was cruel and unusual punishment enjoined by the Eighth Amendment, and set down requirements for securing valid, informed consent for such treatment in the future.[23] Precisely because aversive stimulation is unpleasant, these requirements, which include the right to halt treatment, could lead to termination before the treatment has been able to effect change.[24]

A program that involved aversive stimulation was designed for pedophiles (child molesters) imprisoned at the State Prison at Somers, Connecticut. Volunteer subjects were shown pictures of young children while a painful electric shock was administered to the "groin area." In addition, hypnosis and group therapy were employed in order to inhibit sexual attraction to children. Ninety percent of those who completed the program and were released had remained free of the unwelcome behaviors for an average of ten months when the data were last reported.[25] Critics of such programs, however, make the point that aversive stimulation seems to be employed in treatment of morally objectionable offenses like child abuse and alcoholism. They ask why such procedures are not employed to combat burglary and embezzlement.

Indeterminate Sentences.   The notion that prisons can serve as the site of effective rehabilitative efforts was one of the factors leading to the use of indeterminate sentences. The social scientists who advocated this type of sentence felt that a prisoner should be incarcerated for the period of time necessary to reform him rather than for a fixed period which might be too short or too long.[26] This idea was based on the fallacious premise that prisons are, in fact, capable of reforming criminals, and has led to a system of sentencing which has worked substantial hardship and injustice on countless inmates. Indeterminate sentences generally are much longer and more costly than fixed sentences and create additional emotional strain on both the inmate and his family, who are left to wonder when he will be freed.

Dangerousness. A major justification for the use of indeterminate sentences is the protection of the public from dangerous criminals. Many violent persons seem to "burn out" or calm down about the age of 30 and do not resume their earlier pattern of violent crime. But this eventuality is not predictable when it comes to the individual case. Each offender is unique and some require longer separation from society than others. Or so this justification goes.

Morris views attempts to protect the public from "dangerous" offenders as causing serious inequities. Just as physicians inoculate children against whooping cough although relatively few would contract it ("just to be on the safe side"), so, too, do parole boards try to retain control over the "dangerous" offender. To release someone who then goes out and commits a violent crime will bring disrepute upon the parole board and the entire criminal justice system, not to mention the harm done the victim. Accordingly, like the conservative physician who tries to inoculate as many people as possible against some ailment that strikes relatively few, the parole board is conservative. If it is to err, it is likely that it will err on the side of protecting the public. But how many nondangerous inmates can be kept locked up to protect the public from one who *is* dangerous? It is not an easy question to answer; one dangerous criminal *can* do a great deal of harm.

Kozol et al. attempted to predict the dangerousness of 435 "high risk" offenders using the skills of two psychiatrists and a social worker in each instance. They predicted that 386 of the 435 could safely be released, and 49 would be likely to commit further violent acts. They predicted fairly well. Of the 386, only 31 perpetrated assaults (one, a murder); they erred in only 8% of these predictions. Of the 49 for whom violent crimes were predicted, 17 committed them (including 2 murders). The other 32 stayed out of trouble. In other words, to detain one genuinely dangerous offender it would have been necessary to detain two others who are not dangerous. Is it worth it? Morris argues strongly that no person should be held because he or she is viewed as dangerous. Our ability to predict one's future behavior is too limited, and, more important, punishment should be meted out as a consequence of a crime, not in anticipation of it.

ALTERNATIVES TO INCARCERATION

At various points in this book alternatives have been mentioned to the incarceration of convicted criminals. A period of supervised probation is a frequent sentence for first offenders. The imposition of a fine is another. In a number of jurisdictions persons convicted of crimes against property may sign an agreement to make restitution to their victims, remitting an affordable amount on a regular basis until the debt is paid.

Since as many as 85% of those incarcerated do not represent threats to public safety, and since the costs of incarceration are so high in both personal and economic terms, it seems essential that alternatives to incarceration be devised and implemented on a much larger scale than has been the case to date.

It is hard to determine who comes out ahead in prison systems. The evidence is clear that no one is rehabilitated or reformed as a result of having been incarcerated although some ex-inmates manage to avoid trouble after they have been released. The public is protected only from those in prison; after release many are far more effective criminals and more predisposed to violence. Further, the cost of maintaining a prison inmate is enormously high and is compounded by the cost of maintaining the prisoner's dependents on public assistance. The professional staff, psychologists, social workers, psychiatrists, and physicians, generally find prison work frustrating and discouraging. The system itself makes their effective functioning very difficult.

CAPITAL PUNISHMENT

Capital punishment has a long history in Anglo-American law, antedating by far the practice of incarcerating convicts for long periods of time. Bedau indicates that in North Carolina, as late as 1837, there were more than 25 different capital crimes, ranging from being an accessory to burglary to murder. He suggests that this was partly because the state had no alternative, inasmuch as it had no penitentiary.[27] Indeed, in the 1760s there were as many as 160 capital crimes in England (Johnson puts the figure at 350), and by 1820 the number had risen to some 200, including pocket-picking. Of these, 190 had been made capital offenses between 1650 and 1810.[28]

One way of gauging the progress of a civilization is by noting the decrease in the number of crimes for which the death penalty is exacted. The tendency to reduce the number of capital offenses has reached its logical conclusion in recent years with the *de facto* elimination of capital punishment in the United States. Since 1967 only one person has been executed in this country, and in that case it was only after considerable legal efforts by the prisoner himself to secure his own execution. Whether the cessation of executions is due to a series of recent Supreme Court decisions[29] that have limited the conditions under which the death penalty may be imposed, or to the opportunity these decisions have offered politicians to eliminate the death penalty unobtrusively, is hard to say. The Zeitgeist may be partly responsible. In England, the death penalty was outlawed by Parliament in 1965, following the execution of a "felon" who was later cleared of the crime in question.

Several cases in this country had the effect of awakening public sympathy for condemned individuals whose executions came years after the sentences were pronounced. The long wait and the attendant publicity may have made the public susceptible to the view that execution is cruel and unusual. Surely public opinion is not irrelevant. Solicitor General Bork argued before the Supreme Court that public opinion now *favors* the death penalty, in contradicting one of the assumptions on which the Court had based its ruling in *Furman v. Georgia*.[30] (In that case the Court held that the then-current sporadic imposition of capital punishment rendered it "cruel and unusual" within the meaning of the constitutional prohibition against such punishment.)

On the other hand, Bedau finds "galling" the Court's failure to react to research by social scientists in the years since the *Furman* case.[31] Vidmar and Ellsworth, social scientists who summarized a great deal of that research, seem to feel less confident of its value.[32] They argue that merely counting who supports the death penalty and who does not is not very helpful to those confronted with the task of sentencing. They cite Justice Marshall's dictum in the *Furman* decision that public opinion is not always based on sound information or reason, that it may not be consistent with the Constitution, and that support for the death penalty in the abstract is not necessarily consistent with public opinion in the case of a particular crime, criminal, or circumstances. Having expressed such reservations, Vidmar and Ellsworth cautiously offer some general findings of a series of opinion studies conducted over several decades. They find evidence that proponents of the death penalty feel more threatened by crime and its increase, tend to be more conservative politically and socially, and tend to favor it more for its retributive than for its deterrent value. They question just how informed respondents in these surveys were about the deterrent value of execution and about the ways in which executions are actually conducted. Justice Marshall had argued that if public opinion is to be a guide to changing the law, it should be informed with respect to both utilitarian and humanitarian factors pertinent to the issue. Data which Vidmar and Ellsworth summarize suggest that the public is not well informed in either respect.

For various reasons there appears to have been a shift in public opinion in the direction of support for capital punishment. There are attempts in many states to reinstate the death penalty in some form that will be acceptable to the U.S. Supreme Court. Numerous writers have predicted a rash of executions in the wake of the one in Utah in 1977. At this writing the wave has not materialized.

The reason most often advanced for opposing capital punishment is that any killing is wrong, whether by an individual or by the state. This is an interesting argument, psychologically, in that there are diverse situations in which one person may take another's life (e.g., murder, execution, abortion, self-defense, act of war, or euthanasia), and one can have radically different views of the moral correctness of each circumstance.

While a moral conviction may not seem the most compelling basis for the establishment or abolition of capital punishment, many arguments have been advanced in support of both positions, and we will review and comment briefly on some of them.[33]

Capital punishment has historically been advocated as providing justifiable retribution for heinous acts and as a means of deterring others from committing comparable crimes.[34] Advocates of capital punishment argue that public opinion polls show support for it and that, in a democracy, the people should have the final decision in contested political issues. They argue, too, that in some cases, as when a "lifer" kills a guard or fellow inmate, there would be no way to punish the offender if there were no capital punishment. Zeisel points out, on the other hand, that most lifers have some hope of eventual release and, further, that "a prison . . . has ways of its own of punishing such a double murderer," and that, in any case, such "free murders" are very rare.[35]

Proponents of the death penalty point out that the victim and his family have rights as well as the criminal, and that their rights also ought to be protected by society. In the recent Utah execution which was carried out by selected marksmen, there were those who felt that members of the crime victims' families should be given preference in the selection of the firing squad.[36]

Another argument is that society must have the same right as the individual to self-preservation, and, if it cannot permanently eliminate dangerous, antisocial persons, then it is, in fact, being denied that right.

Moreover, it may be said that since there is no true life sentence (i.e., one without possibility of parole or pardon) in most states, there is no way other than execution to assure the public that vicious killers will not ultimately be released to kill again. Even if a true life sentence were created as a compromise, it would be pertinent to ask whether it makes sense to incarcerate a felon for many years at a cost per year far greater than the cost of attendance at the most prestigious university.

We have not heard advocates of the death penalty urge it, but it could be argued with logic and truth that capital punishment is a more humane form of punishment than living under prison conditions for many decades. Since these advocates generally favor the most severe possible punishment, their indifference to this argument is of no small interest.[37]

Opponents of capital punishment directly contradict many of the proponents' arguments, a fact that will come as no surprise. They question whether capital punishment is a deterrent, noting, among other things, that most homicides involve friends or relatives and that murder has one of the lowest recidivism rates of all crimes.

Furthermore, capital punishment may not only fail to serve as a deterrent, it may actually make convictions more difficult to obtain. Juries, in general, will not hesitate to convict a defendant if they believe him to be guilty; but if there is a death penalty involved, they may be much more hesitant to do so. This is the reason that some states have two trials for capital crimes. In the first trial the issue of guilt or innocence is determined. Following a conviction, a second trial is held to determine whether a death penalty should be imposed.

A number of years ago when the abolition of capital punishment was being debated in the New York legislature, one of the authors sat on the criminal law committee of a local bar association that was considering recommendations to the legislature on this issue. It is interesting to note that almost all of the committee members who favored the repeal of capital punishment were prosecutors, and almost all who favored its retention were defense attorneys! All of those experienced trial lawyers knew that capital punishment makes it more difficult to get convictions.

More support for the position that capital punishment is not a deterrent is the fact that when it was eliminated in individual states, the effect on their murder rates as compared with those of similar states and with their own rates in previous years was generally negligible.[38] Zeisel views the numerous costs and risks of the death penalty as far greater than any deterrent effects it might have. He suggests to those who remain unconvinced of his position and wish for more data that the U.S. Supreme Court has provided us with a natural experiment in which we can compare murder rates in states which reimpose the death penalty with states which do not.[39] (Such research, of course, is far from the ideal design in which independent variables can be manipulated and appropriate controls imposed, and it assumes that executions, in fact, will be resumed in some states.)

Opponents of capital punishment (and some of its proponents, as well) believe that the certainty of punishment, not its severity, is the major source of its deterrent value. Most criminals, however, whether petty offenders or murderers, probably believe (and correctly so) that there is little likelihood of their being apprehended.

A telling argument against capital punishment is that it makes irrevocable the occasional miscarriages of justice which are inevitable in any large number of cases. Proponents counter this argument by pointing out that it could apply to any form of punishment, and that there are numerous procedural safeguards to minimize its likelihood, particularly in capital cases. We agree that there is little that can be done to compensate a person wrongfully incarcerated for many years, but there remains a great deal of difference between the two situations.

To counter the argument that cold-blooded or premeditated murderers must be severely punished, Clarence Darrow argued in the Leopold-Loeb case that he could think of no more premeditated or cold-blooded killing than that committed by the agents of the state in carrying out the death penalty. He argued that the state should be better than the acts of the murderer it seeks to punish; it should not descend to his level.

Another noteworthy argument against capital punishment is that while its supporters urge it as a remedy against professional criminals, its victims, in fact, are often casual offenders and include a disproportionate number of poor and minority defendants.

If capital punishment is truly to be a deterrent and not merely an act of retribution, as a matter of logic its supporters should demand public executions, preferably on prime-time television, to produce a maximum deterrent effect. Indeed, in eighteenth- and early nineteenth-century England public executions were the rule.[40] Nonetheless, while pickpockets were being publicly hanged, their colleagues are said to have been hard at work within the crowd of witnesses.[41] If this is not persuasive evidence against the deterrence theory, consider also the fact that the condemned were generally folk heroes of the day. Exhibited to the public in the days before the execution, they were given flowers and whiskey en route to it; their courage was admired by the crowd as they awaited the rope; and their fate was mourned by the crowd when the rope had done its work.[42] Prime-time television may not be such a good idea, after all.[43]

Whatever the reader's position on capital punishment, the tendency over the years has been to restrict its application more and more. Prior to its *de facto* abolition in recent years, some particularly peculiar statutes were enacted. One was New York's definition of first degree murder which made it a capital offense to kill a police officer who was on duty. This was enacted on the theory that since the police risk their lives daily for the public, they are entitled to special protection. The real effect of this law was a public pronouncement by the state that a police officer's life was more important than that of an ordinary citizen—a college professor, for instance.[44]

The argument that the will of the people should govern in a democracy is countered by opponents of capital punishment who note that the greatest impetus for the reinstatement of the death penalty comes from a public frightened by lurid press accounts of sensational murders.[45] Politicians, particularly those running for office, are rarely able to resist the temptation to capitalize on these public fears and the opportunity they offer for free press exposure. They therefore take a public stand in support of capital punishment as necessary to "make the streets safe."

It is ironic to note that when capital punishment was common, newspapers sold many extra copies by running exposés of the horrors of capital punishment, often describing the events of highly publicized executions in revolting detail. This may be one reason why public support for execution is strong when the sentence is pronounced but grows weaker as the day of execution approaches, and why it is stronger in the abstract than in specific cases.[46]

A final point that should be made is that there are some (admittedly rare) instances of individuals who commit capital crimes *in order to be executed!*[47] There have been murderers who believe that suicide is an irredeemable sin but that atonement while awaiting execution will send them, purified, to Heaven.

At the end of 1975 there were 479 men and women on death rows throughout the country. Of these, 285 had been sentenced during the preceding year, and 151 were condemned in 1974. Fifty-three percent of these people were black; fewer than 2% were women. Most had not graduated from high school.[48] There has been one execution since that date.

The issue of capital punishment will confront us for many years regardless of the outcome of the current legal controversy surrounding it.

NOTES AND REFERENCES

1. Rudovsky, D. *The Rights of Prisoners*. New York: Avon Books, 1973.
2. *Holt v. Sarver*, 309 F. Supp. 362 (1970).
3. *Report of New York State Special Commission on Attica*. New York: 1972. And Jackson, B. A day in the life of the Arkansas penitentiary. *Society* 1972, 9(6), 30–35.
4. Coleman, J. R. Prison guard in Texas for a week. *Fortune News* March, 1978, 8–10.
5. Kaufmann, K. Prisoners, all. *The New York Times* March 25, 1976, p. 35.
6. Sutherland, E. H. and Cressey, D. R. *Principles of Criminology*. New York: J. B. Lippincott, 1960.
7. Mitford, J. *Kind and Usual Punishment*. New York: Vintage Books, 1974.
8. Sommer, R. *The End of Imprisonment*. New York: Oxford University Press, 1976.
9. Ibid., p. 61.
10. Durham, M. For the Swedes a prison sentence can be fun time. *Smithsonian* 1973, 4(6), 46–52.
11. Fowle, F. Study shows prison population rose 13% in 1976 to set a record. *The New York Times* February 18, 1977, A16: col. 3–4.
12. Sommer, R. The social psychology of the cell environment. *Prison Journal* 1971, 51(1), 15–21.
13. Ibid., p. 18.
14. Ibid., p. 19.
15. The Fortune Society accomplishes this by arranging speaking engagements virtually upon request and via its monthly publication, *Fortune News*.
16. Sommer, R. *The End of Imprisonment*, p. 91.
17. See, for example, Milgram, S. *Obedience to Authority: An Experimental View*. New York: Harper & Row, 1974.
18. Milan, M. A. and McKee, J. M. Behavior modification principles and application in corrections. In D. Glaser (Ed.) *Handbook of Criminology*. Chicago: Rand McNally, 1974.

19. Skinner, B. F. To build constructive prison environments. Letter to the Editor, *The New York Times* February 26, 1974.
20. Holland, J. G. Behavior modification for prisoners, patients, and other people as a prescription for the planned society. *Mexican Journal of the Analysis of Behavior* 1(1), 1975, 81–95. See also Trotter, S. Experimental prison opened in Butner, N.C. *APA Monitor* July, 1976, 7(7), p. 5.
21. Opton, E. M., Jr. Psychiatric violence against prisoners: When therapy is punishment. *Mississippi Law Journal* 1974, 45, 605–644.
22. Saunders, A. G., Jr. Behavior therapy in prisons: Walden II or Clockwork Orange? Paper presented at 8th annual convention of the Association for Advancement of Behavior Therapy, Chicago, 1974.
23. For a thorough discussion of these and other cases and their implications, see Friedman, P. R. Legal regulation of applied behavior analysis in mental institutions and prisons. *Arizona Law Review 1975*, 17, 39–104.
24. Ibid., pp. 84ff.
25. Saunders, Behavior therapy in prisons.
26. See, for example, Trotter, S. Patuxent: "Therapeutic" prison faces test. *APA Monitor* May, 1975, 6(5), lff.
27. Bedau, H. A. (Ed.). *The Death Penalty in America* (Revised edition). Garden City, N.Y.: Doubleday Anchor Books, 1967, p. 7.
28. Radzinowicz, L. *A History of English Criminal Law and its Administration from 1750*, Vol. 1. *The Movement for Reform*. London: Stevens & Sons Limited, 1948, pp. 3–4.
29. Among the many in recent years are: *Witherspoon v. Illinois* 391 U.S. 510 (1968); *Furman v. Georgia* 408 U.S. 238 (1972); *Gregg v. Georgia* 49 L. Ed. 2d 859 (1976); and, decided July 3, 1978, *Lockett v. Ohio*, 98 S.Ct. 2954 (1978).
30. Bedau, H. A. *The Courts, the Constitution, and Capital Punishment*. Lexington, Mass.: Lexington Books, 1977, p. 111.
31. Ibid., p. 116.
32. Vidmar, N. and Ellsworth, P. C. Public opinion on the death penalty. *Stanford Law Review* 1974, 26(6), 1245–1270. [Reprinted in a fine collection: H. A. Bedau and C. M. Pierce (Eds.) *Capital Punishment in the United States*. New York: AMS Press, Inc., 1976.]
33. An interesting discussion of moral judgments about capital punishment is given by Kohlberg, L. and Elfenbein, D. The development of moral judgments concerning capital punishment. *American Journal of Orthopsychiatry* 1975, 45(4), 614–640. (Reprinted in modified form and under different title in Bedau and Pierce, *Capital Punishment in the United States*.)
34. Royal Commission on Capital Punishment 1949–1953. *Report*. London: Her Majesty's Stationery Office, 1953, pp. 17–19.
35. Zeisel, H. The deterrent effect of the death penalty: Facts v. Faiths. In P. B. Kurland (Ed.) *1976 The Supreme Court Review*. Chicago: University of Chicago Press, 1977, p. 339.
36. Nordheimer, J. 2 Dozen ask to join firing squad; warden tells of Utah volunteers. *The New York Times* November 11, 1976, 14:1–2.
37. Hamilton and Rotkin attempted to measure perceived severity of various crimes and punishments and found that capital offenses were not always viewed as among the most serious and that capital punishment was not viewed as significantly more severe than a sentence of life imprisonment without parole. For a discussion of these and other noteworthy findings see Hamilton, V. L. and Rotkin, L. The capital punishment debate: Public perceptions of crime and punishment. Paper presented at 84th Convention American Psychological Association, Washington, D.C., 1976.
38. Sellin, T. Experiments with abolition. In T. Sellin (Ed.) *Capital Punishment*. New York:

Harper & Row, 1967, pp. 122–124; Royal Commission, *Report*, pp. 17–24; Zeisel, The deterrent effect.

39. Zeisel, The deterrent effect.
40. Radzinowicz, *History of English Criminal Law,* Chapter 6. In 1846, Charles Dickens witnessed the public decapitation of a murderer in Rome. He describes it in his *Pictures from Italy*, published in 1848.
41. Bedau, H. A. *The Death Penalty in America,* p. 20; Radzinowicz, *History of English Criminal Law*, p. 178 (cites John Laurence, *A History of Capital Punishment*, p. 44).
42. Radzinowicz, *History of English Criminal Law*, p. 172.
43. In recent years there has been litigation concerning the right of television news personnel to videotape or show executions. *The New York Times* reported on January 9, 1977 (44:1–4), that a federal judge in Texas, W. M. Taylor, found for a journalist who had sued for that right. On July 3, 1978 the Supreme Court let stand a ban on televised coverage of executions that had been erected by a lower court *Garrett v. Estelle*, 98 S.Ct. 3142 (1978).
44. Sellin, T. The death penalty and police safety. In T. Sellin (Ed.) *Capital Punishment.* New York: Harper & Row, 1967, pp. 138–154.
45. Bedau, *The Death Penalty in America*, p. 14.
46. Wicker, T. The fifth cartridge. *The New York Times* November 19, 1976, 27:1; Vidmar and Ellsworth, Public opinion on the death penalty.
47. Royal Commission, *Report*, p. 21. It has been suggested that Gary Gilmore, whose execution took place in early 1977, was such a murderer. Nordheimer, J. Death wish is discerned in poetry and killings by doomed convict. *The New York Times* November 15, 1976, 24:1–2. See also Rensberger, B. Death penalty seen as way to die for suicidal type without nerve. *The New York Times* December 18, 1976, 21:1–2; and Solomon, G. F. Capital punishment as suicide and murder. *American Journal of Orthopsychiatry* 1975, 45(4), 701–711. (Reprinted in Bedau and Pierce, *Capital Punishment in the United States*.)
48. Around the Nation: 285 sentenced to death in 1975 throughout U.S. *The New York Times* November 29, 1976, 18:6.

Epilogue

In closing we will describe some of the areas in which law and psychology have come together in the past, or in which we believe they will join in the future. We will also hazard some predictions as to the contributions that psychology and other social sciences may be expected to make to the criminal justice system. Some areas that can be especially frustrating for the psychologist who desires to improve the system will be considered as well.

While there seem to be relatively few people who believe that the criminal justice system is doing a good job and many who would like to see substantial changes in its operations, the critics often have diametrically opposing views as to how the system should be changed.

Some criticize the system for being too slow and uncertain; they would like to see more swift and sure punishment of offenders. Others accuse the system of coddling offenders, and advocate that longer sentences be made mandatory. This "law and order" position is usually taken by political office seekers, some journalists, and, perhaps more understandably, victims and their families. Advocates of this approach lose sight of the fact that it is not possible to safeguard the constitutional rights of the innocent unless we are willing to extend the same safeguards to the guilty. They seem to assume that only guilty persons are ever apprehended or indicted, let alone convicted.

Whether or not the reader agrees with this "law and order" position, it is an important one. Not only does it result in legislation to increase penalties, but, to the extent that it is accepted by the public, it effectively prevents any amelioration of prison conditions. No action to make prisons less destructive or more humane is likely to be taken by legislators without substantial public support.

An example of this can be seen in the current clamor in many states to re-institute the death penalty in some form that the U.S. Supreme Court will find acceptable.

Another point of view is that our prison system is counter-productive and ought to be changed in a direction opposite to that described above. Persons having this opinion are concerned with improving conditions in prisons to make them less destructive to the prisoner and his family.

A more extreme view taken by some is that prison reform is bad in itself. They argue that reforms are cosmetic in nature, that while they may change and even temporarily improve inmates' lives, at the same time they tend to perpetuate a system which is so destructive of human values that it ought to be abandoned and replaced with something totally different. They believe that we need a substitute approach with greater potential for reform of offenders and protection of the public and less emphasis on vengeance and punishment. This view has recently been strengthened by the disappointing results recorded thus far in Sweden, whose progressive approach to incarceration was described in the previous chapter.[1]

Our prisons are becoming increasingly crowded. There is substantial pressure to build more prisons, not near urban centers where most inmates' families might have ready access to their relatives behind bars, but in rural settings where local populations have need for employment and are represented by legislators who can provide it in this form if not in some other.

The suggestion has been made that the great increase in crime during the 1960s was the work of young people who were born during the "baby boom" after World War II. If this is so, as they grow older and the number of young people declines in the next decade, the number of criminals can be expected to decline as well, and the prisons now under construction will stand half empty.[2]

For this reason as well as for others already discussed, it seems to the authors that one of the improvements needed in the criminal justice system is the restriction of its scope of operations to behaviors that are truly antisocial, behaviors that pose a threat to society-at-large. This would include all crimes of violence and aggressive acts against the person or property of others. Crimes created to enforce current notions of morality, such as proscribed sex acts between consenting adults, or crimes designed to force compliance with purely regulatory enactments, for example, the filing of motor vehicle accident reports, ultimately lower the quality of the entire criminal justice system. They overload the courts with a huge caseload of matters that do not belong in a criminal court; they result in the intrusion of the state into the private lives of citizens in areas in which the state has no legitimate interest to protect. Hence, they effectively deprive citizens of personal liberties that ought to be protected in a free society. That it is the nature of any regulatory agency or government to expand its power and regulations over its area of jurisdiction, unless limited by the courts, can be seen by looking at the plethora of regulations issued by any government agency. Nowhere is this propensity more dangerous than in the area of the criminal law. This regrettable tendency has not only resulted in a ruinous contact with the criminal justice system for many productive, law-abiding citizens, but it has placed such burdens upon the entire system as to make it inefficient and unnecessarily costly.

With respect to those crimes which do, in fact, deal with behavior that constitutes a threat to the welfare of society, a better way of dealing with convicted offenders needs to be found. In cases in which the offender is not actually dangerous to others, more emphasis on rehabilitation on an outpatient basis is in order. Other programs, such as those discussed in the previous chapter, including work-release, study-release, and, even more desirable, halfway programs or community service, should be employed far more often than they are at present. To the extent that punishment is necessary as a deterrent, fines or other alternatives to imprisonment should be used more readily. A fine can be a very effective penalty if it is large enough so as not to be regarded as a cost of criminal activity that will be absorbed by profits in a short period of time. Incarceration ought to be limited to the small minority of offenders whose release would constitute a clear and present danger to the public safety. In such cases the conditions of confinement ought to be limited to the restrictions necessary to isolate the offenders; they should not be imposed for purposes of punishment.

Being optimistic and having faith in our species' ability to develop better solutions to social problems, the authors believe that ultimately a better system will be found. Such an advancement will come, however, only after a long series of political struggles in which the pendulum will swing from one side to the other.

The contributions of psychologists to this process of change must be at least two-fold. First, better methods must be developed to deal with criminals, particularly with those who are potentially dangerous. Second, effective public relations campaigns must be developed to enlist the support of an indifferent or even hostile public for such changes. Without substantial public support for a penal reform program, there is little chance that one will be enacted in a democratic society. While such innovations as the use of behavior modification techniques in prisons are not viewed very positively by the authors for ethical and other reasons, they are a positive sign insofar as they represent the beginning of the involvement of behavioral scientists in the penal system and a change in orientation from punishment to reformation.

While the role of psychologists in improving the criminal justice system would seem to be a natural one involving the application of abstract principles of human behavior to specific practical problems (a form of psychological engineering), the role of psychologists in improving our adversary legal system is likely to be much smaller, if not nonexistent. The reason for this is that our legal system evolved slowly over centuries, based on case decisions and *stare decisis*, into its present form. It is concerned not only with finding the truth in a particular contest but also with the larger and, we believe, more important goal of protecting important constitutional rights of defendants. Often, psychologists who are learned in their science but abysmally ignorant of legal theory suggest methods of getting at the truth more efficiently in a trial, but they are methods that totally disregard these legal safeguards. Examples of such suggestions include replacing juries and the adversary system with an inquisitorial system, and changing the order of procedures in a trial or the ways in which witnesses testify in response to questions. If we were concerned only with ascertaining the truth in a particular criminal trial, we could accomplish this in many cases simply by eavesdropping on the conversations between incarcerated defendants and their lawyers. The necessary electronic equipment is readily available. This would solve the problem—until defendants learned that they could not talk to a lawyer in confidence.

Whether psychologists or social scientists hope to improve either the penal or the legal system, it is obvious that they need a sound understanding of the theory and practice of these legal institutions in addition to knowledge of their own specialty. This is the reason that this book presents a primer on the functioning of the criminal justice system *per se* as well as the psychological principles relevant to it. Perhaps the best training in this area would be the obtaining of both the J.D. and the Ph.D. degrees, and, in fact, a few universities now offer combined programs leading to these degrees. Such training may not be essential, however, for only about half a dozen courses in law school directly apply to criminal practice. A forensic psychologist does need special training in these purely legal areas, however, in order to work effectively within the legal system.

There is currently a move afoot in both the American Psychiatric and American Psychological Associations to certify their members as specialists in Forensic Psychiatry or Psychology by setting up specialty boards in these fields. Because of interprofessional rivalries there is a race between the professions to be the first to establish such a board and so to preempt the field. From our (admittedly biased) point of view it appears that such a specialty would be more appropriate for a psychologist, who could advise lawyers concerning a wide range of human behaviors, than for a psychiatrist, whose training in human behavior is limited to the treatment of behavioral or emotional disorders, and whose principal value to a lawyer is in giving expert testimony concerning the mental condition of a defendant.

While the criminal justice system requires many changes and improvements, and psychologists may be expected to play a larger role in effectuating them, all changes are made slowly in a democracy and often in very small increments. Thus, the psychologist's role may be expected to be more one of working within the system than one of changing it.

As Ellsworth and Ross have pointed out, social scientists cannot expect to bring about change by themselves. Lawyers, who are more likely to wield political power and to control the workings of the system, are not always interested in the same issues as psychologists.[3]

Ellsworth and Ross indicate, too, that different styles of research (e.g., public opinion surveys v. experimentation) may be differentially effective in persuading courts, lawyers, or legislators of the need for change.[4]

Probably such pitfalls in the path of interdisciplinary cooperation as jargon and parochialism can best be avoided by persons trained in both fields. However, terminal degrees in both fields may not be necessary, provided personnel are given adequate training to appreciate the special problems and viewpoints of colleagues in the cooperating professions.

Psychologists will continue to be active in prison therapy programs whether behaviorally oriented or more conventional. They will also contribute to probation reports and supervision and serve as expert witnesses. They can be expected to be utilized more often as consultants to attorneys, not only regarding the mental condition of defendants or psychological test interpretation, but also in jury selection and in the evaluation of witness behavior. Their special knowledge of the limitations of human perception and memory enables them to advise attorneys as to how accurate the testimony of a witness is likely to be and what areas might profitably be probed under cross-examination.

In addition to research of the sort described in previous chapters, a most important role of the psychologist in the criminal justice system will be the education of attorneys in the psychological aspects of their profession. In the last analysis, a criminal lawyer is a trial lawyer, and a trial lawyer is a specialist in the art of persuasion. As Louis Nizer pointed out, when a lawyer uses the phrase, "May it please your Honor," he does not mean it literally. What he means is, "May it *persuade* your honor."[5] Hence, an effective trial lawyer needs a good background in the psychology of persuasion and in related areas of human behavior. While many law schools give courses in forensic medicine, and some in forensic psychiatry, most do not yet recognize the difference between the latter and the more general subject of forensic psychology. Nor do most recognize the value to attorneys of training in this branch of psychology.

The authors believe that as the science of psychology matures, we will see fewer and fewer new Ph.D.'s entering academic careers. They will go increasingly into practical and applied fields, among them clinical, industrial, and forensic psychology. We believe that, in the future, psychologists will play a larger and, we trust, a constructive role in the development and day-to-day operations of the American criminal justice system. We hope that some of our readers will be among them.

REFERENCES

1. Goldstein, T. America is fresh out of prisons. *The New York Times* July 2, 1978, E 16:6–8.
2. Idem.
3. Ellsworth, P. C. and Ross, L. Public opinion and judicial decision-making: An example from research on capital punishment. In H. A. Bedau and C. M. Pierce (Eds.) *Capital Punishment in the United States*. New York: AMS Press, Inc., 1976, pp. 154–155.
4. Idem.
5. Nizer, L. *My Life in Court*. New York: Pyramid Books, 1963, p. 582.

Bibliography

CHAPTER 4

Adler, F. The rise of the female crook. *Psychology Today* November, 1975, 9(6), pp. 42ff.

Allport, G. W. *Pattern and Growth in Personality.* New York: Holt, Rinehart & Winston, 1961.

Berkowitz, L. and LePage, A. Weapons as aggression-eliciting stimuli. *Journal of Personality and Social Psychology* 1967, 7, 202–207.

Boggs, S. L. Urban crime patterns. *American Sociological Review* 1966, 30(6), 899–908. Reprinted in D. Glaser (Ed.) *Crime in the City.* New York: Harper & Row, 1970.

Campbell, C. Portrait of a mass killer. *Psychology Today* May, 1976, 9(12), pp. 110ff.

Christiansen, K. O. A review of studies of criminality among twins. Chapter 4 in S. Mednick and K. O. Christiansen (Eds.) *Biosocial Bases of Criminal Behavior.* New York: Gardner Press, Inc. 1977.

Christiansen, K. O. A preliminary study of criminality among twins. Chapter 5 in S. Mednick and K. O. Christiansen (Eds.) *Biosocial Bases of Criminal Behavior.* New York: Gardner Press, Inc. 1977.

Drähms, A. *The Criminal: His Personnel and Environment.* New York: Macmillan, 1900.

Dugdale, R. *The Jukes, A study in Crime, Pauperism and Heredity.* New York: Putnam, 1877.

Edwards, G. Commentary: Murder and gun control. *Wayne Law Review* 1972, 18(4), 1335–1342.

Erikson, E. Ego identity and the psychosocial moratorium. In H. Witmer and R. Kotinsky (Eds.) *New Perspectives for Research on Juvenile Delinquency.* Washington, D.C.: U.S. Department of Health, Education and Welfare, Children's Bureau, 1956, pp. 1–23.

Festinger, L., Schachter, S., and Back, K. W. *Social Pressures in Informal Groups: A Study of Human Factors in Housing.* New York: Harper & Row, 1950.

Fink, A. E. *Causes of Crime: Biological Theories in the United States: 1800–1915.* Philadelphia: University of Pennsylvania Press, 1938.

Fowler, O. S. *Fowler's Practical Phrenology Etc.* New York: Nafis and Cornish, 1845.

Freedman, J. L., Carlsmith, J. M., and Sears, D. O. *Social Psychology* (2nd edition). Englewood Cliffs, N.J.: Prentice-Hall, 1974.

Friedlander, K. *The Psycho-analytical Approach to Juvenile Delinquency.* London: Routledge, 1947. Cited in R. Hood and R. Sparks *Key Issues in Criminology.* New York: McGraw-Hill World University Library, 1970.

Gibbons, D. *Changing the Lawbreaker* Englewood Cliffs, N.J.: Prentice-Hall, 1965. Cited in R. Hood and R. Sparks *Key Issues in Criminology.* New York: McGraw-Hill World University Library, 1970.

Glaser, D. (Ed.). *Crime in the City.* New York: Harper & Row, 1970.

Goddard, H. H. *The Kallikak Family—A study in the Heredity of Feeble-mindedness.* New York: Macmillan, 1912.

Hall, G. S. *Adolescence.* New York: D. Appleton and Company, 1905.

Healy, W. *The Individual Delinquent.* Boston: Little, Brown & Co., 1915.

Hellman, P. One shopper in ten is a shoplifter. *The New York Times Magazine* March 15, 1970, pp. 34ff.

Hood, R. and Sparks, R. *Key Issues in Criminology.* New York: McGraw-Hill World University Library, 1970.

Horn, J. Portrait of an arrogant crook. *Psychology Today* April, 1976, 9(11), 76–79.

Kelley, C. M. *Uniform Crime Reports of the United States 1975.* Washington, D.C.: U.S. Department of Justice, Federal Bureau of Investigation, 1976.

Lewin, K. *A Dynamic Theory of Personality.* New York: McGraw-Hill, 1935.

Lewis, M. Structural deviance and normative conformity: The "hustle" and the gang. In D. Glaser (Ed.) *Crime in the City.* New York: Harper & Row, 1970.

Lombroso, C. and Ferrero, W. *The Female Offender.* New York: Appleton, 1915.

Lunde, D. T. Our murder boom. *Psychology Today* July, 1975, 9(2), 35–42.

Lunde, D. T. *Murder and Madness.* San Francisco: San Francisco Book Company, 1976.

Mednick, S. A. A biosocial theory of the learning of law-abiding behavior. Chapter 1 in S. A. Mednick and K. O. Christiansen (Eds.) *Biosocial Bases of Criminal Behavior.* New York: Gardner Press, Inc., 1977.

Mednick, S. A. and Christiansen, K. O. (Eds.). *Biosocial Bases of Criminal Behavior.* New York: Gardner Press, Inc., 1977.

Meehl, P. E. Schizotaxia, schizotypy, schizophrenia. *American Psychologist* 1962, 17, 827–838.

Milgram, S. The experience of living in cities. *Science* March 13, 1970, 167, 1461–1468.

Newman, O. *Defensible Space.* New York: Collier Books, 1973.

Ordronaux, J. Moral insanity. *American Journal of Insanity* 1873, 29.

Roebuck, J. *Criminal Typology.* Springfield, Ill.: Charles C. Thomas, 1965. Cited in R. Hood and R. Sparks *Key Issues in Criminology.* New York: McGraw-Hill World University Library, 1970.

Rokeach, M. *The Open and Closed Mind.* New York: Basic Books, 1960.

Serrill, M. A cold new look at the criminal mind. *Psychology Today* February, 1978, 11(9), 86ff.

Simon, R. J. *The Contemporary Woman and Crime.* Rockville, Md.: N.I.M.H. Crime and Delinquency Series, 1975.

Steadman, H. J. and Cocozza, J. J. We can't predict who is dangerous. *Psychology Today* January, 1975, 8(8), 32ff.

Stock, R. W. The XYY and the criminal. *The New York Times Magazine* October 28, 1968, pp. 30ff.

Suttles, G. Deviant behavior as an unanticipated consequence of public housing. In D. Glaser (Ed.) *Crime in the City.* New York: Harper & Row, 1970.

Whyte, W. H. Jr. *The Organization Man.* New York: Simon and Schuster, 1956.

Witkin, H. A., Mednick, S. A., Schulsinger, F., Bakkestrom, E., Christiansen, K. O., Goodenough, D. R., Hirschhorn, K., Lundstean, C., Owen, D. R., Philip, J., Rubin, D. B., and Stocking, M. XYY and XXY men: Criminality and aggression, *Science* 1976, 193, 547–555. Reprinted as Chapter 10 in S. A. Mednick and K. O. Christiansen (Eds.) *Biosocial Bases of Criminal Behavior.* New York: Gardner Press, Inc., 1977.

Wolfgang, M. E. *Patterns in Criminal Homicide.* Philadelphia: University of Pennsylvania Press, 1958.

Yochelson, S. and Samenow, S. E. *The Criminal Personality Volume 1: A Profile for Change.* New York: Jason Aronson, 1976.

CHAPTER 5

Bickman, L. Attitude toward an authority and the reporting of a crime. *Sociometry* 1976, 39(1), 76–82.

Bickman, L. Bystander intervention in a crime. Chapter 11 in E. C. Viano (Ed.) *Victims and Society.* Washington, D.C.: Visage Press, Inc., 1976.

Bickman, L. and Green, S. K. Is revenge sweet? The effect of attitude toward a thief on crime reporting. *Criminal Justice and Behavior* 1975, 2(2), 101–112.

Bickman, L. and Green, S. K. Situational cues and crime reporting: Do signs make a difference? *Journal of Applied Social Psychology* 1977, 7(1), 1–18.

Bickman, L., Lavrakas, P. J., Green, S. K., North-Walker, N., Edwards, J., Borkowski, S., Shane-DuBow, S., and Wuert, J. *National Evaluation Program Phase I Summary Report—Citizen Crime Reporting Projects.* Chicago: Applied Social Psychology Program, Loyola University of Chicago (undated).

Criminal Victimization Surveys in Eight American Cities: A comparison of 1971/72 and 1974/75 findings. Washington, D.C.: Department of Justice, National Crime Survey Report, 1976.

Festinger, L. A theory of social comparison processes. *Human Relations* 1954, 7, 117–140.

Gelfand, D. M., Hartmann, D. P., Walder, P., and Page, B. Who reports shoplifters? A field-experimental study. *Journal of Personality and Social Psychology* 1973, 25(2), 276–285.

Greenberg, M. S. An experimental approach to victim crime reporting. Paper presented at 84th Annual Convention, American Psychological Association, Washington, D.C., 1976.

Hindelang, M. J. *An Analysis of Victimization Survey Results from the Eight Impact Cities: Summary Report.* Washington, D.C.: Law Enforcement Assistance Administration, U.S. Department of Justice, 1974; Albany, N.Y.: Criminal Justice Research Center, 1976.

Hindelang, M. J. and Gottfredson, M. The victim's decision not to invoke the criminal justice process. Chapter 2 in W. F. McDonald (Ed.) *Criminal Justice and the Victim.* Beverly Hills: Sage Publications, 1976.

Horn, J. Portrait of an arrogant crook. *Psychology Today* April, 1976, 9(11), 76–79.

Huston, T. L. and Geis, G. Public policy and the encouragement of bystander intervention. Paper presented at symposium on Citizen Response to Crime: Behavior of Victims and Witnesses. 84th Annual Convention, American Psychological Association, Washington, D.C., 1976.

Huston, T. L., Geis, G., and Wright, R. The angry samaritans. *Psychology Today* June, 1976, 10(1), 61 ff.

Jones, C. and Aronson, E. Attribution of fault to a rape victim as a function of respectability of the victim. *Journal of Personality and Social Psychology* 1973, 26, 415–419.

Kelman, H. C. Processes of opinion change. *Public Opinion Quarterly* 1961, 25, 57–78.

Kerckhoff, A. C. and Back, K. W. *The June Bug: A Study of Hysterical Contagion.* New York: Appleton-Century-Crofts, 1968.

Latané, B. and Darley, J. Situational determinants of bystander intervention in emergencies. In J. Macaulay and L. Berkowitz (Eds.) *Altruism and Helping Behavior.* New York: Academic Press, 1970.

Latané, B. and Darley, J. *The Unresponsive Bystander: Why Doesn't He Help?* New York: Appleton-Century-Crofts, 1970.

McDonald, W. F. Criminal justice and the victim: An introduction. Chapter 1 in W. F. McDonald (Ed.) *Criminal Justice and the Victim.* Beverly Hills: Sage Publications, Inc., 1976.

Newman, O. *Defensible Space.* New York: Collier Books, 1973.

Rule, A. At last—Help for innocent victims of crime. *Good Housekeeping* July, 1977, 185(1), 84–93.

Smith, A. E. and Maness, D., Jr. The decision to call the police: Reactions to burglary. Chapter 3 in W. F. McDonald (Ed.) *Criminal Justice and the Victim.* Beverly Hills: Sage Publications, Inc., 1976.

CHAPTER 6

Alex, N. *Black in Blue: A Study of the Negro Policeman.* New York: Appleton-Century-Crofts, 1969.

Allport, G. W. *The Nature of Prejudice.* Cambridge, Mass.: Addison-Wesley, 1954.

Badalamente, R. V., George, C. E., Halterlein, P. J., Jackson, T. T., Moore, S. A., and Rio, P.

Training police for their social role. *Journal of Police Science and Administration* 1973, 1(4), 440–453.

Baehr, M. E., Furcon, J. E., and Froemel, E. C. *Psychological Assessment of Patrolman Qualifications in Relation to Field Performance.* Washington, D.C.: U.S. Department of Justice, Law Enforcement Assistance Administration, 1969.

Bannon, J. D. and Wilt, G. M. Black policemen: A study of self-images. *Journal of Police Science and Administration.* 1973, 1(1), 21–29.

Bard, M. *Training Police as Specialists in Family Crisis Intervention.* Washington, D.C.: U.S. Department of Justice. Law Enforcement Assistance Administration, 1970.

Bem, D. J. Self-perception: An alternative interpretation of cognitive dissonance phenomena. *Psychological Review* 1967, 74, 245–254.

Bickman, L. The social power of a uniform. *Journal of Applied Social Psychology* 1975, 4(1), 47–61.

Chevigny, P. *Police Power: Police Abuse in New York City.* New York: Vintage Books, 1969.

Cramer, J. *Uniforms of the World's Police.* Springfield, Ill.: Charles C. Thomas, 1968.

Crosby, A. Situational testing as an assessment technique in police organizations. Paper presented at convention of the American Psychological Association, Chicago, 1975.

Crosby, A. Implications of police personnel management practices for selection system characteristics. Paper presented at convention of American Psychological Association, Washington, D.C., 1976.

Eisenberg, T. and Reinke, R. W. The use of written examinations in selecting police officers: Coping with the dilemma. *The Police Chief* March, 1973, 24–28.

Festinger, L. and Carlsmith, J. M. Cognitive consequences of forced compliance. *Journal of Abnormal and Social Psychology*, 1959, 58, 203–210.

Fleming, A. *New on the Beat: Woman Power in the Police Force.* New York: Coward, McCann & Geoghegan, 1975.

Freedman, J. L. and Fraser, S. C. Compliance without pressure: The foot-in-the-door technique. *Journal of Personality and Social Psychology* 1966, 4, 195–202.

Inn, A., Wheeler, A. C., and Sparling, C. L. The effects of suspect race and situation hazard on police officer shooting behavior. *Journal of Applied Social Psychology* 1977, 7(1), 27–37.

Joseph, N. and Alex, N. The uniform: A sociological perspective. *American Journal of Sociology* 1972, 77, 719–730.

Kent, D. A. and Eisenberg, T. The selection and promotion of police officers: A selected review of recent literature. *The Police Chief* February, 1972, 20–29.

Kirkham, G. L. A professor's "street lessons." *FBI Law Enforcement Bulletin* March, 1974. Reprinted in *U.S. News and World Report* April 22, 1974, 70–72.

Lefkowitz, J. Industrial-organizational psychology and the police. *American Psychologist* 1977, 32(5), 346–364.

Margolis, R. J. *Who Will Wear the Badge: A Study of Minority Recruitment Efforts in Protective Services.* Washington, D.C.: United States Commission on Civil Rights, 1971.

McEvoy, D. W. Training for the new centurions. Chapter 2 in J. L. Steinberg and D. W. McEvoy (Eds.) *The Police and the Behavioral Sciences.* Springfield, Ill.: Charles C. Thomas, 1974.

Milgram, S. Behavioral study of obedience. *Journal of Abnormal and Social Psychology* 1963, 67, 371–378.

Niederhoffer, A. *Behind the Shield: The Police in Urban Society.* New York: Doubleday Anchor Books, 1967.

Orne, M. T. On the social psychology of the psychological experiment: With particular reference to demand characteristics and their implications. *American Psychologist* 1962, 17, 776–783.

Police Training and Performance Study. Report to the New York City Police Department and the Law Enforcement Assistance Administration, United States Department of Justice. New York: New York City Police Department, 1969.

Reiss, A. J., Jr. *The Police and the Public.* New Haven: Yale University Press, 1971.

Richardson, J. F. *Urban Police in the United States.* Port Washington, N.Y.: National University Publications, Kennikat Press, 1974.

Robin, G. D. Justifiable homicide by police officers. *Journal of Criminal Law, Criminology, and Police Science* 1963, 54, 225–229.

Rokeach, M. *The Three Christs of Ypsilanti: A Psychological Study.* New York: Random House Vintage Books, 1967.

Rokeach, M., Miller, M. G., and Snyder, J. A. The value gap between police and policed. *Journal of Social Issues* 1971, 27(2), 155–171.

Rosenthal, R. *Experimenter Effects in Behavioral Research.* New York: Appleton-Century-Crofts, 1966.

Rubin, J. G. Police identity and the police role. Chapter 6 in J. G. Goldsmith and S. S. Goldsmith (Eds.) *The Police Community: Dimensions of an Occupational Subculture.* Pacific Palisades, Calif.: Palisades Publishers, 1974.

Schlossberg, H. and Freeman, L. *Psychologist with a Gun.* New York: Coward, McCann & Geoghegan, 1974.

Shaw, L. The role of clothing in the criminal justice system. *Journal of Police Science and Administration* 1973, 1(4), 414–420.

Sherif, M., Harvey, O. J., White, B. J., Hood, W., and Sherif, C. *Intergroup Conflict and Cooperation: The Robbers Cave Experiment.* Norman, Okla.: University of Oklahoma Institute of Intergroup Relations, 1961.

Sherman, L. J. A psychological view of women in policing. *Journal of Police Science and Administration* 1973, 1(4), 383–394.

Steinberg, J. L. and McEvoy, D. W. *The Police and the Behavioral Sciences.* Springfield, Ill.: Charles C. Thomas, 1974.

Tenzel, J. H. and Cizanckas, V. The uniform experiment, *Journal of Police Science and Administration* 1973, 1(4), 421–424.

Wall, C. R. and Culloo, L. A. State standards for law enforcement selection and training. *Journal of Police Science and Administration* 1973, 1(4), 425–432.

Zimbardo, P. G., Haney, C. Banks, W. C., Jaffe, D. *The Stanford Prison Experiment: A Slide Show.* Stanford, Calif.: Philip G. Zimbardo, Inc., 1971.

CHAPTER 11

Berman, J. and Sales, B. D. A critical evaluation of the systematic approach to jury selection. Paper presented at 84th annual convention of American Psychological Association, Washington, D.C., 1976.

Boehm, V. R. Mr. Prejudice, Miss Sympathy and the Authoritarian Personality: An application of psychological measuring techniques to the problem of jury bias. *Wisconsin Law Review* 1968, 3, 734–750.

Emerson, C. D. Personality tests for prospective jurors. *Kentucky Law Journal* 1968, 56, 832–854.

Etzioni, A. Creating an imbalance. *Trial Magazine* November/December 1974, 10, 28–30.

Fried, M., Kaplan, K. J., and Klein, K. W. Juror selection: An analysis of voir dire. Chapter 2 in R. J. Simon (Ed.) *The Jury System in America: A Critical Overview*, Vol. IV. Sage Criminal Justice System Annuals. Beverly Hills: Sage Publications, 1975.

Golden, J. Jury selection: Can personality and attitude testing help? *Social Action and the Law* 1973, 1(1), 7–8.

Kalven, H., Jr. and Zeisel, H. *The American Jury* Boston: Little, Brown, 1966.

Mitchell, H. and Byrne, D. The defendant's dilemma: Effects of jurors' attitudes and authoritarianism on judicial decisions. *Journal of Personality and Social Psychology* 1973, 25, 123–129.

Moore, H. A., Jr. Redressing the balance. *Trial Magazine* November/December, 1974, 10, 29–35.

Plutchik, R. and Schwartz, A. K. Jury selection: Folklore or science? *Criminal Law Bulletin* May, 1965, 1(4), 3–10.

Sage, W. Psychology and the Angela Davis jury. *Human Behavior* 1973, 2(1), 56–61.

Saks, M. J. Social scientists can't rig juries. *Psychology Today* 1976, 9(8), 48ff.

Schulman, J., Shaver, P., Colman, R., Emrich, B., and Christie, R. Recipe for a jury. *Psychology Today* 1973, 6(12), 37–44ff.

Shapley, D. Jury selection: Social scientists gamble in an already loaded game. *Science* September 20, 1974, 185, 1033–1034, 1071.

Tivnan, E. Jury by trial. *The New York Times Magazine* November 16, 1975, 30ff.

Zeisel, H. and Seidman Diamond, S. The jury selection in the Mitchell-Stans conspiracy trial. *American Bar Association Research Journal* 1976, 1, 151–174.

CHAPTER 12

Apodaca et al. v. Oregon 406 U.S. 404.

Arenberg, D. Cognition and aging: Verbal learning, memory and problem solving. In C. Eisdorfer and M. P. Lawton (Eds.) *The Psychology of Adult Development and Aging.* Washington, D.C.: American Psychological Association, 1973, pp. 74–97.

Bales, R. F. Task roles and social roles in problem-solving groups. In E. E. Maccoby, T. M. Newcomb, and E. L. Hartley (Eds.) *Readings in Social Psychology* (3rd edition). New York: Holt, 1958.

Ballew v. Georgia 98 S. Ct. 1029 (1978).

Bem, D. J. Inducing belief in false confessions. *Journal of Personality and Social Psychology* 1966, 3, 707–710.

Brehm, J. W. and Cohen, A. R. *Explorations in Cognitive Dissonance.* New York: Wiley, 1962.

Buckhout, R. Eyewitness testimony. *Scientific American* December, 1974, 231, 23–31.

Buckhout, R. and Ellison, K. W. The line-up: A critical look. *Psychology Today* June, 1977, 11(1), 82–88.

Byrne, D. Attitudes and attraction. In L. Berkowitz (Ed.) *Advances in Experimental Social Psychology*, Vol. 4. New York: Academic Press, 1969.

Cohen, J. *Psychological Time in Health and Disease.* Springfield, Ill.: Charles C. Thomas, 1967.

Cray, E. Criminal interrogations and confessions: The ethical imperative. *Wisconsin Law Review* 1968, No. 1, 173–183.

Davis, J. H., Kerr, N. L., Atkin, R. S., Holt, R., and Meek, D. The decision processes of 6- and 12-person mock juries assigned unanimous and two-thirds majority rules. *Journal of Personality and Social Psychology* 1975, 32(1), 1–14.

Doob, A. N. and Kirshenbaum, H. M. Some empirical evidence on the effect of s. 12 of the Canada Evidence Act upon an accused. *Criminal Law Quarterly* 1972, 15(1), 88–96.

Driver, E. D. Confessions and the social psychology of coercion. *Harvard Law Review* 1968, 82, 42–61.

Feneck, N. Dogmatism and the ability to disregard inadmissible evidence. Unpublished doctoral dissertation. Hofstra University, 1977.

Festinger, L. *A Theory of Cognitive Dissonance.* Stanford: Stanford University Press, 1957.

Forston, R. F. The decision-making process in the American civil jury: A comparative methodological investigation. Unpublished doctoral dissertation.University of Michigan, 1968.

Freud, S. Psycho-analysis and the establishment of facts in legal proceedings. In J. Strachey (Ed.) *Standard Edition of the Complete Psychological Works of Sigmund Freud,* Vol. IX. London: Hogarth Press, p. 103. 1959.

Gerbasi, K. C. and Zuckerman, M. An experimental investigation of jury biasing factors. Paper presented at Eastern Psychological Association, New York, 1975.

Gerbasi, K. C., Zuckerman, M., and Reis, H. T. Justice needs a new blindfold: A review of mock jury research. *Psychological Bulletin* 1977, 84(2), 323-345.

Hans, V. P. and Doob, A. N. s. 12 of the Canada Evidence Act and the deliberations of simulated juries. *Criminal Law Quarterly* 1976, 18, 235-253.

Harris, R. Annals of Law: Trial by jury. *New Yorker* December 16, 1972, 117-125.

Hastorf, A. H. and Cantril, H. They saw a game: A case study. *Journal of Abnormal and Social Psychology* 1954, 49, 129-134.

Heider, F. *The Psychology of Interpersonal Relations.* New York: Wiley, 1958.

Hoiberg, B. C. and Stires, L. K. The effect of several types of pretrial publicity on the guilt attributions of simulated jurors. *Journal of Applied Social Psychology* 1973, 3(3), 267-275.

Inbau, F. E. and Reid, J. E. *Criminal Interrogation and Confessions.* Baltimore: Williams and Wilkins Co., 1962.

James, W. *The Principles of Psychology.* New York: Holt, 1890.

Janis, I. L. *Victims of "Groupthink."* Boston: Houghton Mifflin, 1972.

Johnson v. Louisiana 406 U.S. 356.

Johnson, C. and Scott, B. Eye witness testimony and suspect identification as a function of arousal, sex of witness, and scheduling of interrogation. Paper presented at 84th annual convention of American Psychological Association, Washington, D.C., 1976.

Jones, E. E. and Davis, K. E. From acts to dispositions: The attribution process in person perception. In L. Berkowitz (Ed.) *Advances in Experimental Social Psychology,* Vol. 2. New York: Academic Press, 1965.

Kadish, M. R. and Kadish, S. H. The institutionalization of conflict: Jury acquittals. *Journal of Social Issues* 1971, 27, 199-217.

Kalven, H., Jr. and Zeisel, H. *The American Jury.* Boston: Little, Brown, 1966.

Kessler, J. B. Social psychology of jury deliberations. Chapter 3 in R. J. Simon (Ed.) *The Jury System in America: A Critical Overview.* Sage Criminal Justice System Annuals, Vol. IV. Beverly Hills: Sage Publications, 1975.

Larntz, K. Reanalysis of Vidmar's data on the effects of decision alternatives on verdicts of simulated jurors. *Journal of Personality and Social Psychology* 1975, 31, 123-125.

Lawson, R. G. Relative effectiveness of one-sided and two-sided communications in courtroom persuasion. *Journal of General Psychology* 1970, 82, 3-16.

Lerner, M. J., Miller, D. T. and Holmes, J. G. Deserving and the emergence of forms of justice. In L. Berkowitz (Ed.) *Equity Theory: Towards a General Theory of Social Interaction,* Vol. 9 of *Advances in Experimental Social Psychology.* New York: Academic Press, 1976.

Lerner, M. J. and Simmons, C. Observer's reaction to the "innocent victim": Compassion or rejection? *Journal of Personality and Social Psychology* 1966, 4, 203-210.

Loftus, E. Reconstructing memory: The incredible eyewitness. *Psychology Today* December 1974, 8(7), 117-119.

Marquis, K., Oskamp, S., and Marshall, J. Testimony validity as a function of question form, atmosphere, and item difficulty. *Journal of Applied Social Psychology* 1972, 2(2), 167-186.

Marshall, J. *Law and Psychology in Conflict*. Indianapolis: Bobbs-Merrill, 1966.

McGuire, W. J. and Papageorgis, D. The relative efficacy of various types of prior belief-defense in producing immunity against persuasion. *Journal of Abnormal and Social Psychology* 1961, 62, 326–332.

Means, J. R. and Weiss, M. Gestural behavior of the courtroom witness. *The Journal of Forensic Psychology* 1971, 3(1), 12–20.

Merton, R. K. The self-fulfilling prophecy. Chapter 11 in *Social Theory and Social Structure* (revised and enlarged edition). Glencoe, Ill.: The Free Press, 1957.

Michotte, A. *The Perception of Causality*. New York: Basic Books, 1963.

Miller, N. and Campbell, D. T. Recency and primacy in persuasion as a function of the timing of speeches and measurements. *Journal of Abnormal and Social Psychology* 1959, 59(1), 1–9.

Miranda v. Arizona 384 U.S. 436.

Mitchell, H. E. and Byrne, D. The defendant's dilemma: Effects of jurors' attitudes and authoritarianism on judicial decisions. *Journal of Personality and Social Psychology* 1973, 25(1), 123–129.

Münsterberg, H. *On the Witness Stand: Essays on Psychology and Crime*. New York: Doubleday, Page & Co., 1909.

Münsterberg, H. The mind of the juryman. Chapter V in *Psychology and Social Sanity*. New York: Doubleday, 1914.

Münsterberg, H. Untrue confessions. In *On the Witness Stand: Essays on Psychology and Crime*. New York: Doubleday, Page & Co., 1909.

Myslieviec, S. R. Toward principles of jury equity. *Yale Law Journal* 1974, 83(5), 1023–1054.

Nemeth, C. Interactions between jurors as a function of majority vs. unanimity decision rules. *Journal of Applied Social Psychology* 1977, 7(1), 38–56.

Nemeth, C., Endicott, J., and Wachtler, J. From the '50s to the '70s: Women in jury deliberations. *Sociometry* 1976, 39(4), 293–304.

Nemeth, C., and Sosis, R. H. A simulated jury study: Characteristics of the defendant and the jurors. *The Journal of Social Psychology* 1973, 90, 221–229.

Padawer-Singer, A. and Barton, A. H. The impact of pre-trial publicity on jurors' verdicts. Chapter 5 in R. J. Simon (Ed.) *The Jury System in America: A Critical Overview*. Sage Criminal Justice System Annuals, Vol. IV. Beverly Hills: Sage Publications, 1975.

Padawer-Singer, A., Singer, A., and Singer, R. Voir dire by two lawyers: An essential safeguard. *Judicature* 1974, 57(9), 386–391.

Reik, T. *The Compulsion to Confess*. New York: Wiley Science Editions, 1966.

Schachter, S. Deviation, rejection and communication. *Journal of Abnormal and Social Psychology* 1951, 46, 190–207.

Schachter, S. and Singer, J. E. Cognitive, social and physiological determinants of emotion. *Psychological Review* 1962, 69, 379–399.

Schlossberg, H. and Freeman, L. *Psychologist with a Gun*. New York: Coward, McCann and Geoghegan, 1974.

Sears, D. O. Opinion formation and information preferences in an adversary situation. *Journal of Experimental Social Psychology* 1966, 2, 130–142.

Shaver, K. G. *An Introduction to Attribution Processes*. Cambridge, Mass.: Winthrop, 1975.

Shaw, L. Trial by jury: An analysis of the jury's verdict. Unpublished doctoral dissertation. Rensslaer Polytechnic Institute, 1975.

Sigall, H. and Ostrove, N. Beautiful but dangerous: Effects of offender attractiveness and nature of the crime on juridic judgment. *Journal of Personality and Social Psychology* 1975, 31(3), 410–414.

Simon, R. J. *The Jury and the Defense of Insanity*. Boston: Little, Brown, 1967.

Simon, R. J. Murder, juries, and the press. *Trans-Action* 1966, 3, 40–42.

Strodtbeck, F. L., James, R. M., and Hawkins, C. Social status in jury deliberations. *American Sociological Review* 1957, 22(6), 713–719.

Strodtbeck, F. L. and Mann, R. D. Sex role differentiation in jury deliberations. *Sociometry* 1956, 19, 3–11.

Sue, S., Smith, R. E., and Caldwell, C. Effects of inadmissible evidence on the decisions of simulated jurors: A moral dilemma. *Journal of Applied Social Psychology* 1973, 3(4), 345–353.

Thibaut, J., Walker, L., and Lind, E. A. Adversary presentation and bias in legal decisionmaking. *Harvard Law Review* 1972, 86, 386–401.

Toch, H. and Schulte, R. Readiness to perceive violence as a result of police training. *British Journal of Psychology* 1961, 52(4), 389–393.

Valenti, A. C. and Downing, L. L. Differential effects of jury size on verdicts following deliberation as a function of the apparent guilt of a defendant. *Journal of Personality and Social Psychology* 1975, 32(4), 655–663.

Vidmar, N. Effects of decision alternatives on the verdicts and social perceptions of simulated jurors. *Journal of Personality and Social Psychology* 1972, 22, 211–218.

Walker, L., Thibaut, J., and Andreoli, V. Order of presentation at trial. *Yale Law Journal* 1972, 82, 216–226.

Walster, E., Berscheid, E., and Walster, G. W. New directions in equity research. *Journal of Personality and Social Psychology* 1973, 25(2), 151–176.

Zimbardo, P. G. The psychology of police confessions. Paper read at 74th annual convention American Psychological Association, New York, 1966.

CHAPTER 14

Ayllon, T. Behavior modification in institutional settings. *Arizona Law Review* 1975, 17, 3–19.

Banuazizi, A. and Movahedi, S. Interpersonal dynamics in a simulated prison: A methodological analysis. *American Psychologist* 1975, 30(2), 152–160.

Baxstrom v. Herold 383 U.S. 107.

Bedau, H. A. *The Courts, the Constitution, and Capital Punishment.* Lexington, Mass.: Lexington Books, 1977.

Bedau, H. A. (Ed.) *The Death Penalty in America* (Revised edition). Garden City, N.Y.: Doubleday Anchor Books, 1967.

Bedau, H. A. and Pierce, C. M. (Eds.). *Capital Punishment in the United States.* New York: AMS Press, Inc., 1976.

Chaneles, S. Prisoners can be rehabilitated—now. *Psychology Today* October, 1976, 10(5), 129–134.

Clonce v. Richardson 379 F. Supp. 338.

Cloward, R. A. Social control in the prison. Chapter 5 in L. Hazelrigg (Ed.) *Prison Within Society.* Garden City, N.Y.: Doubleday Anchor Books, 1968.

Coleman, J. R. Prison guard in Texas for a week. *Fortune News* March, 1978, 8–10.

Durham, M. For the Swedes a prison sentence can be fun time. *Smithsonian* 1973, 4(6), 46–52.

Friedman, P. R. Legal regulation of applied behavior analysis in mental institutions and prisons. *Arizona Law Review* 1975, 17, 39–104.

Furman v. Georgia 408 U.S. 238.

Garrett v. Estelle 98 S.Ct. 3142 (1978).

Gotkin, J. New words for an old power trip: A critique of behavior modification in institutional settings. *Arizona Law Review* 1975, 17, 29–32.

Gregg v. Georgia 49 L. Ed. 2d 859.

Hamilton, V. L. and Rotkin, L. The capital punishment debate: Public perceptions of crime and punishment. Paper presented at 84th Convention American Psychological Association, Washington, D.C., 1976.

Holland, J. G. Behavior modification for prisoners, patients, and other people as a prescription for the planned society. *Mexican Journal of the Analysis of Behavior* 1975, 1(1), 81–95.

Holt v. Sarver 309 F. Supp. 362.

Jericho: Newsletter of the National Moratorium on Prison Construction.

Johnson, R. N. The state and death. *The New York Times* December 12, 1976, XI:44.

Kaufman, K. Prisoners, all. *The New York Times* March 25, 1976, p. 35.

Kittrie, N. N. *The Right to be Different* Baltimore: Penguin Books, 1973.

Knecht v. Gillman 488 F. 2d 1136.

Kohlberg, L. and Elfenbein, D. The development of moral judgments concerning capital punishment. *American Journal of Orthopsychiatry* 1975, 45(4), 614–640.

Kozol, H. L., Boucher, R. J., and Garofalo, R. F. The diagnosis and treatment of dangerousness. *Crime and Delinquency* 1972, 18, 371–392.

Kurland, P. B. (Ed.). *1976 The Supreme Court Review.* Chicago: University of Chicago Press, 1977.

Levenson, H. Multidimensional locus of control in prison inmates. *Journal of Applied Social Psychology* 1975, 5(4), 342–347.

Lockett v. Ohio 98 S.Ct. 2954 (1978).

Milan, M. A. and McKee, J. M. Behavior modification principles and application in corrections. In D. Glaser (Ed.) *Handbook of Criminology.* Chicago: Rand McNally, 1974.

Milgram, S. *Obedience to Authority: An Experimental View.* New York: Harper & Row, 1974.

Mitford, J. *Kind and Usual Punishment.* New York: Vintage Books, 1974.

Monahan, J. Prediction research and the emergency commitment of dangerous mentally ill persons: A reconsideration. *American Journal of Psychiatry* 1978, 135, 198–201.

Monahan, J. and Geis, G. Controlling "dangerous" people. *Annals of the American Academy of Political and Social Science* 1976, 423, 142–151.

Morris, N. *The Future of Imprisonment.* Chicago: University of Chicago Press, 1974.

New York Commission on Attica *Report,* 1972.

Opton, E. M., Jr. Institutional behavior modification as a fraud and sham. *Arizona Law Review* 1975, 17, 20–28.

Opton, E. M., Jr. Psychiatric violence against prisoners: When therapy is punishment. *Mississippi Law Journal* 1974, 45, 605–644.

Radzinowicz, L. *A History of English Criminal Law and its Administration from 1750,* Vol. 1. *The Movement for Reform.* London: Stevens & Sons Limited, 1948.

Royal Commission on Capital Punishment 1949–1953. *Report.* London: Her Majesty's Stationery Office, 1953.

Rudovsky, D. *The Rights of Prisoners.* New York: Avon Books, 1973.

Saunders, A. G., Jr. Behavior therapy in prisons: Walden II or Clockwork Orange? Paper presented at 8th annual convention of the Association for the Advancement of Behavior Therapy, Chicago, 1974.

Schlesinger, S. E. Psychotherapists in prison: The emperor's new clothiers? Paper presented at Symposium on Psychology and the Criminal Justice System. 48th meeting of the Eastern Psychological Association, Boston, 1977.

Sellin, T. (Ed.). *Capital Punishment.* New York: Harper & Row, 1967.

Shah, S. A. Dangerousness: A paradigm for exploring some issues in law and psychology. Invited address to 84th annual convention, American Psychological Association, Washington, D.C., 1976.

Skelton, W. D. Stress and coping in prison. Chapter 1 in *A Handbook of Correctional Psychiatry,* Vol. 1, 1968. Washington, D.C.: Department of Justice, U.S. Bureau of Prisons, 1968.

Skinner, B. F. To build constructive prison environments. Letter to the Editor. *The New York Times* February 26, 1974.

Solomon, G. F. Capital punishment as suicide and murder. *American Journal of Orthopsychiatry* 1975, 45(4), 701-711.

Sommer, R. *The End of Imprisonment.* New York: Oxford University Press, 1976.

Sommer, R. The social psychology of the cell environment. *The Prison Journal* 1971, 51(1), 15-21.

Steadman, H. J. and Keveles, G. The community adjustment and criminal activity of the Baxstrom patients: 1966-70. *American Journal of Psychiatry* 1972, 129, 304-310.

Stier, S. Prison research. *APA Monitor* 1976, 7(7), 1ff.

Trotter, S. Patuxent: "Therapeutic" prison faces test. *APA Monitor* 1975, 6(5), 1ff.

Vidmar, N. and Ellsworth, P. C. Public opinion on the death penalty. *Stanford Law Review* 1974, 26(6), 1245-1270.

Weiss, K. (Ed.). *The Prison Experience: An Anthology.* New York: Delacorte Press, 1976.

Williams v. Florida 399 U.S. 78.

Williams, W. and Miller, K. S. The role of personal characteristics in perceptions of dangerousness. *Criminal Justice and Behavior* 1977, 4(3), 241-252.

Witherspoon v. Illinois 391 U.S. 510.

Wolpe, J. *The Practice of Behavior Therapy.* New York: Pergamon Press, Inc., 1973.

Zeisel, H. The deterrent effect of the death penalty: Facts v. Faiths. In P. B. Kurland (Ed.) *1976 The Supreme Court Review.* Chicago: University of Chicago Press, 1977.

Zimbardo, P. G., Haney, C., Banks, W. C. and Jaffe, D. A Pirandellian prison: The mind is a formidable jailer. *The New York Times Magazine* April 8, 1973, 38-60.

Zimbardo, P. G., Haney, C., Banks, W. C., and Jaffe, D. *Stanford Prison Experiment.* Stanford, California: Philip G. Zimbardo, Inc., 1972. (Slide and tape program)

EPILOGUE

Ellsworth, P. C. and Ross, L. Public opinion and judicial decision-making: An example from research on capital punishment. In H. A. Bedau and C. M. Pierce (Eds.) *Capital Punishment in the United States.* New York: AMS Press, Inc., 1976.

Nizer, L. *My Life in Court.* New York: Pyramid Books, 1963.

Name Index

Adler, F., 63, 65, 313
Adorno, T. W., 219
Alex, N., 119, 128, 315, 316
Allport, G. W., 61, 70, 128, 313, 315
Anderson, D., 128
Andreoli, V., 222, 321
Arenberg, D., 263, 318
Aronson, E., 93, 315
Atkin, R. S., 318
Ayllon, T., 293, 321

Back, K. W., 70, 93, 313, 315
Badalamente, R. V., 107, 315
Baehr, M. E., 100, 127, 316
Bakkestrom, E., 314
Bales, R. F., 243, 246, 318
Banks, W. C., 317, 323
Bannon, J. D., 128, 316
Banuazizi, A., 291, 321
Bard, M., 113, 316
Barton, A. H., 248, 250, 320
Bazelon, D., 194
Bedau, H. A., 300, 301, 306 307, 312, 321, 323
Bell, L. S., 70
Bem, D. J., 128, 237, 316 318
Berkowitz, L., 67, 93, 264, 313, 315, 318, 319
Berman, J. 214–216, 317
Berrigan, P., 206
Berscheid, E., 257, 321
Bickman, L., 80–83, 86–90, 93, 120, 314–316
Binet, A., 41
Blackmun, H., 245
Bloch, P. B., 128
Boehm, V. R., 205, 317
Boggs, S. L., 313
Bork, R., 301

Borkowski, S., 93, 315
Boucher, R. J., 322
Brehm, J. W., 264, 318
Buckhout, R., 214, 228– 232, 263, 318
Buder, L., 92
Burger, W., 131
Byrne, D., 213, 264, 318

Caldwell, C., 263, 321
Campbell, C., 70, 313
Campbell, D. T., 221, 320
Cantril, H., 230, 319
Cardozo, B., 24
Carlo, G. 68
Cassese, S., 128
Carlsmith, J. M., 128, 313, 316
Chambers, M., 219
Chaneles, S., 321
Chevigny, P., 117, 316
Christiansen, K. O., 48– 49, 69, 313, 314
Christie, R., 206, 209, 2ll–213, 318
Cizanckas, V., 121, 317
Cloward, R. A., 321
Cocozza, J. J., 70, 314
Cohen, A. R., 264, 318
Cohen, J., 263, 318
Coleman, J. R., 305, 321
Colman, R., 318
Conley, J., 253
Cramer, J., 115, 316
Cray, E., 318
Cressey, D. R., 305
Crosby, A., 101, 316
Culloo, L. A., 102, 317
Cunningham, B., 128

Darley, J., 82, 84, 87, 93, 315
Darrow, C., 129, 203, 217, 304
Darwin, C., 37, 38

Davis, A., 206, 208, 209, 216, 232
Davis, J. H., 247, 318
Davis, K. E., 260, 319
Delaney, P., 127
Dickens, C., 307
Doob, A. N., 252, 253, 318, 319
Douglas, W. O., 247
Downing, L. L., 247, 321
Drähms, A., 69, 313
Driver, E. D., 237–239, 263, 318
Dubnikov, A., 70
Dugdale, R., 41, 313
Durham, M., 305, 321
Durk, D., 119

Ebbesen, E. B., 159, 172
Edwards, G., 67, 70, 313
Edwards, J., 93, 315
Eisdorfer, C., 263, 318
Eisenberg, T., 99, 100, 103, 316
Elfenbein, D., 306, 322
Ellison, K. W., 263, 318
Ellsworth, P. C., 301, 306, 307, 311, 312, 323
Emerson, C. D., 204, 205, 317
Emrich, B., 318
Endicott, J., 256, 320
Erikson, E. H., 39, 69, 313
Esquirol, E., 41
Etzioni, A., 216, 317

Feneck, N., 252, 319
Ferrero, W., 69, 314
Ferretti, F., 127
Festinger, L., 70, 85, 93, 128, 264, 313, 315, 316, 319
Fink, A. E., 35, 36, 39– 42, 69, 313
Fleming, A. E., 316

Forston, R. F., 263, 319
Fowle, F., 305
Fowler, O. S., 35, 69, 313
Fraser, S. C., 128, 316
Freedman, J. L., 55, 128, 313, 316
Freedman, M. H., 202
Freeman, L., 128, 231, 317, 320
Frenkel-Brunswik, E., 219
Freud, S., 12, 45, 60, 136, 192, 202, 319
Fried, M., 217–219, 317
Friedlander, K., 60, 70, 313
Friedman, P. R., 306, 321
Froemel, E. C., 127, 316
Furcon, J. E., 127, 316

Galton, F., 41
Garfield, J., 36
Garofalo, R. F., 322
Geis, G., 91, 315, 322
Gelfand, D. M., 83, 93, 315
Genovese, K., 87, 90, 91
George, C. E., 315
Gerbasi, K. C., 319
Gibbons, D., 62, 63, 313
Gilmore, G., 307
Glaser, D., 69, 305, 313, 314, 322
Goddard, H. H., 41, 313
Golden, J., 204, 318
Goldsmith, J. G., 128, 317
Goldsmith, S. S., 128, 317
Goldstein, T., 312
Goodenough, D. R., 314
Gotkin, J., 321
Gottfredson, M., 78, 80, 315
Green, S. K., 82, 83, 93, 314, 315
Greenberg, M. S., 84, 85, 93, 315
Guiteau, C., 36

Hall, G. S., 39, 313
Hall, J. F., 20
Halterlein, P. J., 315
Hamilton, V. L., 306, 321
Haney, C., 317, 323
Hans, V. P., 252, 253, 319
Harris, R., 263, 319
Hartley, E. L., 318

Hartmann, D. P., 93, 315
Harvey, O. J., 128, 317
Hastorf, A. H., 230, 319
Hawkins, C., 255, 321
Hazelrigg, L., 321
Healy, W., 36, 41, 42, 313
Heider, F., 260, 264, 319
Hellman, P., 68, 70, 313
Herbst, M., 210
Herman, R. D., 206
Hindelang, M. J., 72–74, 78, 80, 92, 315
Hirschhorn, K., 314
Hoiberg, B. C., 249, 319
Holland, J. G., 306, 322
Holmes, J. G., 259, 319
Holmes, O. W., 5, 11
Holt, R., 318
Hood, R., 59, 70, 313, 314
Hood, W., 128, 317
Horn, J., 68, 313, 315
Huston, T. L., 90, 91, 315

Inbau, F. E., 263, 319
Inn, A., 126, 316

Jackson, B., 305
Jackson, T. T., 315
Jaffe, D., 317, 323
James, R. M., 255, 321
James, W., 224, 262, 319
Janis, I. L., 219, 244, 319
Janson, D., 127
Johnson, C., 227, 228, 263, 319
Johnson, R. N., 300, 322
Jones, C., 93, 315
Jones, E. E., 260, 319
Joseph, N., 119, 316

Kadish, M. R., 263, 319
Kadish, S. H., 263, 319
Kalven, H., Jr., 210, 214, 261, 318, 319
Kaplan, K. J., 217, 317
Kaufmann, K., 305, 322
Kelley, C. M., 64, 70, 313
Kelman, H. C., 93, 315
Kent, D. A., 99, 100, 316
Kerckhoff, A. C., 93, 315
Kerr, N. L., 318
Kessler, J. B., 244, 248, 263, 319
Keveles, G., 323
Kirkham, G. L., 110, 316

Kirshenbaum, H. M., 252, 253, 318
Kissinger, H., 206
Kittrie, N. N., 293, 322
Klein, K. W., 217, 317
Kohlberg, L., 306, 322
Kohn, I. R., 70
Konečni, V. J., 159, 172
Kotinsky, R., 313
Kozol, H. L., 299, 322
Kurland, P. B., 306, 322, 323

Lamarck, J.-B., 37
Larntz, K., 319
Latané, B., 82, 84, 87, 93, 315
Laurence, J., 307
Lawson, R. G., 221, 319
Lawton, M. P., 263, 318
Lefkowitz, J., 94, 122, 125, 128, 316
Lavrakas, P. J., 93, 315
LePage, A., 313
Lerner, M. J., 259, 319
Levenson, H., 387, 322
Levinson, D., 219
Lewin, K., 38, 69, 314
Lewis, M., 55, 314
Lincoln, A., 129
Lind, E. A., 224, 321
Little, J., 206, 211, 212
Locasso, R. M., 70
Loftus, E., 232, 233, 319
Lombroso, C., 38, 39, 41, 42, 69, 314
Lunde, D. T., 66–68, 314
Lundstean, C., 314

Macaulay, J., 93, 315
Maccoby, E. E., 318
Maness, D., Jr., 78, 79, 315
Mann, R. D., 255, 321
Mansson, H., 226
Margolis, R. J., 104–107, 316
Marquis, K., 227, 319
Marshall, J., 225–227, 229, 263, 319, 320
Marshall, T., 301
Mayer, J., 204
McAlister, E., 206
McDonald, W. F., 93, 315
McEvoy, D. W., 106, 316, 317

McGuire, W. J., 262, 320
McKee, J. M., 305, 322
Means, J. R., 234, 320
Mednick, S., 42, 43, 45–48, 69, 313, 314
Meehl, P. E., 69, 314
Meek, D., 318
Merton, R. K., 263, 320
Michotte, A., 229, 320
Milan, M. A., 305, 322
Milgram, S., 70, 128, 305, 314, 316, 322
Miller, D. T., 259, 319
Miller, K. S., 323
Miller, M. G., 128, 317
Miller, N., 221, 320
Mindszenty, J., 236
Minor, W. W., 70
Mitchell, H. E., 213, 318, 320
Mitchell, J., 210, 211, 219
Mitford, J., 305, 322
Monahan, J., 322
Moore, H. A., Jr., 216, 318
Moore, S. A., 315
Morris, N., 295, 322
Morrison, W. D., 69
Movahedi, S., 291, 321
Münsterberg, H., 38, 203, 224, 225, 235, 240, 241, 255, 262, 263, 320
Myslieviec, S. R., 261, 262, 320

Nagel, S. S., 172
Nemeth, C., 241, 242, 245–247, 254, 256, 320
Newcomb, T. M., 318
Newman, O., 54, 55, 89, 314, 315
New York State Special Commission on Attica, 305, 322
Niederhoffer, A., 94, 316
Nizer, L., 312, 323
Nordheimer, J., 306, 307
North-Walker, N., 93, 315

O'Barr, W., 253
Oliver, J., 297
Opton, E. M., Jr., 306, 322
Ordronaux, J., 69, 314
Orne, M. T., 128, 316
Oskamp, S., 227, 319

Ostrove, N., 263, 320
Owen, D. R., 314

Padawer-Singer, A., 248–250, 263, 320
Page, B., 93, 315
Papageorgis, D., 262, 320
Pavlov, I., 43, 44
Philip, J., 314
Pierce, C. M., 306, 307, 312, 321, 323
Pinel, P., 36
Plutchik, R., 203, 204, 318
Police Training and Performance Study, 106, 316
Powell, L., 245
Prescott, C., 290, 291
Prial, F. J., 128
Priestley, J., 69

Radzinowicz, L., 306, 307, 322
Ray, I., 41
Reid, J. E., 263, 319
Reik, T., 235, 236, 263, 320
Reinke, R. W., 103, 316
Reis, H. T., 319
Reiss, A. J., Jr., 113, 317
Rensberger, B., 307
Richardson, J. F., 127, 317
Rio, P., 315
Robin, G. D., 127, 317
Roebuck, J., 62, 70, 314
Rokeach, M., 57, 125, 126, 128, 314, 317
Rosenthal, R., 117, 317
Ross, L., 311, 312, 323
Rotkin, L., 306, 321
Royal Commission on Capital Punishment, 306, 307, 322
Rubin, D. B., 314
Rubin, J. G., 110, 112, 114, 128, 317
Rudovsky, D., 305, 322
Rule, A., 93, 315
Rush, B., 36, 69

Sage, W., 208, 209, 318
Saks, M. J., 213, 214, 318
Sales, B. D., 214–216, 317
Samenow, S. E., 56–59, 314

Sanford, N., 219
Saunders, A. G., Jr., 297, 306, 322
Schachter, S., 70, 247, 263, 313, 320
Schlesinger, S. E., 322
Schlossberg, H., 115, 121, 128, 231, 317, 320
Schulman, J., 206–209, 211–213, 318
Schulsinger, F., 314
Schulte, R., 231, 321
Schwartz, A. K., 203, 204, 318
Scott, B., 227, 228, 263, 319
Sears, D. O., 262, 313, 320
Seidman Diamond, S., 210, 211, 318
Sellin, T., 306, 307, 322
Serpico, F., 119
Serrill, M. S., 70, 314
Shah, S. A., 322
Shakespeare, W., 17
Shane-DuBow, S., 93, 315
Shapley, D., 213, 318
Shaver, K. G., 264, 320
Shaver, P., 318
Shaw, L., 120, 220, 317, 320
Sherif, C., 128, 317
Sherif, M., 128, 317
Sherman, L. J., 116, 117, 128, 317
Sigall, H., 263, 320
Simmons, C., 319
Simon, A., 41
Simon, R. J., 65, 250, 263, 314, 317, 319, 320
Singer, A., 263, 320
Singer, J. E., 263, 320
Singer, R., 263, 320
Skelton, W. D., 284–286, 322
Skinner, B. F., 44, 306, 323
Smith, A. E., 78, 79, 315
Smith, R. E., 263, 321
Snyder, J. A., 128, 317
Solomon, G. F., 307, 323
Sommer, R., 283, 284, 288, 305, 323
Sosis, R. H., 254, 320
Sparks, R., 59, 70, 313, 314
Sparling, C. L., 126, 316

Stans, M., 210, 211
Starr, B., 39
Steadman, H. J., 70, 314, 323
Steinberg, J. L., 316, 317
Stevens, W. K., 128
Stier, S., 323
Stires, L. K., 249, 319
Stock, R. W., 50, 51, 314
Stocking, M., 314
Strachey, J., 319
Strodtbeck, F. L., 255, 321
Sue, S., 251, 263, 321
Sutherland, E. H., 305
Suttles, G., 53, 54, 69, 314

Taylor, W. M., 307
Tenzel, J. H., 121, 317
Thibaut, J., 222, 224, 321
Thorndike, E., 44
Tivnan, E., 211, 212, 318
Toch, H., 93, 231, 321

Treaster, J. B., 128
Trotter, S., 306, 323

Valenti, A. C., 247, 321
Vaughan, D., 68
Viano, E. C., 93, 314
Vidmar, N., 301, 306, 307, 321, 323
von Liszt, 225

Wachtler, J., 256, 320
Wald, P. M., 161, 172
Walder, P., 93, 315
Walker, L., 222–224, 321
Wall, C. R., 102, 317
Walster, E., 257, 258, 321
Walster, G. W., 257, 321
Warren, E., 185, 238
Weinberg, A., 202
Weiss, K., 323
Weiss, M., 234, 320
Wheeler, A. C., 126, 316
White, B., 247

White, B. J., 128, 317
Whyte, W. H., Jr., 70, 314
Wicker, T., 307
Williams, W., 323
Wilson, C., 84
Wilt, G. M, 128, 316
Witkin, H. A., 50–52, 314
Witmer, H., 313
Wolfgang, M. E., 66, 67, 314
Wolpe, J., 323
Wright, R., 315
Wuert, J., 93, 315

Yochelson, S., 56–59, 314

Zeisel, H., 210, 211, 214, 261, 302, 303, 306, 307, 318, 319, 323
Zimbardo, P. G., 120, 234, 239, 263, 280, 289–291, 317, 321, 323
Zuckerman, M., 319

Subject Index

abortion, 18
accomplice, 27, 38, 184, 188
accessories, 27
accident, 24
accusatory instrument, 140, 144, 150, 152, 153, 155, 157, 158
ACOD. *See* adjournment in contemplation of dismissal
acquiescence response set, 204
acquittal, 27, 50, 146, 155, 170, 173, 179, 197, 199, 201
action
    civil, 4, 142, 158, 171
    criminal, 4, 133, 140, 142, 171
    in equity, 4
adjective law, 9
adjournment, 177
    in contemplation of dismissal, 144, 156
administrative agencies, 6, 7, 16
administrative orders, 31
admissions, 5, 185
adultery, 19, 20, 59
adversary system, 10, 99, 171, 214, 217, 222–224, 310
affidavits, 141
age regression technique, 233
aggregate maximum term, 270, 271
aggregate minimum term, 270
aggressiveness, 51, 52, 67
aided case, 109
alcoholics, 17
alibi, 171, 172
altruism, 87
American Bar Association, 11, 130, 132
American Civil Liberties Union, 213, 279, 297
American Jury, The, 214
American Law Institute, 194
American Psychiatric Association, 189, 311
American Psychological Association, 101, 134, 311

amicus curiae brief, 189
answer, 158
anthropometry, 37, 38
antisocial behavior, 12, 15, 16, 19, 39, 41, 43, 46, 48, 50, 57, 309
appeals, legal, 7, 147, 148, 158, 173, 274–277
appeals, rational and emotional, 221, 238
Apodaca et al. v. Oregon, 245, 263, 318
Apomorphine, 298
appearance ticket, 142, 152, 153
arguments, one-sided v. two-sided, 220, 221
arraignment, 142
    to the charge, 147–150, 153–156, 158, 168
    to the indictment, 144, 148, 164, 168–171
arrest, 141, 142, 147, 148, 150–153, 188
    by citizen, 151
    false, 151
    force in making, 150
    illegal, 19, 32, 153
    record of, 158, 265
    resisting, 150
    search incident to, 151
    trends by sex in, 64
arrested development, 39
arson, 23, 32, 36
assault, 2, 4, 23, 26, 53, 57, 62–64, 72–77, 91, 114, 182, 184
atavism, 38, 39
attempt to commit a crime, 26, 27, 77
Attica, 280, 284
attitude change, 58, 256–262. *See also* persuasion
    in groups, 58
attorney, 17, 31, 132. *See also* lawyer
    assigned, 154, 169
attractiveness, 253, 254
attribution theory, 229, 257, 260, 261
Auburn, 279

authoritarianism, 204, 205, 218, 219
authoritarian personality, 212, 213, 217, 218
autonomic nervous system, 44–46, 48
  parasympathetic division of, 45
  sympathetic division of, 45, 230
auto theft, 53, 64, 77
auto thieves, 59, 62
aversive conditioning, 294, 295, 298

bail, 30, 110, 142, 144, 146, 147, 152, 153, 157–162, 169, 170, 201
  excessive, 9, 158
  factors in setting, 159–162
  pre-arraignment, 152
Ballew v. Georgia, 263, 318
Bambino, People v., 14, 20
bar associations, 17
bar examination, 132, 136
Baxstrom v. Herold, 321
behavior disorder, 192, 193, 205
behavior modification, 135, 293, 310
  in prison, 293–298
    ethical problems in, 294, 298, 310
  techniques of, 294–298
beliefs, self-contradictory, 57
bill of attainder, 8
bill of particulars, 168
Bill of Rights, 8
biofeedback, 44
Biosocial Bases of Criminal Behavior, 42
blackmail, 32
block watchers, 87
blue laws, 15
bookmakers, 18
bootleggers, 19
Bouton, People v., 33
Brawner, U.S. v., 194
bribery, 23
burden of proof, 31, 32, 145, 146, 267
burglary, 32, 50, 53, 62–64, 76–80, 91, 224
burglar, 53, 62
business records, 182
bystander, 71, 80, 83, 84, 86, 90–93
  intervention in crimes, 82, 90, 91

capacity to commit a crime, 28–30
capacity to form intent, 24, 25
capital cases, 154, 303, 304

capital punishment, 29, 36, 67, 300–305. See also death penalty
  as deterrent, 36, 301–304
  as retribution, 301, 302, 304
  in England, 300, 301
career clothing, 121
case law, 5, 6
case study method, 130
catatonic, 25
cause of action, 2, 158
Central Criminal Justice Services Department, 152
cerebral degeneration, 39, 40
certification of psychologist, 133, 134, 137
certification of social worker, 137
certifying boards, 130
challenges of jurors, 162
  for cause, 176, 177
  peremptory, 176, 177
  to the array, 174, 175
  to the poll, 175
character committee of bar association, 132
character disorders, 37
charge of court, 198–200, 251
Chicago 7 case, 213
children, 28, 29, 43, 195
chromosomal testing, 51
chromosomes, 50–52, 59
citizen crime reporting projects, 86–90
civil action. See action, civil
civil commitment to mental hospital, 26
civil liberties, 8
civil negligence, 24
civilian complaint review boards, 127
classification, 21, 59, 61, 62
  empirical schemes of, 60, 61
  theoretical schemes of, 61
clear and present danger, 310
clergymen, 135
clerkship, legal, 132
clerkship, medical, 136
Clockwork Orange, The, 295
Clonce v. Richardson, 297, 298, 321
closing arguments, 146, 221
closure, 110
co-conspirators, 27, 33
cognitive dissonance, theory of, 58, 257
cognitive model of intervention, 82
cognitive set, 218, 219

collateral issues in trials, 188
commercial dishonesty, 68, 69, 76
commissioner of jurors, 174
common law, 5, 27, 32, 195
 English, 3, 5, 10
 Federal, 6
 jurisdictions, 14
communicator, characteristics of, 83
complainant, 91, 140, 150, 184, 187
complaint, 153, 158
 bureau, 150
 felony, 140–142, 149, 157, 169
 misdemeanor, 140–142, 155, 157
concordance rate, twins, 49
conditioned response, 43, 44
conditioned stimulus, 44
conditioning, 43, 44
 classical, 43–45
 instrumental, 43–45
 operant, 44
 Pavlovian, 43
 respondent, 43
 stimulus substitution, 43
confession, 36, 173, 185, 186, 234. See also
  interrogation
 coerced, 185, 236
 compulsive, 185, 235
 false, 185, 234, 235, 237
 involuntary, 185, 235
 recanted, 235, 249
 uncorroborated, 185
 voluntary, 185
confidentiality, 196
conformity, 218, 219, 232, 240
conjugal visits, 292
conscience, 45, 46, 57
consensual sodomy, 19
consistency theories, 256–260
contempt of court, 164
Congress, 7
consolidation of charges, 167, 168
conspiracy, 26–28, 164
conspirators, 34
Constitutional issues, 32
Constitutional rights. See rights, constitutional
Consumer Protection Agency, 16
control groups, experimental, 40, 88,
  207

conviction, 8, 26, 28, 30, 157, 167, 170,
  173, 177, 182, 197, 198, 201, 202,
  265–267
 felony, 22, 267
 misdemeanor, 22
 prior, 156, 160, 161, 182. See also criminal record
cop, polite, 123, 124
cop, tough, 111, 123, 124
corporal punishment, 278, 281
corpus delecti, 23, 25, 31, 140, 183
Correction Law, 269
correctional personnel, 14. See also prison
  guards
correctional system, 14
Corrections, Department of, 270, 271
corrections official, 58
corroboration, 27, 184, 185
 in sex crimes, 184
costs-benefits ratio, 84, 90, 257, 258
co-twin studies, 48, 49
counsel, 9, 25, 165. See also attorney
 assigned, 154, 169
counts of indictment, 198, 199, 201
 concurrent, 199
 consecutive, 199
 duplicious, 167
 inconsistent, 199
 submitted to jury, 200
court, 3, 23, 29, 311
 appellate, 22, 139, 147, 148, 177, 195,
   265, 273
  scope of review by, 276
 Appellate Division of New York Supreme,
   133, 268, 274, 275
 city, 131
 county, 139, 274, 275
 criminal, 29, 30, 33, 140
 district, 5, 139
 family, 29, 166
 federal, 132
 intermediate appellate, 275, 277
 King's, 3
 law, 3, 4
 local criminal, 137, 140, 142, 144, 147,
   148, 150, 153, 157, 163, 165, 166,
   168, 169
 magistrates, 143
 minutes of proceedings, 201

court (*Continued*)
  New York Supreme, 5, 139, 274, 275
    appellate term of, 275
  New York City Criminal, 139
  of Appeals, New York, 275, 277
  of Appeals, United States, 194
  of chancery, 3
  of equity, 3, 4
  of Special Sessions, 143
  order, 155, 275, 276
  superior criminal, 139, 140, 144, 148,
    156, 157, 166
  town, 139
  trial, 139
  United States Supreme, 6, 9, 20, 32, 132,
    133, 175, 220, 245–247, 300, 301,
    303, 308
  village, 139
cranial capacity, 38
crime, 8, 13, 16, 20–22, 25, 27–30, 33, 36,
    38, 40–43, 49, 50, 52, 55–57, 59, 60,
    139, 143, 144, 150, 152, 159, 167,
    271, 272, 309. *See also* offenses
  attempt to commit a, 26, 27, 77
  capital, 29, 159
  characteristics of, 75
  common law, 14
  compounding a, 28
  degrees of, 27, 28
  fighting, 110, 111, 114
  malum in se, 23, 24
  malum prohibitum, 23, 24
  of mental culpability, 23, 24
  of strict liability, 23, 24
  prevention, 111–114
    through environmental design, 55
  principals in, 27
  rate, 53, 61
  records, 54, 89
  regulatory, 309
  reporting, 68, 69, 71, 76–90
    reasons for not, 77
    survey data on, 76
  sex, 17, 19, 57, 184, 309
  statutory, 14
  street, 68, 126
  urban, 53
  victimless, 18, 19, 23

  violent, 29, 39, 52, 64, 65, 74–77, 112,
    309
  street, 29
criminal, 14, 17, 23, 33–70
  action. *See* action, criminal
  acts or omissions, 24, 41, 56, 57, 60
  amateur, 63
  behavior, 32, 34, 35, 38, 39, 41, 46–48,
    50, 52, 53, 56, 57, 61, 62
    patterns of, 62, 63
    theories of, 35–59
  careers, 60, 62, 63, 77
  code, 26, 31
  culpability, inchoate, 28
  culpability, lack of, 31
  dangerous, 8, 65, 171, 299, 310
  facilitation, 26, 28
  female, 34, 38, 63–65, 118
  individual, 60
  intent, 23, 27
  Justice Information and Statistics Service,
    National, 72
  justice system, 10, 12, 13, 77, 127, 129,
    180, 308, 309, 311, 312
    goals of, 13, 20
  law, 12, 17, 21, 22, 50, 129, 198, 309
    adjective, 33, 139
    New York, 31
    procedural, 33, 139
    substantive, 20, 33
  lawyer. *See* lawyer, criminal
  liability, 25, 29, 30, 41
  negligence, 22, 24
  non-dangerous, 65
  offense, 8, 26
  Personality, The, 56
  petty, 34
  procedure, 4, 8, 29, 32
  Procedure Law, 139, 143, 162
  professional, 18, 60, 63, 66
  record, 22, 29, 30, 43, 46, 49, 60, 62, 73,
    102, 152, 170, 183, 188, 226, 267,
    274, 282
    effects on juries, 252, 253
  responsibility, 29–31
  social, 60
  solicitation, 26, 28, 167
  statutes, 16, 20

traits, 41
trial, 29, 30, 149
types, 33, 38, 62
white collar, 59, 284
cross examination, 9, 26, 79, 145, 146, 156,
162-165, 181-183, 186, 188-190,
192, 193
crowding, 288
culpability, 13, 14

damages, money, 3, 4, 92
dangerousness. *See* criminal, dangerous
Danish National Police Register, 42, 51
Davis case, Angela, 206, 208, 209, 232
death, 25
penalty, 21, 29, 67, 177, 275, 277, 300-
305, 308. *See also* capital punishment
arguments favoring, 301-303
arguments opposing, 301-304
public opinion and, 301, 302, 304
decision-making, 220
Declaration of Independence, 278
deductive reasoning, 61
defect of reason, 25
defendant's personal statement on sentencing, 265
defense
affirmative, 31-33
attorney, 30, 129, 143, 158, 165, 166,
169, 171, 177, 185, 187, 197, 202,
265, 266, 273
mechanism, 12
ordinary, 31, 32
personal, 27, 28
defenses, 30, 31, 33, 171
defensible space, 54, 55
degenerate behavior, 39
delinquency, 39, 59. *See also* juvenile delinquent
delusions, 125, 191
demand characteristics, 239, 251, 292
Dennison, Kentucky v., 20
depositions, supporting, 141, 147, 157
depravity, inherent, 40
deterrent, 12, 40, 67
deviant sexual conduct, 151
diagnosis, medical, 21
diagnosis, psychological, 21, 138

dicta, 6
obiter, 6
direct case, 146, 149, 179
direct examination, 145, 186, 188
disbarment, 133
disciplinary proceedings, 133
discovery proceedings, 171, 172
dismissal of charges, 155, 169
dissociation of personality, 235
district attorney, 10, 19, 80, 92, 129, 140,
143, 145, 146, 154, 156, 158, 160-
163, 165, 166, 170, 178. *See also*
prosecutor
divorce, 19
doctoral dissertation, 133
dogmatism, 204, 205, 252
double jeopardy, 9, 143, 155, 276
drug, 73
abuser, 56
addict, 54
law, 16
offense, 17, 23, 62
usage, 16, 56, 68
drunkenness, 62
drunken driving, 22, 31, 64, 167, 168
D.S.W. (Doctor of Social Welfare), 137
due process of law, 9, 10
Durham rule, 194
duress, defense of, 24, 32
duty, 2, 120, 202
dying declaration, 181

economic deprivation, 42, 56
educational level, 57
egalitarianism, 205, 213, 217
electrodermal recovery (EDRec), 46-48
embezzlement, 59
embezzler, 34, 53, 63
emotional contagion, 85, 86
emotional deprivation, 56
entrapment, defense of, 19, 32, 33
environment, 41, 43, 47-50, 87
English legal system, 3
equifinality, 260
equity, juries as preservers of, 261, 262
equity theory, 257, 258
Erie v. Thomkins, 6, 11

escape, 32
  first degree, 32
Escobedo v. Illinois, 186, 202
ethical duty, 10
ethics, 134, 196, 216, 310
  in research, 80, 86, 208, 291
etiology, organic, 193
ethnic minorities, 175, 203, 204
evidence, 10, 11, 31, 131, 163, 168, 173,
    179–188, 193, 196, 198, 285
  admissibility of, 144, 163, 200
  autoptic, 180
  character, 182
  circumstantial, 180, 232
  corroborative, 26
  direct, 180
  documentary, 165, 180
  hearsay, 156, 163, 181, 182, 185
  illegally obtained, 131
  immaterial, 180
  inadmissible, 180, 249, 251–253
  irrelevant, 180
  legal, 156, 163, 166, 199, 267
  legally sufficient, 199
  objections to, 180, 197
    specific, 180
    general, 180
  physical, 165
  planting of, 19
  preponderance of, 31, 32, 267
  real, 180
  rules of, 163, 179–188, 225
  suppression of illegally obtained, 131, 151
  testimonial, 179, 180, 232
evolution, 37, 38
execution, 36, 159, 300, 301, 304, 305
exertion, 260
exhibits, 200
expectancy and witnessing. *See* witnesses
experimenter bias, 241
ex post facto law, 8
extenuating circumstances, 29

fact in issue, 180
faith healer, 134
Family Crisis Intervention Unit, 113, 114,
    117
Federal Bureau of Investigation, 64, 212
Federal Bureau of Prisons, 296, 297

Federal Communications Commission, 7
federal government, 6, 7, 14
feeblemindedness, 35, 40–42
felon, 32, 43
felony, 5, 9, 19–22, 27, 28, 30, 139–141,
    143, 144, 148, 149, 151, 152, 156,
    157, 162, 163, 166, 167, 173, 174,
    177, 201, 266, 268, 269, 271, 272,
    275
  armed, 29, 30, 157
  Class A, 22, 27, 141, 157, 166, 171, 177,
    268, 269
    I, 22, 30, 268, 269
    II, 22, 30, 269
    III, 22, 171, 268, 269, 272
  Class B, 22, 27, 171, 177, 268–270
  Class C, 22, 27, 177, 268–270
  Class D, 22, 27, 268–270, 272
  Class E, 22, 27, 268, 269, 272
  violent, 270
fiduciary, 141
field placement, 137
field work, 137
fingerprints, 151, 265
first impressions, 223
Food and Drug Administration, 283
force, 23, 150, 185
  use of, 32, 117, 126
  use of deadly, 32
forfeiture of office, 21
forgers, 34, 59
forgery, 23
Fortune News, 305
Fortune Society, The, 289
fraud, consumer, 68, 69
fugue state, 235
Furman v. Georgia, 301, 306, 321

gamblers, 62
gambling, 16, 18, 23
Garrett v. Estelle, 307, 321
genetics, 42, 48–52
  and criminal behavior, 49
Gestalt psychology, 256, 257, 260
good behavior, time off for, 272
Good Samaritan laws, 90, 91
"good time," 271
graduate education, 129
graduate school, 53, 129

grand jury, 9, 139, 140, 142–144, 148,
    149, 156, 157, 162–170, 176, 177
  foreman, 162, 167
  minutes of, 169
  oath, 162
  quorum, 162
  runaway, 163, 165
  secrecy of proceedings, 164
Gregg v. Georgia, 306, 321
gross order, 222–224
group
  dynamics, 137, 242, 243, 248
  norms, 243
  pressure, 215, 218, 240, 243, 244
  size, 244
groups, research on, 242–245
groupthink, 215, 244
gun control, 67, 68

habeas corpus, 4, 8
half-way programs, 310
halo effect, 253
Harrisburg 7 case, 206–208, 216
hearing, 267
  felony, 144, 148, 157, 169, 170
  misdemeanor, 147, 157
  preliminary, 142, 143, 149, 156–158,
    162, 176
heredity, 35, 39–42, 50
hijacking, 16
Holt v. Sarver, 305, 322
homicide, 16, 23, 53, 66–68, 113, 114, 161
homosexual, 19
hostage units, 114, 115
hypnosis, 233, 234
hypothesis testing, 61
hypothetical construct, 98
hypothetical question, 189, 193

identity, negative, 39
illegal actions by police, 19
immunity from prosecution, 155, 164, 165
immunity, waiver of, 164, 165
Impact Cities Victim Survey, 71–78
impeachment of witness. *See* witness, im-
    peachment of
impressions, initial, 220, 223
imprisonment, 278–305. *See also* incarcera-
    tion

alternatives to, 92, 299, 300, 310
  effects on inmates' families, 13, 197,
    281, 285
  intermittent. *See* sentences of imprison-
    ment, intermittent
  life, 29, 269, 270, 302
  mandatory, 270, 308
  recidivism and. *See* recidivism
incarceration, 30, 310. *See also* imprison-
    ment
indictment, 140, 144, 148, 156, 157, 162,
    163, 166–168, 177, 201
  amendment of, 168
  multi-count, 170
  sealed, 164, 165, 168
  trial of, 173
  waiver of, 166
inductive reasoning, 61
infancy, 31, 184
infant, 27, 28
infanticides, 38
information, 140–142, 147, 155, 157, 169
  prosecutor's, 140, 166
  simplified, 140, 141, 157
  superior court, 140, 166
information integration theory, 159
injunction, 4
inquisitorial system, 224, 310
insanity, 50, 56, 60
  defense of, 189–192, 196
  plea, 36
insurance, 78, 79
intelligence (IQ), 41, 47, 50–52, 61, 85,
    102. *See also* tests, intelligence
interaction process analysis, 242, 243, 246
interprofessional rivalries, 134
intention, 260
intentionally, 23, 24, 84
interpreter, 153
internal order, 222–224
Internal Revenue Service, 7
internship, medical, 132, 136, 137
internship, psychological, 132–134, 137
interrogation, 235
  circumstances of, 227, 231–233, 236, 237
  demand characteristics of, 233, 237, 239
  techniques of, 186, 235, 239
interrogator, status of, 227, 232, 237, 238
intimidation, 23

intoxication, 31
IQ. *See* intelligence
irresistible impulse, 36, 191, 194, 261
issues of fact, 144, 173, 174, 185
  preliminary, 144
issues of law, 144, 174

jails, county, 22
jails, local, 22
jail time, 271
J.D., 130, 311
jeopardy, 144
Jericho (Newsletter of National Moratorium
  on Prison Construction), 322
Johnson v. Louisiana, 245, 263, 319
joinder of charges, 167, 168
joinder of parties, 168
Judiciary Law, 162, 174, 176
judges, 16, 129, 132, 137, 153, 160, 174,
  198
judgement, 265, 275–277
  modification of, 265, 276, 277
  reversal of, 265, 276, 277
judge shopping, 145
judicial interpretation, 20, 31
Jukes family, 41
jurisdiction, 10, 33, 142, 143, 147, 155,
  167, 267, 274
  appellate, 5
  civil, 5, 139
  criminal, 5, 139
  equity, 5, 139
  personal, 5, 139
  preliminary, 139, 143
  subject matter, 5
  territorial, 5
  trial, 5, 22, 139, 143
jurists, 14
jurors, 179
  alternate, 177, 210
  attitudes of, 204, 256–262
  characteristics of, 241, 242, 254
  examination of, 173
  improper conduct of, 265
  investigations of, 212, 213
  motives of, 256–262
  post-verdict discussions with, 202
  qualifications of, 174
  social status of, 210, 254, 255

jury, 19, 30, 143, 144, 184, 188, 197, 198,
  200, 310
  decision, 220
  deliberations, 239–249
    cohesiveness and, 244, 245
    jury size and, 244–247
    pre-trial publicity and, 248–251
    research on, 240–256
    sex differences, effects of on, 240–242,
      250, 255, 256. *See also* leadership,
      styles of
    unanimity rule and, 241, 243, 245–247
  foreman of, 176, 200, 218, 255
  hung, 218
  petit, 177
  polling of, 201
  preliminary instructions to, 145
  selection, 145, 173–178, 203–219, 248,
    249, 312
    and authoritarianism, 205, 212, 213,
      217, 218
    assessing prejudice in, 204, 205, 208
    attorneys' goals in, 217
    ethnicity a factor in, 203, 204, 208
    stereotypes in, 203, 204
    systematic, 206–216
  size, 244–247
  trial, 167, 173, 197
justice, 2, 10, 17, 40, 91, 131, 144, 155–
  157, 168, 171, 174, 178, 199, 272,
  277
justification, defense of, 31, 32
"just world" hypothesis, 80, 250, 257,
  259, 260
juvenile delinquent, 28–30
juvenile gangs, 55, 62, 63
juvenile offender, 29, 41, 63, 116, 166
juvenile proceedings, 29
juveniles, 29, 41

Kallikak family, 41
kidnapping, 16, 32, 115
kleptomania, 36, 191
Knecht v. Gillman, 298, 322
knowingly, 23, 24

larceny, 23, 62–64, 72, 74–78, 141, 182
  grand, 53
  petty, 36

law, 198, 308
    and order, 308
    unenforceable, 19
law enforcement agency, 186
Law Enforcement Assistance Administration, 297
law enforcement personnel, 18, 151, 188, 271
law, New York State, 21
law school, 12, 17, 129, 130, 132, 136
    admission to, 129, 132
    curriculum of, 130
lawsuit, civil, 2, 3, 5, 10. *See also* action, civil
lawsuit, criminal, 5, 10. *See also* action, criminal
lawyer, 16, 17, 31, 131, 135. *See also* counsel
    criminal, 155, 312
leadership, styles of, 243, 255, 256
leading questions, 186, 188
learning theory, 41, 42, 135, 257, 260
learning, trial-and-error, 44
Legal Aid Society, 130, 154
Legal Attitudes Questionnaire, 205
legal education, 129–133, 312
legally sufficient case, 141, 143, 144, 149, 156, 166
legal profession, 20, 129, 133, 173
legal remedies, 32
legal representation, 26
legislation, 18, 20, 23, 135, 308
legislature, 15–17, 19, 29, 32
    New York State, 268
legislators, 129, 134, 308, 309, 311
Leopold-Loeb case, 190, 235, 304
lesser included offense. *See* offense, lesser included
liberty, personal, 309
lie detection, 45, 46, 104, 105
license revocation, 157
licensing, professional, 133, 134, 136
line-ups, 224, 231
    rigging of, 231, 237, 239
Little case, Joan, 206, 211–213
LL.B., 130
lobbyists, 7
local causality, 260
local ties, 160, 161

Lockett v. Ohio, 306, 322
locus of control, 68, 287
locus of crime, 5
locus penitentiae, 33
logic-tight compartments, 57
loitering, 14, 54, 151
Looking for Mr. Goodbar, 73
lying, 57

malpractice, 277
Machiavellianism, 204
manie sans delire, 36
manslaughter, 63, 64, 67
maturation, 39
M.D., 134, 135, 193
medical school, 129, 135, 136
    admission requirements, 136
    curriculum of, 136
medicine, forensic, 312
memory and hypnosis, 233, 234
mens rea, 23
mental capacity
    to commit crime, 27, 30
    to cooperate with counsel, 26
    to stand trial, 25
mental condition, 25
mental defect, 41, 171, 184, 190, 194
mental disease, 25, 31, 41, 171, 190, 191, 194. *See also* mental illness
mental disturbance, 28
mental examination, 266
mental health professional, 25
mental hospital, 25, 26
    civil commitment to, 26
    criminal commitment to, 25, 26
mental illness, 17, 25, 184, 192, 293. *See also* mental disease
mental incompetence, 26
mentally ill defendant, 25
mental retardation, 41, 52
mental state, 23, 24, 85, 193, 194
    culpable, 23, 31
merger of crimes, 26, 27
middle class, 53
Minnesota Multiphasic Personality Inventory (MMPI), 102
Miranda v. Arizona, 185, 186, 235, 236, 238, 263, 320

misdemeanor, 5, 15, 19, 22, 30, 139–142,
    144, 147, 149, 151, 155–157, 162,
    163, 167, 201, 265, 266, 271, 273
  Class A, 22, 27, 152, 153, 266, 270–
    272
  Class B, 19, 20, 22, 27, 153, 270–273
  unclassified, 22, 270, 272, 273
mistake of fact, 30, 31
mistake of law, 30
mistrial, 177, 198, 201
Mitchell-Stans case, 210, 211
M'Naghten rule, 25, 190, 191, 194
mob violence, 86
modus operandi, 43
moral deficiency, 36
moral insanity, 35–37, 41
morality, 13, 15, 18, 309
moral standards, 16
morals, public, 12, 13, 15, 19, 23, 101
motions, 25, 26, 29, 142, 145, 155, 156,
    163, 167, 169, 199, 200, 265
motion to inspect grand jury minutes, 169
motive, 36, 60, 188
motor vehicle bureau, 16
M.S.W., 137
mugger, 18
Mullaney v. Wilber, 33
murder, 18, 23, 28, 36, 50, 63, 64, 73, 91,
    161, 302, 304
  felony, 50, 59, 66, 67, 73
  premeditated and deliberate (P & D), 50
  rate, 66, 67, 303
  second degree, 29
  victim-precipitated, 67, 73
murderer, 34, 36, 59, 63, 65–67, 184
  mass, 67
"Mutt and Jeff" routine, 237

Napoleonic Code, 5
narcotics addict, 273
National Institute of Law Enforcement
    and Criminal Justice, 86
National Moratorium on Prison Construc-
    tion, 322
National Prison Project, 297
natural law, 1
negligence, 2
neighborhood, 53
  police teams, 112, 113, 117

neurosis, 235
news media, 16, 29, 88, 115, 170, 185,
    283, 304
New York City Housing Authority, 54
Nixon Administration, 270
nonverbal communication, 208, 212, 234
norms, 59, 102, 107
notice of appearance, 169
novel impression, 5
numbers running, 55

oath, 9, 184, 186, 187
  of office, 132, 162
obiter dictum. See dicta, obiter
offenders, 18, 39, 41, 43, 47, 56, 61, 62,
    73, 129
  casual, 60
  first felony, 268, 269
  habitual, 60
  multiple, 43
  persistent felony, 267, 268, 270
  persistent violent felony, 267, 270
  second felony, 171, 266, 268, 269, 272
  second violent felony, 266, 267
  types of, 33
  violent felony, 171
offenses, 14, 21, 22, 29, 47, 52, 62, 74,
    152, 156, 157, 163, 166, 167, 201,
    265. See also crime
  against people, 23, 62, 64, 309
  against property, 23, 62–65, 309
  against public morality, 23
  against the dignity of the state, 23
  aggressive, 16
  classification of, 21–24
  lesser included, 167, 199, 265
  malum in se, 23, 24
  malum prohibitum, 23, 24
  minor, 21, 22, 137, 156
  of mental culpability, 23, 24
  of strict liability, 23, 24
  petty, 77, 139, 141, 150, 171
opening address, 145, 146, 178, 179, 220
order effects, 222–224
order of arguments, 221, 222, 224
  anticlimactic, 222–224
  climactic, 222–224
  gross, 222–224
  internal, 222–224

organized
  crime, 131
  medicine, 135
  psychology, 135
  social work, 135
overt act, 27

paired comparisons, method of 100, 101
Panther 21 case, 213
paranoia, 37
paranoid, 190, 191
  schizophrenic, 125
pardon, 267
parole, 270, 271, 283, 293
parole board, 7, 269, 271, 273, 286, 299
parolees, 56
partial insanity, 191
pathological liar, 46
Patrolmen's Benevolent Association, 103
Penal law, 1, 15, 19, 20, 22–24, 27, 28, 31, 33
  New York State, 192, 273
penalty, 14
penitentiary, 40
penologist, 40
perception by witnesses, 224–234
  psychology of, 224–234
  selective, 225
  unconscious motives in, 225, 226
perjury, 182, 183, 187
  subornation of, 187
personality tests, 204
personal liberties, 132
personal victimization, 72
personnel selection, 95, 122
persons in need of supervision, 29
persuasion
  inoculation against, 221
  psychology of, 220–224, 236, 240, 312
petty thieves, 34
Ph.D., 133–135, 193, 311
phenomenologic reporting, 58
phrenology, 35, 37, 38, 40
physical examination, 266
physician, 41, 134, 135, 192, 196
physiognomy, 38
physiological variables, 42
PINS. See persons in need of supervision
plea bargaining, 145, 166, 170

pleas, 16, 142, 144, 147, 156–158, 168, 170, 183
poisoners, 38
police, 43, 54, 63, 77, 86, 87, 94–128
  academy, 100, 105, 107
    curriculum, 106, 107
    New York City, 106
  auxiliary, 90
  -community relations, 98, 103, 111–113, 116, 118, 120, 121, 123, 126
  corruption, 119
  department, 18, 19, 99, 101, 113, 118, 119
    Chicago, 100
    Menlo Park, 121
    New York City, 86, 94, 95, 115, 119
    Washington, D.C., 105, 116
  emergency line, 88
  officers, 1, 19, 33, 58, 80, 90, 91, 94–129, 150, 152, 153, 174, 181, 231, 304
    attitudes of, 58, 65, 114
    characteristics of, 94, 95, 100, 125
    cohesiveness among, 101, 118, 119
    "cooping" by, 111
    female, 115–119
    job description of, 107–119
    job performance of, 98, 99, 105, 118, 122
    job requirements of, 100, 107
    minority representation among, 95, 103–106, 118
    motivation of, 94
    selection of, 95, 98–106
    shooting by, 126, 127
    socialization of, 107–110
    training of, 94, 106, 107, 123, 125, 231
    values of, 101, 125
    work stresses of, 94, 110, 113, 114, 119, 122
  professionalization of, 55, 95, 121
  pension, 94
  power, 15
  recruitment, 94–98, 101
    standards for, 118
  recruits, socioeconomic status of, 94, 122
  selection of minorities, 102–106, 118

Police (*Continued*)
  training, 101
  uniform, 101, 119–121. *See also* uni-
    forms, effects of
politicians, 18, 129, 137, 304
polygraph. *See* lie detection
population density, 55
pornography, 19
positive law, 1, 2
post-conviction procedures, 265–277
poverty, 47
power
  legitimate, 119–121
  police. *See* police power
  social, 120
precedents, legal, 3, 5, 131
prejudice, 112
  of jury, 173, 174, 176, 182, 183, 198,
    200
preliminary matters, 186
pre-sentence conference, 201, 266
pre-sentence investigation, 148, 266
pre-sentence memorandum, defendant's,
    266
pre-sentence report, 137, 201, 266
President's Commission on Law Enforce-
    ment and Administration of Justice,
    71, 270
presumption, 24, 29
  conclusive, 28
  of innocence, 198
pre-trial procedures, 150–172
pre-trial investigation, 30
pre-trial publicity, 248–251
primacy effects, 221–224
prima facie case, 140, 141, 143, 145, 149,
    156, 169, 178
prior conviction. *See* conviction, prior
prison, 30, 41, 278–305, 308. *See also*
    imprisonment
  behavior modification in, 293–298
  conditions in, 281, 282, 286, 288
  effects of, 40, 286, 288
  escapes from, 285
  guards, 120, 280, 285, 297
  homosexuality in, 280, 286–288, 292
  industry, 282
  inmates, 41, 42, 120
    coping by, 284–286

  deprivations of, 280, 281, 288
  female, 116
  gangs of, 283
  living space of, 288
  release of, 285, 286
  roles of, 285, 286
  vulnerability of, 280, 285, 288
  racial conflicts in, 284
  reforms, 282, 292–299, 310
  rehabilitation in, 285
  security in, 278, 279, 284
  sexuality in, 287
  state, 22, 270
  system, origins of, 278
  system, reasons for, 281, 283
  therapy in, 284, 285, 288, 292–298, 312.
    See also behavior modification in
    prison
  trustees, 280
  violence in, 283, 285
prisoners. *See* prison inmates
prisonization, 282, 283
private housing, 53
privilege, 152, 180, 194–196
  attorney-client, 195, 196
  certified social worker-client, 195, 196
  clergyman-penitent, 195
  husband-wife, 195
  physician-patient, 195, 196
  psychologist-client, 195, 196
probable cause, 151
probationers, 56
probation officers, 137, 266, 274, 283,
    312
probation reports, 312
professional misconduct, 133
professional societies, 133
prognosis, medical, 21
prognosis, psychological, 21
prohibition, 19
prosecutor, 10, 129, 153, 166, 200. *See also*
    district attorney
prostitute, 18, 19, 38
prostitution, 20, 23
protection of public, 12, 309
psychiatric nurses, 134
psychiatric social worker, 137, 138
psychiatrist, 26, 65, 103, 134, 136, 137,
    191, 192, 194–196

psychiatry, 193
  forensic, 311
psychic salivation, 44
psychoanalysis, 136, 137, 257, 260
psychoanalytic approach, 56, 138
psychological education, 133–135
psychological tests, 95–100, 102–105
psychologist, 13, 37, 38, 43, 65, 87, 103,
    123, 132–135, 137, 138, 189, 308,
    310, 312
  clinical, 133, 135, 136, 191, 192, 196,
    312
  forensic, 311
psychology, 308
  forensic, 311, 312
psychopath, 46, 63, 184
psychopathy, 37
psychosocial moratorium, 39
psychotherapist, 137
psychotherapy, 134, 135, 138, 196
psychotic, 191
public housing, 53, 54
public interest, 15
publicity, 29
public
  office, 163, 166
  officials, 4, 10, 18, 19, 31
  policy, 33, 275
  safety, 310
  servant, 32, 33, 111
  welfare, 15
punishment, 12–14, 45, 48, 55, 56, 185,
    258, 302, 308–310
  cruel and unusual, 9, 278, 279
  training, 45
punitiveness, 254
purse snatching, 68
pyromania, 36

quasi-judicial functions, 7
quasi-legislative functions, 7
questions of fact. See issues of fact
questions of law. See issues of law

race, 60, 72–74
Radio Watch projects, 87, 89
random samples, 51
rap sheet, 152

rape, 23, 26, 38, 50, 53, 64, 79, 80, 91,
    182–184, 250
  attempted, 26
rapist, 34, 60, 184, 185
rationalization, defense mechanism of, 12
"reading law," 129
reasonable cause, 140, 141, 143, 151,
    166
reasonable doubt, 31, 32, 158, 178, 180,
    197, 198, 218, 219, 267
reasonable person, 24
recency effects, 221–224
recidivism, 12, 13, 65, 278, 287, 299,
    303
recklessly, 23, 24
re-direct examination, 145, 188
reformation of offenders, 12, 13, 308, 310.
    See also rehabilitation
refusal to aid a police officer, crime of, 23,
    91
regression, 282
rehabilitation, 12–14, 55, 56, 285, 309.
    See also reformation of offenders
reinforcement, 44, 45
release, conditional. See sentences of con-
    ditional discharge
release on own recognizance, 110, 156, 158,
    201
release, unconditional. See sentences of un-
    conditional discharge
reliability, 96
  equivalence method, 96
  stability method, 96
religion, 56, 68, 206, 207, 211
remedy, adequate at law, 3, 4
renunciation, defense of, 33
reparations, 28. See also restitution
requests to charge, 200
re-sentencing, 276
res gestae, 181
residency, medical, 136
restitution, 71, 92, 274, 300. See also re-
    parations
reversible error, 177
rewards–costs ratio. See costs–benefits ratio
Rhode Island State Prison, 291
rights, 2, 120
  basic human, 14, 131, 133
  civil, 8, 22, 131, 282

rights (*Continued*)
  constitutional, 6, 8, 10, 14, 25, 26, 29,
    131, 164, 180, 185, 186, 195, 267,
    308, 310
  inalienable, 11, 278
  of defendant, 153
    to be present at trial, 173
    to communicate with family, friends
      and counsel, 153, 168
    to counsel, 9, 25, 153, 154, 168, 169
    to speedy trial, 142, 155
    to stand mute, 165, 198
  of prison inmates, 282
  primary, 2
  secondary, 2
Right to be Different, The, 293
riot, 58
risky shift, 245
robber, 62
  armed, 62
robbery, 23, 53, 54, 64, 68, 72–78, 80, 91,
    181
  armed, 34, 63
ROC. *See* release on own recognizance
Rokeach Value Survey, 125, 126
role
  identity confusion, 114
  model, 47
  playing, 113, 120
Rosenberg case, 175
rules of construction, 6, 15, 17, 32
rules of evidence. *See* evidence, rules of
rulings of court, 197

Sacco-Vanzetti case, 233
sadist, 184
Samaritans, 90. *See also* bystander
sampling, 214
San Quentin, 288
schizophrenia, 48, 49
scientific law, 61
scientific method, 61, 135
Securities and Exchange Commission, 7
search, 279
  full body, 151, 279
  illegal, 131
  pat down, 151
  unreasonable, 9
  warrant, 9, 151

sealed proceedings, 29
securing order, 142, 144, 147, 158–162,
    170
self-fulfilling prophecy, 117, 231
self-incrimination, 164
sensation-seeking, 111
sensitivity training, 106, 113
sentences, 16, 22, 23, 25, 28–30, 147, 148,
    197, 266, 275
  aggregate maximum, 270, 271
  aggregate minimum, 270
  authorized, 267–274
  concurrent, 199, 270
  consecutive, 199, 270
  definite, 22, 268, 270–272
  execution of, 25, 26
  indeterminate, 22, 29, 268, 270, 271,
    285, 296, 298, 299
  jail, 47
  maximum, 22, 26, 27, 30, 268–271, 273
  minimum, 22, 268–270, 273
  multiple, 270
  nonrevocable, 268
  of conditional discharge, 147, 267, 268,
    271–274
  of death, 268, 275
  of fine, 21, 147, 268, 271, 272, 300
  of imprisonment, 26, 147, 161, 266–272
    intermittent, 147, 268, 292
    mandatory, 270, 308
  of life imprisonment, 29, 269, 270, 302
  of probation, 132, 147, 266–268, 272–
    274, 299
  of unconditional discharge, 147, 267, 268,
    274
  race differences in, 284
  revocable, 268, 273
  suspended, 267, 274
sentencing, 30, 132, 146, 201, 265, 267,
    273
  court's discretion in, 268
sex acts, 16
sex crimes. *See* crime, sex
shoo-flies, 103, 119
shooting by police, 126, 127
shoplifter, 34, 83
shoplifting, 68, 80–84
silent system, the, 279
slavery, 279

slums, 54
small groups, research on, 242-244. *See also* jury, research on
social change, 55
social class, 42, 49, 54, 60, 63, 104, 254. *See also* socioeconomic status
social comparison theory, 78, 85, 86
social exchange theory, 257, 260
socialization, 107, 258
social perception, 124
social reality, 78, 85, 243, 259
social sciences, 308
social scientist, 131
social status, 46, 51, 52, 254, 255. *See also* social class
social work education, 137, 138
social worker, 14, 113, 134, 135, 137, 138, 196
sociological approaches to criminology, 52-55
socioeconomic status, 56, 57, 83. *See also* social status
sodomy, 19, 183
soliciting for prostitution, 20
solitary confinement, 281, 285
special proceedings, 4, 142
specialty boards, 136
Stanford prison experiment, 120, 280, 289-292
stare decisis, 3, 5, 131, 310
START program, 295, 296
state constitution, 6, 15
state licensing agencies, 133
statements, 186
statistical decision theory, 218
statistical tests, 40
status offender, 29
statute, 13, 14, 31, 168
  criminal, 14, 15
  of limitations, 141, 155, 164, 167
  penal, 14, 23
statutory jurisdictions, 14
statutory law, 6
stay of execution, 275
stereotypes, 94, 112, 114, 117, 124, 126, 254, 256. *See also* jury selection, stereotypes in
stop and frisk law, 151
study-release program, 310

subgrouping, 244
subpoena, 163, 190
substantive law, 9
suicide, 36, 305
summations, 146, 196-199
summons, 5, 142, 152, 153
superego, 45, 46
survey research, 208
suspiciousness, 57
Sweden, prisons in, 287, 288
systems theory, 138
systematic desensitization, 294

Tactical Patrol Force, 114
tattooing, 38
tax department, 16
tax evasion, 23, 284
tax fraud, 13
tax system, 13
testimonial capacity, 184
testimony, 180, 186, 197, 224-228, 253
  direct, 165
  expert, 193
  psychiatric, 192
  uncorroborated, 27, 184
tests
  intelligence, 41, 42, 47, 95, 96, 99, 100. *See also* intelligence
  personality, 204
theft, 73-76, 81-84
therapist, 56
therapy, group, 56
thief, 38, 57, 81, 83
  professional, 59
token economy, 294, 295, 297
tort, 4
traffic control, 112, 123
traffic infraction, 5, 21, 22, 139, 140, 153
transactional analysis, 106
treatment, medical, 21
treatment, psychological, 21. *See also* prison, therapy in
Treatment, The (in youthful offender cases), 30
treason, 175
trial-and-error learning, 44
trial by combat, 10
trial in absentia, 173
trial, jury, 144

trial order of dismissal, 146, 199, 201
trial procedures, 173–202
trial record, 277
   sealed, 29, 30
trials, criminal, 10. *See also* action, criminal
trials, separation of, 168
training analysis, 136
true bill, 144, 166
twins, 48, 49
   dizygotic, 48
   fraternal, 48, 49
   identical, 48, 49
   monozygotic, 48
typologies, 59–63
   empirical, 60
   theoretical, 60

unconditioned response, 44
unconditioned stimulus, 44
unconstitutional law, 14, 155, 276
*Uniform Crime Reports of the United
   States*, 64
uniforms, effects of, 119–121
United States Commission on Civil Rights,
   104
United States Constitution, 6–8, 15, 20,
   158, 173, 175, 278, 279
   Amendment Four, 9, 279
   Amendment Five, 9, 164
   Amendment Six, 9, 10
   Amendment Eight, 9, 298
   Amendment Thirteen, 279
   Amendment Fourteen, 9

validity, 96–98, 100, 103, 105, 159
vandalism, 54
vandals, 59
values, deviant, 55
values, instrumental, 125, 126
values, terminal, 125, 126
vehicle and traffic law, 21, 22
Venice, legal system of Renaissance, 234
veniremen, 175, 176
verdict, 146, 174, 198, 200–202, 265
   of guilty, 199
   of not guilty, 199
      by reason of mental disease or defect,
         199
   partial, 201
   special, 199

victimization
   business, 72, 76, 77
   household, 72, 76, 77
   personal, 72, 76
   rates of, 72, 73
   surveys, 71–76
victims, 18, 33, 55, 66, 68, 69, 71–93, 185,
      195, 197, 308
   attempts at self-protection by, 74, 75
   characteristics of, 72–74, 77–79, 83
   compensation to, 71, 91, 92. *See also*
      restitution
   injury and hospitalization of, 72, 75
   relationship with offender, 73, 74, 78
vigilantes, 90
violations, 20–22, 139, 140, 153, 270–272
voir dire. *See* jury selection
voluntary nervous system, 44

waiver of immunity, 163, 165
waiver of indictment, 166–168
waiver of rights, 144, 164
warrant of arrest, 150–152
   superior court, 164
Watergate, 206, 210, 211
wayward minor, 28, 29
weapons, 66, 72, 75, 77, 99
   clubs, 66, 290
   deadly, 32
   guns, 24, 66, 67, 118, 127
   handguns, 66, 67, 119, 121
   ice pick, 66
   knives, 66
   night sticks, 121
   personal, 66
   rifles, 66
   shotguns, 66
Whistlestop projects, 87, 89
Williams, v. Florida, 244, 245, 263, 323
Witherspoon v. Illinois, 306, 323
witness, 84, 86, 91, 92, 143, 156, 163,
      173, 179, 180, 184–186, 194, 224–
      234
   character, 182
   expert, 181, 189, 191–194, 218, 312
      fee of, 190
      qualification of, 189
   grand jury, 164, 169
   hostile, 188

impeachment of, 182, 187, 188
incompetent, 180, 195, 196
ordinary, 181, 188, 189
rebuttal, 146, 172, 182, 193
witnesses
  accuracy of, 224–234
  articulation by, 225
  behavior of, 74, 253, 312
  characteristics of, 228, 230, 231
  credibility of, 188, 197, 232
  demeanor of, 165, 234
  estimates of time and distance by, 225,
    227, 228, 230, 233
  expectancies and, 226, 227, 230, 231
  memory of, 74, 226, 230, 233, 234
  motivation of, 80, 225–228
  perceptiveness of, 225, 229, 230

preparation of, 186, 187
recall by, 224, 226, 227, 230, 233
rehabilitation of, 188
sex differences among, 228, 253
sources of error by, 225, 229–233
tasks of, 228–233
work-release programs, 310
Wounded Knee trials, 206
writ, 3
  of mandamus, 4
  of prohibition, 4

XYY syndrome, 50–52, 59

youthful offender, 28, 30

Zeitgeist, 37, 300
zygosity, 48